AT THE EDGE OF THE ABYSS

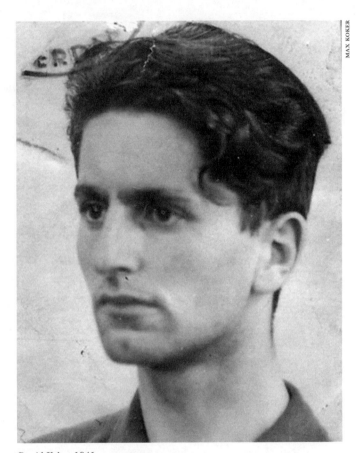

David Koker, 1941

At the Edge of the Abyss

A Concentration Camp Diary, 1943–1944

Robert Jan van Pelt
New York, June 2012.

David Koker

EDITED BY Robert Jan van Pelt

TRANSLATED FROM THE DUTCH BY Michiel Horn AND John Irons

Northwestern University Press • *Evanston, Illinois*

Northwestern University Press
www.nupress.northwestern.edu

N ederlands letterenfonds
dutch foundation for literature

The publishers gratefully acknowledge the support of the Dutch Foundation for Literature.

Book interior composed in New Baskerville, a modern interpretation of the original type cut in 1762 by British type founder and printer, John Baskerville.

Printed in the United States of America

10   9   8   7   6   5   4   3   2   1

Library of Congress Cataloging-in-Publication Data

Koker, David, 1921–
    [Dagboek geschreven in Vught. English]
    At the edge of the abyss : a concentration camp diary, 1943–1944 / David Koker ; edited by Robert Jan van Pelt ; translated from the Dutch by Michiel Horn and John Irons.
       p. cm.
    "Originally published in Dutch by G. A. van Oorschot as Dagboek geschreven in Vught, 1977."
    Includes bibliographical references.
    ISBN 978-0-8101-2636-7 (cloth : alk. paper)
    1. World War, 1939–1945—Personal narratives, Dutch. 2. Koker, David, 1921— Diaries. 3. Prisoners of War—Netherlands—Biography. 4. Vught (Concentration camp) I. Pelt, R. J. van (Robert Jan), 1955– II. Horn, Michiel, 1939– III. Irons, John, 1942– IV. Title.
    D811.K573513 2012
    940.53'18092–dc23
    [B]

2011026584

CONTENTS

My heavily marked-up copy of David Koker's diary, published in the Netherlands in 1977, is one of my prized possessions. David, as I got to know him from his diary, his letters, and his published writings, from the stories and testimonies given by family and friends, has become for the last three years a steady companion. The result of this relationship is the book now before you, the reader. I hope and trust that, for you also, David's diary will become a book you will treasure, and that David will become a friend.

David came into my life as the result of a chance encounter in Amsterdam, three years ago, between Nina Koker-Tordjman, the wife of David's brother Max, and Justus van de Kamp. Nina asked Justus, who was the coauthor of a history of the Philips workshop in the Vught concentration camp, if he might have any suggestions about how to make available an English-language edition of David's diary. "You better talk to my wife, Karen Polak, who works at the Anne Frank House," Justus told her. Nina told Max, who traveled to Amsterdam to meet with Karen. She had no publishing contacts in Great Britain or the United States, but suggested "my Dutch cousin in Toronto might be able to help." Thus I became involved. I knew the diary, and having completed a few weeks earlier the manuscript of a book, I was looking for a new project.

My qualifications as a onetime student of Dutch-Jewish history and as a historian of German concentration camps were useful assets. But was I ready to spend a couple of years working on the history and legacy of a single person? As a historian, I always had been attracted to topics of more epic dimensions. I decided that I needed to meet Max before I could answer this question. A few weeks after Karen had established contact, my wife, Miriam Greenbaum, and I crossed the Atlantic. In Max and Nina, we recognized kindred spirits. During the day we spent in the Koker house, we came to feel very close to the thoughtful Max, who carried not only the burden that came with the loss of his father, Jacques, and brother, David, in the Holocaust and his own survival of five concentration camps, but also the freely accepted responsibility for the most important legacy of his brother: the diary written in the Vught concentration camp. And we came to love the attentive Nina, who had embraced not only Max but also his difficult inheritance, given him two sons, and created a beautiful home that provided space not only for the living but also for the memory of David. Yes, David was present, not only in photos but especially in a bold and beautiful painting created by Max that portrays a chain of people dancing at the edge of an abyss—an image inspired by a poem David translated from Hebrew into Dutch. For many hours Max bore witness to the life of his brother and his hopes for the future of his diary. By the day's end I knew I wanted to be involved. The brother had made me love the brother.

I drafted a prospectus for presentation to potentially interested publishers and showed it first to Peter Hayes, the eminent historian of the Third Reich. Hayes suggested that I approach Northwestern University Press. Director Donna Shear and editor Henry Carrigan Jr. embraced the project, and with the help of Wouter van Oorschot, the publisher of the Dutch edition of the diary, and my agent, Beverley Slopen, contracts were drafted, agreed on, and signed. Francis van der Maarel was helpful in clearing up some particular problems in the early phases of the negotiations.

Having reached agreement, it was important to organize the translation. Barbara Mazzotta of the Nederlands Letterenfonds (Dutch Foundation for Literature) helped arrange financial support for the translation, and through the Letterenfonds I identified Michiel Horn as perfect for the job. Not only did he have a fine feeling for the nuances of David's language but also as fellow historians we shared essential values in working with a historically important text. And, luckily, he also lived in Toronto, which made it possible to regularly meet in person. Michiel began work in the spring of 2009, and for a year I marveled at the enthusiasm and dedication with which he undertook the translation. Initially we had agreed that the translation would contain only prose translations of David's poems. Early in 2010 Michiel changed his mind. David's lyrics deserved better, he decided, and with help of the Letterenfonds he found John Irons in Denmark, who quickly agreed to translate David's verse. Both Michiel's and John's renditions faithfully evoke the richness and at times complexity of David's language.

While Michiel and John translated David's words, I researched David's life before and after the period covered by the diary. I conducted many lengthy oral histories with Max, with David's cousin Michal Elata (formerly Roza Koker), with David's friend Frederika (Fré) Samson, with his Zionist comrade Sieg Gitter, and with Henry and Corrie Schogt, friends of David's best friend, the late Karel van het Reve. Miriam and I spent a wonderful day with Toet Hiemstra-Timmenga, who had provided support for the Vught inmates during the war and had deciphered and transcribed David's diary after the war. Two evenings spent with Ruth Hoogewoud-Verschoor and her husband, Frits Hoogewoud, taught me much about the Radical Zionist ideas that defined David's perspective between 1938 and 1940.

Archival work was necessary to understand the situation in Vught, and since both the original manuscript of the diary and most documents are preserved in the Nederlands Instituut voor Oorlogsdocumentatie (Netherlands Institute for War Documentation), or NIOD, I had the pleasure of spending a lot of time in its magnificent library and archive. NIOD director Marjan Schwegman welcomed me, and Hubert Berkhout, David Barnouw, René Pottkamp, and the late Dick van Galen-Last were always ready to help me. Hans de Vries, who had done important work on the history of German concentration camps in the Netherlands, became a key comrade in the search for the facts. Jeroen van den Eijnde, director of the Nationaal Monument Kamp Vught (Camp Vught National Monument), and Guido Abuys of the Herinneringscentrum Kamp Westerbork (Commemoration Center Camp Westerbork) responded speedily to many queries. Rochelle Rubinstein helped me to negotiate the Central Zionist Archives in Jerusalem, while Regina Klaassen got me a copy of the wartime aerial view of Vught preserved in the collection of the Kadaster (Land Registry Office) in Zwolle. On the basis of this view, University of Waterloo graduate student David Takacs produced the beautiful diagram of Vught that allows us to understand the physical context of David's diary. In order to understand the last months of David's life, I believed it necessary to travel to Lower Silesia to see the remains of the Langenbielau camp and the Hagenuk factory. Wojciech Smolen accompanied me to Bielawa and Dzierżoniów and helped me identify both sites. In Munich and Dachau Ulrich Fritz, Kay Kufeke, and Robert Sigel were helpful in establishing the final resting place of David's body.

The many research trips to the Netherlands (2008–10), a journey to Israel (2009), and the trip to Poland (2010) were possible thanks to research grants provided by Adel Sedra, dean of the Faculty of Engineering, University of Waterloo, and the Social Sciences and Humanities Research Council of Canada. Judy Jolly, Eitan and Saskia Mazor, Wim and Ineke van Pelt, Michal Elata, and Amitai and Ada Spitzer provided practical and spiritual support in Europe and Israel. For most of the time spent in the Netherlands, an ancient, light-filled house located along the Rapenburg canal in Leiden provided a convenient and cheerful base of operation. Anneke Boot, cat Colette, the cordial spirit of the late Dick van Peype, and an ever-ready bottle of Marc de Bourgogne provided an environment in which the findings of each day's research became the occasion of frequent debate and speculation.

Early on in this project Michiel and I became curious about the identity and fate of the inmates David encountered in Vught. With the help of the card index of Vught inmates preserved at NIOD, the Digital Monument to the Jewish Community in the Netherlands, the Memorial Book of the German Federal Archives, the Central Database of Shoah Victims' Names of Yad Vashem, the power of Internet search engines, and Miriam's dogged refusal to let go, it proved possible to do so. Ruth Aproot Polomski, Ophir Baer, Ben-Zion Beeri, Anneke Boot, Michal Elata, David Ellman, Ellen Goudsmit, Marten Hofstede, Remke Kruk, Philip Schrijver, Tilly Schuller-Bosman, Gerald Stern, Julie and Marlon Stufkens, Mart van Lieburg, Jan van Muilekom, and Ernst Verduin provided valuable help in providing missing information.

Throughout my research I profited from conversations with academic colleagues, including Doris Bergen, Frank Bialystok, Joël Cahen, Evelien Gans, Alain Goldschlager, Lloyd Hunt, Michael Marrus, Marieke Meeuwenoord, Dan Michman, and Bettine Siertsema. Rick Haldenby, director of the University of Waterloo School of Architecture, recognized the importance of this work and, as with my earlier research on Holocaust-related topics, supported it as a legitimate research undertaking for a professor in the School of Architecture.

When research gave way to writing the two biographical essays, the footnotes to the diary, and the biographical entries on the inmates David met in the camp, Michiel and his wife, Cornelia Schuh, provided many editorial suggestions. Max read every page, identified and corrected some blatant errors, and doggedly insisted that I would not only get the facts but also the tone right. Miriam subjected every draft that issued from the printer to detailed criticism and returned each iteration of the manuscript with observations, queries, and suggestions—written in a hardly legible script. As a result, she was forced to read all those scribbles back to me as I made notes in my own illegible handwriting.

Many people at Northwestern University Press were involved in the transformation of the finished manuscript into a book. Without the wise guidance and unstinting loyalty of Henry L. Carrigan Jr. and the attention to detail of Peter Raccuglia, this project would not have flourished in the two years that separated the signing of the contract and the submission of the final text. Marianne Jankowski captured in her art direction for the cover the friction between the spirit of David Koker and his fate—a friction that was to shape his diary. When in the late 1930s the young David dreamed about his own future as an author, he probably did not imagine that seventy years later the future of the book would not only be dependent on the skills of the author, on the trust of an editor, and on the vision of a designer, but also on the skills of those charged with the task of carving a niche for the book in a saturated market. Yet I think he would have appreciated Rudy Faust's strategy to ensure that *At the Edge of the Abyss* will be stocked by bookstores from coast to coast. There is no doubt that the meticulous David, with his attention to detail, would have appreciated the both sympathetic and critical manner in which copy editor Mike Ashby and project editor Gianna Mosser picked up the many (small) mistakes and inconsistencies that had crept into the text as it had evolved over a seventy-year period.

This edition of the diary would not have been completed if it had not been for the support of all those mentioned above, and I am beholden to each and every one. Most important, I am grateful to Max and Nina for having pulled me into the wake of their love for David and their devotion to his legacy.

Robert Jan van Pelt

Translating David Koker's diary was not easy, but it was extremely worthwhile. I want to thank Robert Jan van Pelt for inviting me to undertake the task. He deserves my thanks, too, for being constantly available to discuss points of translation as well as history. Max Koker repeatedly provided essential information on the Vught concentration camp and was always willing to assist. I am grateful to Marion Aptroot, Lyse Hébert, Mariam Leitman, Cornelia Schuh, Anne de Thy, and Kalman Weiser for help with tricky points of translation from several languages. As translating poetry is a skill I haven't mastered, I'm very glad that John Irons took on the translation of David's poems. Finally, the help of my wife, Cornelia Schuh, a superb amateur copy editor, was even more valuable this time than it usually is.

Michiel Horn

AT THE EDGE OF THE ABYSS

David Koker's diary, entry of January 29, 1944. The letter to Nettie begins on the eighteenth line from the top. "Lieve Nettie, je krijgt dit wrschl. heel gauw onder ogen" (Dear Nettie, You'll probably soon be reading this).

Introduction: David Koker and His Diary

"Dear Nettie, You'll probably soon be reading this. I suddenly happened to see a possibility . . ." the twenty-two-year-old Dutch-Jewish student David Koker wrote in his diary on January 29, 1944.[1] For more than eleven months David, or Dick as his family called him, had been incarcerated as prisoner number 15,169 in KL Herzogenbusch, a German concentration camp known as Vught because of its proximity to the village of Vught, in the Netherlands.[2] David had begun his diary on February 12, 1943, the day after his arrest and that of his parents and his younger brother and their deportation from Amsterdam to Vught. "This diary reaches beyond the end of the war!" he wrote in early March 1943. "I could be reading from it to Nettie, with an image available to me, an image full of remarkable things, full of the most astonishing as well as incomprehensible facts. Reading from it to Nettie is a big, heavy thought, charged with tenderness."[3] Nettie David was his girlfriend. A German-Jewish refugee, since November 1942 she had been living in hiding in Amsterdam.[4]

On January 22, 1944, one of the civilian employees of the Philips Electronic Corporation, which operated a large workshop in the camp, agreed to take the exercise books that contained many months of David's diary to the village and deliver them to Karel van het Reve, David's best friend who belonged to the informal network that supported Nettie.[5] One time earlier he had found an opportunity to smuggle a part of his diary to Karel, who had shared it, as David intended, with Nettie.[6] But now David faced a difficult dilemma: did he want Nettie to read this second part of his diary, which contained a candid record of his relationship with Hannelore (Hannie) Hess, or not? "I have a sweetheart here in the camp, whom I find extraordinarily attractive physically," he had recorded seven months earlier. He described her as "a girl of 18 with the appearance of a 23-year-old."[7] David and Hannie became steady companions, and he confessed to his diary that he could not stop thinking about her. "I have the strength to be very open with her, about 'personal' matters and about everything that inspires my thoughts and feelings. And she always knows exactly the right moment to give me the stimulus to keep on speaking, by means of some pleasant words, a sweet anticipatory or assenting gesture, or a friendly question. . . . In love with her? It's because of that unknown, almost uncomprehended something that exists between us. That newness, not yet habitual. And also the wonderment each time we reveal something of ourselves to each other."[8]

When he wrote this on October 14, 1943, he must have thought that Nettie would find out about it only when, upon his return to Amsterdam, he would read it to her—a reading that would allow him to frame these observations and other expressions of his love for Hannie with appropriate explanations. But things had changed between October 14, 1943, and January 22, 1944. On November 27, David's birthday, his close friend Alfred Spitz had received a letter from Auschwitz. He read it in the presence of David and Jan Hendrik (Hein) van Wijk, a non-Jewish prisoner who was employed as a statistician in the Philips workshop. David recorded the text of the message. "Three people (his fiancée and her parents) are living with Moves. And Moves's business is working overtime." Alfred and David knew the meaning of the coded message: in Dutch Yiddish "*moves*" [pronounced moe'vess] means death. David noted in his diary that "up to this point we took a very optimistic view of Poland: camps, perhaps even better than here, no concentration camps, after all, labor action. The weak won't survive it. But beyond that everything seems quite favorable." Now they came to the conclusion that only a small percentage of those deported had been put to work. "And the rest: wiped out. The world has changed. Now we know where we're at. . . . We're standing at the edge. In the middle of life. But we can't move a step, because before us is an absolute void."[9]

Discovering the fate of those who had been deported to Poland forced David to reconsider the likelihood of his return to Amsterdam. During the spring he had occasionally despaired of the future. "I'm so worried, so fearful whether Nettie and I will see each other again someday, or whether, after the war, I'll still fit into what I've built up with Karel and the others. I'm even afraid that everything is irrevocable, that my life from now on will travel along unknown paths and that I won't see any of them again."[10] Such early moments of pes-

David Koker's diary, entry of November 27, 1943. The passage about standing on the edge begins on the twenty-eighth line from the top. "Wij staan op de grens. In het volle leven. Maar we kunnen geen stap verzetten, want voor ons is een volmaakte leegheid" (We're standing at the edge. In the middle of life. But we can't move a step, because before us is an absolute void). Significantly the last sentence is partly obscured by a large blot of ink—one of the few to occur in the diary.

simism had passed, but after November 27, 1943, he realized he very probably would not see Nettie and Karel again. As a result the purpose of his diary had changed: it was to represent him if he were to die. Very likely there would be no shared reading: if the text reached Nettie, she would be reading it alone. Should he send it or not? In the end, he decided to follow the example of Van Wijk, who in a New Year's Eve speech to his fellow prisoners had confronted them with the fate of those who had been deported from the camp—"friends from whom we've heard nothing more and from whom we'll never hear again."[11] David recorded on January 6, 1944, that Van Wijk's speech had created great commotion: "In my view that still has the advantage of making people face the situation squarely, instead of calmly walking across their worn-out feelings of grief and acquiescence. It's not that bad to open up old wounds, some wounds have no right to heal."[12] And so he sent Nettie the full record of his life in the fall of 1943, "the whole history," as he wrote her, "with all its ups and downs. As free and open as I could write it down for my own purposes. Because I didn't think you people would be reading this before the end of the war. That has been a great advantage, of course. That's the only way I was able to let myself go completely." He warned her that his feelings had gone "quite far" and that she would be reading the diary "after things have clarified themselves"—that is after the relationship with Hannie had come to an end. To which he added that, "in more than one respect, to this point this journal is a finished whole."[13] And so he entrusted the exercise books to the messenger who smuggled them out of the camp and took them to Karel. It is not clear if Karel handed Nettie the pages that recorded David's flirtation and later infatuation with Hannie. As Karel had a great sense of loyalty to David, he might have decided to hold back these pages and wait to see if David would return after the war.

David did not return to Amsterdam. He died in German captivity. But the diary survived. First it was in Karel's safekeeping, and then it was in the possession of David's younger brother, Max, who received it upon his return to Amsterdam from Vught, Auschwitz, Langenbielau, Dörnhau, and Wüstegiersdorf concentration camps, before it finally passed into the archival collections of the State Institute for War Documentation (RIOD).[14] The diary, which consisted of a collection of pieces of paper and exercise books, attracted the attention of Aaltje (Toet) Hiemstra-Timmenga, a RIOD employee who was

charged with collecting material about the history of German concentration camps on Dutch soil.[15] During the German occupation
Toet had been a resident of the village of Vught. Together with her
mother, Eelkje Timmenga-Hiemstra, she had been deeply involved
with setting up an informal organization dedicated to aid the inmates
of the nearby concentration camp and to help family members trace
the movements of inmates from Vught to other camps. After the
liberation of the camp she had entered it to secure historical documents and begin sorting them. Toet was interested in any material
on Vught; the pieces of paper and exercise books Max had brought
to RIOD appeared to her to be a major historical source. She had a
passion for cryptography and paleography and hoped to decipher
David's writing and organize the material into its proper chronologi-
cal sequence. In 1948 Toet convinced the director of RIOD, historian Louis de Jong, to officially charge her with the transcription,
to be undertaken in collaboration with Max. De Jong had attended
the same high school as David and had met him on a few occasions
before his own escape to England in May 1940. He supported the
project. The result was a typed transcript: one copy for the RIOD
archive, one copy for Max, and one for Karel. By this time Nettie had
lost touch with David's brother and friend, and as a result she did not
receive the transcript of the diary that had been written for her.[16]

For a number of years it appeared that the diary would be accessi-
ble only in Toet's transcription. Both Max and Karel were busy establishing their careers in the Netherlands, and neither had the time or
the contacts to push for its publication. In 1954 Karel earned a Ph.D.
with his dissertation on Soviet literary criticism, and in 1957 he was
appointed to the chair of Slavic literature at the University of Leiden.
After becoming a professor, Karel approached Max: "Max, hasn't the
time come to publish the diary?" Max responded, "But what about
the publicity when it appears?"[17] He resisted publication at this point
because he feared its impact on his mother, Judith Koker-Presser, who
never recovered from the death of her older son and suffered his loss
day and night. She had survived Auschwitz but had returned a broken woman, and her depression had deepened when she learned
that both her husband, Jesaja (Jacques), and David were dead. Max
had told her that David's diary had survived and had invited her to
read the typed transcript, but she never did.

Yet the diary refused to remain buried in the RIOD archives. Professor Jacob Presser, who had been David's history teacher in high

school, read it and, like Toet, immediately recognized its great historical value. He quoted extensively from the diary in his seminal history of the Holocaust in the Netherlands, published in 1965. Presser believed David's diary occupied a unique place among the contemporary testimonies from the camps. "We are aware of no other camp document that sounds so subdued: a superficial reading may suggest that Koker did not see the horrors surrounding him, with a more attentive reading one discovers them all right, even if they are hinted at rather than described. Nor do we know a second source in which so much justice is done to the enemy, the camp guards, in which the humanity of these people, generally exhibited to us as monsters and all too often behaving that way, has been sought—and found."[18]

According to Presser, David's diary lacked the photographic sharpness of the concentration camp diary kept by the Dutch-Jewish journalist Philip Mechanicus in Westerbork camp.[19] But David's diary more than compensated for this by "its lyrical touch and its sensitive focus."[20] Presser was also struck by the fact that David, who had written poems before his internment, continued to compose poems in the camp. Presser could not resist printing a few of them that expressed the way the persecution affected the soul of one of the hundred thousand who had been put outside the law, isolated, robbed, and imprisoned—to be subsequently deported and murdered.

> My memory refuses to dismiss
> all that was dear to me—it is retained
> perhaps, too, scores of years will ease the pain
> of loss, humiliation such as this
> though here it has become forever plain
> how paltry and how sick at heart life is.[21]

The first major review of Presser's book was written by the popular politician, journalist, and public intellectual Johannes (Han) Lammers in April 1965. Lammers explicitly articulated what Presser had only hinted at: the miserable unwillingness of many Netherlanders to protect the Jews in their midst. Believing in the necessity of Dutch society to reform itself, Lammers called on the Dutch to "come clean" on the issue of their own role in the destruction of the Jewish community, forcing the Holocaust into the center of Dutch political discourse. Remarkably Lammers's review opened with one of David's sonnets written in Vught and published by Presser:

So seated at my twilight windowpane
I write the verse that ends my useless day
the wind flings round and steely drops that spray
the window's eardrums time and time again.

My sense is spare and dismal as the sound
of sudden gusts of wind and splashing rain
my poem then? God knows what it may mean—
for unexpressed remains what's most profound.

And yet: it is the tenderness maybe
with which I sometimes wait and think of lines
that stops this place from suffocating me.

And down the drainpipes I hear water seep
and write the verse that in the silence cries
when in weak moments I can sometimes weep.[22]

Lammers observed that the last two lines of the poem perfectly described Presser's book. Asking about the identity of the poet, Lammers noted that the poems and the diary extracts made clear that David had been a "remarkable and beautiful human being." He added the following thought. "Unique as he is, David Koker is multipliable, by a thousand, ten thousand, a hundred thousand, millions."[23] Twenty years after the Allied armies opened the gates of Bergen-Belsen, Buchenwald, and Dachau, David became the symbol of every murdered Jew.

Max and Karel, responding to the new interest in the fate of the Dutch Jews during the German occupation and inspired by Lammers's focus on David, once again considered the publication of David's diary. Convinced that Presser's endorsement had created an audience for it, they agreed that it would be desirable if Karel undertook the task of preparing it for publication. Judith's health was deteriorating, and without articulating this explicitly, Max and Karel knew that she might die by the time the manuscript would be ready. They agreed that Karel should begin work on a critical, fully annotated edition of the diary.

By the mid-1960s Karel had acquired fame in the Netherlands as an essayist, journalist, and public intellectual, and he had a devoted following who would purchase anything that appeared under his name. Max was convinced that a scholarly edition by Karel would ensure that David's diary would be noticed. But Karel could not find time to work on it. As a result of his many obligations and his ongoing activism for Russian dissident writers, he was stretched too thin. In early 1976 Max confronted him, and he admitted he had done nothing. Max proposed dropping the idea of a critical edition, publishing the diary with just a few notes and a general introduction by Karel that would include a short memoir of his friendship with David.[24] Karel approached his publisher, Geert van Oorschot, who offered him a contract. Then Karel turned to writing the introduction to the book. "I am older now than our combined ages at the time he died. Because it is not known how and where he died I catch myself fantasizing from time to time: considering the possibility that he survived and is stuck somewhere, unable to communicate—insanity, illness, a Russian administrative mistake." He recalled that David had been his dearest friend and said that he continued to dream about him. "He is in Amsterdam. He visits people whom I also see. But he doesn't come to my place, and I don't understand that. I want to do something about it, to see him and restore our past relationship, but for one reason or another that doesn't work. He doesn't want it, and I don't know why."[25]

Published in 1977, *Dagboek geschreven in Vught* (*Diary Written in Vught*) was immediately hailed as a classic.[26] "A single book can earn a writer a permanent place in literature, but to do that it has to be exceptional," literary critic Ivan Sitniakowsky wrote in a review. "I do not think that, after reading the book, anyone will dispute that *Diary Written in Vught* fulfills that condition."[27] So David would remain symbolically alive in the pantheon of Dutch literature.

A few weeks after its publication, on May 4, 1977, David's diary acquired celebrity status when Dutch public television broadcast a thirty-minute program entitled *Naar aanleiding van een dagboek* (*In Response to a Diary*). The program was the introduction to the national commemoration of the war dead. Usually a historical documentary preceded the broadcast of the solemn ceremony that was watched by most Dutchmen. This time Dutch television broke precedent by focusing on a single individual: David. The filmmakers hoped to pull in young people for whom the war existed only in the stories of parents and teachers. The camera followed Max, Karel, and Joel Cahen, the son of another inmate of Vught, as they visited the site of the former camp, which now housed a military base in the former SS barracks, a community of south Moluccans (exiled from Indonesia because of their support of the Dutch colonial regime in the 1945–49 War of Independence) in the former concentration camp barracks, and a youth prison in the former camp prison, the so-called Bunker. Readings by Max, Karel, and Joel of selected entries from David's diary were interspersed with interviews of soldiers in training, exiles without hope of ever returning to their homes, and young criminals incarcerated because of their crimes. The result was, at times, heartrending.

The diary went through two printings in its year of publication (1977), appeared in magazine format for high school students (1985), and in an expanded edition that contained an epilogue by Max (1993). This afterword related what had happened to David after February 8, 1944. The present English-language edition is the direct result of the continued devotion and commitment of Max and his wife, Nina, to David's legacy.[28]

Yet Max's and Nina's commitment is of limited importance. As the Roman poet Terentianus Maurus wrote eighteen centuries ago, "The fate of books depends on the receptiveness of the reader."[29] The future of David's diary depends on those who read it. And it is well worth reading. Above all: the very existence of David's diary is exceptional. While the number of postwar memoirs written by Holocaust survivors is enormous, and the number of diaries and notebooks written during the Holocaust by Jews while they were at home, or in a ghetto, or in hiding is substantial, the number of testimonies that were written in the inner circles of hell, in the German concentration camps, and that survived the war is small. And even those that survived are often fragmentary. Renata Laqueur's pathbreaking study of concentration-camp diaries and notebooks lists, in addition to her own diary written in Bergen-Belsen, fourteen titles, six of which were written by Jews.[30] Since Laqueur finished her study, a few more records of concentration-camp life written by Jews during their imprisonment have been found and published, but the total number of authentic, contemporary firsthand accounts of life in the camps remains negligible.[31] This, of course, is a problem if we consider the great importance of the concentration camps in the history of the Holocaust and their crucial significance for our understanding of the twentieth century as what the philosopher Zygmunt Bauman has aptly defined as "a century of camps."[32] By itself this already recommends David's diary to our attention.

David's diary is a fascinating document worthy of close and sympathetic attention. But it does not always offer an easy read. While David's prose and poetry are of high quality, the diary is a rough draft. Normally a book is the final product of a continuous process of editing. This is true not only of texts that are written to be published but also of those that are composed for more private purposes. Anne Frank prepared more than one draft of her entries. She was a perfectionist, and with her revisions carried out in the relative tranquility of her hiding place she was able to maintain good aesthetic control over the whole, even if her arrest and subsequent deportation and death prevented her from choosing the final form.

David's diary is an unedited first draft written under extremely difficult circumstances and never submitted to the process of editing and revising. Densely filled with David's handwriting, the sheets of paper and the exercise books do not show the kind of deletions, changes, and additions that marked the manuscripts of his poems written before his incarceration. The roughness of the draft is its singular strength because the topics David describes and analyzes are themselves very harsh. Unlike Anne Frank's diary or Etty Hillesum's letters, David's diary is not a source of optimism or spirituality. Instead he mercilessly probes the abyss that opens around him and within himself. At times he embarrasses the readers of his diary by showing the spiritual nakedness, abjectness, and shame of both himself and others, pulling us into the core of the Holocaust as a world-shaming event as only a raw, unedited text can do.

David's diary covers almost a year. The long temporal span not only allows the reader to understand life in Vught as it developed over time but also traces the spiritual evolution of the writer. And thanks to David's enormous skills of observation, reflection, and writing, this journey into the strange world of the Nazi concentration camp is very rewarding because it reveals a rich social universe that even includes the man who was responsible for what the Germans euphemistically labeled the Final Solution of the Jewish problem in Europe. On February 4, 1944, David recorded that the day before he had been eye to eye with Reichsführer-SS Heinrich Himmler.

> A slight, insignificant-looking little man, with a rather good-humored face. High peaked cap, mustache, and small spectacles. I think: If you wanted to trace back all the misery and

David Koker's diary, entry of February 4, 1944. The first line reads: "H. voorop. Een klein onaan-zienlijk, nogal goedmoedig uitziend mannetje. Hele hoge pet, snorretje en een kleine bril" (H[immler] at their head. A slight, insignificant-looking little man, with a rather good-humored face. High peaked cap, mustache, and small spectacles).

horror to just one person, it would have to be him. Around
him a lot of fellows with weary faces. Very big, heavily dressed
men, they swerve along whichever way he turns, like a swarm
of flies, changing places among themselves (they don't stand
still for a moment) and moving like a single whole. It makes
a fatally alarming impression. They look everywhere without
finding anything to focus on.[33]

How many of the six million Jews murdered in the Holocaust faced
the man responsible for their fate? I recall a photo that shows Himmler speaking to Chaim Rumkowski, the elder of the Jews of the Łódź
ghetto. And how many of them created an immediate record of that
encounter—a record that survived the catastrophe? I don't know of
any record—except the entry in David's diary.

In the diary we find fascinating portraits of the SS men, of high,
middle, and low rank, drawn *sine ira et studio*. The Roman historian
Tacitus believed that the true historian is characterized by his ability
to write about the most terrible crimes and offenses "without indignation or partisanship," and in his descriptions of the Germans and
their Dutch collaborators David showed himself to be a true historian.[34] And he wrote without sentimentality about his fellow inmates,
both Jewish and non-Jewish.

As readers encounter the inmates who make their entrances and
exits on David's stage, they may want to know more about them
and, most important, if they survived their incarceration in Vught
or their deportation to other camps, or not. Whenever possible this
edition of the diary provides basic biographical information about
the inmates David encountered or friends and family members about
whom he worried while in Vught.[35] The Germans may have considered the inmates numbers, but we may remember the teacher Samuel Aardewerk (1910–43), the physician Salomon Zwaap (1906–44),
and all the other inmates who appear in the diary as David encountered them: not as dead people on leave but as individuals whose lives
had purpose and meaning and who acted at times with courage and
compassion, and at times with cowardice and malice. David did not
suppress the confusions, conundrums, and embarrassments that he
witnessed, and neither does this edition.[36]

David's diary does not only give dignity to many individuals who
shared its author's fate; it also saves Vught from being merely a symbolic site within some parallel universe of night and fog that oper-

ates under its own laws. One of the obstacles to understanding life in the German concentration camps is the way survivors, witnesses, and even scholars have chosen to understand those places in mythic terms. The concentration and death camps are "*Hell made immanent,*" the Jewish critic and philosopher George Steiner observed. "They are the transference of Hell from below the earth to its surface."[37] Steiner suggested that one should read Dante's *Inferno* to understand the camps—and many others have tried to conceptualize the camps in a similar fashion.[38] But such rhetoric suppresses the historical contingency that determined the origin and operation of each of the camps and ignores the complexity of human relations within the camps. David's diary provides an antidote to the tendency to depict the camps as a separate universe or another planet, disconnected from our day-to-day world. In this it aligns with the autobiographical novel *Fatelessness,* written by the Hungarian-Jewish survivor, writer, and 2002 Nobel Prize winner for literature, Imre Kertész. At the end of the story, the protagonist György Köves observes the late-afternoon light in Budapest and suddenly remembers the concentration camp from which he had just returned. "It was that peculiar hour, I recognized even now, even here—my favorite hour in the camp, and I was seized by a sharp, painful, futile longing for it: nostalgia, homesickness."[39]

Kertész's shocking notion of an ex-inmate's nostalgia for Auschwitz, Buchenwald, or the *Arbeitskommando* Tröglitz near Zeitz, and his memories of what he provocatively defined as "the happiness of the concentration camps"[40] challenged the dominant view in the memoirs and testimonies that camp life was always and everywhere infernal. But Kertész wrote *Fatelessness* twenty years after his liberation from the camps. A diary like David's, which was written in the camps, allows us to test both Steiner's thesis and Kertész's paradoxical assertion. Were the camps a universe of torture only? Was there happiness in the camps? And if so, did that happiness resemble the happiness in our world, or did it have different characteristics? Of course, Vught was a "regular" concentration camp, not an extermination camp. There were no gas chambers. Using Steiner's analogy of the concentration-camp system with Dante's Hell, Vught occupied one of the outer circles. While only a few hundred of the more than twelve thousand Jews who were admitted to the camp survived the Holocaust, almost all who did not survive died elsewhere: in the trains to the east, in the gas chambers of Sobibor and Auschwitz, or in the countless larger and smaller camps where Jews who had survived the selection in Auschwitz were worked to death. Certainly conditions in Vught were bad. In the transit camp of Westerbork Philip Mechanicus noted in his diary that those who arrived in that camp from Vught "considered themselves very lucky." He observed that those coming from Vught must have been starving. "They were insatiable. They were made a fuss of, as befitted men who had managed to escape death and the grave—martyrs of their race."[41] Yes, Vught was a bad place, and while David's restrained account does not stress the bondage, hunger, and especially filth that marked life in Vught, it does not camouflage them either. But at the same time Vught was a place where life went on. And David's description of his flirtation with Hannie allows us to believe that there were moments of normalcy in the camp: boy meets girl and so on—an extraordinary feat in a concentration camp made possible by the fact that the Philips workshop employed both men and women (the latter were considered indispensable because their smaller fingers allowed them to do detailed technical work).

Amid the squalor there was love, and there was beauty. "Yester-day morning I walked between barracks 41 and 42," David wrote on his twenty-second birthday. "The air we're walking through is mild and misty. The trees glisten. With every breath you take, you feel the world to be more spacious and yourself more free." Near the hospital barrack he saw a toddler, imprisoned as a hostage with his parents. "He hasn't been walking all that long. And he doesn't do so with any great confidence. He stretches his little arms out and stumbles along the white, misty field like a small dark bird. In this perfect and clean cold we feel ourselves to be so real. And our presence in this enclosed piece of the world so unreal. And these mixed feelings themselves become reality again in that tiny hostage, who totters so uncertainly across the vaguely misted meadow."[42] Like Imre Kertész's protagonist, György, David remained capable of recognizing the beauty and mira-cle of life. And he proved capable of creating beauty within the camp. David was a published poet.[43] When he arrived in the camp, he was determined to continue writing poetry. On the third day of his incar-ceration he wrote that "this afternoon I jotted down my first lines of verse. No matter how odd it sounds: I've got the opportunity to write something here. I would almost say: the circumstances are favorable for my kind of poetry, quite aside from the content. If I get through this, then it may all turn out to have been very fruitful. In the way that things are fruitful for me. Destructive in a certain sense."[44] And, as his diary shows, he proved able to distill beauty from the madness and misery that surrounded him, writing "verse that in the silence cries / when in weak moments I can sometimes weep."[45]

We must not underestimate the difficulty of producing poetry in a concentration camp. David observed on various occasions that the camp compromised the raw material of poetry, the author's ability to understand his own perceptions and emotions. "It's impossible to express how empty I am here."[46] After a few months he noted that "thoughts keep going around in the same circle. Our receptiveness lies open and shrinks and hardens at the surface. Because life has become a nothingness, a void."[47] On June 3, 1943, David noted that "our feelings are like skin that has been stretched very tight—you get that with wounds sometimes—and then becomes insensitive and oversensitive at the same time. Then feelings don't have any color, as it were. . . . I often think: you have here the highest degree of consciousness and of unconsciousness. The nuances between them, which used to make life so rich and full of possibilities, are absent."[48] From his very first day in the camp, David noticed that he had difficulty in keeping a firm grip on his experiences. He knew if he proved unable to hold fast to his feelings, he would lose his own integrity and his ability to communicate, after the war, with those who had not shared his ordeal. On May 10, 1943, he recorded a conversation with Spitz. "I asked Alfred Spitz (and I was thinking of Nettie): 'Do you think that, if you survive this business, you'll be able to pick up your life again together with those who are dear to you (he's engaged) and to commit yourself anew to the work that's dear to you?' He said: 'No.'"[49] It was a disturbing response, because David had come to realize that a confidence in his ability to share the experience of the camp with others was not only important for the future but also the key to survival in the present. On June 3, 1943, he wrote: "Lately this line has been running through my head: *Wer spricht von Siegen? Überstehn ist alles* ("Who speaks of victory? Survival is everything").[50] Everything, certainly the contact with our friends, is actually nothing more than maintaining past relationships, in principle, with an eye to resuming those relationships after the war in their original form." But so much of what he experienced in the camp did not really register. "It's possible, of course, that everything will be stored in our unconscious mind and will manifest itself after the war. To activate that unconscious experience must be the task of this diary."[51]

David's diary provided a bridge between his life before his incarceration and the life he hoped to live after leaving the camp. He knew he was losing his grip on reality in Vught—quite literally risking insanity. In the early 1940s the Austrian-Jewish refugee Soma Morgenstern reflected on his own experience in the French internment camp of Audierne, located on the coast of Brittany. After the outbreak of war he had been interned there as an "enemy alien." Morgenstern observed that the concentration camps tear and destroy "the softest tissue of life: memory . . . Much has been talked, chattered, written and smeared about the suffering in concentration camps, but none has observed the greatest danger of this mass grave of the mind, above all the mind. How can one explain that people locked up in dungeons do not disintegrate as quickly (and some do not do so at all) as people in a concentration camp?"[52] To Morgenstern the key issue was the tyranny of the present. "There is a plenitude of the present. Not a crack opens up to allow in a bit of past and a bit of future. That is why one loses one's memory . . . A concentration camp is full of the present. Full to the level of madness."[53] Morgenstern wrote this beautiful analysis shortly after he had escaped from Audierne. His analysis is well composed and shows the opportunity of careful reflection offered by a measure of distance from the camp. David Koker never had that opportunity: he died in the system. His diary offers the raw material for an essay on the loss of one's sense of reality in a concentration camp.

David did not only keep a diary in the camp. He also wrote and received letters (some of those are excerpted in this edition). When the camp was established (January 1943), its regulations stipulated that every inmate was allowed to send and receive one letter per week.[54] Later the SS restricted prisoner correspondence with the outside world, but David made full use of every opportunity. Thirty-two of these letters survive. Written in the knowledge that they would be read by censors, they offer limited access to David's state of mind. However, David also maintained a secret correspondence. Each inmate was allowed to receive a food parcel every week. Whenever they could, Karel, his girlfriend, Jozien (Tini) Israël,[55] and their friend Frederika (Fré) Samson dispatched food parcels to Vught, and they often hid letters, written on small pieces of thin paper, in loaves of rye bread.[56] David referred to these letters as *Leckerbissen* (German for "treats"). He kept them in his diary, and thirty-three have survived.

David also found a way to mail secret letters from Vught. The camp contained a number of prisoner workshops operated by Dutch corporations such as the Escotex textile factory and the Philips Electronics Corporation. David persuaded civilian employees of Escotex and Philips to take his letters out of the camp. The single secret letter written by David that survives was written in March 1943. Remarkably, it was the very letter in which David informed Nettie about the existence of his diary, and that it was to be his gift to her and Karel. "For each of you I intend something different with it. For you it has to be the record of *my* experiences and thoughts, for Karel a record of experiences and thoughts in general."[57]

As David's diary reveals, in spite (or perhaps because) of the feelings of emptiness and the flattening of his ability to experience sorrow and happiness, he did adapt relatively well to the camp and its regime. Thanks to his intellect and flexible disposition, David acquired a somewhat privileged position that allowed him to observe his environment and himself with a certain distance. Had he gone insane he would not have been able to continue his diary. Had he become incapacitated by depression, he would not have been able to build up the social network that saved both him and his family from early transfer to Westerbork, which, as we know now, would have resulted in deportation to the Sobibor death camp.

Historians of the Holocaust know that the best—that is, the most useful—testimonies of camp life were produced by those who enjoyed a position of privilege and who, as such, were somewhat sheltered from the full horror of the camp. David was able to observe the beauty of a November morning, to recognize the paradoxes of camp life, to maintain his diary, write his letters, and compose his poems because, at least while he was in Vught, he was not at the bottom of the camp's social ladder. He was "somebody": he was known by other prisoners, and not only because many knew he was keeping a diary. His rise in Vught, very modest in absolute terms but of vital importance given the implications of remaining part of the anonymous mass, arose from a combination of servility and ambition that he both recognized and condemned in himself. "I wish I didn't try to do things quite so well," David wrote shortly after his arrival in Vught. "I have no negative attitude towards what they order us to do. I give in and hope to make something of it in accordance with the German regulations. I want to have a job here: out of ambition. Everywhere I show up, I want to join in the work. In the vanguard. No matter whether it's good or bad. I wish I were less of an apple polisher. Less ambitious."[58]

Three weeks later he recorded his desire to associate "with anyone who's highly placed, regardless of his quality. An ambition of the lowest kind. And without the means to make it effective. And other things accompany it: attitude to authority, etc. And what's bad: I know this so well and am trying to kill it."[59] Yet he did not do so: at times his instinct for adapting to the situation in the camp trumped his moral sense. Initially his ambition provided him with the satisfactory and morally unambiguous position of being first a teacher and, after some time, from April to June 1943, the head teacher of the many children interned in the camp. But David had already realized in May that the position of teacher was only temporary. "Drukker and Spitz are saying, and I don't think they're wrong: 'They're going to empty this place. This will become an Aryan labor camp.' That sounds plausible." David knew that, two days earlier, Spitz had started to work in the Philips workshop, which, until then, had employed only non-Jewish prisoners imprisoned in a separate part of the camp. So there might be room for Jews in an "Aryan" labor camp, "useful" Jews, like Spitz and perhaps himself. And so, without transition, he jotted down: "I want an important job. I'm going to see Lehmann tomorrow."[60] Arthur Lehmann, a German-Jewish refugee, was chief of the internal administration and chief camp clerk. Since he decided who would work where, he was a very powerful man. He was happily married to Gertrude Lehmann-Sternberg, also imprisoned in Vught. David got to know both of them, and through them he acquired some measure of influence.

This proved to be no small matter. In the summer of 1942 the Germans had designed Vught as an internment and labor camp for Jews, but in the spring of 1943 they changed its purpose, and Vught became an anteroom to the death camps in the east. In April David noticed a seemingly small change in the designation of Vught: the SS men had ceased to refer to it as "reception camp," and now they were calling it a "transit camp." He noted that "all of us have explanations for that, and they would be very reassuring if we believed them, only we don't believe them."[61] For David the new designation meant that everyone faced deportation to Poland, a dreaded prospect even if no camp inmate could imagine what was happening there. On May 10, the day he decided to approach Lehmann, he wrote: "This last week we've been living in one great abiding fear. In fact, almost in a certainty. I'm preparing myself for deportation. A few days ago: woken at 4 a.m. To listen to an important announcement. I was petrified with fear. My heart was beating laboriously, was almost frozen. People to the dining-hall. There's a transport to Westerbork. Old and sick people."[62]

The transport with 1,280 people left the camp on May 8. In the next couple of months another six transports left Vught, reducing its Jewish population from over 8,600 inmates at the beginning of May to 4,276 by the end of June. David witnessed and described the drama of these departures without becoming involved. However, when early in July the camp administration decided to include his younger brother, Max, in a transport of youngsters who were to end up in Sobibor, David panicked and decided to use his access to Lehmann to change Max's fate. But he could not get to Lehmann, protected by *Kapos* (inmate functionaries) from the masses of inmates who were trying to petition him. Then David saw Lehmann's wife and showed her the summons of deportation Max had received. She went up to her husband and presented David's request. "He shakes his head. Half an hour later I ask again. Negative once more." David decided that he would stay put. Another opportunity offered itself. "Mrs. Lehmann comes towards us and says: 'Give me the summons for a moment.' Motions us to come along with her and then says: 'You can go, it's been fixed.' We ask her to repeat this. I congratulate everybody, go to the barrack, throw myself on my bed and immediately fall asleep."[63] In the staccato language of this entry we can sense the terror and agitation of that day, and perhaps also David's awareness that, in pleading with Lehmann for Max's release, he had accepted the legitimacy of his authority and, by implication, of the whole system.

Three months later David had become part of "the system." By the end of October he and his family had survived the deportation of 80 percent of the inmates. Before the departure of each of the trains, he witnessed the negotiations about who would leave and who would remain. His heart had begun to harden. "You need to have the strength to sacrifice people if it can't be avoided. I'm slowly learning this. And now the fact is that someone or other has to go, and that it should be exclusively a matter of what is best for everybody"[64] he wrote at the end of September. In early November the prisoner administration was ordered to draw up another list of inmates to be deported to the east, which, as we know today, meant Auschwitz. Of the slightly less than fifteen hundred inmates only half would remain. The Philips workshop now became a last refuge. Alfred Spitz, who had been instrumental in setting up the workshop, and Hein van Wijk, who had acquired great influence within it, were to decide who would be protected by employment at Philips. David had become their friend, and he joined them in their deliberations. "The old system: we don't take someone's husband. Then the wife leaves. Then we put another woman in her place. And then *her* husband stays," David wrote on November 11. The telegraphic brevity of the account and its lack of more meditative circumspection reveal the terrible pressure of the situation. "Meanwhile young assembly-line girls come to inquire whether they've been approved to stay. And if they've been approved, whether others have been approved as well. Or whether others can be considered. Especially sisters . . ." Their decisions meant the difference between life and death, even though they did not know with certainty that death was almost inevitable for those who left. But the prospect of deportation was bad enough. "To all these matters I bring an *angry* but nevertheless *abstract* sense of responsibility. I *have* to do this, this is my job, it has to do with people, but it makes absolutely no difference who exactly is doing it."[65] Only after the departure of the train with 1,152 inmates did David allow himself to reflect on the moral implications of his participation in drawing up the lists of those who were to remain behind. "When you've played at being providence for an evening, you go to bed with a moral hangover and great doubts."[66]

If there was doubt on November 20, there was greater resolve a week later when, as a result of the letter Alfred Spitz had received from Auschwitz, David realized that the refuge offered by the Philips workshop was only temporary, and that all were doomed. "Disdain for one's own fate and for that of others is the necessary basis for every great style of life. . . . I'm well on the way here to become some kind of Nietzschean, without any rhetoric, by the way. Without being indifferent to it, I can make peace with doom. Above all I can reconcile myself to it when I see so much that's small and ugly go to ruin. That doesn't exclude pity. And it certainly doesn't exclude making an effort to hold on to life. But otherwise . . ."[67]

After November 15, 1943, David Koker was part of a small remnant of the original camp, at least so far as its Jewish inmates were concerned: 92 percent of the Jews who had arrived in Vught since January were now gone. Most of those who had left had been murdered in Poland. He was a survivor who, especially in November, had worked hard to keep his family safe from deportation. Willy-nilly he had become an inhabitant of the moral landscape that Primo Levi has identified as the "Gray Zone," an area of collusion and sometimes even collaboration between privileged prisoners and the SS.[68] Yet, it must also be said that he had lost all sentimentalism about his own fate. Shortly after his arrival in the camp, David wrote that "it's still incomprehensible to me that, with all my precious talents, this has happened to me and the ultimate can still happen to me."[69] Eleven months of camp life had killed all traces of self-pity, and he speculated about his fate with an almost flippant cynicism when he speculated about the bitter end of those who had been held back, "when the last few of us as sordid / smoke-pall from the stack ascend."[70]

David Koker and His Family

In his diary David offers a self-portrait with many fissures and gaps. He doesn't offer much information about his earlier life, as a son and brother, as a high school and university student, as an observant Jew and Radical Zionist, as an editor and poet. In the same way that this edition attempts to provide basic biographical information about the inmates David met in the camp, it must provide a somewhat more substantial biography of David and his family.

The year is 1935, the day Friday, the time sundown, and the setting is the second-floor four-room Koker apartment at 13 Biesboschstraat, located in the newly constructed Rivers Quarter at the southern edge of Amsterdam. The Kokers are Jesaja, who is known by his family and friends as Jacques (48), his wife, Judith (42), David (13), and his brother, Max (8). At sundown Jacques leaves for the small B'nai Teiman (Children of the South) synagogue, where he serves on the board. Judith prepares dinner. David reads, and Max plays outside. Upon Jacques's return the family gathers for the Sabbath meal, after which they pray and sing together—Jacques was an accomplished tenor and a connoisseur of the music of the Amsterdam Ashkenazi community. And he was also a lover of books. Following the observances the members of the Koker family sit around the dining table, each reading a book of their choice. David was a voracious reader. A precocious young man with literary aspirations, he read not only adventure stories but also the greats of British, French, German, and Dutch literature.[71] Like the majority of Dutch Jews, neither Jacques nor Judith socialized with non-Jews, but David had some very close

MAX KOKER

Jacques, Max, David, and Judith Koker on the Damrak, Amsterdam, 1930

non-Jewish friends, and they were welcome to join in the evening of
quiet reading. In a poem written in 1940 David described the atmosphere of such a Sabbath evening.

> We looked up at each other from our reading
> quite simultaneously. And through our eyes
> there passed the very same serene surprise
> that everything could be so good and pleasing.
>
> Within these walls, where joy all haste is spurning,
> where in their sunlike, unassuming shine
> white, slender Sabbath candles now are burning,
> life's smallest things can seem both whole and fine.
>
> Glimmering light-spots dancing on the ceiling
> the table of a never-ending white,

with dishes motionless and softly gleaming,
the wine, the pure white bread. Oh how this sight

expressed such solemn presence, nonetheless
seemed so aloof. We find ourselves constrained
for just one instant by bright giddiness
yet to what's innermost have been ordained,
and like the things around us self-contained

have we become as we observe each other,
re-find ourselves in space so bountiful.
Each in his solitude and yet together—
such was our Sabbath, and so wonderful.[72]

At ten in the evening the books are closed, and conversation begins
about the things read or the week just passed. The next morning
Jacques, David, and Max attend the Sabbath service. Judith kept her
distance from the synagogue. Her father, a diamond worker, had
been, like so many in his trade, an ardent Socialist. He was also an avid
reader of the writings of the atheistic philosopher Baruch Spinoza.
Judith had absorbed her father's values, and when she married the
more religious Jacques it was on the understanding that she would
not join in public worship but would help him to maintain a Jewish
household in the cultural sense of the word. Around noon Jacques
and his sons return home for a lunch of herring and sardines, and
after an afternoon nap Jacques sings again—but now he entertains
his family with selections from his repertoire of operatic arias. Then
he reads aloud from selected masterworks of Dutch literature such
as Hildebrand's *Camera Obscura,* the sketches of Amsterdam Jewish
life written by Volksrebbe (People's Rabbi) Meijer de Hond (a rabbi
who attended to the poorest of the poor and was a family friend), and
novels by Dickens, which were sure to entertain young and old alike.
A short ceremony bringing Sabbath to an end is followed by a simple
supper and the arrival of uncles and aunts eager to engage in a little
socializing and a game of cards.

The Koker family spent the Sabbath as Jews; the Koker men enjoyed Sunday morning as proud citizens of Amsterdam, Jacques often
taking his sons for a show-and-tell history lesson through the city.[73]
He discussed the architectural splendors of the canals, the modern
technology of the railway station and the harbor, and the monumen-

tal synagogues erected in the seventeenth century by Sephardic Jews who had arrived as refugees from Spanish-annexed Portugal and Ashkenazi Jews who had fled the ravages of the Thirty Years' War in Germany and the Chmielnicki pogroms in Poland. Jacques explained to the boys how the Jews—including their own ancestors[74]—had found a new home in what was at that time the most cosmopolitan city in Christendom and which, in the twentieth century, had remained a place of wide and unprovincial intellectual horizons.[75] But Jacques wanted to give the boys a fair picture of the city, warts and all. He told them that much of the wealth of the West India Company had come from the African slave trade, and the Portuguese Jewish community that had built the largest and most beautiful synagogue in Europe had disgraced itself by banning Spinoza from its midst instead of accommodating him as a fellow Jew of heterodox disposition. He also discussed politics with them. Jacques was a self-made man who had risen by virtue of education and initiative from poverty to the limited and uncertain prosperity of the petite bourgeoisie. He embraced the ideals of the Vrijheidsbond (Liberty Association), a somewhat libertarian political party located on the center-right of the Dutch political spectrum that stressed the importance of personal freedom and initiative.

While each time the Koker men explored a different section of the city, they were careful always to arrive at the neo-Venetian Calvinist church on Keizersgracht when Burgemeester (Mayor) Willem de Vlugt entered his place of worship. And there the four participated in a weekly ritual. Jacques tipped his hat, and David and Max took off their caps as De Vlugt passed by: "A good Sunday to you, Mr. Mayor!" "Thank you, sir, thank you young men, and a good Sunday to you all!" the mayor replied as he tipped his hat. And Jacques told his sons: "Remember, he is *our* mayor."[76]

The Kokers knew that they belonged in Amsterdam and in the Netherlands. This did not mean they were blind to the anti-Jewish prejudice that existed in Dutch society. Many Christian Netherlanders believed that Jews were richly endowed with disagreeable qualities such as pushiness and avarice. Social contacts between Jews and non-Jews were characterized by a certain aloofness toward the Jews: they were not admitted in major clubs, and there was a common understanding that Jews should not rise above a certain level in public life. By and large they remained effectively excluded from the highest levels of government and the civil service, although there were a few notable exceptions like Chief Justice Lodewijk Ernst Visser. But Dutch Protestants also had strong prejudices against Catholics, and vice versa, and Christians had strong prejudices against Socialists and Liberals.

All this existed within a culture of so-called pillarization. Dutch society consisted of a number of distinct groups or "pillars," each characterized by its own religious and political ideas, which were also reflected in the economic, social, and cultural choices people made. In sports and leisure activities, in literature and the arts, in their choice of newspapers and radio broadcasters, people organized themselves according to the preferences of the pillar with which they identified. These power blocs were represented in Parliament by their own political parties and in the economy and society by their own professional organizations, trade unions, and school systems. Jews were too few in number to form their own pillar, and this made them politically invisible in Dutch society. Since they could not belong to the Catholic or various Protestant pillars, they belonged either to the Socialist or, like the Koker family, to the Liberal pillar

Priests and ministers did not hesitate to use the pulpit to incite the faithful to remain within these groups, reinforcing feelings of mistrust toward those who adhered to other pillars. By and large, the prejudice against the Jews was perhaps somewhat stronger in degree but not different in kind from the prejudices among the pillars. The bourgeois, middle-of-the-road, and commonsensical character of society in the Netherlands was largely immune to the anti-Semitic hysteria that arose in France in the 1890s and in Germany in the 1920s.[77] As a result Dutch politicians never initiated a national debate about the position of the Jews. And so Jacques and Judith were not mistaken in feeling at home in Amsterdam and displaying their local patriotism on the walls of their apartment by way of a collection of framed engravings of the city's canals and major monuments.[78]

They did not just feel at home. In fact, like the other 65,000 Jews of Amsterdam, the Kokers had a proprietary feeling toward Amsterdam—a city they affectionately called Mokum or Mokum Ollef, derived from the Hebrew word *makom* (place) or *makom aleph* (first place).[79] It was still indisputably the first place in the Diaspora, the Jerusalem of the West, and a true home in the world. Today, of course, this is difficult to imagine. A few years later, to be a Jew of Amsterdam meant a sentence of deportation and death. Of the 65,000 native Jews

and 15,000 German-Jewish refugees who lived in the city in 1940,
eleven percent of the city's population, only 5,000 remained alive in
1945. Most of the Jews were taken away while their neighbors stood
impotently by.

Jacques was an Amsterdam patriot, but he was not nostalgic for the
age of Rembrandt. He actively participated in the transformation of
Amsterdam into a modern city. In the 1920s Mayor de Vlugt, a former
contractor, oversaw the construction of the largest and most beautiful
urban project in modern Dutch history: the district of Amsterdam
Zuid (South). The Kokers were among the first to move from the old
city to the Rivers Quarter section of the new district.[80] First they rented
an apartment on Amstelkade, and later on Biesboschstraat. Initially
few were willing to follow the Kokers' example, and there were lots of
vacant dwellings. After 1933 German-Jewish refugees made use of the
rental opportunities: the Otto Frank family leased an apartment on
Merwedeplein, a couple of hundred yards from the Kokers, and the
parents of Nettie David moved into an apartment on Roerstraat, just
around the corner. Because of the distance of the new district to the
synagogues of the old center, Jacques established the B'nai Teimon
synagogue in a converted garage on Amstelkade and, after the community had grown sufficiently to support a new building, he pushed
for the construction of a large, modern, and, most important, archi-
tecturally significant synagogue on nearby Lekstraat. Trained as a calligrapher and designer and employed as a manager in the firm of
Lindenaar and Kapsenberg, an atelier that produced jewelry, Jacques
knew that beauty mattered. The result was a light-filled modernist
box typical of the International Style.[81]
    The cosmopolitian architecture of the Lekstraat synagogue did
not, however, really fit the character of the community that built it.
From a global Jewish perspective, the *species hollandia judaica* (Dutch
Judaic species) was characterized by a detachment from Jewish communities elsewhere—a segregation that most Dutch Jews understood
as a form of "splendid isolation" but which those who were concerned
about the future of Jews everywhere tended to define as narrow provincialism.[82] The glory days of the Jewish community in the seventeenth century had been followed by a century of stagnation and
then one of assimilation into Dutch society and dissimilation from
the larger Jewish world. The integration of Jewish children in Dutch
public schools had led to the rapid decline of Portuguese and Yiddish

as communal languages, and as a result the Dutch Jews became Jewish Netherlanders and, as such, both indifferent and irrelevant to the larger, more vibrant Jewish communities in east-central and eastern Europe. Dutch Jews felt at home in the Netherlands. At the end of the Passover Seder meal they said not the customary "Next Year in Jerusalem" but "Next Year in Amsterdam."[83]

From 1933 to 1939 David attended the Vossius Gymnasium, a very demanding secular high school located in Amsterdam Zuid. There he made the friends who would support him and his family with food packages and secret letters during his incarceration in Vught: Tini Israël, Fré Samson, and, most important, Karel van het Reve.[84] Karel and David stimulated a passion for literature and poetry in each other, writing poems together, writing poems for each other, and mercilessly criticizing each other's work. As David explained in an article he contributed to the Vossius student magazine *De ventilator* (*The Fan*), he believed that in critically analyzing Karel's work, and that of others, he would be able to achieve his own individuality.[85] As a sixteen-year-old he was, of course, fascinated and at the same time troubled by the changes he noticed in himself.

MAX KOKER

David Koker and his fellow classmates at the Vossius Gymnasium, 1938. David is first on the left in the back row; Karel van het Reve is fourth from the left in the back row; Tini Israël is on the extreme right.

> What was it that the unknown god once said:
> fathom yourself: his precept I obey,
> this brings dishonor on me, since I may
> from sheer self-fathoming end up half-dead.

David knew that what he found within puzzled not only him but also others.

> The finest experts of the human heart
> can't make me out, I'm quite a thing apart.
> They say that from them I perhaps should quit:
> you, sir, don't fit our system one small bit!"[86]

David may have felt like a stranger to others, but in the eyes of many he was a very attractive young man, with his wavy hair, triangular face, and, as his cousin Roza (Rootje) Elata-Koker remembered in 2009, "beautiful eyes."[87]

David and Karel loved books, and they read widely and voraciously. Karel's Communist upbringing ignited a lifelong passion for Russia and Russian literature. David focused on Dutch literature—probably because he hoped to make a contribution to it. He discovered in the poet and essayist Jan Greshoff (1888–1971) a voice that spoke to him personally. Greshoff asked a question that intrigued David as he embraced the idealism that comes with mid-adolescence: how to live a life marked by compromise? Greshoff accepted and celebrated compromise, suggesting the grace of a limited happiness that would come at the price of loneliness.[88] In 1938 David wrote in *De ventilator* a review of Greshoff's recently published volume of essays *In alle ernst* (*In All Seriousness*). It offered, David believed, an oasis in an increasingly Fascist world that celebrated the power of the organized community.[89] For a sixteen-year-old, David had a remarkable understanding of the meaning of loneliness and solitude in Greshoff's oeuvre and the historic significance of Greshoff's position in an age that offered little space for the private and the individual. The review appeared at a time when various Dutch writers had joined together to produce two volumes with essays in his honor, one written by established writers and the other by "the youngest generation." One of the contributors noticed David's piece and included it in the second volume.[90] David had become a published author.

Greshoff spoke to David the aspiring poet. The essayist, critic, and journalist Menno ter Braak (1902–40) was David's role model as the engaged man of letters. Positing in an age of bad faith the ideal of the Man of Integrity, Ter Braak held up an always critical, often caustic, but at the same time empathic mirror to Dutch society in a series of monographs and columns that appeared in the liberal daily *Het vaderland* (*The Fatherland*).[91] Ter Braak sought to "unmask" what he saw as the rampant laziness of thought, especially when it carried the mask of reason and intelligence. He was often merciless, especially when sloppy thinking united with moral cowardice. In late 1938 he wrote a scathing article entitled "The Treason of the Flags." When British prime minister Neville Chamberlain and French prime minister Édouard Daladier "saved" the peace of Europe in the fall of 1938 by sacrificing Czechoslovakia's territorial integrity to Hitler, Netherlanders everywhere hung out flags. "The Dutch nation . . . displayed flags, because in Munich they had silently throttled the neck of another small nation: Czechoslovakia."[92] Unlike his compatriots, Ter Braak did not celebrate the fact that war had been averted. The price, surrendering to Hitler's demands, had been too high.

David read and admired this piece, as he read and admired almost everything Ter Braak wrote. One essay that shaped David's life was "The Jewish Spirit and Literature," published in 1939. The non-Jewish Ter Braak tackled the problems created by the emancipation and the assimilation of the Jews with intellectual courage, integrity, and empathy. He was a relentless critic of anti-Semitism and an opponent of National Socialism, but he did not deny that "the Jewish question" was both real and difficult, and that it expressed itself in literature. Assimilation, Ter Braak argued, had too often produced Jewish writers, or more appropriately "men of letters," who adapted well to European civilization but who were unable to speak with an original and authentic voice because they were uprooted from their own vital tradition. Among these writers he included Stefan Zweig, Lion Feuchtwanger, and Emil Ludwig. In his view, only a few assimilated Jewish writers had developed an authentic voice: Julien Benda, Lev Shestov, and Franz Kafka.[93] David recognized in Ter Braak's analysis his own struggle to find his place and voice. And Ter Braak, who read one of David's poems published in *Vulpes* (*The Fox*), the official, principal-approved student magazine of the Vossius Gymnasium, recognized in the young man someone who could become either just another "man of letters" or a true writer. He contacted David, and they met for a long conversation in Ter Braak's newspaper office—the high point in David's prewar intellectual life.

In his admiration for Greshoff and Ter Braak, David did not push the envelope of what could earn the understanding of his peers and the approval of his teachers. In the last year of high school, however, he became aware of the work of the eminent Russian-Jewish scholar, writer, and Zionist thinker Jacob Klatzkin (1882–1948), and this discovery opened a new and exciting political and intellectual horizon that was irrelevant to his non-Jewish peers, and off-putting to the great majority of Dutch Jews. David believed that Klatzkin's *Krisis und Entscheidung im Judentum* (*Crisis and Decision in Jewry*), published in 1921, offered a blueprint for his own life as a member of the Jewish people who were facing, in the rise of National Socialism, the greatest challenge since the beginning of emancipation.[94] Klatzkin analyzed the crisis of European Jews in the wake of World War I. He thought that the Balfour Declaration (1917), which promised the Jews a national home in Palestine, and the prospect of full Jewish emancipation resulting from the collapse of the autocratic Russian, Austro-Hungarian, and German empires (1918) threatened the future of Jewish culture and religion in the Galut (exile). In order for Jewish life in Europe to survive, Jews had to accept and even embrace the antagonism they generated, refuse the offer of equal rights, and voluntarily return to the situation before the emancipation, "with all its advantages and disadvantages." Only in a "new ghetto" would they be able to maintain their own culture "in springlike purity." Jews should abandon the claim that they could be good Jews *and* good Germans, good Jews *and* good Frenchmen, and accept, instead, a painful choice: "either Jew or German, either Jew or Frenchman."[95] Jews in the Galut should have the courage to tell the majority: "An unbridgeable abyss exists between you and us. Your spirit is alien to us, as are your myths and sagas and your national heritage."[96] Jewish existence in exile should remain an anomaly, a source of conflict, and Jews should heroically accept "the persistence of the Jewish question, and not its solution." Such a life demanded intellectual rigor, willpower, discipline, and stubbornness, fostered by a small elite that would shape and govern the new ghetto. "Only an elite, a small band of idealists and fanatics, are able . . . to be the bearers and the protectors of Judaism in the tragic insolubility and double anomaly of the contemporary Galut."[97]

Klatzkin's ideas fired David's political imagination. And they led David into a world that would remain radically separate from the social life he had built up at the Vossius Gymnasium. He may never have expressed the thought that "an unbridgeable abyss exists between you and me" to Tini, Fré, and Karel, but he kept them out of the almost cultlike world that filled his imagination and commanded his loyalty—a semisecret realm that accommodated a three-year-long rebellion against his Dutch-Jewish upbringing at home and his Dutch national education in the public school system.

David Embraces Radical Zionism

David's rebellion began on November 30, 1937. Three days after David's sixteenth birthday Jacques celebrated the completion of "his" synagogue. The new building confirmed the position of the Rivers Quarter as a new center of Judaism in Amsterdam. The day marked a high point in Jacques's life. It also brought him unexpected disappointment. In Judaism a boy officially becomes an adult at the age of thirteen. Yet a thirteen-year-old adult is a contradiction in terms. The board of the Lekstraat synagogue realized this. They knew that the long-term future of their synagogue depended on their own willingness to welcome and accommodate the adolescent members of their community as bearers of much-needed fresh energy without demanding total conformity from the outset. Therefore they built, next to the main sanctuary, a special youth synagogue that would ensure a graduated transition of the young members into the adult community. Refusing the separate and subordinate place of youth within the community, David joined the Mizrahi youth organization Zichron Ja'akov instead.

The Zionism created by Theodor Herzl was purely secular and hence heretical in the views of devout Jews. Shortly after the First Zionist Congress in the Swiss city of Basel (1897), the Lithuanian rabbi Jacob Reines conceived that Orthodox Jews might embrace a Zionist agenda if it were to accommodate and celebrate traditional Jewish religious and cultural values. To that end he founded the Mizrahi movement, which adopted the motto "The land of Israel for the people of Israel according to the Torah of Israel."[98] Eastern European Jews brought Mizrahism to Antwerp, and in 1914, when they fled into the neutral Netherlands to escape the German occupation of Belgium, they introduced it to the Dutch-Jewish community.

In the 1920s the Dutch Mizrahi movement found itself between the anvil of the anticlericalism of Dutch Zionists and the hammer of the anti-Zionism of much of the Dutch-Jewish community, and it attracted few followers. However, its youth organization, Zichron Ja'akov (In Memory of Jacob [Reines]), prospered. Zichron welcomed boys and girls on a basis of equality, breaking with the view prevalent in Dutch-Jewish circles that the Jewish education of girls should focus simply on how to keep a kosher kitchen. In Zichron, youths did not learn about Judaism and Zionism but *lived* it in a subculture that fused puritanism and messianism. Zichron offered exciting programs that merged Jewish religious education, Zionist ideology, and instruction in modern Hebrew, or Ivrit, which was the official language of the Jewish community in Palestine.[99] The members conducted services with an eastern European élan that did not exist in the Dutch synagogues. The Dutch-Jewish establishment considered Zichron with great suspicion, even hostility, but many Jewish youngsters, unhappy with the hierarchical organization and the pomp and circumstance of Dutch-Jewish religious life, or simply seeking to create some distance between themselves and their parents, loved it.[100]

In the Amsterdam branch of Zichron, David found a religious and cultural milieu that seemed like a breath of fresh air. In Zichron he could present himself as his own man, transcending his subordinate status as Jacques's son. And Zichron also allowed him to widen his horizon. The club was the most important component of the Joodse Jeugdfederatie (Jewish Youth Federation), a national organization that brought together all Zionist youth societies in the Netherlands and that acted as their representative to the outside world. Participating in summer camps of the Jewish Youth Federation, David would discover the Dutch-Jewish communities outside his native city.

When David left the Lekstraat synagogue and joined Zichron he was in his middle adolescence, a period when young people often test limits, committing themselves to values and principles of conduct that clash with those taught at home before finding a place in the social order. They may feel the urge to create a relationship of personal loyalty to a leader of their choice, one their parents often object to.[101] In Zichron David met a group of young men who were from five to twelve years older than he and who became his mentors and heroes. Given their age, they should already have left Zichron, but they continued to hang around. They had also read Klatzkin, and inspired by him they called themselves Radical Zionists.[102] The group included the

energetic Jaap Meijer, the learned Jozeph Melkman, and the charis-
matic Lion Nordheim. Applying Klatzkin's ideas to the rapidly wors-
ening conditions for Jews in Germany, Poland, Romania, and other
countries, they had become convinced that the project of assimilation was in shambles and that the Jewish community in the Netherlands would not be spared. They believed that Jews should give up
the illusion that they were Jewish Netherlanders, or even Dutch Jews;
they were Jews who happened to be living in the Netherlands.[103]

The refugee crisis caused by the Nazi seizure of power in Germany
in 1933 revealed difficulties in the relations between Jews and non-
Jews in the Netherlands. On the one hand, Dutch Jews felt the need
and moral obligation to show solidarity with Jews who fled Germany,
and this implied that they ought to oppose the Dutch government's
restriction of asylum.[104] On the other hand, most were afraid to challenge the government and chose to treat the refugee issue as one of
relief and charity only. The Radical Zionists believed that Dutch Jews
ought to declare an unconditional identity with the German Jews,
and by implication with Jews everywhere, even if it were to lead to
their isolation in Dutch society. After the Dutch government decreed
on May 7, 1938, that, in principle, no more refugees would be admitted, and that all who had arrived since March 1 would be treated as
"unwelcome aliens" and returned to Germany,[105] Meijer and Nordheim called on Jewish youth to draw the correct conclusion. "We do
not ask the Dutch government to admit them, because we are not
'*schnorrers*' (beggars). But we appeal to the Jews, including Dutch Jews,
at last to take control over their own destiny, the destiny of our own
nation, a nation of unwelcome aliens. . . . This nation will not bow its
head, not even for the sake of its security, or agree to its extinction. It
knows only one response to persecution: to go its own way, however
difficult it may be."[106] The fortieth anniversary of Queen Wilhelmina's
reign in August of 1938 led them to articulate the principled position
that, as Jews, they could not participate in the patriotic festivities.

Klatzkin had assumed that a spiritual aristocracy consisting of people who refused to bend, compromise, or concede would have to
lead the Jews back from assimilation, acculturation, and seculariza-
tion into self-imposed isolation. In this spirit Nordheim gathered a
small group of people who would become that avant-garde in the
Netherlands. David was its youngest member. They met on an almost
daily basis in the cellar of the house of a member's parents, and therefore the group became known as the Catacombs. They debated Klatz-

kin's views, the provincialism of the Dutch-Jewish community, and the moral cowardice of rank-and-file Dutch Zionists. They were not afraid to offend. It is not surprising that the members of the Cata-combs were unpopular, since not only secular Zionists but also mem-bers of the Mizrahi movement and many other Dutch Jews regarded the self-appointed elite of Dutch-Jewish youth with irritation and disapproval.[107]

David's turn to Radical Zionism and his membership in the Cata-combs led to a rift with Jacques, who had taught him a vision of Jew-ish history that stressed the continuity and security of the Amsterdam Jews. Before 1938 the relationship between Jacques and David had been easy. But from the beginning of 1938 to the beginning of 1941, when German persecution would bring them together again, father and son were almost like strangers, an alienation that was also influ-enced by Jacques's increasing despair about the future of the Jews in Europe.

Yet the distance between Jacques and David was a blessing in dis-guise for Judith. A quiet and modest woman, she had enjoyed the bond between her husband and his sons when times were good. When a break developed in the relationship between Jacques and David she stepped into the breach, and mother and son began to confide in each other. They forged strong ties that would continue in the camp, when David often sneaked into the women's section to see her. "Mother was ill for a few days and my days were empty," David wrote in May 1943: "Something drives me towards her. . . . It's something I experience an urge to do every afternoon, but not an urge arising of tenderness, rather out of a need whose character I'm unable to determine. Partly of a moral character, but also to give every day a fixed point."[108] Indeed, from 1938 until their separation on June 6, 1944, in Auschwitz-Birkenau, Judith would be a source of strength and consolation to David.

For three years David maintained a fire wall between his Dutch world centered on Karel van het Reve and his Jewish world centered on Lion Nordheim. All the same, in the early spring of 1939 these two worlds touched when David decided to apply for admission to the sociography program at the University of Amsterdam. Tini Israël had discovered sociography, a field that embraced social geography and ethnography.[109] Karel became interested in it because he fancied Tini, and David then got interested in it, and not only because he could not bear to be separated from Karel. Although a committed Radical Zionist, David did not like all the implications of Zionism. As an aspiring intellectual, he felt no attraction to Youth Aliyah, which took teenagers to kibbutzim in Palestine, or to Hachshara (literally, "preparation"), which prepared young people of university age for agricultural work. David was unwilling to abandon a future as an educated man. Sociography seemed to offer an opportunity to reconcile opposites. Henri Nicolaas ter Veen, the chair of the department of sociography, was a specialist on the formation of societies in the polders (areas reclaimed from the water).[110] David recognized that there were many parallels between polder settlements and the *moshavim* (villages) in Palestine: both developed virgin lands and both created instant communities. He believed that, as a sociographer, he might take a leading role in the Zionist project.[111]

In May 1939 David passed the examinations that concluded his secondary education and gained him admission to the university. Despite his achievement, David felt in no mood to celebrate: the British government had just issued a white paper limiting Jewish immigration to Palestine to seventy-five thousand over the next five years and making it dependent on Arab approval starting in 1944. This effectively meant the rescinding of the Balfour Declaration and the end of the prospect of a Jewish national home in Palestine. Jews all over the world protested. In Amsterdam, the Radical Zionists did not join the protests. They weren't beggars, after all. Klatzkin had taught them the power of facts, and the members of the Catacombs began to chart a course that acknowledged the new situation, a course that was to be announced at the annual meeting of the Jewish Youth Federation scheduled for next September. Accepting the truth that their own generation would find it difficult if not impossible to emigrate to Palestine, Nordheim persuaded David and the others to shift their focus from settlement, and the politics that would make it possible, to the preservation of Zionism as an idea. They would connect to the long history of the Jewish longing for Zion, which was untouchable. "We must separate the Zionist movement from current politics, with which it was connected up to now, perhaps out of necessity," Nordheim wrote in the summer of 1939. "We must discover Zionism as the Jewish struggle for the Messiah. It did not arise half a century ago but at the beginning of the Galut."[112]

In June and July the Kokers began to plan for David's entry into the university. Money was tight, and therefore Jacques, Judith, and David

David Koker, 1939

agreed that he would live at home rather than find a room near the university, and use his bicycle to commute. But they also agreed that he needed more space. During his high school years he had shared a room with Max; now Judith suggested that she and Jacques yield their own bedroom to David. He would be able to live there as if he had moved out, free of the obligation to socialize with the other members of the Koker household. Jacques agreed, and the parents relocated to the sitting room.

David moved into his new room at the beginning of September, on the weekend that Germany invaded Poland, and Britain and France declared war on Germany. Many Netherlanders, expecting their own country to remain neutral, observed the hostilities from the sidelines and more or less dispassionately. Few liked Nazi Germany, or for that matter Germany, a country admired and envied for its accomplishments but feared for its dominating influence on Dutch economic and cultural life. Furthermore, although there was a small Dutch National Socialist movement that favored Germany in the war, a larger number of people adopted a pro-British and pro-French stance. As for Poland, it was a distant country with an authoritarian government that was terra incognita to most Netherlanders. David and his fellow Radical Zionists took a different view of the war against Poland, for they felt great solidarity with Polish Jewry. They realized that a German occupation of Poland would mean a catastrophe for the Jews living there. No strangers to anti-Semitism, the Polish Jews were to undergo that affliction in an immeasurably more virulent and deadly form.

David saw with great clarity that the fate of Polish Jewry was to determine the fate of all Jews, including himself. He was not equally sure about the way the increasingly uncertain future of the Netherlands was to shape his own position. In early 1939, when war appeared imminent, the same Radical Zionists who had counseled Jews not to join in the festivities surrounding Queen Wilhelmina's Jubilee determined that Jews who were citizens of the Netherlands ought to serve in the Dutch armed forces when called up to do so.[113] On August 28, 1939, the Dutch government mobilized the armed forces. At that time David was seventeen and not eligible to be conscripted. Turning eighteen in November, however, he faced the prospect of military service. And while he did not question his legal obligation to serve, he was unsure that this was politically right.

As a member of the Catacombs, David had been initiated into the inner sanctum of Radical Zionism. Now that he was a university student, he was expected to take positions of responsibility in the movement. David knew how to write, and in September 1939 Nordheim arranged for his appointment as joint editor of two monthly magazines. The first was *Pitchon peh* (*Giving a Voice*), published for the members of Zichron. David immediately changed the course of the magazine, expanding its role from being a magazine for internal use to one that also served the spread of Radical Zionist ideas into the Jewish community at large.[114] In the October issue, David and his fellow editor Jacob Vleeschhouwer accompanied a description of a rabbi's life in the provinces with a sharply worded editorial in which they indicted Jewish life in the Galut: one with little dignity and no energy. It illustrated "the great spiritual disarray in which our people find themselves and which can become fatal if we are unable to discern the Galut-element in our own mental lives and, as far as possible, to eliminate it."[115] But David's stewardship of *Pitchon peh* ended after two months. The November issue carried a terse announcement that he had resigned as editor because he was too busy.

David was indeed busy. In September he had also become an editor of *Tikwath Israel* (*The Hope of Israel*), the monthly magazine of the Jewish Youth Federation. His first contribution to *Tikwath Israel* was a report on the annual meeting of the Federation held in mid-September—the occasion Nordheim used to announce the appropriate response to the white paper and to the war. David described the speech as the beginning of a new epoch in the history of the federation. For the first twenty years of its existence, Zionism had been the means and the Jewish homeland in Palestine the end, but for an indeterminate time to come Zionism would have to carry the burden of being both means and end.[116] David and his fellow editors of *Tikwath Israel* endorsed Nordheim's vision. If Zionism had focused before on the building of the Jewish homeland in Palestine, it must now focus on life in the Galut without, however, endorsing the Galut. "Let us join the long succession of generations who were capable of bearing the sorrow without losing the feeling of freedom."[117] By looking backward, the Zionists would keep the flame of the return to Palestine alive.

David embraced this change in policy. He hastily penned an article for the November issue of *Tikwath Israel* about the emancipation of the Jews during the French Revolution, and the price they had to pay for it. "It is good to show . . . how much they demeaned themselves in order to be assimilated, and how frantically their descendants exert themselves to remain assimilated."[118] In January 1940 he considered the meaning of Palestine at a time when entry to it would be severely restricted for years to come: "Palestine means to us what it has meant to our people for 2,000 years." David defined the core of the Jewish nation as the memory of a shared past in Palestine and an anticipation of a shared future in Palestine. It was therefore the symbol of Jewish nationality and history.

> To see Palestine as the symbol of our existence as a people means: realizing this symbol in everything. Knowing that Palestine is our fatherland and we are on the way there means calling no other country our own. By means of the symbol we realize that we are a people. When we see Palestine in this way: as a symbol of our existence as a people, and when we realize this idea in our life by way of a positive Jewish attitude that rejects the Galut, we thereby continue a centuries-long tradition.[119]

In the same January 1940 issue David published a polemical article that was to land him in trouble. He had read that five hundred Czech Jews, who had reached Palestine after the outbreak of the war, were going to join the Czech Legion in France. David was appalled. He understood their anger against the Germans and their wish to fight them, but he could not understand that a Jew who had arrived in Palestine would want to return to the Galut. David thundered that "an action like that can only be described as treason." These Jews did not owe Czechoslovakia any loyalty, particularly because some Czech politicians had called for the expulsion of the Jews long before the German occupation of the Czech lands in March 1939. Alluding to Ter Braak's image of the "treason of the flags," David concluded that Jews had no choice but to "turn our backs on the Galut and to be aware that the flags waving there are not our own."[120]

This bold and contentious assertion enraged the Jewish and Zionist establishments. Many Dutch Jews had become increasingly worried that Nordheim and his fellow Radical Zionists were providing Dutch Nazis with pretexts to push for some local version of Germany's anti-Semitic Nuremberg Laws. At the beginning of 1939 the mainline Zionist organization had threatened to break its ties with the Jewish Youth Federation, and the national Mizrahi organization had disavowed Zichron. The Radical Zionists found themselves isolated within the Jewish community as a whole. This only strengthened their belief that they were on the right path, and they decided not to change it.[121] However, Abel Herzberg, a prominent lawyer, a key member of the Jewish establishment, and the leader of the mainstream Zionists, who had been seeking for some time to break the Radical Zionists, thought he had found a way to do so when he read David's article. He brought a charge against David before the Zionist Council of Honor—the court of discipline that had jurisdiction over all Zionist organizations in the Netherlands. The trial was scheduled for May 12, 1940.

As he awaited the proceedings, David dropped out of the sociography program. He had become disappointed with courses that struck him as pedestrian, and Karel and Tini had begun to attend lectures on Russian history and literature. More important was that David's choice of sociography had been prompted by his desire to gain skills that would be useful in Palestine. By 1940 the prospect of emigration to Palestine had moved from the near to the distant future, and Nordheim had stated that, for the time being, the preservation and ultimate redemption of the Jewish people was to rest on a reconnection to its own history in the Galut. David therefore decided to study history. Until the beginning of the new academic year he would keep himself busy by improving his Hebrew.

The First Years of German Occupation

In the early morning of May 10, 1940, the German armed forces invaded the Netherlands. The Kokers were at home and remained there for the four days of hostilities that ensued. Unlike some three thousand Jews, they did not try to reach Great Britain. And, unlike three hundred Jews, they did not commit suicide. On one occasion a few bombers of the *Luftwaffe* attacked Amsterdam, but the damage was slight and the Rivers Quarter remained untouched. At the time of the invasion David was preparing for his trial before the Zionist Council of Honor. But the Dutch government ordered the closure of all schools and public institutions on May 10, as well as the cessation of all other civic and organizational activities. David's trial was postponed. After the capitulation of the Dutch armed forces in the Netherlands on May 14, the Zionists faced bigger issues than David's article. They never set a new date for the trial.

Queen Wilhelmina, the royal family, and the cabinet had fled to England, creating a government in exile that was committed to continuing the war, putting the wealth of the Dutch colonies, the navy, and the merchant fleet at the disposal of the Allies. In the absence of a legitimate government, administration fell to the College of Secretaries-General, an informal gathering of the senior civil servants overseeing the Dutch governmental ministries. The college had no standing in Dutch law and the secretaries-general, who had never carried political responsibility, were ill prepared for their new roles. The Germans exploited the power vacuum in the occupied Netherlands by establishing a civilian administration led by Arthur Seyss-Inquart, an Austrian Nazi who had been instrumental in the *Anschluss* of 1938. He aimed to trigger in the Netherlands a process of Nazification in which the Dutch people would participate voluntarily.[122] Hence Seyss-Inquart decided to govern through the College of Secretaries-General.

It was a cunning decision. The secretaries-general took pride in being loyal servants of an elected government, servants who had never resisted directives. In an early conversation with German military authorities, the secretaries-general made clear that they were ready to cooperate with the Germans, but that they were concerned "about the Jewish question."[123] They did not articulate their fear that the Germans would persecute the Jews. Instead they chose to speak in generalities. They assumed, they said, that the Germans would respect the Hague Land Warfare Convention, which stipulated that the occupying power "shall take all the measures in his power to restore and ensure, as far as possible, public order and [civil life], while respecting, unless absolutely prevented, the laws in force in the country."[124] The German commander assured them Germany would not violate Dutch law, and the heads of the Dutch civil service inferred that the Jews were safe.

The leadership of the Jewish community also assumed that the Germans would honor the convention. Probably this was wishful thinking: after all, the Germans had shown in Czechoslovakia and Poland that they did not much care about international law. But most thought that the Netherlands was "more civilized" than eastern Europe, that the Dutch Jews were "more civilized" than eastern-European Jewry, and that the Germans would therefore act in a "more civilized" manner than they had in the east. The best course, it seemed, would be to adopt a policy of avoiding confrontation, in the hope that the Germans would leave the Jews alone.

This position was influenced by two thousand years of precedent. Through retreat or submission, the Jews had survived in dangerous times. One famous example took place during the Roman siege of Jerusalem in 70 C.E. After the famous Rabbi Yochanan ben Zakkai had failed to persuade the Zealots defending the city that continued resistance would end in catastrophe, he left the city and successfully petitioned the commander of the Roman army to allow him to build an academy in the small village of Yavneh. This academy became an important religious center that was instrumental in the survival of the Jewish religion and people.

Six weeks after the beginning of the occupation, the same Abel Herzberg who had initiated the proceedings against David wrote that the Dutch Jews should withdraw into a "Yavneh" of their own making. This village, in his view, symbolized "a transitional form" in which a national identity could be preserved without the aid of politics. As a consequence of the German occupation, Jewish politics of the kind that had been embodied in the Zionist movement had come to an end for the time being. Herzberg entreated Jews to remember Yavneh while returning "to the core of all our work! To Judaism, to Jewish culture, to the spirit, history, and essence of Judaism."[125]

Herzberg's article triggered a debate in the Jewish community. Many Jews believed that Yochanan ben Zakkai had acted cowardly, and some stated this openly. Herzberg responded by saying that in avoiding a battle that could not be won, the rabbi had been more courageous than the Zealots. His was "a pathos that was more quiet, more inward, without glitter and without the dramatic gesture, continuing to burn within the boundaries of a self-imposed reasonableness."[126]

In some ways Herzberg's Yavneh was a variation on the theme of Klatzkin's voluntary ghetto. But if Klatzkin's withdrawal from non-Jewish society was a political act connected to the ideal of achieving a Jewish homeland in Palestine, Herzberg's proposal was apolitical, even antipolitical.

David apparently opted to heed Herzberg's advice and follow the example of Yochanan ben Zakkai. It corresponded, of course, to the turn to history that he had taken a year earlier. During this period David turned to Nettie David, whom he had met in Zichron. Her

MAX KOKER

Nettie David (left), Tini Israël (right), and Fré Samson (kneeling), 1943

father had been a successful businessman in Germany before his flight to the Netherlands, and Nettie had grown up in a sophisticated and cosmopolitan milieu in which David felt at home. The two developed a close intellectual companionship that remained, however, a private affair. It appears David kept Nettie out of the eye of friends and family. Neither Karel in his written recollections about his friendship with David nor Fré or Max in conversations have shed light on the nature and intensity of the relationship. Nettie died in 2000 and did not leave any testimony about her relationship with David.[127] No letters survive from the years of the relationship before Nettie and David were separated as the result of David's arrest and internment in Vught. All we know is that, while in the camp, David wrote about his deep longing for Nettie, and that he wrote the diary for her.

While Nettie may have provided an emotional center for David, the creative and academic center of his "Yavneh" was the legacy of the Dutch-Jewish poet Jacob Israël de Haan (1881–1924). In 1940 David began systematically to read and collect the works of the brilliant, famous, and notorious journalist, writer, and lawyer Jacob Israël de Haan. He had discovered De Haan's work while at the Vossius Gymnasium, but before the beginning of the German occupation David's main literary focus had been on Greshoff and Ter Braak. In the context of Yavneh as the symbolic location of Jewish life in the German-occupied Netherlands, the concerns embodied in the work of those two writers appeared less relevant. The work of De Haan spoke to David as he withdrew into an increasingly isolated Jewish community.

De Haan's life was full of bizarre twists and turns.[128] Raised in a devout Jewish household, he became an ardent Socialist at twenty, acquired notoriety as the author of an openly homosexual novel at twenty-three, and, at twenty-six, married the non-Jewish physician Johanna van Maarseveen, who was eight years his senior.[129] At the age of twenty-nine he began to rebuild a Jewish identity through the creation of a series of magnificent Jewish-themed poems.[130] He adopted the middle name Israël, and in his midthirties found a spiritual home in Mizrahi Zionism.

De Haan moved to Palestine in late 1918 as the correspondent of the *Algemeen handelsblad,* a high-quality Dutch newspaper with cultural aspirations; his wife remained in the Netherlands. In Palestine, De Haan tried to obtain a senior position in the British administration or the Jewish Agency, but failed to do so. Sir Ronald Storrs, the British governor of Jerusalem, in his memoirs describes De Haan as a "tragic, haunted figure" who was "a difficult subject to place. . . . Facially he was an intellectual version of Vincent van Gogh, whose dreadful glare of an unknown terror sometimes blazed in his eyes also."[131] Rejected by the British and Zionist establishments, De Haan sought shelter in the Arab community. There he enjoyed the friendship and love of male adolescents. At the same time, he took up the cause of the ultra-Orthodox Jews in Jerusalem who opposed Zionism as a heretical, secular ideology. His liaisons with Arab boys and his public support for Jewish anti-Zionism made De Haan a despised and hated figure among the Zionists, one of whom assassinated him in 1924.[132]

David was fascinated by this obviously torn individual and felt great affection for him.[133] In this he stood alone: the literary and the Jewish establishments both considered De Haan's legacy too toxic. But to David, De Haan was no mere "man of letters": his voice was authentic. In the summer of 1940 David contacted De Haan's widow, who had received all her husband's manuscripts after his death. Johanna van Maarseveen liked the young enthusiast. They began to meet regularly, and soon she appointed David executor of her husband's literary estate. She lent David all her husband's manuscripts and promised him that, upon her own death, he would inherit everything, including the rights of publication.[134]

David began to prepare a small book containing a selection from the articles that De Haan had written as the Palestine correspondent of the *Algemeen handelsblad*. It appeared in 1941. In his introduction, David described De Haan as a man who was driven by a dialectic of *Beauty,* represented by the Arabs (and specifically by the "earnestness and beauty of the children") and *Sanctity,* represented by the "intimacy and self-discipline" of the pious Jews who had embraced the sinner. David noted that De Haan had been unable to bring these two principles together in a synthesis, and that he lived the conflict between beauty and sanctity in every moment, thinking of young men when he prayed, and thinking of the security of piety when he was with the boys. This split was tragic, David observed, but De Haan's honesty about his own needs and desires made him heroic.[135] If Greshoff had taught David the value of compromise, De Haan taught him to appreciate contradiction. It was a lesson that was to serve him well in Vught.

In 1941 David began to organize De Haan's literary estate with an eye to assembling a critical edition of all De Haan's poems. The project ended abruptly when the Kokers were arrested. David and Van Maarseveen had prepared for such an eventuality: Karel would try to save David's work and turn it over to her. He broke the seal on the Koker apartment, entered it, and removed the De Haan material (he also took such personal and priceless possessions as the family photos reproduced in this book). In 1946, when it was clear that David would not come back, Karel and Van Maarseveen donated the documents to the Bibliotheca Rosenthaliana, a major collection of Hebraica and Judaica that is now part of the library of the University of Amsterdam. There it caught the attention of the critic Kees Lekkerkerker, who gained permission from Van Maarseveen to continue the work David had begun. However, Lekkerkerker's two-volume edition of De Haan's collected poems, published in 1952, did not credit David.[136] Nor did the historian of the Dutch-Jewish community Jaap Meijer, who relied on David's work in writing his De Haan biography, acknowledge David's crucial role in saving De Haan's legacy and preparing the ground for his own book.[137]

In 1940 David also became interested in those Jewish poets living in Palestine who wrote in the Hebrew language. By this time he had reached such a level of competence in Hebrew that he could consider translating contemporary poetry from that language into Dutch. His collaborator was his Hebrew teacher, Jozeph Melkman. Lion Nordheim, who had created his own Yavneh through a series of small books that sought to make Jewish writing and Jewish culture available to a Jewish public, and who had accepted David's edition of De Haan's letters from Jerusalem, invited David and Melkman to publish those translations in his series. The result was a small volume that contains a learned introductory essay on Jewish poetry in Palestine, twenty poems printed in both Hebrew and Dutch, and brief biographies of the poets.[138]

One poet, Isaac Lamdan, impressed David with particular force. In "The Chain of Dances" Lamdan brings together the major issue faced by David and the Dutch Jews: the preservation and celebration of the continuity of Jewish history in the presence of the abyss. Lamdan's central metaphor is that of a chain that is unbroken and continues from generation to generation, a chain of dancers holding one another and bearing the load of history, who dance with eyes closed because they don't want to see the abyss below them, knowing that, if they open their eyes, "the chain would crumble into the

MAX KOKER

The Chain of Dances, *painting by Max Koker, 1995. Max painted this scene based on Lamdan's poem (of the same title) in honor of his brother, David, who in 1941 published a Dutch translation of the poem.*

deep."[139] Lamdan's poem became a lodestar to David, who found in it his determination to carry on the legacy of the Jewish people. After David's death, Max saw in it a call to preserve his brother's legacy. A few years ago Max painted *The Chain of Dances* in homage to his brother. His wife, Nina, chose the colors.

By late 1937 David had turned his back on the world represented by his father. For two and a half years he was caught up in the intense world of Radical Zionism, but in the course of 1940 he realized that the ready-made identity offered by the Jewish Youth Federation and the Catacombs no longer suited the person he had become. In late 1940, as he would write in his diary a couple of years later, he began to consider Zionism as an "erratic way" of achieving Jewish conscious-ness. "Not with words does the Jewish people propagate itself, but with songs."[140] In this sentence David declares himself to be the son of Jacques, who had sung his faith on Friday evenings and his joy on Sat-urday afternoons. Singing had been at the core of the Koker house-hold, and to that household he now returned to find the refuge that would allow not only him but also the Jewish people and Judaism to survive spiritually. But he brought with him in this return the experience and insight he had gained from Nordheim's mentorship: especially the idea that the basis for Jewish life in an increasingly difficult environment could be found in an understanding of the historical continuity of the Jewish people in the Galut.

In March 1941 David published a five-page article on the Jewish family and its Jewish tradition. "What connects us more closely to the Jewish people and to its past than the Jewish family, where the past lives on in rituals and symbols? Preserving the Jewish people means: continuing its past in whatever form." David characterized the Jewish family as "the only natural and completely Jewish community that is possible in the Galut." And for that reason the family circle was the symbol of two thousand years of continuity, and a writer's attitude to the family was the litmus test of his Jewish identity. "A man of letters whose origins are Jewish can only be called Jewish if his attitude towards the Jewish people, as it is revealed to him in the form of the family, and towards the past of the people, as it survives in the rituals and symbols of that family, gains positive expression in his writings."[141]

The publication of *Menorah 5702: Joods jaarboek* (*Jewish Yearbook*) in September 1941 confirmed David's return to the family hearth. Editors Hugo Heymans and Jozeph Melkman state in their introduction that their aim was to provide a mirror to the Jews, and to provide support on the difficult road ahead. They included David's Sabbath poem. "And through our eyes / there passed the very same serene surprise / that everything could be so good and pleasing."[142]

When David's poem appeared in print, the Germans had completed the first phase of their assault on the Dutch Jews, violating the Hague Land Warfare Convention with every decree they issued.[143] In September 1940 they asked for a list of all public servants who were wholly or partly Jewish. Since this information was not available from the existing records, the College of Secretaries-General instructed all public servants and elected public officials to declare whether or not they had Jewish grandparents and, if so, how many. There were many misgivings about this, but very few people, whether non-Jews or Jews, refused to submit the "Aryan declaration." An attempt to legitimate the action of those who wished to refuse making the declaration failed when the supreme court ruled by majority vote that no basis existed for refusal. As the court had every reason to believe that the declaration would be used against those who had identified themselves as Jewish, the ruling betrayed a lack of insight and moral courage. This was compounded when a letter expressing objection to any dismissals of public servants that might result from the declaration was ultimately not sent to Seyss-Inquart. This decision was taken by the two associate chief justices, Chief Justice Lodewijk E. Visser having recused himself because he was Jewish.[144] All those who had registered as Jews, just over twenty-five hundred in total, were suspended from their duties in November and then dismissed.[145] There were few protests in the civil service, but student strikes took place at the Universities of Delft and Leiden in protest against the dismissal of Jewish professors and lecturers (university teachers were public servants). The Germans closed both institutions.[146]

More menacing to the Jewish community was the registration of all those who met the official definition of Jewishness. Anyone with at least three Jewish grandparents, or anyone who was a member of a synagogue or who was married to a Jew and who had one or two Jewish grandparents, was regarded as Jewish. By early 1941 the Dutch authorities had registered 140,522 full Jews, 14,549 half Jews (those with two Jewish grandparents), and 5,719 quarter Jews (people with one Jewish grandparent). The Kokers registered as full Jews and received identity cards marked with a *J*. Once the Jews had been identified their assets were registered.

The systematic isolation of the Dutch Jews was interrupted by an episode of violence. After an incident in Amsterdam in which Dutch Nazis had attacked Jews who had shown the insolence to resist, 600 German security police raided the Jewish Quarter of Amsterdam on February 22 and 23, 1941. They picked up between 425 and 450 male Jews, forced them to run a gauntlet, and then shipped them off, first to Buchenwald concentration camp near Weimar, where some of them died, and from there to Mauthausen, near Linz. All but one of the Amsterdam Jews taken to Mauthausen were murdered within days of their arrival.[147] Reacting with outrage to the raid and more generally to the growing persecution of the Jews, municipal employees, metalworkers, and longshoremen in Amsterdam launched a strike that paralyzed the transportation systems and industrial production in the provinces of North Holland and Utrecht. The Germans crushed the strike ruthlessly.[148] Cowed into compliance, the great majority of

Dutch citizens turned to their daily affairs, grudgingly enduring the German presence for the duration.[149]

The mass arrest and the strike represented a watershed for the Jews. From then on they were outlaws who could be arrested and sent to Mauthausen or any other camp at will. In addition, Jews could no longer deal as individuals with the occupiers: the Germans would deal only with the newly appointed Jewish Council, chaired by the wealthy businessman Abraham Asscher and the prominent academic Dr. David Cohen. On March 12, 1941, Seyss-Inquart stated publicly that Jews did not form part of the Dutch nation and that he sought the complete elimination of Jews from social and economic life. The Germans worked hard to achieve that goal. In 1941 the Jews lost access to public parks, restaurants, cafés, theaters, cinemas, swimming pools, concert halls, public libraries and museums, and they were restricted to a few facilities that were available only to them. Jewish children were expelled from the public school system and forced into hastily created Jewish schools. Jews could shop only during specified hours of the afternoon, when stocks of goods that were dwindling in any case were often sold out or in short supply. Travel was first curtailed and later prohibited. By the late spring of 1942, Jews were forced to turn in their bicycles, radios, and telephones. At that time, too, they were no longer permitted to visit non-Jews and were not allowed to leave their homes between 6 p.m. and 6 a.m. Jewish businesses were expropriated, Jewish land was seized, Jewish employees were laid off, the licenses of Jewish professionals were withdrawn, and all pension claims had to be cashed in at a token surrender value. Jewish financial assets had to be deposited with a well-established bank, Lippmann, Rosenthal & Co., which the Germans used as a tool of despoliation. The only way for a Jew to earn anything was by means of casual labor. "Mauthausen" was the threat that hung over anyone who resisted, and everyone knew that "Mauthausen" meant death.[150] Few Dutch gentiles took much notice of the Jewish plight, however. They knew they were not targeted; too many felt little or no solidarity with their Jewish compatriots and even less with the refugees who had immigrated before the war. The pillar system that structured Dutch society by means of a contract of mutual indifference showed its fatal weakness.

Being male and twenty years old, David was very much at risk, since Germans randomly arrested Jewish young men from time to time and sent them to Mauthausen. On three occasions he left Amsterdam seeking shelter elsewhere. Once he and Max stayed with their paternal uncle Jacob Koker and family in Hilversum, about sixteen miles east of Amsterdam. On a second occasion he cycled with Karel to Mook, a village south of Nijmegen near the German border, where they stayed for three weeks. Later David stayed in Leiden for several weeks. At this time he also obtained a forged identity card with the name of Hugo van der Brugge. This identity card was not marked with a "J." It does not appear that he ever used it to evade arrest. But after his incarceration in Vught he would use "Hugo" when he wanted to refer to himself in the censored letters addressed to Karel and his other friends. When David was arrested, he carried his official identity card, which he had to surrender in Vught and which was destroyed after his deportation to Auschwitz. His forged papers survived the war in the care of Karel van het Reve. It carried the photo reproduced as the frontispiece of this work.

David was still registered at the University of Amsterdam, but by September 1941 it was clear that his academic future was uncertain. Jewish students already registered were allowed to continue for the time being, but no new Jewish students were admitted. David knew it was only a matter of time before students like him would be forced to leave. He hoped to obtain his first degree before he was expelled, but he was not to reach that goal. He still lacked a few courses when the university, acting on German orders, compelled him and other Jewish students to leave in August 1942. By this time Karel had left the university voluntarily to apprentice himself to a graphic designer and printer. To practice his newly acquired skills, he designed and printed a few small books in editions of ten to twenty copies. One of these was a volume of David's poems.[151]

David was worried not only about his own future but also about the future of fifteen-year-old Max. His formal schooling had come to an end, and he was working as a custodial assistant in a Jewish domestic-science school. Max had not yet learned German, and David believed knowledge of that language might prove to be of vital importance.[152] He taught Max basic grammar and syntax, gave him a dictionary, and began to read Heinrich Heine's *The Harz Journey* with him. This is a rather satirical account of a three-week trip Heine had made in the fall of 1824. The Germany Heine described was an innocent and ineffectual country—very different from the Third Reich. Yet at times the texts David and Max read together were sadly relevant. From Heine's

Ideas: The Book of Le Grand they translated Heine's description of hell as a huge kitchen with a massive stove on which stood three rows of iron pots in which Christians, Jews, and pagans simmer for their sins. The Jews "were sometimes teased by the devils, and it was very comical when a fat, puffing pawnbroker complained about the excessive heat, and a little devil poured a few bucketfuls of cold water over his head, to show him that baptism was a true refreshment to the soul."[153]

Meanwhile the screw continued to tighten. In March 1942 the Germans prohibited marriages and extramarital relations between Jews and non-Jews. On April 29, 1942, the cochairmen of the Jewish Council were summoned to the Zentralstelle für jüdische Auswanderung (Central Office for Jewish Emigration), the local branch of Adolf Eichmann's operation in Berlin. The deputy head of the office, Ferdinand Aus der Fünten, told them that, beginning on May 3, all Jews had to wear a yellow star with the label "Jood." In spite of this, David found the inner peace to compose the long "Festive Writing" of twenty stanzas for Karel's twenty-first birthday on May 19. David recalled how, in the past, words had come easily to him but that, for a year now, his poetry had been "quite austere," and he had recently been unable to write any poems at all.

> Times are unfavorable, that's for sure:
> people are hungry, are uncertain too
> of a tomorrow, of what lies in store,
> they're frightened: more than two years that's been true.

David remembered the lighthearted spirit of his earlier work, full of irony and militancy.

> With God and Satan I would lark and play,
> at Metaphysics I would poke such fun.
> My song would mock itself by day
> and in the evening chase girls every one.

Such affirmations of life and thought were now things of the past. Yet he had decided not to wallow in self-pity and stoically accept the bitter changes that had happened:

> You have to take life as it is, don't fret,
> in one sense everything's to your advantage.

> Just let things come, don't always try to manage.
> And spare yourself annoyance and regret.

At the same time, he acknowledged that acceptance did not mean insight, and certainly not insight into his own heart:

> I am past master at all self-deception,
> one would be pushed to find a match for me.
> What I persuade myself turns into poetry—
> and each verse offers me a new perception
>
> about myself. The matter's most confused,
> as is quite clear if these lines are perused.
> But then, to know one's heart, to know one's head,
> need still not mean one knows oneself as yet.

Even as the Germans determined that David's identity could be summarized in the proper noun "Jew," David continued to ask the question, who am I?

Destruction

A few weeks after David had penned his gift to Karel, Adolf Eichmann in Berlin, Wilhelm Zöpf, Eichmann's representative in the Netherlands, Willy Lages, the head of the Central Office in Amsterdam, and his deputy, Aus der Fünten, began to draft plans for the final phase of the liquidation of the Jewish community in the Netherlands: the deportation to the Polish death camps. On June 11 Eichmann chaired a meeting in Berlin that Zöpf and his counterparts from Brussels and Paris attended. Eichmann announced that military reasons had caused problems with the deportations of German Jews, begun in the fall of 1941, and that during the summer 15,000 Jews from the Netherlands, 10,000 Jews from Belgium, and 100,000 Jews from France were to be sent to Auschwitz instead. Of these Jews, 90 percent had to be between sixteen and forty years of age and able to work. A few days after the meeting it became clear that the Germans would not be able to arrest and transport more than 40,000 Jews of the right age group from France during the summer: the Vichy government put up a fight to prevent the deportation of French Jews. Eichmann reviewed the situation and concluded that Lages and Aus der Fünten would be able to deal with a higher target. Unlike in France, in the Netherlands there was no collaborationist government to consider.[154] On June 20 he called Lages with the order that the initial number of Jews to be deported from the Netherlands was to be 40,000, not 15,000, and that the deportations were to start by mid-July. These 40,000 constituted 90 percent of Jews of between sixteen and forty living in the Netherlands. Six days later Aus der Fünten informed Asscher and Cohen that the Jewish Council had to call up Jews for what he called labor deployment in Germany. On June 28 the Dutch newspapers reported that all Jews would be leaving the Netherlands.

The Jews felt menaced, and at this time some decided that it was time to go into hiding. One of them was Otto Frank, a stateless refugee since November 1941. He had no illusions about the future. He realized that the Jewish Council would most likely try to sacrifice German-Jewish refugees in order to protect Dutch Jews from deportation. He moved his family from his apartment in the Rivers Quarter to a hiding place behind his office on Prinsengracht. Today a bronze statue of Anne Frank commemorates the departure of the Frank family. The statue gazes down Biesboschstraat toward the apartment of the Kokers.

To prepare for the deportations, the Germans forced the Jewish inhabitants of many parts of the country to move to Amsterdam. Most of the more than twenty-five hundred Jews living in Hilversum arrived by truck on June 15. Among them were David's uncle Jacob, his aunt Sara, and his cousin Roza (Rootje). The room they found was so small that Jacques and Judith took in Rootje, who stayed for a few months. She joined David in his project of organizing De Haan's papers and preparing a second volume of his dispatches from Jerusalem. But books by Jewish authors or dealing with Jewish themes were no longer being published in the summer of 1942. The only Jewish publication allowed to appear was the *Joodsche weekblad* (*Jewish Weekly*), the mouthpiece of the Jewish Council. Its content was limited to the latest German orders, the council's urgent advice to comply with these orders, articles about "safe" topics such as Jewish liturgical music or the Talmud, and numerous advertisements offering backpacks, bread boxes, and other items useful to people facing deportation.

The Germans took direct control of Westerbork Central Camp for Refugees on July 1, 1942. Located on the moors in the northeastern province of Drenthe, Westerbork was built in 1939 by the Dutch government (and financed by the Dutch-Jewish community) in response to the refugee crisis that had begun with the *Anschluss* and sharpened after the *Kristallnacht* pogrom of November 1938.[155] Until the end of June 1942 the camp had functioned as a refugee camp for German Jews and had remained under Dutch supervision. Now the German security police took over, renaming it Polizeiliches Durchgangslager Westerbork (Westerbork Police Transit Camp). Within a few weeks a seven-foot-high barbed-wire fence guarded by seven towers surrounded the camp. Dutch Railways constructed a spur line connecting the camp with the main line into Germany. A train departing Westerbork could reach the Auschwitz station in Upper Silesia in a little over two days and the Sobibor station in the Generalgouvernement (General Government, the name given to the rump of Poland that had not been annexed to Germany or the Soviet Union in 1939) in three.

With a transit camp in place, it was Aus der Fünten's job to fill it. He relied on a combination of a threat—any Jew not obeying orders to show up for transfer to Westerbork would be sent to Mauthausen—and the cooperation of the Jewish Council. The so-called *Sperren* (literally, "suspensions"), which were official German exemptions from deportation, were an essential part of the operation. By focusing the attention of the Jewish leadership on the *Sperren,* Aus der Fünten believed that the security police would be able to remove the rest of the Jewish population without too much fuss or bother. The Jewish Council walked into the trap. Its leadership expected deportations to be relatively slow, and the war to end soon, and they therefore believed that the system of *Sperren* would enable them to save as many Jews as possible.[156] Asscher and Cohen were given seventeen thousand five hundred *Sperren* for use by the Jewish Council, to cover its members and employees of the Jewish Council and their immediate families as well others it might designate. A key concern was to include in this group those crucial to the reconstruction of the Jewish community after the war. Obviously, at least to Asscher and Cohen, this group did not include members of the Jewish proletariat. Another fifteen thousand exemptions were granted for special groups such as Jews married to non-Jews, baptized Jews, diamond workers, so-called *Rüstungsjuden* (armament Jews) who were employed in industries that were useful to the German war effort, and a few hundred Portuguese Jews who claimed that they were really Celto-Iberians and as such of pure Aryan descent. German officials weighed the merits of this spurious bit of ethnology for some time, meanwhile exempting those who had submitted this claim from deportation. Thus, some 23 percent of the Jews living in the Netherlands were, for the time being, to be issued an exemption. Jacques obtained a *Diamantsperre* for himself and his family. Because the Germans had a great appetite for diamonds, and because the skills involved in the industry were highly specialized, the German authorities had not included diamond workshops in the confiscation of Dutch-Jewish enterprises in 1941, and in July 1942 they exempted three hundred diamond merchants and five hundred diamond workers and their spouses and children from deportation. Jacques was not involved in the diamond industry, but as a manager of a jewelry manufacturer he was able to gain registration as a "diamond Jew." Initially David was protected by Jacques's exemption, but he knew that he would lose this protection on November 27, 1942, his twenty-first birthday. He therefore tried to get a job as a nurse in Apeldoornse Bos, the Jewish institution for the aged and mentally ill located forty-five miles east of Amsterdam.[157] This job came with a *Sperre:* it would also allow David to keep an eye on his eighty-six-year-old grandmother, Rosette Koker, who had been living there since 1939.[158] But David failed to pass the physical: it appears he had a problem with his lungs. Then he approached the Jewish Council through the head of its cultural department, Meijer Henry Max Bolle. Could he offer a course on Jacob Israël de Haan? Bolle was very much concerned about the education of the Jews who were still in Amsterdam. In the fall of 1942 he ran thirteen courses on Jewish law, liturgy, religion, art, philosophy, and history. He had supported Herzberg's legal action against David in early 1940, but since the beginning of the occupation much had happened, and he did not hold that matter against David. In fact, Bolle considered the young poet a valuable asset to the Jewish community because of his books on modern Hebrew poetry and De Haan, and he issued him a Jewish Council exemption. By this time Nettie, too, had obtained an exemption, in her case as a *Rüstungsjude,* sewing raincoats for the German army in the Hollandia-Kattenburg plant.

When the Jewish Council called up 4,000 Jews for deportation to Germany in July 1942, many refused to show up. On July 14 the Germans raided the Jewish Quarter and arrested 700 Jews as hostages, threatening to deport them to Mauthausen. This led the Jewish Council to urge all who had not shown up to come forward, reminding them of the likely fate of the 700 hostages. They did not speculate about the fate of the 4,000. Later that day the first deportation train pulled out of Amsterdam station, carrying 962 people to Westerbork. By the beginning of August so many Jews were refusing to heed the summons that the security police began organizing dragnet operations. Central in these so-called *razzias* (from the Arab word for "raid") was a special battalion of Amsterdam police formed in the summer of 1942 by Police Commissioner Sybren Tulp. Jews with valid exemptions would be allowed to go free, but anyone without an exemption, or whose exemption was subject to doubt, would be taken to the Hollandse Schouwburg (Dutch Theater), a spacious building on Plantage Middenlaan that had been seized by Aus der Fünten to be the assembly point for detainees. Aus der Fünten decided whether a Jew should go to Westerbork or not, but he also took advice from the head of the liaison office of the Jewish Council, the Austrian-Jewish refugee Dr. Edwin Sluzker, whose office had a branch in the building that employed up to eighty clerks at a time.[159]

Those who were not released were taken by streetcar to Muiderpoort station and from there by train to Westerbork. Deportation trains to Poland typically left Westerbork on every Tuesday. "Men and women, old and young, sick and healthy, together with children and babies, are all packed together into the same wagon," Philip Mechanicus wrote in his diary on Tuesday, June 1, 1943. Sanitary facilities consisted of a single barrel. "When the wagons are full and the prescribed quota of deportees has been delivered, they are closed up. The Commandant gives the signal for departure—with a wave of his hand. The whistle shrills, usually at about eleven o'clock, and the sound goes right through everyone in the camp, to the very core of their being. So the mangy-looking snake crawls away with its full load."[160] A total of ninety-three transports shuttled 58,380 Jews to Auschwitz, 34,313 to Sobibor, 4,894 to Theresienstadt, 3,751 to Bergen-Belsen, and 150 to Buchenwald and Ravensbrück. Less than 5 percent of them were alive at the end of the war.[161]

In August 1942 the *höhere SS- und Polizeiführer* (Higher SS and Police Leader) in the Netherlands, Hanns Albin Rauter, decided to establish a concentration camp near the village of Vught, south of the city of 's Hertogenbosch, in order to facilitate the isolation and removal of Jews from Dutch society. As he explained in a letter to Himmler written on September 24, by October 15 "Jewry in the Netherlands will be declared outlawed," and all remaining Jews without a so-called privileged status were to be interned in either Westerbork or what came to be known as Vught.[162] The larger part of Vught was to serve as a *Judenauffangslager* (reception camp for Jews), where those who had diamond and armament exemptions could be interned and employed in large workshops operated by the SS. A smaller part of the new camp would be a special compound, separated from the Jewish camp by a barbed-wire fence, which was to serve as a *Schutzhaftlager* (protective custody camp) for people arrested for resistance activities. The inmates in the two sections of the camp were to have a different status. The Jews were to be civilian internees and remain subject to the Jewish Council and the Central Office, headed by Lages and Aus der Fünten. The inmates in the protective custody camp were to be official concentration camp *Häftlinge* (prisoners). The capacity of the camp was five thousand inmates.[163]

By the fall of 1942 David's world was becoming very small. Eighteen months of persecution and the cynical system of exemptions had almost totally destroyed the social fabric of the Jewish community, setting those with exemptions against those without them. In such a situation the only social structure resilient enough to remain intact was the family. David, who had clearly sensed this in March 1941, acted upon his conviction in the fall of 1942, when the parents of Tini Israël offered him a hiding place. By that time, many of David's friends and associates had gone into hiding, among them most of the members of the Catacombs, as well as Nettie, who had narrowly escaped the arrest of the Jewish staff of the Hollandia-Kattenburg factory in November 1942. David refused to follow her lead because he did not want to be separated from his family.[164]

The 1942 *Report of the Commander of the Security Police and Security Service for the Occupied Dutch Territories,* issued in January 1943, stated that the deportations had been speeded up because of the available transportation opportunities and "because of the increasing psychological and technical problems of a radical solution that seemed likely in the future." It noted that some thirty-five thousand Jews had exemptions, and that a significant number of them would be "concentrated in the Vught camp."[165] By the time the report appeared, Vught had opened its gates. David Cohen, Edwin Sluzker, and Conrad Blüth of the Jewish Council had visited the camp and, as Cohen reported to the Jewish Council, they had gained the impression that those sent to Vught would be exempt from further transport.[166] A first group of four hundred and fifty, the majority of them diamond workers and their families, arrived on January 16, 1943. Three other transports soon followed: on January 20, January 27, and February 10.

MAX KOKER

David Koker, summer 1942

While the Germans were continuing to arrest and deport Jews, the Jewish Council continued to operate. At no point did Asscher, Cohen, or any of their aides suggest that Jews might do well by going into hiding. Instead they announced several new courses for those who were still in Amsterdam. A list released on January 25 included one by David on "Jacob Israël de Haan: An Attempt at a Characterization of His Life and Work."[167] The course was scheduled to begin on Thursday, February 11, at 4:30 p.m., in the headquarters of the Cultural Department. The first class was canceled by the German authorities, however, and David stayed home in frustration.

On the evening of February 11, 1943, officers of the special battalion of the Amsterdam police force trained to conduct *razzias* left their barracks to fill another transport to Vught. The target was 420 Jews, all of whom had exemptions. A police truck carrying a couple of squads drove to the Rivers Quarter, and pairs of policemen fanned out over the neighborhood. They took one person from Eemsstraat and one from Oude IJsselstraat, four from Roerstraat, five from Waal-straat, five from Vechtstraat, six from Lekstraat, and nine from Bies-boschstraat. At number 13, two officers ascended the staircase and knocked on the door of the second-floor apartment, the home of Jacques Koker and his family, waking the four inhabitants. They got up, dressed, turned off the gas, picked up the backpacks they had pre-pared for such an eventuality, and left their home for the last time.

The Koker family and their police escort walked down the street to an air raid shelter adjacent to a ten-year-old high-rise that symbol-ized Amsterdam's ambition to be a modern city. In the shelter, which served as a temporary holding pen, the Kokers joined the others who had been picked up. After all the hunters had delivered their prey, they forced the Jews onto cars and trucks that transferred them to the Hollandse Schouwburg. The auditorium was crowded with dia-mond workers and their families. Jacques was in a state of shock and Judith was in tears. David took the initiative of trying to negotiate a possible return home. With a mixture of arrogance and trepidation he approached the senior German official in charge, Friedrich Streich. He tried to explain to him that their arrest must have been a mis-take, that Jacques's diamond exemption was still in force, and so on. Streich refused to deal with him. David did not take *nein* for an an-swer. Streich began to shout. Realizing that neither insistence nor charm was going to work, David went to talk to a clerk in Sluzker's liai-son office. The latter informed him that the arrest of Jacques, Judith, and Max was final. The recent announcement of the defeat of the German Sixth Army at Stalingrad, he reassured David, meant that the war would end soon. Vught might turn out to be a relatively good place to spend the remainder of the war. Then David showed him his own Jewish Council exemption. The clerk said that it appeared to be valid and that David should ask for an interview with Sluzker.[168]

While David waited for Sluzker to arrive, he wrote a note in which he mentioned his exemption. "He most respectfully requests you to do whatever is possible so that he will receive his freedom again, and he will be forever grateful to you."[169] We can surmise that he wrote this note because he was aware that a long line of people were wait-ing to see Sluzker, and because it was important that Sluzker see him first, since it appeared that the transport for Vught would soon be leaving. David was known in the Jewish Council, and he must have expected that he would be able to jump the queue, talk to Sluzker, and convince him to overrule the deportation order for Jacques, Judith, and Max. But something went wrong. The next day David wrote that he had "bad luck all the way down the line," and a week later he referred to "the mishap of Thursday evening," which he blamed on his "indecisiveness and lack of courage."[170] Did Sluzker not arrive, and did a clerk refuse, in Sluzker's absence, to exempt the whole family from transport to Vught? Or did David see Sluzker but fail somehow to secure his family's release? We don't know. What we can be sure of is that when Jacques, Judith, and Max were told to ready themselves for departure David faced a terrible choice: should he remain in the theater in the near-certainty that he would be released either that night or within a couple of days? He would have a place to go: Tini's parents would hide him. Or should he join his family, thereby nullifying his exemption?

Jacques was crushed by the arrest and disoriented by the chaos in the theater. Judith appeared lost, and Max was too young to take care of his parents by himself. David must have realized that the well-being of the Koker family depended on his presence as a support and an advocate. In addition he must have realized that he faced a crucial test of his own integrity. His hero Menno ter Braak had announced before the war that he refused to live in a country under Nazi rule. When Dutch radio announced the surrender of the Dutch armed forces on May 14, 1940, Ter Braak committed suicide. He had been true to his word. David himself had proclaimed in 1941 that the family was the core of Jewish history. If he walked away from his family, he would be violating his most fundamental belief. He might save his life but at the price of losing his soul. When the guards began to push those who were being taken to Vught toward the street, David must have decided that he could not stay behind and chose to join his family on their journey.[171]

Outside, on Plantage Middenlaan, the Kokers and 416 other Jews were forced to get into specially chartered streetcars. Guarded by German security police and Dutch policemen, they traveled to Muiderpoort station, where a train consisting of an engine and a few third-class carriages stood ready. Everyone was assigned a place. David and Max were separated from their parents, and as the train pulled out of the station, Max suggested that they try to escape. David told his younger brother that their parents needed their support. After a couple of hours the train halted at the small station with the odd name of Vught-De IJzeren Man (Vught-The Iron Man), named after a nearby recreational park.[172] The Jews disembarked. When the Germans counted them, it was clear that none of those who had boarded the train had escaped. Carrying their luggage, the 420 Jews walked to the newly constructed concentration camp. Upon their arrival, they handed over their backpacks, and the men and women were separated. When the moment came to say good-bye, Judith proved to be remarkably stalwart and determined. After fifty years of an extremely sheltered life, she had apparently decided, somewhere along the way between Amsterdam and Vught, to meet head-on whatever was to come her way. Jacques, by contrast, was passive and apparently resigned to his fate as he walked to the empty barrack assigned to the Koker men along with some fifty other internees.

A few hours later David made another important decision. He noticed he had difficulty in recalling the details of his arrest, and he evidently hoped that the discipline of recording his experiences would enable him to maintain his grasp on events and on himself. It is also likely that he realized that, in an unexpected way, he could live up to his vocation as a historian. In late 1939 he believed that he would interpret Jewish history. Now he realized fate had chosen him to be a witness. David found a piece of paper and a pencil, and began to write: "*Thursday, February 11.* Picked up between eleven and twelve p.m."

Notes

1. Diary, January 29, 1944.

2. In official SS parlance, the abbreviation KL stood for *Konzentrationslager* (concentration camp). Ordinary Germans usually used the sharper-sounding abbreviation KZ, pronounced "kah-tset," which suggested that the concentration camp was a special kind of Z, or *Zuchthaus* (prison). Schmitz-Berning, *Vokabular des Nationalsozialismus,* 351, 367.

3. Diary, March 6, 1943.

4. David consistently used the common Dutch spelling "Nettie," a practice followed in this book, when referring to the German-born Netty in his diary or letters.

5. The conclusion that a civilian worker employed in the Philips workshop smuggled the diary out of Vught is based on inference.

6. This inference is based on a letter to Fré Samson that David wrote at approximately the same time as his diary entry of January 29, 1944 (at this time inmates were allowed to receive and send two censored letters per month; many of the letters David sent survived). David informed Fré that Hugo had written him to say that he had completed "the second part of his memoir" and would visit his friends soon. "Hugo" was a coded reference to himself (forged identity

papers he had obtained in 1941 but never used carried the name Hugo van der Brugge), "his memoir" was the diary, and the "visit" the delivery of his diary to his friends. We may infer that the first part of the memoir was the first part of David's diary that his friends had received earlier. I believe that the first dispatch occurred at the end of July 1943. From June 3 onward David had made his entries in an exercise book. The last entry is dated July 27. Remarkably enough, the exercise book contained nine pages that David did not use. Considering that David never wasted any paper, we must assume that he found an opportunity on July 27, or in the days that followed, to smuggle this exercise book, and the earlier parts of the diary written on loose sheets of paper, to Karel. Letter, David Koker to Fré Samson, January 1944, Koker family archive, Santpoort-Zuid, Netherlands.

7. Diary, July 7, 1943.

8. Diary, October 14, 1943.

9. Diary, November 27, 1943.

10. Diary, April 3, 1943.

11. Hein van Wijk, "Toespraak op oudejaarsavond 1943," copy of ms., collection of Robert Jan van Pelt. Translated by Michiel Horn.

12. Diary, January 6, 1944.

13. Diary, January 29, 1944. The relationship between Hannie and David seems indeed to have come to an end by late January. Hannie survived the war and built a new life in New Zealand. See entry on the Hess family in the appendix.

14. The RIOD (Rijksinstituut voor Oorlogsdocumentatie) was conceived in London by the Dutch government in exile. As a Radio Free Orange broadcast explained on March 28, 1944, its purpose was to collect, among other things, journals and diaries written during the war. Anne Frank heard the broadcast and wrote the next day, "Of course, they all immediately ran toward my diary." Anne Frank, *De dagboeken van Anne Frank*, 594. Originally reporting directly to the Dutch government, the RIOD became a wing of the Dutch Academy of Sciences in 1999. At that occasion it changed its name to NIOD (Nederlands Instituut voor Oorlogsdocumentatie). The Koker diary and the secret letters that David received while in the camp are preserved as file 1657 (Koker) in collection 244 (diaries) of the NIOD archive. In 2009 NIOD scanned the Koker diary, and since September 2010 it has been available on the NIOD website (www.niod .knaw.nl). Click on *zoeken in collecties* (search in collections), then click on *zoeken in de dagboekencollectie* (search in the collection of diaries); type "David Koker" in the search box, then click on the pdf document symbol, and an 85 MB pdf file will appear. Sadly the letters that also belong to file 1657 were not scanned.

15. Toet Hiemstra-Timmenga, oral history conducted by Robert Jan van Pelt, August 19, 2008, Heerenveen, Netherlands.

16. Nettie survived the war, mourned David's death when it became clear that he would not return, and then turned to a future without him. In 1949 she married Leo Hess, a German-Jewish camp survivor; together they built a new life in the United States. See entry on Nettie David in the appendix.

17. Max Koker, oral history conducted by Robert Jan van Pelt, August 5, 2008, Santpoort-Zuid, Netherlands.

18. Presser, *Ondergang*, 2:382. Translation by Michiel Horn. An abridged version appeared in the United States as *The Destruction of the Dutch Jews*. The quotations do not appear in this edition.

19. Mechanicus, *Year of Fear*.

20. Presser, *Ondergang*, 2:394.

21. Diary, April 2, 1943. Translations of David Koker's poems in this edition are by John Irons. See ibid., 395.

22. Diary, July 21, 1943. See ibid.

23. Lammers, review of *Ondergang*.

24. Max Koker, oral history conducted by Robert Jan van Pelt, August 5, 2008, Santpoort-Zuid, Netherlands.

25. Van het Reve, "Inleiding," 7.

26. A few months before the publication of the book Karel had published what he believed to be the key entries in the literary journal *Hollands maandblad*: February 11, 1943; February 13, March 27, March 28, April 2, April 7, April 24, May 10, September 1, September 30, November 7, November 27, and February 4, 1944. D. Koker, "Dagboek geschreven in Vught."

27. Sitniakowsky, "Uniek dagboek van Koker uit kamp van Vught."

28. Impressed by the diary's reception in the Netherlands, the well-known German literary agent Ruth Liepman-Lilienstein (herself a Holocaust survivor) promoted the book to the Swiss publishing house Walter-Verlag, which bought the German-language rights in the spring of 1978. Later that year the broadcast of the American television series *Holocaust* triggered a nationwide debate in West Germany about the persecution and destruction of the Jews, and this turned into a flood of publications about the Shoah. Knowing that he could not get a German translation of the diary into the bookshops before early 1981, editor Bernd Jentzsch got cold feet, and he canceled the contract because, as he wrote to Liepman, the time for another book on the Holocaust had clearly passed. Obviously Jentzsch, who was (and continues to be) an excellent poet, writer, and essayist, did not have a prophetic gift. By the time Max and Karel had recovered from their disappointment, Etty Hillesum's *Het verstoorde leven* (*An Interrupted Life*) had captured whatever foreign market existed for a Dutch Holocaust diary not written by Anne Frank. Liepman lost interest in the project, Karel was fully occupied with teaching and writing, and Max was focused on keeping the Dutch steel industry in the black. And so David Koker's reputation remained limited to the Netherlands. Letter, Bernd Jentzsch to Ruth Liepman, May 2, 1979, Koker family archive, Santpoort-Zuid, Netherlands.

29. Terentianus Maurus, *Terentiani Mauri De litteris,* 1:93.

30. Laqueur discusses the diaries of the non-Jewish concentration-camp inmates Floris Bakels (Vaihingen / Dachau), Karl Asdolf Gross (Dachau), Heinrich Eduard vom Holt (Dachau), Edgar Kupfer-Koberwitz (Dachau), Jacques Lamy (Buchenwald), Nico Rost (Dachau), Simone Saint-Clair (Ravensbrück), and the Jewish concentration-camp inmates Abel Herzberg (Bergen-Belsen), David Koker (Vught), Hanna Lévy-Hass (Bergen-Belsen), Philip Mechanicus (Westerbork), Gerty Spies (Theresienstadt), and Louis Tas (aka Loden Vogel, Bergen-Belsen). Laqueur, *Schreiben im KZ*.

31. The most important journals written by Jewish concentration-camp inmates not mentioned by Laqueur are those by Etty Hillesum (Westerbork), Ana Novac (Auschwitz and Plaszow), and Klaartje de Zwarte-Walvisch (Vught). Novac's journal was heavily edited by the author after the war but contains an authentic core.

32. Bauman, "Century of Camps?"

33. Diary, February 4, 1944.

34. Tacitus, *Annals of Imperial Rome*, 32.

35. This information can be found in the notes if David mentions the person only once, and in the appendix if David mentions the person twice or more.

36. In the Dutch edition of the diary, Karel van het Reve chose to mask the identities of those inmates who, in David's account, are described as acting in a less-than-honorable manner: while David had provided their names, Karel supplied only initials. When Karel's edition appeared some of those people were alive, and his decision made sense at that time. Thirty-three years later, all the people whose identities Karel found it necessary to suppress have died. This edition seeks to identify and provide basic biographical information on all the inmates who appear in the diary, whether as major or minor figures. This is done in loyalty to David's work.

37. Steiner, *In Bluebeard's Castle*, 46ff.

38. Arendt, "Image of Hell," 292; also Arendt, *The Origins of Totalitarianism*, 433ff.

39. Kertész, *Fatelessness*, 262.

40. Ibid., 263.

41. Mechanicus, *Year of Fear*, 22ff.

42. Diary, November 27, 1943.

43. Koker and Melkman, *Modern-Hebreewse poëzie;* D. Koker, "Sjabbath," 113.

44. Diary, February 14, 1943.

45. Diary, July 21, 1943.

46. Diary, March 1, 1943.

47. Diary, May 23, 1943.

48. Diary, June 3, 1943.

49. Diary, May 10, 1943.

50. This line is from Rainer Maria Rilke, "Requiem—Für Wolf Graf von Kalckreuth," in *Gesammelte Werke*, 2:343

51. Diary, June 3, 1943.

52. Morgenstern, *Flucht in Frankreich*, 50.

53. Ibid., 289.

54. Letter, Dr. David Cohen to W. Diamand, January 27, 1943, collection 250g (Vught), file 872, NIOD archive, Amsterdam.

55. Tini came from a Calvinist farming family in Zeeland. In this region biblical surnames like Israël were not unusual for non-Jewish families.

56. Fré's father, Frits Samson, developed a method of introducing the paper into the bread: He took a long, thin knife, folded the paper around it tightly, and inserted the knife into the bread. The paper went in and remained inside when he pulled the knife out. Fré Samson, oral history conducted by Robert Jan van Pelt, August 9, 2008, Santpoort-Zuid, Netherlands.

57. Letter, David Koker to Nettie David, March 1943, collection 244 (diaries), file 1657 (Koker), NIOD archive, Amsterdam.

58. Diary, February 23, 1943.

59. Diary, March 15, 1943.

60. Diary, May 10, 1943.

61. Diary, April 17, 1943.

62. Diary, May 10, 1943.

63. Diary, July 4, 1943.

64. Diary, September 30, 1943.

65. Diary, November 11, 1943.
66. Diary, November 20, 1943.
67. Diary, November 27, 1943.
68. Levi, *The Drowned and the Saved,* 36–69.
69. Diary, February 15, 1943.
70. Diary, January 6, 1944.
71. David's favorite writers were Shakespeare and Dickens (Great Britain); Villon, Baudelaire, Verlaine, and Rimbaud (France); Heine, Nietzsche, Rilke, Kafka, and Thomas Mann (Germany); Gorter, Couperus, De Haan, Van Bruggen, Elsschot, Greshoff, Slauerhoff, Du Perron, and Ter Braak (Belgium and the Netherlands).
72. D. Koker, "Sjabbath," 113.
73. An excellent history of Amsterdam is Mak, *Amsterdam.*
74. Jacques's ancestors had settled in Amsterdam in the early eighteenth century; Judith's family came from the northern province of Groningen.
75. In the 1930s Klaus Mann wrote an essay in which he suggested that Amsterdam was characterized by a tension between, on the one hand, the solidity of the patriciate and, on the other, a mood of adventure generated by the imprint of the Dutch colonial empire on the city and the presence of the Jewish community. See Mann, "Amsterdam," 326–28.
76. Max Koker, oral history conducted by Robert Jan van Pelt, August 5, 2008, Santpoort-Zuid, Netherlands.
77. See Johan Huizinga, "Nederlands geestesmerk," in *Verzamelde werken,* 7: 279ff.
78. For an excellent English-language introduction to Dutch-Jewish relations before the war, see Johan Cornelis Hendrik Blom and Joel J. Cahen, "Jewish Netherlanders, Netherlands Jews, and Jews in the Netherlands, 1870–1940," in Blom et al., *History of the Jews in the Netherlands,* 230–95.
79. Van de Kamp and Van Wijk, *Koosjer Nederlands,* 399. Note that in Hebrew the letter aleph (A) also denotes the number 1.
80. Biesbosch (literally, "rushwoods") is a large freshwater tidal area in the southern Netherlands.
81. The commission went to the twenty-eight-year-old Jewish architect Abraham Elzas, a dedicated modernist who worked as an assistant to Le Corbusier. See Elzas, "De synagoge aan de Lekstraat"; Van Voolen and Meijer, *Synagogen van Nederland,* 60ff.
82. The term *species hollandia judaica* was coined by Sigmund Seeligmann. See "Die Juden in Holland," 253ff. See also Brasz and Kaplan, *Dutch Jews as Perceived by Themselves and Others,* and Leydesdorff, "De Nederlandse Joden."
83. M. H. Gans, *Het Nederlandse jodendom,* 5.
84. For a biography of Karel van het Reve, see Verrips, *Denkbeelden uit een dubbelleven.*
85. D. Koker, "Kritiek in dienst van de gemeenschap," 17.
86. These poems are quoted by Karel van het Reve in his "Inleiding," 13.
87. Michal Elata, oral history conducted by Robert Jan van Pelt, July 13, 2009, Herzliya, Israel.
88. Eduard Hoornik, "J. Greshoff: Dichter en moralist," in Hoornik, *Kritisch proza,* 7ff; Greshoff, *In alle ernst,* 216, 232ff.
89. D. Koker, "In alle ernst," *De Ventilator,* 16.

90. D. Koker, "In alle ernst," in *De jongste generatie*, 28.

91. The standard edition of Ter Braak's work is Ter Braak, *Verzameld werk;* an excellent biography is Hanssen, *Menno ter Braak.*

92. Ter Braak, "Het verraad der vlaggen," in *Verzameld werk*, 4:652.

93. Ter Braak, "De Joodse geest en de litteratuur," in *Verzameld werk*, 4:463–79.

94. Lewin, *Vorig jaar in Jeruzalem*, 277.

95. Klatzkin, *Krisis und Entscheidung im Judentum*, 104ff, 106, 111.

96. Ibid., 118ff.

97. Ibid., 186, 188, 190.

98. The Mizrahi Manifesto, as quoted in Mendes-Flohr and Reinharz, *Jew in the Modern World*, 436. The word "Mizrahi" stands for Merkaz Ruhani (Spiritual Center).

99. Hoogewoud-Verschoor, "First Years of the Zionist Youth Movement," 314ff; Giebels, *De Zionistische beweging*, 86.

100. Jozeph Melkman (Michman), interview by Hetty Berg, May 25, 1999, Joods Historisch Museum, Amsterdam. Gitter, "De Mizrachistische jeugd"; Gitter and Meier, "De sjoeldiensten van Zichron Jaäkov"; Gitter, "Zichron Jaäkov en de Joodse Jeugdfederatie."

101. Erikson, *Identity*, 233ff, 248.

102. On the Dutch Radical Zionists, see E. Gans, *De kleine verschillen;* Hoogewoud-Verschoor, "Idealisten en fanatici:," 36–48; Lewin, *Vorig jaar in Jeruzalem*, 267–86.

103. On Nordheim, see Hoogewoud-Verschoor, *Lion*. Nordheim's key writings defining the program of Dutch Radical Zionism include "More Derech"; "Humanisme en zionisme"; "De verdorde beenderen"; "Om de Joodse traditie."

104. See Moore, *Refugees from Nazi Germany.*

105. Berghuis, *Joodse vluchtelingen in Nederland*, 223–24.

106. Meijer and Nordheim, "De trots van Israel," 118ff.

107. See, for example, Hoofdbestuur der Nederlandsche Mizrachie, "Onze verantwoordelijkheid"; S. Ph. de Vries, "Openingsrede"; De Wolff, "Spanningen tusschen"; Convenant-Commissie in de Nederlandse Mizrachie, "Rapport."

108. Diary, May 13, 1943.

109. Steinmetz, "What Is Sociographie?"; Ter Veen, "Van anthropogeografie tot sociografie"; Van Peype, *Wat is sociologie?*, 45ff; Gastelaars, *Een geregeld leven*, 66–87.

110. Ter Veen, *De Haarlemmermeer als kolonisatiegebied.*

111. Sieg Gitter and Lea Neubauer, oral history conducted by Robert Jan van Pelt, July 22, 2009, Herzliya, Israel.

112. Nordheim, "De heerschappij van het geweld," 4ff.

113. Kleerekoper, "Het Tsionisme en het staatsburgerschap," 63.

114. [Koker and Vleeschhouwer], "Onze taak." Translation by Michiel Horn.

115. [Koker and Vleeschhouwer], "Het Galoeth in verval," 14ff.

116. D. Koker, "De 20ste algemene vergadering," 10ff. Translation by Michiel Horn.

117. "Voorwoord der redactie."

118. D. Koker, "Franse stemmen over de emancipatie," 21. Translation by Michiel Horn.

119. D. Koker, "Wat betekent Palestina op het ogenblik voor ons?" 70ff. Translation by Michiel Horn.

120. D. Koker, "Strijd voor het Galoeth," 69. Translation by Michiel Horn.

121. Hoogewoud-Verschoor, "Idealisten en fanatici," 44ff.

122. Kwiet, *Reichskommissariat Niederlande;* De Jong, *Het Koninkrijk der Nederlanden,* 4:16ff, 49ff, 127.

123. See Hilbrink, *"In het belang van het Nederlandse volk . . . "*

124. Friedman, *Law of War,* 1:321.

125. Herzberg, "Jabne en Jeruzalem," in *Verzameld werk,* 3:48.

126. Herzberg, "Toen de eerste bres geslagen werd," ibid., 52.

127. Telephone interview and e-mail exchanges with Nettie's daughter Evelyn Berger-Hess, June 4 and 21, 2009.

128. For a biography of Jacob Israël de Haan, see Meijer, *De zoon van een gazzen.*

129. J. de Haan, *Pijpelijntjes.*

130. J. I. de Haan, *Het Joodsche lied.*

131. Storrs, *Memoirs,* 443.

132. The story of De Haan's end is told in a novel: Zweig, *De Vriendt Goes Home.*

133. D. Koker, "Woord vooraf," in J. I. de Haan, *Brieven uit Jeruzalem,* 8. Translated by Michiel Horn.

134. Max Koker, oral history conducted by Robert Jan van Pelt, August 5, 2008, Santpoort-Zuid, Netherlands.

135. D. Koker, "Woord vooraf," 7ff.

136. J. I. de Haan, *Verzamelde gedichten.*

137. Meijer, *De zoon van een gazzen.* In his book on De Haan's life in Palestine, Ludy Giebels notes David's role in preserving his legacy. Giebels, *Jacob Israël de Haan,* 28.

138. Koker and Melkman, *Modern-Hebreewse poëzie.*

139. Isaac Lamdan, "The Chain of Dances," in Yudkin, *Isaac Lamdan,* 213.

140. Diary, March 1, 1943.

141. D. Koker, "Het Joodse gezin," 1–2. Translation by Michiel Horn. The *Rondschrijven* was a mimeographed circular letter sent by the Dutch Zionist organization to each of its branches with topics for discussion in their meetings.

142. D. Koker, "Sjabbath," 113.

143. Excellent English-language studies are Presser, *Destruction of the Dutch Jews;* Peter Romijn, "The War, 1940–1945," in Blom et al., *History of the Jews in the Netherlands,* 296–335. Also Warmbrunn, *Dutch Under German Occupation.*

144. De Jong, *Het Koninkrijk der Nederlanden,* vol. 4, pt. 2:764–65. The decision of the court shocked Visser, who was dismissed soon afterward. His colleagues did not protest. Visser died of natural causes in February 1942. M. H. Gans, *Memorboek,* 806ff.

145. There was one notable exception: Hans Max Hirschfeld, the secretary-general of trade, industry, and merchant shipping, German-born but fully assimilated into Dutch society, had three Jewish grandparents but in no way identified with Jews. In spite of constant attacks on him by Dutch and German anti-Semites, he was maintained in his position by Seyss-Inquart, who valued Hirschfeld's extraordinary ability, energy, and dedication. De Jong, *Het Koninkrijk der Nederlanden,* vol. 4, pt. 1:163–68.

146. Ibid., 780–803.

147. Kogon, *Theory and Practice of Hell,* 180–81.

148. Warmbrunn, *Dutch Under German Occupation,* 106ff; De Jong, *Het Koninkrijk der Nederlanden,* vol. 4, pt. 2: 861ff.

149. Warmbrunn, *Dutch Under German Occupation,* 112ff.

150. On the use of Mauthausen as a means to terrorize Dutch Jews into obedience, see H. de Vries, "Sie starben wie Fliegen," 16ff.

151. Verrips, *Denkbeelden,* 145ff.

152. Max Koker, oral history conducted by Robert Jan van Pelt, August 8, 2008, Santpoort-Zuid, Netherlands.

153. Heinrich Heine, "Ideas: The Book of Le Grand," in *Harz Journey,* 92.

154. Klarsfeld, *Vichy-Auschwitz,* 78–81, 410–11.

155. On Westerbork, see Boas, *Boulevard des Misères;* Dick Houwaart, *Westerbork: Het begon in 1933,* 2nd ed. (Kampen: Kok, 2000).

156. On the use of the *Sperren* in the cat-and-mouse game the Germans played with the Jews, see Presser, *Destruction of the Dutch Jews,* 164–69.

157. Letter, director of the Apeldoornse Bos to David Koker, August 30, 1942, Koker family archive, Santpoort-Zuid, Netherlands.

158. Jacques's mother, Rosette Koker-van der Reis (1856–1943), became a widow at an early age. She sent some of her five children to the Jewish orphanage, but she raised Jacques herself. When David was a child, he visited his grandmother regularly, but by the time he was a teenager she was drifting into dementia. Along with the other residents of the Apeldoornse Bos, she was taken from the institution during the night of January 21, 1943, and murdered in Auschwitz on January 25.

159. On Sluzker's activities, see Lindwer, *Het fatale dilemma,* 30ff, 105ff.

160. Mechanicus, *Year of Fear,* 26ff.

161. See the statistics given in Hirschfeld, "Niederlande."

162. Letter, Rauter to Himmler, September 24, 1942, in In 't Veld, *De SS en Nederland,* 1:825.

163. For English-language accounts of the history of Vught concentration camp, see Presser, *Destruction of the Dutch Jews,* 464–78; H. de Vries, "Herzogenbusch Main Camp." Also Stuhldreher, "Deutsche Konzentrationslager"; De Moei, *Joodse kinderen;* H. de Vries, "Herzogenbusch (Vught)."

164. Max Koker, oral history conducted by Robert Jan van Pelt, August 4, 2008, Santpoort-Zuid, Netherlands.

165. In 't Veld, "Jahresbericht 1942," 322, 329.

166. See H. de Vries, "Herzogenbusch (Vught)," 133ff; meeting minutes, Jewish Council, January 25, 1943, NIOD archive, collection 182 (Jewish Council), file 1c.

167. List of courses offered by the Bureau Culturele Zaken van de Joodsche Raad, January 25, 1943; NIOD archive, collection 182 (Jewish Council), file 33a.

168. Reconstruction of David's action while in the Hollandse Schouwburg is based on his diary entries of February 11/12 and February 18, 1943, on a letter written by David Koker on February 11/12, 1943, and on a series of oral histories with Max Koker held in August 2008. Diary, February 11/12, 1943; letter, David Koker, February 11/12, 1943, Koker family Archive, Santpoort-Zuid, Netherlands.

169. Letter, David Koker, February 11/12, 1943, Koker family Archive, Santpoort-Zuid, Netherlands.

170. Diary, February 11/12, 1943; February 18, 1943.

171. Reconstruction of David's dilemma is based, in addition to the sources already listed in note 168, on a letter David wrote to Fré Samson eight months

later in which he marveled at the fact that his family was still together. "From that perspective, I am not sad that I joined them at that time." Letter, David Koker to Fré Samson, November 1943, collection 244 (diaries), file 1657 (Koker), NIOD archive, Amsterdam.

172. Until May 1938 this station had serviced a large recreational park with man-made beaches surrounding an artificial lake. This body of water had begun as a sandpit in the nineteenth century. For decades a steam-driven dredging machine nicknamed the Iron Man had done the digging, and the name had stuck. In January 1943 the station was put back in operation to service the concentration camp that had been built adjacent to the park.

Aerial view of Vught concentration camp, September 1944. The Vught camp, oriented north-south, was constructed close to three small outworks constructed in the nineteenth century as part of the system of fortifications protecting the approach to the city of 's Hertogenbosch. The camp itself consisted of an area for the SS and a prisoners' compound. This photo, taken by an Allied reconnaissance plane, shows Vught after its official closure as an SS concentration camp on September 5, 1944, and before the arrival of Allied forces on October 26, 1944. At this time the German army used Vught as a prisoner-of-war camp. The original photo showed some perspectival distortion that was corrected for this publication. Courtesy Kadaster Geo-Informatie, Zwolle, Netherlands.

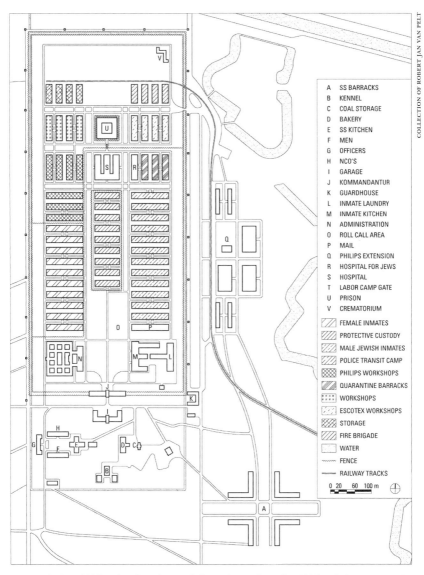

A   SS BARRACKS
B   KENNEL
C   COAL STORAGE
D   BAKERY
E   SS KITCHEN
F   MEN
G   OFFICERS
H   NCO'S
I   GARAGE
J   KOMMANDANTUR
K   GUARDHOUSE
L   INMATE LAUNDRY
M   INMATE KITCHEN
N   ADMINISTRATION
O   ROLL CALL AREA
P   MAIL
Q   PHILIPS EXTENSION
R   HOSPITAL FOR JEWS
S   HOSPITAL
T   LABOR CAMP GATE
U   PRISON
V   CREMATORIUM

FEMALE INMATES
PROTECTIVE CUSTODY
MALE JEWISH INMATES
POLICE TRANSIT CAMP
PHILIPS WORKSHOPS
QUARANTINE BARRACKS
WORKSHOPS
ESCOTEX WORKSHOPS
STORAGE
FIRE BRIGADE
WATER
FENCE
RAILWAY TRACKS

0 20 60 100 m

Drawing by David Takacs based on the aerial photo taken in September 1944 and plans contained in collection 250g (Vught), file 4 of the archive of the Netherlands Institute for War Documentation (NIOD)

DAVID KOKER'S DIARY

WRITTEN in VUGHT

David Koker's diary, entry of February 11/12, 1943. The first line reads "Donderdag 11 Feb. 's Avonds tussen 11 en 12 gehaald. Geschikte maar angstige, en ongeschikte agent. Ik hoorde ze aankomen" (Thursday, February 11. Picked up between eleven and twelve P.M. One police officer decent but anxious, and one unpleasant. I heard them coming).

Winter

(February 11, 1943–March 20, 1943)

By February 11, 1943—the day that David Koker began to keep a diary—deportations from the Netherlands had been going on for almost seven months. Forty-nine trains had taken more than forty-four thousand Jews to Auschwitz. Officially, the deported were sent to "the east" for the purpose of the Arbeitseinsatz im Osten (labor deployment in the east). However, with the deportation, on January 22, of all the residents of the Jewish psychiatric hospital in Apeldoorn to Auschwitz, the official German explanation of the purpose of the transports had become incredible. And indeed, of the forty-four thousand Jews who had been deported, some forty thousand had been killed on the day of their arrival in Auschwitz.

Thursday, February 11 [1943]. Picked up between eleven and twelve p.m. One police officer decent but anxious, and one unpleasant. I heard them coming. Quarrel with the unpleasant one. Hollandse Schouwburg. Quarrel with Streicher.[1] Bad luck all the way down the line.[2] On the way in the streetcar thought about the fact that every experience (especially a very serious one) seems like a dream when it happens, as it does when you reflect on the event afterwards and on the reflection. These words don't communicate it, they convey nothing of the impotence you feel as you consciously undergo what is happening. You see what's happening to you as if you're looking

1. David is referring to SS-Hauptsturmführer (captain) Friedrich A. G. Streich, who, working in the Amsterdam branch of the Zentralstelle für jüdische Auswanderung, oversaw the registration and transport of detainees. He often came to the Schouwburg [theater] to supervise the comings and goings. Streich had the authority to release detained Jews. Throughout his diary David made greater or smaller mistakes in the spelling of personal names. Sometimes he did not remember a name properly. Thus Streich became Streicher and Fleminger became Vleming. Sometimes he did not know the correct spelling. Thus Meisler became Meissler and Färber became Ferber. The translation of the diary preserves David's spelling of personal names. The accompanying footnote or biographical note in the appendix will provide the correct spelling.
2. See "David Koker and His Diary," 61–2.

through a window. Slept in the train. Leave? So immensely miserable and yet so indifferent towards it. After walking slowly for two hours, reached camp. Glad it was dark. It must have been a sad procession. Limping people, crying children. Camps: very recent construction, a nice smell of stucco, and lime on the ground. Just like in a new house that you might go to look at.

In the air-raid shelter and in the [police] car, people displayed more gallows humor (where are we being driven to? To the *ashmedai* [devil]). In the theater in a nervous, fidgety mood, here [I feel] down. Mother wept. I kept making contrived cynical remarks, literarily contrived, but for the first time I felt cynicism coming from the heart. Here I felt deeply wretched. Tears in my eyes now and then.

Speech by Süsskind,[3] everyone is staying here etc., etc.[4]

People who've been here for a while, very content. You live here among the military, who dominate life by their presence, without having direct contact with them. The atmosphere makes me think of Fleet Prison, or of a kibbutz.[5] People alternate between optimism and despair. They like to make comparisons with home. The Germans are businesslike. They talk among themselves in an argumentative tone. A fierce reasonableness.

3. See the entry on Richard Süsskind in the appendix. Süsskind was murdered in Auschwitz.

4. Süsskind's assurance that those interned in Vught would stay there was meant to remove the fear that Vught was to be, like Westerbork, just a way station to Poland—which in early February 1943 meant Auschwitz; Sobibor became a second destination in early March. The Jews who were initially interned in the camp were told that they should build a stable community because the Germans officially labeled the Jewish section a reception camp; initially only Jews with exemptions from deportation were sent to Vught. Yet in a letter of December 17, 1942, to Reichsführer-SS Heinrich Himmler, SS-Obergruppenführer (General) Oswald Pohl, the de facto chief of the concentration-camp system, referred to Vught as a transit camp. Letter, Oswald Pohl to Heinrich Himmler, December 17, 1942, collection 250g (Vught), file 2, NIOD archive, Amsterdam.

5. When the Koker boys were younger, Jacques Koker often read to them from Charles Dickens's novels. The description in *The Pickwick Papers* of Samuel Pickwick's unhappiness during his ordeal as an incarcerated debtor in Fleet Prison made a great impression on David and Max. "There is no disguising the fact that Mr. Pickwick felt very low-spirited and uncomfortable—not for lack of society, for the prison was very full, and a bottle of wine would at once have purchased the utmost good-fellowship of a few choice spirits, without any more formal ceremony of introduction; but he was alone in the coarse, vulgar crowd, and felt the depression of spirits and sinking of heart, naturally consequent on the reflection that he was cooped and caged up, without a prospect of liberation" (Dickens, *Pickwick Papers*, 636). Unlike the Kokers, Mr. Pickwick was released after three months. David's suggestion that life in the camp might also compare to life in a kibbutz reveals his increasing detachment from the radical Zionist ideology that he had embraced in the late 1930s.

This afternoon [February 13, 1943] lay on my bed. If we stay here it's tolerable, but I must have something to do. You have to deaden yourself to a lot of things. Sensitivity to background noise, for example. But I'm already getting used to it. In life you can quickly change your plans. People are grimly doing their best. They formulate their rules for behavior: community, discipline, being content, etc. But this can also lead to pushiness. There is one man who gratuitously bosses others around to a remarkable degree, who gets good results that way and stays unlikable. Otherwise dependence on management. No arguments between Dutch and German Jews.[6] I almost cried because of the ban on letter writing. If it wasn't for that and fear about the future, I could bear this quite nicely. I miss Nettie a lot, difficult to say why, but that whole business is difficult. I'd really like to write to her. I want to know what she's thinking and feeling.[7]

6. There were tensions between Dutch Jews and German-Jewish refugees from 1933 onward. Many Dutch Jews did not like the attitude of the refugees, whom they identified first and foremost as "Germans" or "Prussians" (generally unpopular). Furthermore, they also feared that the arrival of the German Jews would give rise to anti-Semitism in the Netherlands. German-Jewish refugees arriving after the November pogrom of 1938 (*Kristallnacht*) blamed the Dutch-Jewish leadership for its collusion with the Dutch government in agreeing to the refugees' internment in a large camp in the desolate location of Westerbork, in Drenthe province near the German border. The camp was paid for by the Dutch-Jewish community. After the beginning of the occupation tensions continued, and German-Jewish refugees believed that the Jewish Council, established in 1941, had little interest in their fate. When the first deportations began in June 1942, the Germans decided that Westerbork would be a transit camp, but the Jewish Council decided who was to be deported from there. The Jewish Council ordered the first two trains to be filled with German-Jewish refugees interned in Westerbork. The refugees who had been interned in the camp for three years felt betrayed by the Jewish Council, which was clearly determined to sacrifice German Jews to protect Dutch Jews. In response, they decided to resist the policy of the Jewish Council. The German-Jewish inmate Kurt Schlesinger, who ran the internal administration, approached Westerbork commandant SS-Obersturmführer (First Lieutenant) Erich Deppner, and the two agreed that two thousand of the three thousand German-Jewish refugees in the camp would obtain the status of *alte Kampinsassen* (long-term camp residents) who were not to be deported, and that the senior German-Jewish inmates such as Schlesinger would determine who should be included in the transports. The Dutch-Jewish journalist Philip Mechanicus observed in his diary that in Westerbork the German Jews formed "an almost exclusive association for the protection of the interests of the German Jews. . . . In this way they have, in point of fact, handed over the Dutch Jews to the Germans to suit their convenience." Since there were no German-Jewish *alte Kampinsassen* in Vught, and since the German-Jewish inmates who ran the internal administration of the Jewish section of the Vught camp did not have the power to decide who would be deported and who would stay, relations between German Jews and Dutch Jews remained tolerable. See Boas, *Boulevard des Misères,* 41; Mechanicus, *Year of Fear,* 33.
7. See the entry on Nettie David in the appendix.

You have to learn to organize your meals.[8] Up to now I've done a good job of that. Haven't felt hungry. Because of the primitive conditions I feel pity for Father, who is perplexed to be in such strange circumstances but who is managing all right otherwise. Mother is in worse shape.

We went visiting this afternoon ("to the women" is the rather unpleasant description; it's valued very highly, of course, and the privilege is often revoked by way of punishment).[9] The women are bullied by the SS men. Everything over there is even less well equipped than here. We walked between the barracks on a road shaded by nice young pines. An African village. For the men it's more like a town in the American West. Everything gets very dirty here. I'm trying to keep my clothes as clean as possible. The more your clothes have to put up with, the more you like them.[10] This afternoon there was a pretty girl I didn't know but who kept smiling at me and actually did know me, from the [Jewish Youth] Federation apparently. I think I'll pay her some attention. If I dare. I need something like that. I'd be happy if I had Nettie's picture here. Even happier if she were here. I've thought about that already. I'm so egotistical in these matters. Lea Theeboom is here too.[11] Nicely *gesperrt*.[12] When I spotted her I was glad. At least I'm not the only one. That's the way I am. In this atmosphere of urgent chumminess, my officiousness and sensualism have an opportunity to come forward. I speak with everyone about our prospects, console people and want to be consoled by them. Much of the pose I had adopted has disappeared here. If I survive this it will have been a weird stage [in my life].

This evening we're sitting at dirty tables. There are four small lamps, candles on each table. People are huddled together, they talk about their homes, or about the situation and the prospects here. Small groups of people everywhere, like a club evening, a lot of noise.

8. In concentration-camp jargon the verb "to organize" refers to the acquisition of an object, clothes, food, or cigarettes, by any means. This may mean purchasing, bartering, begging, swindling, or stealing.
9. The Jewish women were housed in a special section of the camp, separated from the men's section by a barbed-wire fence.
10. Until July 21, 1943, the Jewish inmates of Vught wore their own clothes, not the striped prisoner uniform of the inmates of the *Schutzhaftlager* (protective custody camp).
11. Lea Theeboom (1919–43) was a teacher of stenography. She was murdered in Sobibor.
12. The German verb *sperren* (obstruct, suspend, or stop) and the related noun *Sperre* (suspension) acquired great importance for Jews in the summer of 1942. See "David Koker and His Diary," 56–7.

One or two are sleeping. Time here passes both very slowly and very quickly. In the course of a day you can't determine whether it's one or the other. If you think about it afterwards, only a couple of things will have happened, and everything has been nothing. People are cynical, embittered, sentimental, friendly, indifferent, everything together. Their lives are shaped more by the awareness that they're in this together (a formulation that has great value for them) than by the consciousness [that they're confined]. Tonight I met Dr. Schrijver, internist and graphologist, an amiable, peculiar old gentleman I hope to become better acquainted with.[13]

The Germans are military men, not anti-Semitic, not pro-Semitic, they have promised to perform an allotted task and they do it.[14] They replace conviction with a sense of duty. They use their *yads* ["paws," to hit people]. That's military style, you sense it clearly. Historically it must have been that way.

The prisoners on the other side are having a tough time, they look starved.[15] Uniforms are draped around them, ripped, tied up with rope. When you see them walking in line it's terrible. No pity, love rather. They're not trying to arouse pity. Guys from Mauthausen (Amersfoort?).[16] They look like people in pictures and descriptions from Dickens. Some of them have to be carried to roll call.

---

13. See the entry on Joachim Schrijver in the appendix.

14. Strictly speaking, the two companies of the SS-Wachbataillon Nordwest (SS Guard Battalion Northwest), which guarded Vught, did not consist of military men, i.e., members of the Wehrmacht, or, for that matter, even regular members of the Waffen-SS. Most of the unit's five hundred members were Dutch volunteers who did not have to meet the usual stringent SS physical and racial requirements.

15. David is referring to the inmates of the *Schutzhaftlager*, which was located in a fenced-off section in the middle of the *Judenauffangslager*. In his diary he usually employs the nouns *gevangenen* (Dutch), *Häftlinge* (German), or *heftlinge* (a Dutch-German word of his own creation) to designate these mostly non-Jewish inmates. In this translation these people are referred to as "prisoners."

16. Beginning in February 1941, the Germans used Mauthausen concentration camp in Austria as the primary destination of Dutch Jews who had been arrested either for violations of German decrees or as hostages. Hence "Mauthausen" came to stand for "concentration camp." In the SS categorization of concentration camps, Mauthausen belonged to the fourth, or harshest, category. In the Netherlands, the German Sicherheitsdienst (SD, Security Service) transformed a small camp built for the Dutch military near Amersfoort into a *polizeiliches Durchgangslager* (police transit camp) in August, 1941. A concentration camp in everything but name, "Amersfoort" became a symbol of the German terror regime in the Netherlands. By the spring of 1943, 8,522 Netherlanders, of whom around 10 percent were identified as Jewish, had been imprisoned in the camp. In late 1942 the Germans decided to close Amersfoort by the spring of 1943, to transfer 600 prisoners to concentration camps in Germany, and send the rest to a special fenced-in section in the center of the new concentration camp near Vught. Between January 13 and March 2, 1943,

Witticisms: Jopie, I bet you never thought you'd lie on top of me! If you don't like it here, why don't you go home?

They had *shul* [synagogue] here too. Only our Lord was able to get anything out of it. [Like being in] a noisy circus tent.

Sunday, February 14 [1943]. People older than 55 have to leave here. Perhaps Father will be allowed to stay. I feel deathly ill. I placed stones around a flowerbed and allowed Lezer to abuse me.[17] Yesterday evening in somber conversation with Dr. Schrijver, who is sad about all his lost and pointless years. "What you've had so far doesn't matter." "Our time to study will come again." "But everything is so senseless." Complains about people and their conversations. We talked about European politics in a way that's theoretical (in contrast with the tendentious and customary). He was in touch with Siegfried van Praag and [Jan] Romein.[18] Has a lot of respect for their friends. An open, lively, immediate manner of speaking. Was startled when I said I was a university student. Opposite me at the table sat a coal heaver, who ate six bowls of soup and had just gotten out of prison.

I've wanted to write this down for quite a while. Nettie and I often talked about it, the notion that nothing [bad] is going to happen to us (my family and me). Well, now it has happened, but it's like this: whatever happens to us we at once incorporate into the image of our daily lives, we lack the ability to see exceptional things in their exceptionality. So preeminently prosaic are we; Nettie *is* able to see things that way. Father, who in this case has the advantage of age, said it was a strange sensation to be behind barbed wire. But I said he shouldn't feel it that way.

The moments when I'm writing are the only things I really remember. Beyond that the day flows away like water. This afternoon I jotted down my first lines of verse. No matter how odd it sounds: I've got

they transferred 2,850 inmates to Vught. The section of the concentration camp where they were housed in nine barracks was known as the *Schutzhaftlager* (protective custody camp). Some 12,000 people were incarcerated in this section of Vught camp at different times. Approximately 7,500 were released and 4,500 sent on to camps in Germany.

17. The translator Jozef Lezer (1904–43) was murdered in Auschwitz.

18. At the Vossius Gymnasium, an elite secondary school in Amsterdam, David was a classmate and friend of Jan Erik Romein (1921–91), son of the prominent Marxist journalist and historian Jan Romein (1893–1962) and his wife, the cultural historian Annie Romein-Verschoor (1895–1968). David often stayed at the Romeins' cottage in Groet, located near the North Sea at the edge of the dunes. Siegfried E. van Praag (1899–2002) was a prominent journalist, novelist, and essayist who introduced the work of Franz Kafka into the Netherlands.

the opportunity to write something here. I would almost say: the circumstances are favorable for my kind of poetry, quite aside from the content. If I get through this, then it may all turn out to have been very fruitful. In the way that things are fruitful for me. Destructive in a certain sense. I can't imagine that I won't make it through. But death *is* the only unimaginable thing. We're living in a rarefied atmosphere here. Rarefied because of the plentiful and pointless talk (that sick feeling you have when you hear a lot of talk around you). But rarefied above all because of all the pointless speculation about the future. With everything people do here, they say: at home I do this, at home I have that. Somebody puts on a necktie: at home I've got twenty-four ties, at the very least. The few days I've been here I've already become less sensitive to the talk. Here's a strange thought: once again to live in a community where people don't shout at each other. Met two Zionists here, from the Noar.[19] I knew the name of one of them, came looking for me to establish a Zionist group. Talkative and argumentative young men, who naturally approached me in the conviction that I am one hundred percent Zionist. I will accommodate myself to them. This evening somebody's reading from the *Joodse weekblad*.[20] Everyone listens closely. Harmonica. Skits, jokes.

Monday, February 15 [1943]. The thought that Nettie and I can't write to each other makes me feel desperate at times. What might she be doing? Will I see her again? I try to conjure her up in my mind's eye. I'm as far from her as I used to be. Nettie. People went to bed late yesterday, after telling jokes. Farting and sharing pleasantries. I couldn't stand it, even though I often had to laugh. To a high degree I'm experiencing the old paradox here: natural inclination towards

19. Noar Haowed (Working Youth) was the youth wing of the Socialist-Zionist organization Poale Zion (Workers of Zion). As a member of the Mizrahi youth club Zichron Ja'akov, David was skeptical about Noar's Socialist ideology.

20. *Het Joodsche weekblad* (*The Jewish Weekly*) was the only Jewish paper allowed after February 1941. It was published under the auspices of the two cochairmen of the Jewish Council, Abraham Asscher and David Cohen. Its main purpose was to transmit, via the Jewish Council, instructions from the Germans to the Jewish population. When in the fall of 1942 some Jews began to hide to escape deportation, many issues of the paper carried on the front page a message by Asscher and Cohen that read, "The Jewish Council of Amsterdam again urgently draws the attention of all Jews to the necessity of being continuously aware of the announcements, measures, and decrees that are of importance to him [*sic*]. These are constantly published in the official organ of the Jewish Council of Amsterdam. Everyone needs to ensure, in his own best interests, that he takes weekly notice of the messages published in 'The Jewish Weekly.' Readers of this newspaper have the duty to spread this announcement as widely as possible."

contact with people, at the expense of everything: taste, prestige, self-respect, *and* inability to convey this. I engage in the same chitchat as all the others, try to put people in a friendly mood, especially those who are in charge here (not with any particular object in mind, but solely out of servility. I've always liked to associate with the great ones of the earth.) In short, [I] talk nonsense and can't stop myself. Only in dealings with people who amount to something can I be something myself. I feel so slimy here. I'm someone who tells jokes that no one hears. You know what that's like. Then again: it would be good not to be shouted at by a butcher anymore. To have to learn about community from him . . . Ever more people here are claiming the right to shout. But no one's as good at it as the butcher.

The most junior officer here, R[u]d[olf], used to be a coal dealer in Breda. A very decent fat guy. [From] Thuringia.

Today a speech from Bernhard de Vries, who always calls me friend, talks to me, and seems to like me a lot.[21] Tried to collect money for communal smoking paraphernalia. The good fellow thought he was back in the diamond exchange. A nice diamond type, has been secretary of the exchange. He has a lot of grief here, defenseless among all these yahoos.

Father is extraordinarily clumsy and helpless. Quarrel this morning. He probably won't be staying here because he worked with diamonds.

This morning people had to hand in any leather overcoats they had.

The butcher is selling cigars in an American auction.[22] It's a jolly affair here inside.

This afternoon a discussion with the education section. Meissler, the barrack leader, is an exceptionally nice man.[23] Small, rugged, with

21. It is clear that David is referring to Barend de Vries (1883–1943), a well-known member of the board of the Amsterdam Diamond Exchange—in Dutch-Jewish circles men with the name Barend were often called Bernhard. In the card index of Vught inmates there are cards for both a Bernhard and a Barend de Vries; the former card has no information except that he lived before his arrest at Herculesstraat 9 in Amsterdam. This was the home of Barend de Vries, who was childless. David's description of Bernhard makes it clear that he referred to Barend de Vries. Seen the entry on Barend de Vries in the appendix. De Vries was murdered in Auschwitz.

22. In the Netherlands, a so-called American auction normally occurs as part of charity fund-raising. An item is put up for auction. The first bidder puts the amount of his or her bid on the table. Subsequent bidders put down only the difference between their bid and the previous one. The auction ends when no further bid is forthcoming, with the item going to the last bidder.

23. David is referring to Maijer Meisler. See the entry on the Meisler family in the appendix. Maijer Meisler was murdered in Auschwitz.

lank hair clinging loosely to his head, an organ grinder.[24] Hoarse, talks a lot, listens "actively," putting his arm around your shoulder.

This morning quarreled with a man who challenged me about a seat at a table, not for himself but because that table was intended for the administration. I had to sit there, however, because Father was entitled to sit at it. I called him a troublemaker, which always makes people angry. Later I got half a bowl of soup from him.

The boys of the *buitendienst* [men who were working outside the camp] had to lie in the mud for two minutes because they were talking.

Everyone here shouts at everyone else because everyone feels called upon to maintain order. People live here according to the mores of the community, of order, etc. Anyone who mouths these words, no matter how, can count on success. On the other hand, sometimes people are obstinate. Won't remove their caps until the officer is very close to them. Moreover, where talking is concerned they're incorrigible. When an officer is chewing them out, they just have to talk to each other. Then I enthusiastically call out *shhh* along with the others, which makes even more noise but seems to be tolerated. At these moments you sense a mixture of fear and meddlesomeness in yourself. Also irritation towards the ghetto and a few other things.[25]

Today felt a bit hungry for the first time. Laziness is more to blame for this than a shortage of food. Actually an exceptionally large amount today. A very tolerable macaroni soup in a very large bowl. Other days cabbage soup over and over again, with large chunks of turnip, loathsome. Yet nutritious all the same. The bread is not inadequate. Is handed out in the evening and has to do for the following morning.[26]

24. In the Netherlands organ grinders are mostly tough and assertive men who, with chutzpah, make it almost impossible for those who pass by to do so without putting a coin in their bowl.

25. David more than once refers to the poor Jews from the old Jewish area of Amsterdam as "the ghetto." The city had no real ghetto, and while the neighborhood was officially identified from 1941 on as the Jewish Quarter, it did not operate like the German-imposed ghettos in Poland. It did not house Jews exclusively, nor did all the Jews in Amsterdam live there. It was not physically separated from the rest of the city, and neither entry to nor exit from it was controlled.

26. Until the late summer of 1943 the food in Vught was very bad. Cabbage soup was the staple. In the morning and evening the inmates received hot beverages euphemistically known as "coffee" and "tea" and a few slices of bread. Three times a week the inmates were given a slice of sausage and a spoonful of jam, and four times a week an ounce of margarine. Occasionally they received a slice of cheese. See Arthur Lehmann, "Das Lager Vught (16.1.43–20.3.1944)," collection 250d (camps and prisons), file 633, NIOD archive, Amsterdam, 16.

Monday [apparently Tuesday, February 16, 1943]. Nice breezy weather. Inspected for fleas this morning. I washed myself all over with cold water, just as I did the day before yesterday. Wrote a short letter for Nettie.

The conversation topic of the morning is: yesterday evening a gang of laborers, diamond workers, systematically [denounced] "the bosses."[27] They were having a fine old time, gossiping and name-calling. The whole thing made a *sultry* impression. [Spitefully] pleased that the gentlemen would be coming here too. "I can already see Hakker on his belly, crawling through the mud," one of them said. Everybody was yelling at them. I shouted: "Shut up, you louts!" Bernhard de Vries read them a hysterical little lecture. And these are members of the leading S[ocial] D[emocratic] trade union![28] This is the sediment in the stream of the class struggle.

Our friends from the other side encourage us during roll call. Heads high, guys! Take care of yourselves! Things are okay! This morning after roll call, held in the cold at 8 a.m., the guard said: "Good, we're through." Anyway, the [Thuringian] coal dealer let us go at once.

Last night a fellow, a professional variety show artist,[29] presented French chansons by [Maurice] Chevalier, [Charles] Trenet, among them *Valentine* and *Boum* (the latter with very nice lyrics). A big hit! Applause is not allowed. But there's always someone who slips up. Just cigarettes, the guy shouted. Maxi [Koker] gets his guitar.

The man I called a troublemaker gave me a bowl of soup with a big piece of meat yesterday evening. Also to Maxi and the first-aid man,

27. The so-called bosses in the diamond trade were brokers who assigned jobs to the diamond workers. They were generally unpopular.

28. Both Barend (Bernhard) de Vries and David had reason to be disappointed in the behavior of the diamond workers. They were considered to be the elite of the Dutch proletariat. The Algemene Nederlandse Diamantbewerkers Bond (General Dutch Diamond Workers' Union, ANDB), established in 1894, was the first modern labor union in the Netherlands. It successfully negotiated minimum wages, health and disability benefits, and unemployment insurance, as well as an eight-hour workday and a week of paid holidays annually. The union was also dedicated to the cultural education of its members. The ANDB was the avant-garde of the workers' movement in the Netherlands: it was the nucleus of the Nederlandse Verbond van Vakverenigingen (Dutch Association of Trade Unions, NVV) and a core constituent of the Dutch Social Democratic movement. Its beautiful and monumental headquarters, designed by the famous Dutch architect Hendrik Berlage and described at its opening in 1900 as bearing witness "to strength immovable as a rock, to determination and gravity of purpose," boldly embodied the union's claim to social, political, and cultural preeminence.

29. David is referring to Max Groen. See the entry on Max Groen in the appendix.

with both of whom he had also quarreled. With meat as well. You're probably thinking I won't do anything for you. . . . We're all a bit irritable, I said. Of course, he said. We're good friends now.

Maxi wants me to sing when he plays the guitar, but that doesn't appeal to me with this audience. On the other hand, I would have an occasion to go over to the women some evening. If I could only establish contact with Nettie! I think about that all day. That, and whether I'll get out of this alive. I'm thinking this: today my longing for her is stronger than before. Probably I've already passed beyond the realistic image of our relationship. At times I think: when I go to see Mother, she'll say: Don't be startled, but Nettie is here too.

Next to me a German Jew who was turned in at Marnixstraat[30] by the man with whom he wanted to take refuge and to whom he had given his money, a business connection who used to come to dinner at his place. His wife is in the hospital now, her wrists slashed. Daughter is engaged to Hans Krukziener.[31] It's a small world.

Strange rumors are going around. Schools burning in Amsterdam. Armored cars in the streets, eight-hour curfew, they say. Sim[feropol?] has fallen, they say, Sev[astopol?] surrounded. Tomorrow Blüth will come.[32] Find out what's true. I'm afraid.

The appearance of the prisoners on the other side is terrible.[33] Yellow faces, fixed gazes. All the same, they take more, far more liberties than we do. Singing about Blonde Mientje, although they're just about collapsing.[34] Shout RF [Red Front, a Communist battle cry.]

---

30. The headquarters of the Amsterdam police were located on the corner of Marnixstraat and Elandsgracht. One of its departments, the Office of Jewish Affairs, played a key role in the German persecution of the Jews. Established on June 1, 1942, this department had the special task of enforcing full compliance with all anti-Jewish measures and, after the beginning of the deportations, the search and arrest of Jews who had failed to present themselves for deportation by going into hiding. Netherlanders who desired to denounce hidden Jews often would send anonymous letters to this office. Almost all policemen working in this department were committed Nazis. De Jong, *Het Koninkrijk der Nederlanden*, 6:247ff.; Meershoek, *Dienaren van het Gezag*, 273ff.

31. The legal name of Hans Krukziener was Hans Cutzien (1921–44). Cutzien was murdered in Auschwitz.

32. See the entry on Conrad (Kurt) Blüth in the appendix.

33. These were the inmates who were previously incarcerated at Amersfoort concentration camp and were now held in the *Schutzhaftlager* section of the camp. The regime in Amersfoort had been terrible.

34. "Blonde Mientje heeft een hart van prikkeldraad" (Fair-Haired Mina Has a Heart of Barbed Wire) was a Dutch soldiers' song that became popular during the general mobilization of 1939. Blonde Mientje refers to Queen Wilhelmina. The melody of "Blonde Mientje" was taken from the German marching song "Erika," composed in 1939 by Herms Niel.

Two rumors are doing the rounds. The people who stayed in the theater and came later, sent back. Other rumor: the whole theater and the diamond exchange are full of people.[35]

The discussions about "the bosses" continue.

Had a conversation with Dr. Schrijver about the Jewish question, which he denies exists. I can readily appreciate the attitude of assimilated Jews. Veldman's cousin butted in and tossed off a few federation slogans, which was very awkward.[36] Talked about tradition.

The *Unterscharführer* [SS sergeant] said to Süsskind: "Today we officially lost Rostov [on the Don River], but we'll get it back."

Blüth was here today but was unapproachable. Accompanied by two officers. What am I going to do with my letters? I think about that all day.[37]

The officers here are mostly from Mauthausen. The commander as well.[38] Fear. One of the officers seems to have said that he really wanted to be with the Stukas [dive-bombers] or go to the eastern front "to be one of Adolf's best soldiers." He didn't get permission and because he kept insisting was put in the brig for a few days.

Someone stole our butter today. Meissler secretly searched the luggage and found it, taken out of its paper package, in the same kind of bottle I have as well. The boy seems to have come clean during interrogation. I still have to hear how Meissler targeted him. The backpacks have arrived.

35. The diamond exchange was not used as an assembly point, but the rumor that the theater was full of people may have been true. At times more than a thousand Jews lived in the building for weeks on end.

36. David is referring to slogans of the Jewish Youth Federation, which preached the bankruptcy of assimilation.

37. Like all inmates, David was allowed to send and receive two letters or postcards each month. These were censored. David wanted to send more letters and circumvent the censor.

38. David is referring to SS-Hauptsturmführer (SS captain) Karl Walter Chmielewski (1903–91). A sculptor by training, Chmielewski joined the SS in 1932. He served in Sachsenhausen (1936–39) and became in 1940 *Schutzhaftlagerführer* (leader of the protective custody camp) of the Gusen subcamp of Mauthausen. Chmielewski oversaw the murder of many of the two thousand Jews sent to work in Mauthausen's stone quarries. His motto was that "a good prisoner lasts only three to four months in a concentration camp; anyone who lasts longer is a crook." In September 1942 he was transferred to Vught, and in January 1943 he became the commandant of that camp. In October 1943 the security police arrested Chmielewski, and he was tried by an SS court in Berlin for corruption and theft. He was sentenced to fifteen years. He then became a prisoner of various concentration camps. In May 1945 he went into hiding as an agricultural laborer. In 1951 a Munich court sentenced him to one year incarceration for perjury, and subsequently he was arrested for crimes committed in Gusen. In 1961 a court in Ansbach convicted him for 282 murders committed in Gusen and sentenced him to life imprisonment. He was released for reasons of health in 1979. Bauer et al., *Justiz und NS-Verbrechen*, 17:160ff.

The days are empty, empty. Work-filled hours have become inconceivable. Not a single fixed point in the day. Because even the things that count as fixed points in the other life are fleeting here. Meals take a long time, one table still has to get their food when another is already finished. Besides: people will eat all day if they've got anything. Perhaps the only fixed points: the roll calls. But people are so passive during them that they have no real significance.

I actually continued with a poem: i.e., wrote one stanza definitively and added a nice new line:

> I noted the brief glance of rapt attention
> You gave me as I was about to pass.
> We've sized each other up, no false intention
> And both of us know what that signifies,
> So don't be sad and frightened, my young lass.

I nurture the hope of being able to do some writing here. But very downcast if I repeatedly say the last line to myself. It's still incomprehensible to me that, with all my precious talents, this has happened to me and the ultimate can still happen to me.

It already seems like a year since I did anything. Doing nothing seems a natural state of affairs. People here are speculating in every possible way about whether the Germans will do anything to us, if they'll leave, yes or no. People here are wearing high caps with earflaps, made available by the Jewish Council. People look like farmers on Sunday. I really dislike the design. So I still haven't succeeded in getting hold of one. Although I did try to get one.

February 17 [1943], Wednesday. All day yesterday I kept hold of the thought that it was Tuesday. Anyway, I'm afraid to lose track of days and other information here. Today is Truusje's birthday.[39] A year ago we had an enjoyable dinner together. The specter that haunted us then was Mauthausen.

Yesterday the people from Amstelveenseweg: the bald men had to present themselves for a roll call.[40] It really startled me. People feared they would have to go to the other side.[41] They were sent back and

---

39. David is referring to Geertruida (Truus) van Amerongen. See the entry on the Van Amerongen family in the appendix.

40. The jail in Amsterdam used for Jews was located on Amstelveenseweg. Those who had been held there had shaved heads.

41. The "other side" is the protective custody camp.

had to present themselves again this morning. They're still not back. That doesn't necessarily mean anything, because it's happened before and then all they were asked was whether there were any "criminals" and after that they were sent back.

Rumors: yesterday morning people said: armored cars are driving through Amsterdam. A couple of hours later: there are riots.[42]

A transport of six hundred people last night. Around five o'clock.[43] Largest part: people with *Wehrmacht* exemptions.[44] Haven't spoken to them yet. I did see them enter in the dark, trudging outside our windows. You could see their blankets, light against the darkness of everything else. People wake up at five here. Some get up at that time, among others Meissler's brother, who shaves every morning and also showers.[45] By six most have gotten out of bed. They force each other to get up because of the noise they make. I always stay in bed awhile. But not for long, like at home. In any case, physically I feel particularly fit here. No quiet and no possibility to come to your senses and to feel your fatigue. Anyway, life here is physically, spiritually *unconscious*. Words mostly take the place of feelings here. But [they] contain and bring a mighty inspiration.

When the prisoners had to leave yesterday afternoon, one person said to another: "Guy (guy is a much-used word here, people also speak of the guys from Amstelveenseweg), guy, if you have to go, think of me. And if you want to keep on living, then you *will* keep on living." And then you think: I'll make the same wish right back and even more. Simply because the words always seem to be available, a very direct and simple tone prevails here.

Yesterday evening I couldn't get comfortable indoors. There was a full moon, clear stars, a dark blue, high sky. Fluffy clouds here and there. Someone from the Ordedienst [service responsible for order]

42. These were indeed only rumors.

43. Trains that brought Jews from Amsterdam generally arrived around 5 a.m. They were received at the station by SS guards, members of the Ordedienst (OD), and members of the luggage unit. The new arrivals always brought excitement: the internees hoped to encounter family and friends and also hear news of the outside world. See Arthur Lehmann, "Das Lager Vught (16.1.43–20.3.1944)," collection 250d (camps and prisons), file 663, NIOD archive, Amsterdam, 29ff.

44. In September 1942 the Germans designated thirty-eight hundred Dutch Jews as so-called *Rüstungsjuden* (armament Jews). These were people who worked in factories or workshops that served the German army by making uniforms and raincoats. This category also included some diamond workers and some people who traded in metals or rags.

45. David is referring to Albert Meisler. See the entry on the Meisler family in the appendix. Albert Meisler did not survive the Holocaust.

stood at the gate.[46] The only thing, he said, that gives you comfort on a night like this is that your wife is watching the moon as well, that she's here breathing the same air, that she's also thinking about all of this. He got married last August. We talked for a long time. I said that for people like himself, people who had a work environment, people who in a certain sense were complete, there was not as great a need to think about the future as for me, who because of my work was focused on that future. He conceded this at once.

Yesterday evening Bernhard de Vries talked about his travels, very interesting. Without prompting he promised to tell us much more.

Pity. Yesterday Father followed me with every step I took. *Literally.* So helpless. Very sad to see.

On the other side they don't have any sick people during roll call. Only the living and the dead. The dead don't need to show up, although they also say the same thing here. But here it isn't true. Sick people are brought in wheelbarrows or are carried. One got lashed on the back because he got too close to the fence. Yesterday it suddenly occurred to me: *"We don't know whether laws are right, etc."*[47] I almost wept.

Maxi is moping around because he's got nothing to do.

There's a short fellow here, of *modest* proportions, spectacles, an unassuming face. Neurotic. Everybody pulls his leg, everybody (me too) detests him. People need to despise someone. Because of their own sense of human dignity.

Ever more stories about the guard, who is so friendly and disappointed.

I'm afraid to force myself on Dr. Schrijver. In any case, as I see myself, I am too smarmy. That's because I don't know what others know or don't know about me.

People are asking me about my diary. They approve of it. In general people here have a lot of understanding for others' comings and

46. Controlled by *Lagerälteste* (senior inmate) Richard Süsskind, the Ordedienst was responsible for internal security. The OD enforced the separation between the men's and women's camps, oversaw the roll calls, guarded the storage rooms with the inmates' possessions as well as the warehouse with the food supplies. The OD assisted, under German supervision, with the arrival and departure of transports at the Vught and Vught-De IJzeren Man railway stations and the transfer of newcomers between these stations and the camp.

47. David is trying to quote from the beginning of part 5 of Oscar Wilde's *The Ballad of Reading Gaol:* "I know not whether Laws be right, / Or whether Laws be wrong; / All that we know who lie in gaol / Is that the wall is strong; / And that each day is like a year, / A year whose days are long." See Wilde, *Complete Works,* 857.

goings. Thereupon the pros and cons of a diary, mine in this case, come under discussion. "Are you also going to write that there's not a single cigarette butt to be found in the dust here (it's being swept up at this very moment)? That would be amusing to get into the record." Indeed, it is amusing. This heavy addiction to cigarettes is incomprehensible to me. Just one drag makes people here happy.

The chatter about the "bosses" seems to have been aimed especially against Van West, whose name was found on a list [of detainees], or so they say.[48]

The roll calls still constitute the most eventful moments. People are well along the way to learning how to arrange themselves in rows of five and how to make right turns. At the beginning they sometimes turned the wrong way. It's also becoming a bit quieter around here. Although complete silence is of course impossible. Cursing under one's breath is permitted, of course.

Ate well yesterday. People were quite touched by the meal. Bread, butter, herring, and liverwurst. At moments like that life is good. And being together with people is bearable.

One good thing here is the cooperation. When someone gives an order and it's reasonable, then people do it. The other side of the coin, of course, is that everyone feels called upon to give orders about something. All this is rooted in the realization, or in the slogan, that there must be order. With a few exceptions, people here have real insight into what is good for them.

This diary has the positive outcome that it's teaching me the power of facts. I focus on incidents in order to make notes about them. Yet there are still too many generalities in it, too few completed anecdotes. But that will come. It's remarkable that I just don't come up with general reflections. I look around and notice that I haven't seen the surroundings yet, as it were.[49] Drab walls, many fairly small windows, through which great streams of light enter. At the tables a few

48. Jesajas van West (1883–1943) was murdered in Sobibor.
49. Vught contained two kinds of barracks. Those in the Jewish section were large, one-story brick buildings measuring 265 by 50 feet. Each was divided into two wings. Each wing, controlled by a *Blockälteste* (senior barrack inmate), consisted of a vestibule, a room with 10 toilets, a washroom with 6 large washbasins and 48 taps, a dayroom with tables and benches and in one corner the so-called kitchen, and a dormitory filled with triple-decker beds that had been obtained from military dormitories on the French Maginot Line. All rooms were provided with fireplaces, but in general only the dayroom had a stove. Each wing was meant to house 225 inmates. The non-Jewish prisoners were housed in wooden barracks that had the same general arrangement as the brick barracks but were smaller and had a capacity of 150 inmates per wing. See Arthur Lehmann, "Das Lager Vught (16.1.43–

people sit or stand motionless. White poles support the low roof. No one here has anything to do, except for a few people in a corner that has been marked off with benches and is called the kitchen. Nobody's allowed to go there, and nobody does. People sit and stand here the way you see old people together on park benches. Or as if they were waiting to be allowed to enter somewhere. But there's nothing.

The other day there were a few old newspapers that people seized on eagerly, although most had already read them in Amsterdam. Anything in print enjoys a huge amount of attention. The stove is a beloved meeting place. Many gray-haired people stand around it. I look around me: incapacity to experience the present. This coolness, this thinness, this calm and collected busyness. Our eyes are turned inward. Our visual faculty is unequal to the reality we inhabit. There ought to be something in us that makes us realize the image becomes permanent the moment we take it in. Right now it is thin, fluid, might just as well not be there. I started this diary partly as a struggle to make the image permanent. Not on paper, but in me. So far I don't see much in the way of results.

The prisoners stood around for five hours this morning.[50] Without knowing what was happening to them (eight to twelve thirty). Then the fat officer showed up and shouted: "These people have to eat, don't they? Knock off!" At one thirty they had to return and after a while got the order to get their luggage. Great haste. I helped Swaap, the first-aid worker, roll up his blanket.[51] Dr. Schrijver absentmindedly took my blanket.[52] I let him do it. They had to go to the other side, we heard, had to put on prison garb, had to take it off again and seem to have been transferred to the first brick barrack, on our side. There seems to have been a panic among the women.

This afternoon we visited Mother. Who had received a parcel from Samson: sausage, bread, butter, cheese spread.[53] Just in time. Also saw

---

20.3.1944)," collection 250d (camps and prisons), file 663, NIOD archive, Amsterdam, 16; "Concentratie kamp bij Vught (Kromvoort)," ms., NIOD archive, Amsterdam, 1.

50. David uses the noun *gevangenen* and is referring to the *Schutzhäftlinge.*

51. David is referring to Salomon Zwaap. See the entry on the Zwaap family in the appendix. Salomon Zwaap was murdered in Auschwitz.

52. David's entry is rather terse. While Dr. Schrijver had been sent to Vught to be imprisoned as a *Häftling* in the *Schutzhaftlager,* Dr. Zwaap was supposed to be interned in the *Judenauffangslager.* It appears that on February 17 both were to be transferred to the *Schutzhaftlager* but that this order was revoked—probably because Dr. Schrijver was the father of three half-Jewish children, and because Dr. Zwaap did not belong there.

53. David is referring to Frederik (Frits) Edward Samson. See the entry on the Samson family in the appendix.

the NSB women.[54] They are abusive: numskulls, idiots. One of them told anyone who wanted to listen that she had been a domestic with a Jewish family for years and had never been fed there. They look like the cleaning women who used to clean the school after four. The women used to be under the supervision of their own people. But [there was] disorder.

The women won't take orders from each other.[55] The ghetto rule the roost.[56] There's an enormous amount of theft. Aptroot says to anyone who cares to listen: my wife only has to turn her back and . . . He's here with three small children and talks about them a lot. He is 32, looks like 25, and honestly acts like 17.[57] But a warmhearted, pleasant lad of 17. This afternoon he, Max, and I, each with a spoon, ate from the same bowl. He's with the outside work crew now, walks around in overalls and says that he works so hard.

The aforementioned transport came. That's why we had to stay inside all day. Maxi was so bored he wept. When we got outside I heard that Rostov had fallen, Kharkov surrounded, Reydon dead.[58] Also rumors about others, S. Olie and others.[59]

54. David is referring to the *Aufseherinnen* (female guards) of the women's camp. These women were generally Dutch nationals who belonged to the Nationaal-Socialistische Beweging (National Socialist Movement, NSB). They had a terrible reputation. Jan van de Mortel, a non-Jewish prisoner who served these women as a batman, confirmed David's judgment. He observed that they were possessed by two things: "an implacable hatred against every decent woman and an insatiable hunger for men." Van de Mortel, *Kamp Vught*, 75.

55. David had run out of paper, and therefore he wrote the remainder of the entry of February 17 and that of the days that followed on the back of three forms that had lost their use. The first form was a document that attested that Jacques was exempt from deportation because of his involvement in the diamond industry. The second form was the first page of a three-page document sent to Jews who were called up for deportation. This page was a preprinted travel authorization issued by the Zentralstelle für jüdische Auswanderung that allowed the holder to travel to Westerbork on February 12, 1943. The third form was the third page of the forementioned document. It provided instructions on how to list all one's assets.

56. David is referring to Jewish women from the bottom of the social hierarchy.

57. David is referring to Isidoor Simon Aptroot. See the entry on the Aptroot family in the appendix.

58. Hermannus Reydon (1896–1943) was a well-known National Socialist who had been leader of the NSB in Amsterdam and political editor of the Dutch Nazi daily. He was appointed as secretary-general of the Department of Popular Enlightenment and Arts on February 1, 1943. Six days later he was shot by a member of the Dutch resistance group CS-6. He died of his wounds in August 1943.

59. Simon Paulus Olij (1900–1975) was Dutch champion boxer (heavyweight) in 1926, 1927, and 1928 and a member of the Dutch Olympic team in the 1928 Olympic Games, held in Amsterdam. Afterward he became a constable in the Amsterdam police. Olij became a member of the Dutch Nazi Party in 1940, and in 1942 volunteered for work at the Zentralstelle für jüdische Auswanderung. Olij became the face of the collaboration of the

There were a few people about whom I heard, upon inquiry, that they had worked for Cohen.[60] They went and asked about Nettie for me. Her mother was picked up this past week and she herself a few days later. At first I believed that and went to look for her. Later I knew what it meant . . .[61] It makes quite a difference. I was happy and sad at the same time. The goal now is: to see her again. As I jot these thoughts down I picture her reading them one day.

Thursday, Feb[ruary] 18, [1943]. The water here is a big problem. It's very hard, with a lot of iron deposits, and therefore undrinkable when it comes from the tap. You have to boil it first. Then the iron sinks to the bottom. Then you need to strain it through a piece of cloth. So far we haven't been doing this. And we don't boil it either, but we don't drink it just like that. In the evening, sometimes in the afternoon as well, we make tea in Meissler's pot. Because community is the uniting and dividing principle and human beings can't live without collectivity and destruction, we've got a small group who get tea and a large group to whom we give nothing. Bernhard de Vries is sometimes moved to tears if we give him tea. Actually he more or less makes a claim to it. He knows how to press his case in a modest manner. In any case he needs it in the evening to take his sleeping medication. Aside from him the recipients are Aptroot, Meissler because it's his pot, Meissler's brother because Meissler's the leader, Paul Meissler because he's his son. If we're still here this summer, it'll become difficult.

Father is in charge of the administration of this barrack, together with a Mr. [Simon] Viool, whom I don't care for so far.[62] Father allows this fellow to push him into the background. I urge him on, but he's very passive and slack.

For the time being Maxi doesn't seem to be able to get hold of the guitar they have here. He had a ukulele this morning, but that's useless. I still hope to be able to sing here some time. There's going to be a piano.

Amsterdam police in the arrest of the Jews. In 1947 a Dutch court condemned Olij for his role in the genocide and sentenced him to death. His sentence was commuted, and in 1954 Olij was set free. Meershoek, *Dienaren van het gezag*, 231ff.; Van Opzeeland, *Ben Bril*, 53.

60. Dr. David Cohen was cochairman of the Jewish Council. See the entry on David Cohen in the appendix.

61. Nettie had gone into hiding.

62. The diamond merchant Simon Viool (1897–1943) was murdered in Sobibor.

Yesterday something funny happened that was explained to me only today. At the end of the roll call there was a great burst of laughter farther along. It appears that Süsskind, the senior camp inmate, a really big cheese, had come running and shouted: so who here gave the order to leave? Whereupon the *Unterscharführer*, the easygoing [Rudolf] said: "Me," and laughed along with the crowd. Whether Süsskind laughed I don't know.

I still have to jot down a verse written on the prison wall:

> *in dit bajes / zit geen gajes / Hollands glorie / Godverdorie.*
> in this cooler / there's no riffraff / Holland's pride / Goddamn.

One of the guys who are gone now told me that. Instead of Leezer, who was also among the prisoners, there's a new big shot now, Krieker, a nice man.[63]

I have to record here what offenses the prisoners had committed: one of the first-aid men was engaged, had bought a few pieces of furniture and stored them with a goyish [gentile] sister-in-law. One was a gramophone, with a radio receiver built in.[64] By accident Leezer happened to be in a store just before three.[65] Dr. Schrijver had a sister living with him who wasn't registered there. Ensel (the soup man) has a coal business on Rapenburgerstraat and was accused by two goyish black marketers of having made clandestine deliveries to them.[66] Acquitted. Taken into custody by another police agency, Marnixstraat office: "Jew, you just had to blacken the reputation of two Aryans, didn't you!" Now people are saying that if their offenses are judged to be minor, they can stay here. May their offenses be judged to be minor.

People here are gradually starting to resent those who have a small job. For example, those who are helping in the kitchen. Everybody wants to do something. Bernhard de Vries went to stand at the door to register the new people and is now extraordinarily angry that this work is being done a second time inside. De Vries is a well-traveled

---

63. David is referring to Abraham Krieker. See the entry on the Krieker family in the appendix. Abraham Krieker was murdered in Sobibor.

64. From April 1941 onward Jews were not allowed to own radio receivers.

65. From July 1942 onward Jews were permitted to enter non-Jewish stores only between 3 and 5 p.m. Because of the scarcity of food, little remained on the shelves by the afternoon.

66. The coal merchant David Abraham Ensel (1905–43) was murdered in Sobibor.

man who seems to have a beautiful collection of etchings. Also a library of art history books. He's having a hard time getting used to things here. Every once in a while he blows his top, gets up on a bench and starts screaming that people have to be quiet. Until the startled community has to get him to simmer down.

The only acquaintances I've found among the new arrivals are the Duizend family.[67] Wijreblijst.[68] Not exactly the best people from my circle, I had already grieved for you, Joey comments. Now you can grieve together! said another.

This morning a torn, dirty newspaper, Monday's edition. Great commotion. Somebody read it out loud. Rostov was abandoned, evacuated according to plan. Cologne, etc.[69]

It becomes known that parcels are coming.[70] Kharkov evacuated. Emotions are high. "Now the war will soon be over."[71] We receive three big parcels from Nico and Lea.[72] We needed them very badly. Three big hunks of cheese, a pound and a half of butter, etc., etc.

---

67. See the entry on the Duizend family in the appendix. The Duizend family was murdered in Sobibor.

68. David is referring to the so-called Weinreb list. In late 1941, when the situation for Jews in the Netherlands had become very difficult, the Jewish confidence man Fryderyk [Friedrich] Weinreb (1910–88) told friends that the Germans had granted him permission to leave German-occupied Europe in a special train and take thirty families with him. Between thirty-seven hundred and four thousand four hundred Jews lined up to be included in this group, and they paid Weinreb a hundred guilders each to get their names on the list. Nothing came of it, but Weinreb cleared three hundred and fifty thousand guilders. When the deportations began in the summer of 1942, Weinreb claimed to be administering a list on behalf of a completely fictitious German lieutenant general von Schumann. Those on the list would be allowed to emigrate when this should become possible and would receive a Weinreb *Sperre* that would exempt them from deportation. Believing Weinreb, thousands lined up to have their names included. The Sicherheitsdienst allowed Weinreb to pursue this activity, assuming that those who trusted the validity of the Weinreb *Sperre* would not go into hiding and would thus be ready victims for deportation. See Grüter, *Een fantast schrijft geschiedenis.*

69. On the night of February 14, 1943, 243 Royal Air Force bombers attacked Cologne.

70. In the first six months, when the food supply in Vught was very poor, parcels sent by family members and friends proved an important source of nutrition. As fewer Jews remained at large, fewer parcels arrived. From mid-1943 onward, all parcels came from Jewish family members who lived in mixed marriages, from half Jews, or from Gentile friends.

71. In a number of conversations held in August 2008, Max Koker stressed that the Koker family and most other Dutch Jews whom he met in early 1943 believed that the war would end soon. The destruction of the German Sixth Army at Stalingrad and the German withdrawal from the industrially important Donets Basin in early 1943 seemed to point to a larger German defeat in the summer. An attitude of holding on and holding out seemed prudent, and the Kokers expected to be liberated while still in Vught.

72. Nico Presser was one of David's uncles. Lea was his wife. They survived the war in hiding.

Cigars and cigarettes. A nervous mood. Eighty parcels for our barrack. Comparisons are made with Sinterklaas.[73] If everyone weren't happy I would simply be sad. As you open the parcels up, you sense the concern that people feel for you. Maxi senses it just as strongly. But maybe everything will soon be over.

Two shocks yesterday. I thought or better: it was thought in me: you can become familiar with death too. That can be normal as well. So: that's possible too. Cold terror. This morning the consolation. From the new transport I heard that some people had stayed in the Schouwburg and that some of those who had Jewish Council exemptions had been set free. One of the many errors, then, that I made on Thursday evening.[74] But suddenly: in every life every fate has been decided. Something I always knew. But never as emotionally as now. *"Nóos anthrópoi daímon"* [Man's mind is his fate].[75] No need to blame myself for any error, because everything is in me and from me. Very concretely: the mishap of Thursday evening can be blamed on my indecisiveness and lack of courage. But these are mine. *These are me.* And so in every life every fate has been decided.

In a lighthearted and optimistic mood because of Kharkov. I think of Nettie. Maybe we'll see each other again soon. Sometimes it can really bother a person that he didn't do things better. I could have gotten away. In the evening during dinner it's sometimes hard to take. That's the worst time.

Books have arrived as well. Because of my cultural past I was appointed distributor of a few grubby cheap paperbacks, some novels from the last century, a couple of fat children's books. Real prison literature. Mr. Herman Bak,[76] who must be well into his sixties, is now reading Karl May.[77] Another is reading a book for preschoolers.

73. The festival of Sinterklaas (Saint Nicholas) is a secular celebration in which Dutch people of all backgrounds, including Jews, participate. The festival includes a parade in which the saint, in full episcopal gear, riding a white horse, and attended by Moorish servants, formally enters every city, town, and village to be received by the mayor, the municipal council, and hosts of children. On December 5, Saint Nicholas Eve, children (and more recently also grownups) receive presents and sweets.

74. David is referring to the evening of his arrest.

75. David, who was reasonably competent in Greek, is referring to Heraclitus, fragment 114 (Kahn), *Éthos anthrópói daimón* (Man's character is his fate). See Kahn, *Art and Thought of Heraclitus,* 260–1.

76. David is probably referring to the diamond cutter Joachim Bak (1882–1943). He was murdered in Sobibor.

77. The German author Karl May (1842–1912) wrote adventure stories set in exotic places. His principal audience was adolescents and young adults. One of his admirers was the young Adolf Hitler, who attended a reading given by May in 1912. Hitler was particu-

The *Scharführer* [SS staff sergeant], (the thin one), has a remark-able face.[78] One could say, soulful eyes. But a hardened sensitivity as it were, he looks meditative, seems (but that's undoubtedly ap-pearance) not fully attentive to what he's doing, when he's counting people he looks past them, it's as if his eyes had attached themselves to something fresh and new. And that's generally the impression he makes. Something of a disappointed, sulky child.

A young man, Beek, a teacher, asked for me.[79] Brother of Phil Beek.[80] Wants to do cultural work here. We chat a bit through the open win-dow. He outside, me inside. The emptiness is oppressive. Thursday al-ready. Maybe later we'll be able to say: this time did not exist.

Friday, Feb[ruary] 19, [1943]. The birthdays of Aptroot (we gave him a piece of cheese) and Süsskind (who was honored and congratu-lated and cheered at roll call this morning, and who's proving to be better than expected). He smoked in the barrack, together with Lehmann,[81] and was threatened with four weeks on the other side by the *Oberscharführer* [SS sergeant first class].[82] For his birthday!

The women are coming here, but children above the age of three are leaving the women. That is hard, but it seems to be because of hygiene. There must be scenes in the women's barrack.

The big event: we're allowed to write a postcard. I wrote one to Fred[erika Samson], c/o Hulstein etc.[83] I'm completely satisfied! Busy

larly impressed by May's powerful imagination, which allowed him to write with great force and plausibility about places he had never visited and people he had never encountered. Hitler believed his own imagination to be similar to May's, and his own pronouncements on subjects like America or the Jews, about which and whom he had little factual knowl-edge, to be accurate. Hitler's views were unknown to David, of course. When younger, Da-vid had read some of May's books in a Dutch translation, and like all boys, he had enjoyed them tremendously.

78. Probably David is referring to SS-Oberscharführer (sergeant first class) Menne Saa-thoff (1914–48).

79. David is referring to Josephus Nicolaas Beek (1921–43). He was murdered in Sobibor.

80. See the entry on Philip Beek in the appendix. Philip Beek died in Buchenwald.

81. David is referring to Arthur R. Lehmann. See the entry on the Lehmann family in the appendix.

82. This may have been SS-Oberscharführer Franz Ettlinger, who was responsible for the Jewish section of the camp.

83. The reference is to David's close friend Frederika (Fré) Samson. This card does not survive. Fré destroyed all of David's cards and letters during a police raid on her par-ents' house in the spring of 1943. Most of the letters had been illegally smuggled out of Vught—probably by civilian employees of Escotex. Fré Samson, oral history conducted by Robert Jan van Pelt, August 9, 2008, Santpoort-Zuid, Netherlands.

day, because I had to translate a lot of postcards into my best German, then I had to censor them, and finally sort them. My tendency to bureaucracy and high-handedness came to the fore. I worked really hard at this, and it made me tired.

Will probably get a job in the post office.[84]

Sang with Maxi yesterday. "Das Wandern," "Dans le jardin de mon père," "Hans und Liesel."[85] People were enthusiastic.

Met an odd fellow today, Van der Sluis's brother-in-law. A feeling of affinity. Used to be a tenor.[86] Gave me some hints about singing.

Generally, it seemed to me, people had little to write about. Parcels, especially smoking materials. Often they don't know what to do with the very limited space. One wrote: I'm here in Vught. Stay healthy (signed) Meier. Now I'll soon hear something from Nettie.

The word difficult has experienced a shift of meaning, from doing with difficulty to: not really possible. I've encountered that here. I said of something: that's difficult, whereupon someone barked at me: all right, so it's difficult. While I meant, that's not really possible. In ordinary circumstances something like that wouldn't happen, but people's nerves are exposed here. Quarrels take place frequently. About everything: often between old and young. But others too. Earlier this week a boy came to get more food. The man in the kitchen said: you mustn't let your father eat it. People talked about that. Whereupon the father wanted to get some of his own back and asked who had been talking. And that he thought it low etc., etc. Then Krieker gets between them and says: fellows, what's up? Or Meissler puts his arm around someone's shoulder. Two remarkable things: people are quick to call each other "guy" and are almost immediately on a first-name

84. The post office was a subsection of the Judenschreibstube (Jews' Secretariat). Every inmate in the Jewish section of the camp was allowed to write one letter every two weeks. These letters had to be written on a sheet issued by the camp authorities and sold for four Dutch cents. Postage cost another 7.5 cents. The sheet carried a printed summary of the rules of correspondence and also mentioned that a release date had not yet been determined, and that "visits to the camp are forbidden. Requests for visits are futile." The sheet contained two spaces reserved for the censor's stamp and a note by the SS noncommissioned officer in charge of the correspondent's barrack. Incoming letters were not to exceed four sides with fifteen lines each and were to be written clearly. Inmates could receive an unlimited number of food parcels, but these were not to contain alcohol or letters. See Arthur Lehmann, "Das Lager Vught (16.1.43–20.3.1944)," collection 250d (camps and prisons), file 663, NIOD archive, Amsterdam, 19ff.

85. David and Max performed Franz Schubert's "Das Wandern" (Wandering), the children's song "Dans le jardin de mon père" (In My Father's Garden), and Franz von Woyna's love song "Hansel und Liesel" in a small concert given in their barrack. Max Koker, oral history conducted by Robert Jan van Pelt, August 8, 2008, Santpoort-Zuid, Netherlands.

86. Like his father, Jacques, David was a tenor.

basis and are very familiar. I myself use many people's first names without being asked, put a hand on somebody's shoulder right away. It all has to do with having lost a piece of our individuality, so to speak.

Yesterday evening I thought in a great burst of emotion: at all stages of the conscious, thought is aimed at restoring the synthesis of the unconscious. But then this must be a type of thought that is itself at the stage of the unconscious. People here are in many respects dissatisfied. That keeps them from being unhappy. When they make their beds or fetch food or something like that, they say: Well, well, if only my mother could have seen this. And that can be understood both ironically and literally at the same time.

Orthodoxy is better represented here than might have been expected. Many people use a lot of Jewish religious terms. And not altogether in jest.

If you haven't seen it, you can't picture it. People stand around in groups or by themselves, or walking by twos, between the barracks. No meaning and no sense, that they're standing there. A few hang around with their hands in their pockets, standing in the doors and looking into the distance, cigarette smoke in the air. Children, running between groups, digging in the sand. Some stand by the barbed wire and look outside. Sometimes prisoners are working there. They shout something to us and then we turn as if by coincidence and continue strolling. To the other barbed-wire fence. Look out for a while over there, as though we're waiting to be released. And then back again. Stop every once in a while, digging in the sand with a foot. Or looking at the sky, which is smooth and cool. Great moving lines of wild ducks. I often look at them in the morning, during roll call. All of this is not sad, not impotent. Because all feelings are too weighty for this rarefied atmosphere.

This morning the fat guy in the kitchen claimed that (just as in the army) there was camphor in the food.[87] At his table, he said, men had assured him that their sexual drive wasn't great. That could be true.

Some of the women had to sleep on benches last night. I've seen all of the cleaning women by now.

This morning great excitement: two opulent parcels from Lea and Nico and a very tidy package. Nice wrapping paper around it: cardboard box, and inside it a tin, butter, cheese, rye bread. Frederik[a]'s signature on it. A letter from Fred[erika] and on the back one from

87. Rumors circulated in all camps that the Germans added bromine to the food to reduce the inmates' sex drive.

Nettie.[88] I couldn't believe what was happening. A young and lucid feeling. Signed: your Nettie. This is all very strange. I'm grateful to her. This morning gave someone a message for Cohen. Through Meissler's intervention. Also for Nettie. To write to me often. That'll make life bearable. I pity her. At this moment I can't picture her very well.

Otherwise it is *not* unbearable here. We were at the table this afternoon, feasting from our parcels in happy luxury. I said to Krieker, and I wasn't just saying it the way I often do here: "Perhaps these are the happiest Jews." And we talked about this seriously for a while.

Just like everywhere else they call me Kokertje [little Koker, or Koker Junior] here. I don't mind that. That's what they call me wherever I haven't been able to make a name for myself.

There's a man wandering around here. Cohen with a terribly big nose.[89] Thin and tall with his pants tucked into his garters. He's supposed to be a big *gijnponem* [joker] and was going to lead the cabaret yesterday. Because of the departure of De Vries and those with him it had to be canceled, which made him complain bitterly. Today he said: "Would you believe it? the cabaret is canceled again" That was

88. The food parcels sent to David often included secret letters written by his non-Jewish friends Fré Samson, Karel van het Reve, and Tini Israël. David referred to these letters as *Leckerbissen* (German for "treats"). Written on small pieces of thin paper, the letters were hidden in loaves of bread. Fré's father, Frits Samson, developed a method of introducing the paper into the bread: he took a long, thin knife, folded the paper around it tightly, and inserted the knife into the bread. The paper went in and remained inside when he pulled the knife out. David kept this letter, like many others, and was able to get it smuggled back to Amsterdam with an installment of his diary. "Sunday, February 14, 1943 / Dear David, / We received your postcard with your farewell greeting. We were happy to hear from you and send you greetings and best wishes from all your friends. / All the best, also to your parents and your brother. / Fré." "Dear David, / You can imagine my great consternation when I heard you had left for Vught. Because on Friday I arrived home at 7 p.m., I didn't hear about it until Saturday morning, while I was quietly reading [Jacob Israël] de Haan's essays. What are you up to? Are you teaching? I really hope you'll find an occupation that fits your profession. Also: Hugo was here and was no less shocked by this news. / With very best wishes to you and also your parents and Max, from your Nettie." Letters written by Frederika Samson and Nettie David, February 14, 1943, collection 244 (diaries), file 1657 (Koker), NIOD archive, Amsterdam.
89. At the time of this entry, the Jewish section of Vught counted twelve adult men with the surname Cohen. These included the furrier Abraham à Cohen (1899–1945), the diamond merchant Alexander Eduard Cohen (1882–1944), the debt collector Herman Cohen (1897–1943), the presser Joseph Cohen (1898–1944), the diamond worker Mozes à Cohen (1893–1945), the merchant Mozes Cohen (1888–1943), and the diamond cutter Salomon Cohen (1894–1943). Comparing David's description of Cohen to the wonderful photo of a large-nosed and witty-looking Salomon Cohen preserved in the archives of the Algemene Nederlandse Diamantbewerkers Bond and posted on the Digital Monument to the Jewish Community in the Netherlands, I believe we can tentatively identify him as the man David met in the camp. Cohen was killed in Auschwitz.

his part of the *tsores* [distress] of the entire day. The fact is that the whole crew has moved again. The women too! When we had stood for two hours, it became apparent that our barrack had to be divided up among the other barracks, a complete disorganization (our barrack was exceptionally disciplined and we were proud of that). Big panic. Aptroot, Meissler, the three of us, let all the others go ahead of us and after a lot of trouble we ended up in the OD barrack, where we are at this moment with our friends from the kitchen. A good many of those here are loud, highly uncivilized young people, but the advantage is, first, that there aren't that many of them. Besides, a number of them are always away on duty. Furthermore, this barrack is very tidy. Even the toilets, which in the other barrack were unimaginably disgusting. On the other hand, the atmosphere is rather unpleasant, since all these fellows, being in a kind of military service that is an extension of the German command, are quite full of themselves. They talk of service and take the matter (even such an unpleasant matter) seriously in a boastful way. Aptroot says: "Your father won't be able to stand it here." Behind me a man is using his knife to draw a map of Russia on the table, lecturing the gentlemen of the kitchen.

The OD leader is a diamond worker from Amsterdam with an intelligent, clear, constantly changing face.[90] High forehead, hooked nose, wavy hair combed back. This evening he gave a speech with a lot of diamond-workers' rhetoric.[91] For a long time the OD nursed the wish to have their own barrack, they who are called upon to serve as an example to the community, to serve their neighbors etc., etc. To this point there had been little discipline, that was going to change now. Insisted that the OD must not steal. The man likes to hear himself talk, a little general. He closes with an appeal "in the interest of the public interest." The public interest has become an abstraction, to be used independently of any particular objective.

In the evening, roll call at sundown. The sky slowly changed from blue to lilac. A large sun hangs behind the watchtower. Flights of ducks go calmly back and forth.

We stand there for an hour in rows of five. Exercises while we stand there. Move it, back and forth. And the evening so calm. A purple glow over us all.

90. David is referring to the diamond worker Leendert Overste (1895–1944). Overste was murdered in Auschwitz.

91. The Amsterdam diamond workers were well organized and took pride in their solidarity.

Meissler is best of enemies with Dresel: a pushy Berliner with a crooked, thin-lipped mouth.[92] And riding pants. He addresses everybody as: "Mensch" [Hey, you]. Everybody hates his guts. They call him Kalman Knaak.[93] He can't count, either. Maxi heard him make a mistake in counting the other day. He rants at Meissler, who shouts back and smiles at his men when he has the advantage. Right in front of us he yelled at Dresel: "Big mouth and nothing to back it up." We enjoyed that.

Then there's Lehmann, a little fellow with glasses and a cowlick. Bemused face, neurotic, walks and looks like an old professor so I keep wanting to say "Herr Professor" to him.

Sunday [February 21, 1943]. Roll call at 8:30 this morning. Nice late rising. I needed that. At midnight Overste woke up the OD (I don't really want to use that acronym, in speaking, indicates too much familiarity), I got up to get a drink, was able to find some dregs of coffee for my raw throat. The water is the worst problem here.

A message from Barber this morning.[94] To help to register newly arrived Westerborkers.[95] They were in a barrack whose floor hasn't been finished yet. Packs on the tables. Sleeping with their hands under their foreheads. Children. A mournful chaos. Registration in the fierce cold in the bedroom. I wrote down:

> D. Koker,
> poet and bureaucrat.

Was properly tired. This afternoon the women paid us a visit.[96] After that waited at Lehmann's for an hour and a half, only to go back to our barrack without having accomplished anything. There the bad news was waiting for us: Meissler is going to be the leader of the Westerbork barrack. The kitchen's leaving with him. Now we're truly

92. See the entry on Willy Dresel in the appendix.
93. In the 1930s Kalman Knaak was a popular comic actor in operettas, mostly in the Netherlands.
94. See the entry on Jakob Samson Barber in the appendix. Barber was murdered in Auschwitz.
95. On February 20, the first of four transports of Jews arrived in Vught from Westerbork. Jews who had been taken to Westerbork but who were in the manufacture of furs, or who had worked in the diamond business, were transferred to Vught.
96. While the mens' and womens' sections of the camp were separated, the Germans occasionally allowed the wives and children to visit their spouses, grown sons, or fathers and brothers, and vice versa.

lost and forsaken. The OD barrack is a bit like the Tulp barracks.[97]
Ill-mannered, arrogant young men. Always on duty. Last night two
guys were talking. I've seldom heard two people describe an absurd
situation with so much spite and so much conviction (especially in
the tone; the description doesn't do justice to it). Completely serious. Sometimes you had to wonder. "Have you heard that the OD is
being issued rubber truncheons? Yes? Boots as well. To be able to get
right in there. Overste will be assigned a bodyguard. Twelve men. A
horse. No, that's not true. They say the OD is being considered for
the eastern front." And then: "Oh my God, my grandmother should
have seen this. Some people are coming from Den Bosch to join the
OD. We'll have to sing while we march. We're getting different food.
We have to be well fed."

Monday [February 22, 1943]. I walked along the barbed wire yesterday. I heard three shots. I saw the gun smoke. Two SS soldiers,
laughing: "Hey, get to work!" Moments later: "Merciful God." More
laughing. I'm afraid. (I can't check whether I've already written this.[98]
I registered the Westerborkers yesterday. Enjoyable work, actually. I
wrote down: D. Koker, poet and bureaucrat. Because that's the way it
is. There are a lot of Oostjoden [eastern Jews] among them.[99] With
kippot [skullcaps]. Yesterday evening they served us lard. Many people
turned it down.[100] Yesterday afternoon I had to accompany people.)

Because Meissler had to leave, the OD barrack doesn't have a
leader. Father took care of it yesterday evening and he didn't do
badly. People were full of praise and wanted to make him permanent
leader. He refused in prudent self-restraint. A working-class boy, who
is an optician but also studies philosophy and psychology, urged me

97. Sybren Tulp (1891–1942) was a Dutch National Socialist who, after a military career
in the Dutch colonies, became chief commissioner of the Amsterdam police in 1941. He
made the Amsterdam police force into an efficient tool for the Germans, creating a special
battalion to conduct mass arrests of Jews. This unit was housed in barracks on Cornelis
Troostplein. In early October 1942 Tulp suddenly died after a short illness. In recognition
of his achievements, Reich Commissioner Arthur Seyss-Inquart named the police battalion
after its founder. Thereupon the unit's barracks were referred to as the Tulp Barracks.
Meershoek, "Amsterdam Police."
98. This suggests that David's entries of the preceding days may already have been
smuggled out of the camp.
99. Many Jews had left eastern Europe earlier in the century, some of them coming to
the Netherlands.
100. Lard was a staple in the diet of Dutch farmers and workers and was also served to
soldiers and prisoners. It was not kosher and hence could not be eaten by observant Jews.

to try to get him to stay on. I talked him out of it. I also made the acquaintance of one Van der Hoek, whom I recognized as Jopie van der Hoek, a classmate of fifteen years ago.

Anyway, we're leaving too. Our luggage is in Meissler's barrack. A filthy barrack, but as far as the people are concerned a disciplined one. On the other side of the small and not-unpleasant-looking square. Yesterday evening Overste kicked up a row, against us, against the kitchen. And I must say he had a point. We're letting him down badly. Too bad that he uses such uncommonly coarse language. That makes the chaos even greater. Genuine pandemonium yesterday evening. The respectable people want out. It got to the point that people warned each other not to go too far. Because otherwise the Germans will take charge of it [the Jewish section of the camp] And then God have mercy on us all.

A crumpled newspaper: Thursday [February 18, 1943]. Kharkov evacuated, according to plan, by the way. The troops in Novorossiysk, who were decimated, have now been thrown back towards the [Black Sea] coast.

The night was terrible: people who apparently were supposed to stay awake had gone to bed, so that there was a lot of ruckus at midnight, 2, 4, and 6 o'clock to get them out. And after that the usual quarrels.

Strange to be writing this. I'm uncertain that it was last night. There's nothing here to mark the time. I have a fierce headache. The days are empty and full. Undifferentiated: full. Pulverized by noise, by your own conversation, by walking back and forth. It lasts for hours and it never happened.

Because of the disorder of the last few days even the daily roll calls have gone by the board. You stand there for a moment, then you're gone. No officer, or only in the distance.

This morning stood around for a long time. The fat officer, who was at the center of a circle of six Jews and who conversed most pleasantly during the entire women's visit, walked back and forth a bit. Everybody was talking. He's a person you can take a few liberties with. Yesterday he taught us various commands. "And when I say: 'stand still,' then you'll stand still, and even if the devil appears you don't turn your head." At the end he ordered a right turn, whereupon the gathering, in line with ancient Jewish custom, came to stand nose to nose. Thereupon he allowed us to break up. I often think of the old militia. People here don't have the slightest inclination to do things the proper way.

So this morning the whole family stood around in the cold fog for half an hour. Coughing and sniffling before the officer showed up, jumping on the spot like in gymnastics. Because our feet were cold. Süsskind demonstrated, in front of the group, in his short leather coat. He's an agreeable chubby fellow after all: "I care about only one thing: I want it to be really cold at the end of February." He has a round, smiling face. A somewhat arrogant posture. Recently he almost hit a man who had ordered a number of diamond workers to carry suitcases (he sometimes hits people for real. You can't imagine this place without German methods.) The diamond workers are not allowed to do heavy work.[101] Sometimes they think they've gone crazy. They're mollycoddled so much. "They say we're built too delicately."

In front of the group yesterday: punishment carried out. They shaved a strip down the middle of a man's head. He had bought tobacco for the prisoners, and had been warned repeatedly. It was done by an OD man. Accompanying speech from Prof. Sickbock, in which he used the word community five times in not more than four minutes.[102] Of course it remains a difficult problem: people are often forced to do things in the interests of a group that they can't do individually. That is to say, of course, that people are in a false position: they're serving the Germans and are put under duress by them.

Tuesday [February 23, 1943]. Advertisement in J.W. [*Joodsche weekblad*]: "Young, lonely artist seeks an independent, easygoing, sweet-tempered girl, with the aim of marriage after compatibility has been established, etc."[103]

Panic yesterday. All clothes had to be handed in. I was desperately unhappy. In the end it appeared: the *Oberscharführer* (we call the offi-

---

101. The Germans intended to use their skills in workshops that were to be set up in the camp.

102. Professor Joachim Sickbock is a character in *Tom Poes*, a greatly beloved and highly readable Dutch comic strip written and illustrated by Marten Toonder (1912–2005). It is populated by anthropomorphic animals, central among them Olivier B. Bommel, a dim but amiable bear, and Tom Poes, a perspicacious cat who rescues Bommel from trouble he has often made for himself. Professor Sickbock is a brilliant but malicious goat, desperate for fame. David gently pokes fun at the brilliant, goateed Lehmann when he compares him to Sickbock.

103. The message and structure of this ad are similar to those of many other ads in the marriage section of *The Jewish Weekly*. This ad stands out because of the unusual self-description of the person who placed the ad and the particular qualities of the girl he hopes to find. Did David read this as a description of himself and Nettie? *Het Joodsche weekblad*, February 19, 1943, 2.

cers by their titles, as though we were students in their school), in the
end it appeared the *Oberscharführer* was afraid that the high authority
who was going to come today (first people said Seyss-Inquart, now they
say Rauter)[104] would criticize the absence of closets.[105] We had to hand
in all our clothes so we could stuff the remainder more easily into our
beds. A little conspiracy with the *Oberscharführer,* in fact. But we didn't
know that yesterday evening. So we all put on two sets of clothes. So
that we were overheated. The rest handed in as a neat parcel. People
initially believed we wouldn't see it again. They're a bit more optimistic
now. Rumors, gradually approaching certainty: Kiev has fallen![106]

This morning roll call at seven. Got up just after five to fix up the
matter of the luggage. Exhausted. Roll call pretty much in the dark.
Quarrel between Süsskind and a man in which the latter shouted
across the silent square: "I don't give a damn for what you say!" Süsskind seems to have hit him. The man hit back. The fat officer began
to yell like crazy. Hit the man in the face. Held his revolver under the
man's nose: "You know what this is? I'll shoot you!" The *Oberscharführer* was brought into it: "This man attacked Süsskind! Really, I'll shoot
you." The matter is still current. The *Unterscharführer* made a speech
in which he made the people out to be fools: "You don't know what

104. The head of the German occupation administration in the Netherlands, Reichs-
minister Dr. Arthur Seyss-Inquart (1892–1946), never visited the camp. SS-Gruppenführer
Johann (Hanns) Baptist Albin Rauter (1895–1949), head of the SS and the police in the
Netherlands, inspected the camp three or four times. Born in the Czech lands, Seyss-
Inquart grew up in Vienna and became a lawyer and, in the 1930s, a senior official in the
Austrian Republic. A known sympathizer with the Nazis, he attained, with pressure from
Hitler, an appointment as federal chancellor in March 1938, and immediately invited the
German army to occupy Austria, triggering the so-called *Anschluss.* Subsequently he became minister without portfolio in the German government, deputy governor general of
occupied Poland, and in May 1940 head of the German civil administration in the Netherlands. He remained in this position until Hitler's death, when he became minister of foreign affairs in the Dönitz government. Tried in Nuremberg, Seyss-Inquart was sentenced
to death and executed in 1946. Born in Austria, Rauter fought in World War I. An early
member of the Austrian Nazi Party, he fled to Germany in 1933. There he made a career
in the SS. In 1940 he became Generalkommissar für das Sicherheitswesen (General Commissioner of Security Forces) in German-occupied Netherlands and as such the enforcer
of Nazi rule. He oversaw the deportation of one hundred ten thousand Jews to the camps
in Poland and the transfer of three hundred thousand Dutch men to Germany as forced
laborers. Severely wounded in an attack by the Dutch resistance (March 1945), he was unable to evade arrest at the end of the war. Tried by a Dutch special court, he was sentenced
to death and executed.

105. The standard German concentration-camp barrack, as approved by the SS leadership, provided each inmate with a locker for his or her personal belongings. The barracks
in Vught did not provide lockers.

106. In fact, the Red Army did not enter Kiev until November 6, 1943.

you owe this man, who works day and night for the welfare of all. For your wives and children." This last bit he repeated several times. Definitely a reasonable man.

The sergeant slapped the man hard. Asked Süsskind to do the same, whereupon Süsskind turned on his heel and walked off without saying a word.

Süsskind's behavior is judged variously by different people. Without using German military manners to some extent, you can't manage here. And Süsskind combines in clever fashion reasonableness, friendliness, severity, and harshness. Yesterday he happened to come upon a quarrel between Overste and someone else. Both showered him with arguments. Finally, when they had finished, he told them what needed to be done, looking past them as he enumerated the points. And walked off without waiting for an answer. To look at, he's sturdy but not big. Stout without being fat. I know few fleshy people on whom it looks so good. He always walks around in a leather jacket, riding boots. Smooth hair. Plump face that would look bloated on someone else. What I wrote about the hostility between Dutch and German Jews, that it doesn't exist here: it does exist. But in an unusual form. It's aimed against Süsskind and also against his associates Dresel, Lehmann. More particularly against their military habits, which are, however, essential, as I said. People are faced with something [unpleasantly] real. On the other hand, people are aware that essential things are at issue, so that they air their misgivings surreptitiously, as it were. But there are misgivings, something to which the strong exclusiveness of the German-Jewish attitude contributes. I sometimes feel misgivings myself.

A strange day today. Up at five, line up at seven, sick with fatigue. The entire camp had to be clean, paths and streets raked and scrubbed. Speech by Süsskind: those who "slack off" will go to the prison camp (language Germanizes here in a worrying fashion).[107] Whoever speaks to the women will be shot. The diamond workers had to join us. I myself raked the paths in front of the children's shelter.[108] What a miserable sight. Weeping children, screaming for their moth-

107. David notes that Süsskind uses the verb *drukken.* This was derived from the German verb [*sich*] *drücken* (to avoid one's responsibilities). Dutch teachers used to fight a battle against the Germanization of the Dutch language, the all-too-ready adoption of German words.

108. By May 1943, two barrack sections housed 284 infants and toddlers aged up to three years and their mothers. One barrack section housed 102 boys aged four to five, and one barrack section 80 girls aged four to five.

ers, messing around between the redbrick barracks. It often makes me think of the renovated part of the ghetto, Uilenburgerstraat.[109] New and dirty. The NSB women are walking around, yelling. At the children as well. And you can rake all you like, the children walk across it. But that doesn't matter, as long as you're occupied.

Because of the visit, the officers are more nervous today than the people. Their promotions depend on it. Now and then I took garbage to a dump with a wheelbarrow. [Saw] a shoe with a rubber heel. Prisoners there. Scrounging for food. Asked me to run an errand. I said: don't give us a hard time. I wish I weren't such a coward. I wish I were less compliant. That if the Germans order something to be cleaned, I weren't so prompt in the execution. I wish I didn't try to do things quite so well. I have no negative attitude towards what they order us to do. I give in and hope to make something of it in accordance with the German regulations. I want to have a job here: out of ambition. Everywhere I show up, I want to join in the work. In the vanguard. No matter whether it's good or bad. I wish I were less of an apple polisher. Less ambitious.

Yesterday a boy told me that he had spent a month in Russia. I asked him to tell me more. Streets in Stalingrad half again as wide as Ceintuurbaan.[110] Apartment blocks three or four times as big as in Amsterdam. Common entrances for a large number of households, six floors. Impression: New York. Four households live around one chimney, which draws much better than ours. They have one bathroom. Bath and shower. If a household becomes bigger, the factory makes a larger, roomier apartment available. When people become old or physically disabled, they automatically get to live on a lower floor.

The destruction we saw in the newsreels affected only a small part [of what was there].[111] Enormous factory complexes and bridges. Interesting stories about wages. Entry wage. It can be raised through

109. The Uilenburg and Marken areas formed the heart of the Jewish neighborhood. By the beginning of the twentieth century these two areas had become the worst slums in the Netherlands. In 1911 the Amsterdam city council voted to undertake an extensive program of urban rehabilitation. This led to the demolition of most of the substandard housing in these neighborhoods and the construction of workers' housing. The client was the society Handwerkers Vriendenkring (Circle of Friends of Manual Workers), a society established in 1869 with the aim of emancipating Jewish workers.

110. Ceintuurbaan, located in the nineteenth-century part of Amsterdam, was one of the few broad avenues in that city.

111. David is referring to the destruction that resulted from the battles shown in the *Polygoon journal*, the weekly news program shown in Dutch cinemas.

performance. It can *drop* if you don't advance, but then *increase* if it appears as a result of a psychotechnical test that [a] laborer is working at full capacity and can't do any better. Slackers are punished with reductions of salary and coal. Average income that enables you to buy what you could buy for 30 guilders before the war.[112] He was there in '38. The armament industry employs a lot of people. Children in day-care center. Big parks. Playgrounds also for children five years of age, for example.

An apartment block has small front yards and a common backyard. There are playgrounds with swings and so on.

Theater performances. Childish. The devil and the good farmer. Just as in literature, fairy stories are greatly beloved. Tolstoy is much read. Pushkin only by more educated people. Jews who live a traditional life have to be in the ghetto. In Stalingrad this is just as modern as the rest. It's no disgrace to live there. Societal anti-Semitism exists, just as in the Netherlands. In Kiev, of course, the ghetto is old, musty, like the whole city. For the people the GPU meant something like the price control agency here.[113] People have to be careful. No feeling of pressure. On the other hand, a large espionage apparatus. When he arrived there, they knew everything about him. In which organizations he, his father had been. That his grandfather had supported the royal house. And this without visiting his acquaintances. He was skeptical, but it did overwhelm him. [When he got back to the Netherlands] he didn't want to sell *VAB* anymore.[114]

Thursday [apparently Wednesday, February 24, 1943]. The visitors didn't come yesterday. The same game today. Camouflage the luggage. No walking around in the barrack, so it won't get dirty. Sit on a bench in your overcoat. Try to sleep. Some are looking out the window, to see whether Rauter and his associates are coming. Shouts: he's in the next barrack. Or: they're in the hospital barrack. Silence for a moment. Then a buzz once more, and screams to puncture it. Boredom that would make you weep if you had tears to weep with. Outside everything has been nicely raked, and inside there are small

---

112. At the end of the 1930s the average Dutch worker made between thirty and thirty-five guilders (equivalent to between twelve and fifteen United States dollars) per week.

113. The GPU (Gosudarstvennoye Politicheskoye Upravlenie, State Political Directorate) was the Soviet secret police from 1922 to 1934.

114. *VAB* refers to the anti-Communist Social Democratic weekly *Vrijheid, arbeid, brood* (*Freedom, Labor, Bread*).

puddles on the floor because of the cleanup, *saubermachen* as it's called here. Rauter has indeed been here. Only not in our barrack. Asked whether it was better here than in Westerbork. And what the meals were like. And said that the Jews were looking good. "I feel sure a lot of parcels are sent here." He praised the tidiness. "Is it this clean here every day?" "You can come any day," the *Oberscharführer* lied proudly.

This afternoon a parcel from Dürerstraat, prepared with evident love.[115] Crêpes.

Today I decided not to chase after jobs anymore. Tomorrow I'll go to Süsskind. But that will be the last time. After all, I'm too good to be a doormat for these people. I've already shown enough servility. The ease, the determination with which others do something like that. I always make a dismal impression. Perhaps Meissler can do something.

Today we were definitely supposed to move to Meissler's barrack. But once again it didn't happen.

Thursday [February 25, 1943]. It seems that yesterday wasn't Thursday but Wednesday. I hope to pay better attention in the future. Yesterday cabaret under the leadership of a "good" [though] unsympathetic entertainer. A guy named Josefsohn played the mandolin.[116] Others accompanied him with jazz-style noises. There were songs composed in Westerbork. Remarkable Westerbork love song, of which I'll get the words.[117] Also a song about transport. With desperate affirmations of loyalty to the Netherlands. Westerbork *has had a culture* that's worth studying. That's how they woo at Westerbork, the entertainer said about the love song. The people who are here [the Westerborkers] keep saying: back when we were in Westerbork. Much better meals there, better organization, etc.[118] That's all really true. There

---

115. Albrecht Dürerstraat 46, Amsterdam, had been until the summer of 1942 the home of Lion Nordheim, his wife, Jeanne Nordheim-van Amerongen, their friend Jaap van Amerongen and his wife, Loes van Amerongen-Asscher. See the entries under Lion Nordheim and the Van Amerongen family in the appendix.

116. David is referring to the German-Jewish refugee David Josephsohn (1927–44), who was murdered in Auschwitz.

117. It is not clear to which song David is referring. Only in late 1943 did inmates form the Westerbork cabaret. The famous "Westerbork Serenade," performed by the singing duo Johnny and Jones (Max Kannewasser and Arnold van Wesel), was composed at that time.

118. There is a certain irony in David's observation about the nostalgia of the former Westerbork inmates for the camp that was, in fact, an anteroom to Auschwitz and Sobibor. When German-Jewish refugees began arriving in the Netherlands in 1933, they quickly

was a village there, where more remarkable people came together under more remarkable circumstances than are commonly found in a village. Everything was included in the total picture and considered normal: symptom of a genuine culture. Painful to think that this has been liquidated by a single command.[119] It makes you wonder about *this* place. I was very much afraid yesterday. Talked to the lad who lives on Roerstraat and knows Nettie.[120] Nice, intelligent boy, whom I told a lot, as always: too much. But okay. Also got better acquainted with that Beek fellow from Haarlem, the teacher, a slimy type who talks about God.[121]

From all appearances, we really will move into Meissler's barrack today. Gone from the shouting, quarreling, thieving OD guys with their abusive leader. The kitchen boss here is Bialik,[122] a nephew of Chaim N. Bialik's,[123] or so he claims, but when my newfound friend Max Splitter[124] says that he's lying, that may be true.

Today we've been here for fourteen days. Amsterdam is unimaginable. But that's not because it's Amsterdam, but because you can't measure the time here. Because everything that happens here is already so long ago. That time, for example, that Leezer chewed us out. Or the time that we visited the women, etc., etc. Everything just a few days ago. But long, long past. You can't measure the days with getting up and going to bed. Because we get up during the night at six. And we go to bed at nine. And all day long we don't know what time it is, like fish in stagnant water, who see the light appear and then disappear again. Anyway: like everything else the light here lacks nuance.

earned the nickname of *Bei-unser* (back-homers). This referred to their habit of comparing whatever they encountered in their country of asylum with the allegedly superior conditions back in Germany. The often-heard remark "Bei uns in Deutschland war alles besser" (Back home in Germany everything was better) irritated Dutch people in general and Dutch Jews in particular.

119. Around February 15, 1943, only a few Jews arrived from Dutch cities in Westerbork; at the same time, four hundred Westerbork inmates were sent to Vught, which at that time also received many transports from Amsterdam. If an observer wanted to create a causal link between the drop of arrivals in Westerbork, the transfer of inmates from that camp to Vught, and the rapid growth of Vught, he might have come to the logical (but as it would turn out erroneous) conclusion that Westerbork would be closed. Letter, Guido Abuys to Robert Jan van Pelt, February 18, 2009

120. Nettie David lived on Roerstraat.

121. David is referring to Josephus Nicolas Beek.

122. See the entry on Abram Moisze Bialek in the appendix. Bialek died in a subcamp of Dachau

123. Chaim N. Bialik (1873–1934) was a famous Hebrew poet.

124. Max Splitter was a partner in a family business. See the entry on the Splitter family in the appendix. Max Splitter died on a death march.

No sunrise: a foggy morning emerges from a foggy night. And usually the featureless day ends in a gray evening, and it ends in a night in which you can no longer see a thing. The trees are dark against a flat sky. The branches are damp. The windows are always and forever fogged up. And everywhere the soil is moist underfoot. We're located between sandy stretches and woods. The wind is empty here. Without odor, without mildness. Bleak and scornful. But it's rarely very windy in these parts. Even through the wind we have no contact with the rest of the world.

The *Oberhauptscharführer*[125] ripped up the postcards on which we had worked so hard. We had asked too eagerly for food. Slandered the hotel's good name. But I gave messages for the furriers to deliver.[126] Fortunately many people don't know what has happened.

The Splitters are German Jews, but not refugees from Hitler.[127] In Westerbork they always had two candles on Friday evening. One of them was praying this morning with *talles* [prayer shawl] and *tfillim* [phylacteries]. In reaction to this Father starts to pray as well.

Father is very grumpy the last few days. Offended by the smallest thing. Yesterday I got a little soup from someone without knowing that the man had offered it to Father first but had forgotten about it. Father was insulted to the core etc., etc. Whenever he's looking for something, he's despair personified. I wouldn't want to go camping with you, I say to him. We had a row this afternoon because he was looking for a pair of scissors.

As though to contradict what I've written so far: it has become beautiful, clear weather. Smooth blue sky. The sun shines on the barracks. Spring!

I don't know why, but today I had to keep thinking about the people who went to the other side. I'll never forget how they came in, with but one concern: getting their luggage in good order quickly. An endearing attention to their possessions. Already entirely adjusted to their new existence. I'm writing this because I became conscious of

125. There was no such rank in the SS. David may be using the designation of *Oberhauptscharführer* ironically: the Dutch were amused by the German habit of adding the adjective *ober-* (superior) even to lowly occupations such as that of waiting on tables. The literal translation of this fictitious rank of *Oberhauptscharführer* is: Superior (*ober*) chief (*Haupt*) troop (*Schar*) leader (*Führer*).

126. This is an important sentence as it reveals that David used Escotex employees who were not inmates of the Vught camp to smuggle both letters and his diary to Amsterdam.

127. David is mistaken here: as noted before, the Splitter family came from Galicia, which used to be part of the Austro-Hungarian empire.

it only later and didn't write about it at the time. Why I have to keep thinking about it, I don't know.

Maxi's already a big man here. Through young Meissler he has gotten a job in the warehouse, works there all day, has a note so that he can pass everywhere and is so busy that he may not have an opportunity to go to the women. This morning I started a poem:

When off to work in morning dark the band
of prisoners on the other side departs
there is a singing loud and clear that starts
and all around over the peaceful land
is heard: I love you dearly, Nederland.
When streaks of gray the darkness part
many we see find standing up too hard
for the SS governs with iron hand.

Friday [February 26, 1943].[128] Yesterday received five parcels, from Tini and Fred[erika] and Karel.[129] Prepared with great care. Unbelievable. Eight loaves of rye bread. Brown beans. A loaf and a half of whole wheat. Two or three jars of jam. Lots and lots of butter. Sausages. Bouillon cubes. Deventer honey cake. Mother was with us when we unpacked everything. Very emotional. I long for letters. They really could have written them.[130] Max was greatly impressed. Max Querido appears to be on the other side.[131] He shouted for him. Maxi carried on a conversation with Aptroot at the top of his voice, so that Querido could hear it. I've hardly ever seen Maxi so upset. All these things affect me less. I'm fairly indifferent to the welfare of other people. That saddens me a lot.

Kiev hasn't fallen yet. According to people in the [recently arrived] transport, they [the Soviets] still have 40 kilometers [25 miles] to go. On the other hand, some say it *has* fallen.

128. An advertisement published by Joachimsthal Bookshop in the February 26, 1943, issue of *Het Joodsche weekblad* announces that David Koker and Jozeph Melkman's *Modern-Hebreeuwse poëzie* (*Modern Hebrew Poetry*) remains available. David Koker's edition of Jacob Israël de Haan's *Brieven uit Jeruzalem* (*Letters from Jerusalem*) seems to have sold out. *Het Joodsche weekblad,* February 26, 1943, 2. This was the last time that David Koker's name appeared in print before the end of the war.

129. Tini Israël, Frederika Samson, and Karel van het Reve.

130. In fact a letter was hidden in one of the loaves of rye bread. See the diary entry of February 28.

131. Max Jacob Querido (1925–44) lived close to the Kokers and was a friend of Max's. He was murdered in Auschwitz.

Something terrible yesterday: scarlet fever has broken out in the Westerbork barrack. The *Oberscharführer* has promised, with his well-known generosity, to shoot anyone who enters or leaves it. People are mortally afraid of infection. Quite right.

Now there's measles among the babies. Yesterday afternoon the ladies visited us. But a number of men walked over to the women and talked with the women through the open windows. It seems to have been less a failure of discipline than a misunderstanding. The OD is responsible. Therefore they have extra punishment. What we all got was bad enough. Squat for more than an hour, initially with our hands held up high, later in the neck. Of course we didn't do it all that exactly. When the *Oberscharführer* wasn't looking we got on our knees and put our hands down. We had a lot of fun. Extinction is a favorite term here. Witticisms filled the air. Lehmann initially sat there nicely with his hands up, but he began to feel ill. Was supported by a couple of people. It looked as if we were lining up for a group photo. Neumann, the administration barrack leader, popularly known as Neusman [Noseman], did no more than keep his head bowed, enjoyed that a lot, refused to sit down and turned quite red because of the effort, because that position naturally required much more effort.[132] This kind of measure doesn't make people unhappy. The Westerborkers: "Why did we have to come to Vught?" They said: "Poland can't be any worse." And yet we don't feel down. For myself: I'm completely insensitive to these things. That is no virtue, I believe. But anyway insensitivity. I don't feel humiliation, even when I'm subjected to it deliberately. I feel it more when I *suspect* contempt. In any case, I do reproach myself for adapting to everything so easily. Worse: no visits to the women for 14 days. Less bad: into bed at 8 p.m. Highly irritating: the mutual blame game. Süsskind's cursing. In future the OD will be allowed to hit people. Hallelujah! Father desperate yesterday. Went to bed in darkness in the new barrack. I wish I were dead. I can't stand these things. Inauthenticity has become natural. And people don't want to make an effort.

This morning [we had to] camouflage the luggage again. Another visit. They say Christiansen.[133] So first a walk this morning in the cool

132. See the entry on Josef Neumann in the appendix.

133. Luftwaffe (air force) general Friedrich Christiansen (1879–1972) was commander of the German forces in the Netherlands from May 1940 to April 1945. His qualifications for the position seem to have been his East Frisian birth, which meant that he was "racially" related to the Dutch, and his initial training as a sailor. Also it may have made sense to Hitler to

sunlight. And now we're sitting around inside. And the same boredom as on the other days. Reading newspapers. The Germans seem to have had successes in Tunisia.[134] The idea that the war will end soon has disappeared here as people have become used to the camp. Nor do they speculate as freely as they used to.

A lot of people have colds because of yesterday. People discuss the *Oberscharführer* in the customary picturesque terms, but also with a certain understanding. What I had already thought myself, they say often here: [this is] a German disciplinary measure that's also applicable in the army. In many ways people are quite reasonable. To each other as well. Quick to quarrel, that's true. But with no ill feelings afterwards. I often quarrel with people, too. That's progress, because at the outset I often allowed people to push me aside.

Began a new sonnet this morning. The terza rimes of the other one have to be fundamental and I'm a bit afraid of them. The new version is:

> Along the paths they patiently push barrows
> or rake painstakingly the meager sand
> the light hangs in a sunny grace that hallows
> over the houses of the camp.

Yesterday the barrack leaders naturally had to ensure that the group carried out its knee bends in an orderly fashion. Meissler did that in a very amusing way. Hands up in the air. Whispering: *Götz von Berlichingen.*[135]

Saturday [February 27, 1943]. According to the wishes of the *Oberscharführer,* the OD is not sufficiently military and so now drills daily. It's not going at all badly and it looks nice. There's always a few civil

appoint a Luftwaffe general, since the country was to be an important Luftwaffe base in the war against Britain. Impulsive, irascible, and lacking all diplomatic skills, Christiansen proved to be the wrong man to pacify the Dutch.

134. In the Battle of Kasserine Pass, fought in the second half of February 1943, German troops commanded by Field Marshal Erwin Rommel routed poorly led American forces.

135. In German, just referring to Götz von Berlichingen equals saying "Kiss my ass!" Meisler alludes to the vigorous reply made by the eponymous hero in Goethe's play *Götz von Berlichingen* when a herald summons him to surrender his castle to the imperial army: "Surrender? Unconditionally? Are you talking to *me*? Am I a bandit? Tell your captain: for his Imperial Majesty I have, as always, all the respect due to him. But your captain, tell him he can kiss my ass!" Goethe, *Götz von Berlichingen,* 146. Translation by Michiel Horn.

ians [i.e., other internees] standing at the fence, looking on in wonderment. People make a lot of jokes. Overste will be given a horse. There's someone who can do a really great imitation of a horse.

On the list I see there's a Jeanette David here.[136]

I heard this about Lehmann: when we all had to kneel, the clerical staff were exempt. At that point he ran over to the place where the clerical staff normally assembles and sat there all alone. This, the manner in which he raised his hands high, and his expressive face made many people laugh. But he did it to get others [of the clerical staff] to come as well, because he wanted no exceptions. After a while he had to be held up because he almost fainted.

Two parcels yesterday from Karel, Tini, Frederika. Another parcel today. This morning I was cooking twice, a kind of sausage stew that I gave to Father in its entirety because there was so little. Officially we're not supposed to cook, they keep telling us, but they can't stop it. There's always a group of people around the stove. You smell clothes being singed. The pans and pots are arranged [on its wide top] in the most efficient way, because the largest number possible have to occupy the least possible space. Anywhere on the stove is good, but the process can't be completed unless your container is on the hottest spot. When it's there at last, you have to stay at the stove, because as soon as someone sees his chance, he'll shove it to the rear. So that some pots stay on the stove for hours. Once some water of mine—in the OD barrack—was on the stove for two hours and in the end was pushed off, onto the floor. That happens too.

A bad day yesterday. I got up, my eyes ached, and in the course of the day they got worse. Dizzy, cold, shivering. Temperature not elevated. Too bad. I'd like to be sick. Couldn't sleep last night because of the cold. Traded blankets with Maxi. If I turn my eyes they ache. My head [hurts too].

Father made a scene in the middle of the night, woke everybody up. This morning I talked with Meissler about arranging to give him some small job. This way he's going to go crazy.

Just now I traded five sugar cubes for a cup of warm lemonade. That did me good, because this morning I woke up with an ache in my chest. A real flu feeling. Stayed in all morning today. Read *Levensinzicht* [*Understanding Life*], a Rilke anthology.[137] Oh, God, I heard

136. The furrier Jeannette David (1924–43) was murdered in Sobibor.
137. David is referring to a Dutch-language reader of selected letters written by Rainer Maria Rilke (1875–1926) and published in 1940.

myself say. Rilke of all people. Gorgeous passages in it, alongside much I don't care for. What I do care for, I'll get back to later. In any case a surprise. Rilke has the same difficulty in expression that I do, that is, the inability to see things simply. Because things don't strike us as simple, not because we are profound but because we lack poetic force. And for that reason the mystification, which is literary mastery, not genuine force. A world of senseless surmises, without content and comprehension. All that turns into word, thought. But that's not everything. It remains somewhat fluid, hazy, boundless. At the same time, beautifully concrete things about tempo in the arts, about Paul Cézanne, wonderfully told anecdotes. Beautiful things, but once again unformulated, about love.

Airplanes flew over last night. For a good hour. We listened in a mood of pious attention. Nobody was allowed to speak. This morning people said: the *Unterscharführer* had spent the time in a barrack out of fear. Not impossible, because just over a week ago Amersfoort was bombed.[138]

Also a dream last night: there was an "exalted visitor" again. He was a big fellow with an enormously tall, gray, fantastic Russian cap: Christiansen. I thought: he's so exalted that an ordinary military model is no longer sufficient.

Sour, walleyed, unshaven, drunk, but not very. A couple of less important gentlemen, with smaller caps. In other ways the same. Accompanied by a woman, who said to everybody: "Terribly lazy!" She was on our side. The company seated themselves on the podium and at once the woman called me up from the audience. We entered a small room. She wasn't good-looking, but there was something "loose" about her, easygoing, something decadent, too. Every gesture with the same ease. At a certain moment she took the pen, and marked the lines of her face with ink. That was something which didn't surprise me. Just the sort of thing she would do. She had Leo Seligmann's letters with her.[139] (I forgot to write about them, I received them yesterday and was amazed) and said: this way there's little chance [of getting out]. We have to flesh it out. We discussed it for a long time. Were frighteningly intimate.

138. On February 13, 1943, Mustang fighters of the RAF conducted a raid on the barracks of the SS Guard Battalion Northwest, which guarded Amersfoort camp. Six SS men died, and eleven were wounded.

139. See the entry on Isaac Leo Seeligmann in the appendix.

Shul in the post office yesterday. Lehmann and Barber from the [Jewish camp] leadership. Additional this morning: Pacz,[140] Hanoch.[141] The Oostjoden set the tone here.

Sunday [February 28, 1943]. And on *shabbes* [Saturday] morning we had another *shul* service. But then the *Oberscharführer* came in and said: "So what's this, eh?" And then we had to break it up, because it was time for "work." This fiction is rigidly maintained here. Also the fiction that we aren't prisoners.[142] That's why we haven't been assigned numbers. The Oostjoden calmly continued in an empty barrack, and when someone said something about it later, one of them told us about Uganow and Ruppin, who were in prison, one because he had studied the Torah, the other because he had said [a prayer?]. It was preferable to get into trouble because of the Torah. Said how God takes pity on us in the torments that he allows us to suffer. Like a father who lets his son be operated on and feels more pain than the child itself. And all this said with unbelievable clarity and expressiveness. He's not handsome. His hair and beard were cut off in Ellekom,[143] and they're still short. His face therefore looks too narrow. Glasses. Great curved lines in his face. But with a detached and open gaze. He spoke to someone who said something about everybody going up to Jerusalem. About the impossibility. Very reasonable and realistic. Talked about Ellekom. They took all his clothes except what he was wearing. When, however, a man threw his *tfille* [phylactery] away, he jumped at him and said: I came here to work, but if necessary also to die. A couple of hours later, on some pretext they kicked and beat him so terribly while he was down on the ground that his body was one massive contusion and he thought he would die that very day. After that they took him to the commanding officer, to whom he said that he had traveled on the Sabbath for the first time in order to work here. But had he known how things were done here,

140. The identity of Pacz is unclear. It is possible that David is referring to one of the many Pachs in the camp.

141. The German-Jewish refugee Gerhard Hanoch (1900–43) was murdered in Sobibor.

142. David is referring to the fact that the Jewish inmates are not *Schutzhäftlinge* (protective custody prisoners).

143. Kamp Palestina (Palestine Camp) in Ellekom, northeast of Arnhem, was a small camp attached to a training school for Dutch SS men. Most of the inmates were Jewish refugees in the Netherlands. The conditions in this camp were absolutely atrocious. The trainees practiced their newly acquired torture skills on the inmates. Presser, *Destruction of the Dutch Jews*, 229ff.

he wouldn't have come. The gentlemen looked at each other, left the room for a while, and returned a few moments later. "Why are the Jews of Europe waging war against us," the commanding officer asked. "I don't know anything about that," he said. "So who is Litvinov Finkelstein?"[144] "Not a Jew," he said, "but a Russian statesman who has the ability to lead his country and has therefore been placed in a high position." "Why are the American Jews [waging war on Germany]?" "In order not to undergo the same fate as us." "What does it say in the Talmud? Not to beat people to death. It does say that you shouldn't eat the meat of an animal if you can't elevate it into a higher form of life."[145] Ten commandments etc. He also said: If Germany hadn't persecuted the Jews, it would have won the war long ago. Nowhere on earth more patriotic Jews than in Germany. Subsequently he was marked out for good treatment and got kosher meals.

They sit together at a table, which I privately call "the pious Russian table."[146] There they pray, study, give praise to God. Yesterday we did a really beautiful job of singing *hamavdil*.[147] An unforgettable *havdalah*.[148] Two candles, the light brightening their faces. Their shadows on the wall, their shapes framed by the glow. Afterwards people sang. Maxi accompanied me on the lute as I sang "Od lo nutka."[149] The Oostjoden sang the refrain. And all but embraced me. "That is the future," they shouted: "A song for when we're on the way home." I myself was very touched. Bialik, the man from the kitchen who says

144. Maxim Litvinov (1876–1951) was born as Meir Henoch Moiszewicz Wallach-Finkelstein. In the 1930s he was the Soviet minister of external affairs. For the Nazis, Litvinov's Jewish background was proof that the Soviet regime was dominated by Jews. In 1939 Stalin replaced Litvinov with the non-Jewish Molotov, who then signed the Ribbentrop-Molotov Pact. During the period of Soviet-German cooperation, Litvinov was in the political wilderness, but he returned to favor when Germany attacked the Soviet Union on June 22, 1941, becoming ambassador to the United States.

145. This is a reference to the Talmudic commentaries on Deuteronomy 12:20. "When the Lord thy God shall enlarge thy border, as he has promised thee, and thou shalt say, I will eat meat, because thou longest to eat meat; thou mayst eat meat, to thy heart's desire." Talmud Yoma 76; Chulin 16b; Pesachim 49b. The central idea is that animals do not know freedom. If their energy is consumed by a human being who is free and hence able to choose the good, the energy of that animal is "elevated."

146. David is alluding to Thomas Mann's novel *The Magic Mountain*. In it, Joachim Ziemssen tells his cousin Hans Castorp that the sanatorium where he resides has a "good Russian table" where the "nicer" Russian residents of the sanatorium eat, and a "bad Russian table," attended by the more uncivilized Russians.

147. A hymn to end the Sabbath.

148. The religious ceremony marking the end of the Sabbath.

149. "Od lo nutka hashalshelet" (Yet Is the Chain Unbroken) is a song that became popular in the Yishuv, the Jewish community in Palestine before the founding of the State of Israel.

he's [Chaim] Bialik's nephew (he does come from Odessa), sang a bit for me (he is an unfriendly and reportedly unreliable man, but I've captured his heart) and [he] promised me some extra food.

In a parcel from Karel, a note was concealed between two slices of rye bread. I had given them to Mother. Got the note back today: it was nice.[150]

Roll call for half an hour to an hour this morning. The sky was bright. A few thin clouds like those bits of paper you often see stuck to new items but which gradually disappear. We were bathed in a strong, yellow light. Icy cold. Hoarfrost on the trees. People are sensing [the coming of] spring. The poem's going to be like this:

> The early dew tells of a spring to follow
> and from the plain rise vapors pure and damp
> the light falls in the sunny grace that hallows
> over the reddish houses of our camp.

This afternoon a parcel from Se[e]ligman[n]. Touched me. A feeling of guilt.

There's a man here, Waag, who is a great comedian.[151] Yesterday evening after eight he presented a poem from his repertoire. He is gauche but with a tendency to virtuosity that you occasionally come across. He can do a very nice Han Hollander imitation.[152] He did it again yesterday afternoon. Although all days are actually much the same here, it's genuinely Sunday afternoon this afternoon. Krieker and Viool are playing cards. Meier, the troublemaker, whom we left in the other barrack amid the quarrels, will be paying us a visit to drink a cup of tea.[153] Krieker is smoking a cigarette. Everything is certainly in its place.

---

150. The note survives. In it, Karel assures David that "I have organized and neatly packed all your scholarly materials. The last piece I grabbed was that letter from [Jacob Israël] de Haan (which you copied). It was left on the table." Karel also advises his friend: "If you're able to free yourself or get into an advantageous position, do it." Letter, Karel van het Reve, February 23, 1943, collection 244 (diaries), file 1657 (Koker), NIOD archive, Amsterdam.

151. The diamond cutter Herman Waag (1906–44) probably died in Auschwitz.

152. Hartog [Han] Hollander was a famous and extraordinarily effective radio sportscaster who covered Dutch soccer. See the entry on Hartog Hollander in the appendix. Hollander did not survive the Holocaust.

153. It is not clear to whom David is referring.

Met here: Dr. Knoche.[154] With whom I went for a bit of a walk. We both belong to the teachers' group, which got together this morning for the first time, under the leadership of Verduyn,[155] a pleasant former member of the AJC.[156] This much: one Ph.D., one Dr. Knoche, one Koker, will guide children aged 6 to 12 and instruct them.[157] Besides these also the tedious Beek, who always thinks he's better informed, and the even more tedious Duizend.[158] With nasal voice. Made for the job.

When you speak with Oostjoden, it's always something. Major conversation with Bialik, who [never] lets anyone else get a word in edgewise. Hoarse voice. Reasonable questioning tone. Large, fat. "The Jew knows no borders. If he lives on one square meter, he still praises God for his existence and his meals." He's a Zionist, of course. Having a

154. See the entry on Gerhard Dagobert Knoche in the appendix. He was murdered in Auschwitz.

155. David is referring to Abraham (Albert) Verduin. See the entry on the Verduin family in the appendix. Albert Verduin probably died on a death march.

156. The AJC was the Arbeiders Jeugd Centrale (Central Organization of Working-Class Youth).

157. From the arrival of the first transport on January 16, 1943, children under sixteen made up approximately one-fifth of the population of what was initially known as the *Judenauffangslager* Vught. It appears that the first initiative to create a school in Vught was taken by Albert Verduin and Josephina Gersons-van der Hove. They quickly gathered a number of volunteers, including David, who were willing to help with the schooling of the children. The effort was stymied by the lack of space to hold classes, lack of furniture, and the lack of teaching materials. By the end of April the number of children under thirteen had reached almost 1,000, and the Jewish Council became involved in the efforts to improve the children's education. It commissioned a report on the educational situation in Vught. This report mentioned that 170 children from four to six years of age were instructed by 13 teachers, and 772 children of primary school age were instructed by 47 teachers. There were also 37 support staff. The children needed tables and benches, and the report suggested that they could be obtained from the now-empty Jewish schools in the provinces (from which the Jewish population had been sent to Vught in April). The report noted that there was no information about the schooling of those of middle- and high-school age. Two other reports mentioned, however, that the lack of activity and the consequent boredom of the 281 boys and 318 girls aged thirteen to seventeen were a source of great concern. They were difficult to control, and the reports expressed the fear not only that there would be conflict among the youngsters but also that they would cause conflict with the Germans. The discipline provided by vocational schooling was expected to help deal with these potential problems. Boys were to be given the opportunity to learn trades like carpentry, tailoring, shoemaking, and so on, while girls were to be taught sewing, child care, and cooking. By early June 1943, the proposal to strengthen the education of the younger children had become irrelevant, for almost all children under the age of thirteen had been sent to Westerbork. Most of those thirteen to sixteen years old were transported in July. Various mss., collection 250g (Vught), file 864, NIOD archive, Amsterdam.

158. David is referring to Joseph Duizend. See the entry on the Duizend family in the appendix. Joseph Duizend was murdered in Sobibor.

few assimilated Jews conquer Palestine is nothing. But making it into a Jewish country [is the challenge].

Monday [March 1, 1943]. Ferber and I are the best of friends.[159] I thought of you all night, he said yesterday, in reference to "Od lo nutka." [When he gets out], his first run is going to be to Eretz Israel.

Two dreams: Every night I know beforehand that I'm going to dream. Then I resolve to remember. That works, because I'm awake a lot of the time. First dream (from the night before last): We were going to be "sent through" and were in Amsterdam for that reason. I was standing on the edge of the Amstel, and threw myself into it, to kill myself, observers thought, but in reality to save myself. I went into Leo S's place, but his wife had just gone into labor.[160] An old-fashioned birthing room complete with scalloped-edged linen cloths.[161] Ancient aunts. I've come at a bad time, I said. Actually you have, L. S. said, in his typical fashion, but, looking around, perhaps you haven't. I stayed for a little while, then had to flee again. I traded jackets with someone who resembled that handsome, supercilious young man in the administrative office, the one who always walks around in his equestrian costume but who wasn't quite so supercilious at this moment. I walked under the awning of the Amstel Hotel and reached freedom that way, emerging from a feeling of oppression so great—the image of Poland lay over everything—that I can't find words for it.

The second dream was from last night: I was walking with Nettie along Middenweg, which is where we last walked together. She was weeping and her face was very small. "That it is you who has to go to Poland now. You, who always laughed so hard about me [about my fear] that I had to go." She didn't say that last line. It was something in that spirit. Also in the spirit of: "You, who always laughed so hard in order to avoid dealing with my fear." It shows how our recollection of dreams is an interpretation of a feeling, an intimation, which is actually the dream. Not a certain event, but simply an intuition that poses an event as a possibility. That was the dream. It really moved me. Several times when I was awake I thought: I must remember this.

159. David is referring to Chaim Färber. See the entry on the Färber family in the appendix. Chaim Färber was murdered in Auschwitz.
160. David is referring to Isaac Leo Seeligmann.
161. At the time almost all Dutch children were born at home.

Brother Waag is most amusing.[162] Red, smooth hair, a big nose that is slightly turned up at the end. A meditative smile in which his entire face takes part, and large, brown, melancholy eyes. "You don't have a leg to stand on, sir. You call people names. I put more trust in physical violence." Or during a roll call which doesn't add up because one man is missing, and we have to stand around for a long time: "Why don't they just shoot two people, then we'd be through here."

At the moment there's a huge quarrel going on. People won't be quiet. And at last Meissler called them swine. Swine, sow, shit, these are the current symbols here. Loudmouth is also a favorite word.

People can be so petty here. This evening those younger than 17 got extra bread. One man: "My son is 17 and gets nothing and Paul M[eisler], who is 16 (in fact, he turns 17 on Thursday), does get bread." Yesterday there was a fight because the kitchen staff scraped the butter wrappings clean and "no doubt saved the butter for themselves."

Sang yesterday evening. But without rehearsal, so sang badly. Although people were very pleased and happy. On request I closed with "Hatikvah,"[163] at which point everybody got to their feet and sang along as best they could. I had introduced it with a short speech. Two people were offended by it, one of them Boas,[164] who looks like the housekeeper of Mrs. De Haan.[165] They had sensed Zionism. Actually I'm not a Zionist at all, but because of my longing for a positive Jewish consciousness I constantly end up in Zionist territory. Zionism is the easiest, the crudest, and the most erratic way of getting there. It is given to the occasional individual to *approach* the goal along another route. If he makes a public appearance, however, if he has to *speak* about his Jewishness, then at once he seems to be a Zionist. And that causes much confusion. The truth about the Jewish people cannot be systematized, cannot be socially formulated. In no way does it serve any endeavor, [it] is only an ineffable, insubstantial posses-

---

162. The reference is to Herman Waag. See note 151.

163. "Hatikvah" (Hope) was a song composed in 1878 by the Polish-Jewish poet and Zionist Naphtali Herz Imber (1856–1909). It became the unofficial anthem of the Zionist movement and in 1948 the national anthem of the State of Israel.

164. David could be referring either to the diamond worker Benjamin Boas (1897–1943) or to the diamond worker Emanuel Boas (1901–43), or to Louis Boas (1922–43). All three were killed in Sobibor.

165. Johanna van Maarsseveen was the widow of Jacob Israël de Haan. See "David Koker and His Diary," 45–6.

sion of certainty. To speak about it is difficult. To sing is easier. I said yesterday evening: not with words does the Jewish people propagate itself, but with songs. People are very much enthralled. It's incredible how much conscious Jewish life there is among the people, and how it can be activated.

Another remarkable thing. Many people rejected their portion of blood sausage.

This morning we were doing the rounds on behalf of education. The barrack hadn't been cleaned yet. Walked around all morning. I don't see much happening with this education scheme. I don't aspire to a job in this field at all.

Remarkable how sex is totally in the background here. A conversation between Krieker and Meissler (very personal) dealt with this. The husbands and wives here feel, one would almost say, a conjugal love for each other. That they can't be with each other is cruel. When luggage has to be taken from one part of the camp to another, lots of men volunteer in the hope of catching a glimpse of their wives. Then the women stand together alongside the road to look and wave. Because talking is prohibited and therefore often impossible. Yet people reconcile themselves to it amazingly well. Lots of notes are exchanged. Maxi is often with Mother, because he's allowed to pass everywhere. That's very nice for Mother, because Father and I don't have the flair that [some] others have for getting past the guards.

It's impossible to express how empty I am here. Everything I always thought about, all my "positions," which were always *associated* with all the phenomena of reality that cropped up, they are gone and gone. There's nothing left besides camp life. There's no posture you can adopt to confront it, there's only more or less intensive participation, sometimes even nonparticipation, but then not based on the possession of anything.

My few good moments are in camp life, with Rilke, with the Oostjoden, with my poems. But especially the last of these are more laborious than ever. I've never realized how weak, how dependent I am, how devoid of any content *of my own*. I'm an instrument that can make a big sound when a gust of wind blows up but defenseless and without power of its own when the days are windless and deathlike.

Bialik has good stories about [what happens] when the transport lists in Westerbork are made public. He speaks so singularly, so helplessly, with a schematic sentence structure. He takes the same kind of pleasure in everything he says, tragic or comic. Everything with the same clumsy emotiveness. As if he were juggling great burdens in his hands. He has small, dreamy eyes in his large, heavy head, and while he's speaking with you it's as though he were looking past you, looking past you at the many things he has to say. When he's telling stories he looks at people long and menacingly, challenging them, pushing out his lower lip as if waiting for the admiration of others. And at the same time he speaks with a great lack of emotion.

Heard Süsskind talk yesterday morning in a melancholy way about his conversations with the *Oberscharführer*, who doesn't believe in victory any longer.

Tuesday [March 2, 1943]. Again this morning . . .

Wednesday [March 3, 1943]. Yesterday morning accompanied the rest of the teachers' group in strolling back and forth near the education barracks. But nothing doing. The day before yesterday the *Oberscharführer* stopped us when we were doing that, and when we said we were teachers: "Yeah, right, you look like the teacher type," and disappeared after uttering a few threats. As far as I'm concerned I won't mind if this education project doesn't get off the ground.

I was too despondent yesterday to write anything. It was due to very concrete things: two full jars of jam were broken. Food in parcels had spoiled. As a result the whole day a bleakness that led to new gloom concerning the whole state of affairs.

Otherwise yesterday was a day of encounters. In the afternoon made the acquaintance of T[eeboom],[166] a cousin of Philip's.[167] He told me how Philip had behaved towards his family. And that the family was fully able to appreciate the Schaik section as a middle-class social circle.[168] And yesterday Maxi hooked up with a cousin of Bennie Meyers's.[169] Someone who was actually the spitting image of that

---

166. The tailor Hartog Teeboom (1905–44) died in Auschwitz.

167. David is referring to Philip de Vries. See the entry on Philip de Vries in the appendix.

168. It is unclear what David has in mind in mentioning the "Schaik section." He may be alluding to Josephus Robertus Henricus (Josef) van Schaik (1882–1962), the Dutch minister of justice from 1933 to 1937. Van Schaik framed the increasingly restrictive asylum policy of the Dutch government toward Jewish refugees.

169. See the entry on Benjamin Theodoor Meijers in the appendix.

lad. And just as uncouth and friendly as Bennie always depicted his family. A really strikingly accurate characterization.

A game of chess with Paul Meissler in the semidarkness yesterday evening. Lost after a few moves. I was not a little peeved.

I have to say a few things that have been on my mind. About the orders during roll calls. I keep forgetting them. People don't have the slightest feeling for German. Overste, the commanding officer of the OD, gives an order: *richt uit,* his pronunciation of *richt euch* [straighten yourselves]. People turn that into *licht uit* [lights out]. *Rührt euch* [move] is another order, one that is often mistaken for the first and is usually rendered as *rusthuis* [old-age home]. Willie Dresel, who keeps track of the roll calls, gives his orders in a friendly fashion, and always makes errors in counting [*tellen* in Dutch], has been given the cute nickname William Tell.

"Taught" this morning and afternoon. Among small and scrawny children. Hurt my throat yelling amid the noise, very attentive and interested. Strange experience. Went for a walk this afternoon. With one of the girls on my arm. Like a real social democratic teacher. This morning told the story of Mordecai and Esther.[170] The children not very interested but paid attention all the same. Arithmetic this afternoon. Yesterday translated one of the *Oberscharführer*'s orders [into Dutch]. Something similar this morning.

Conversation with Vleming, Süsskind's secretary, a pleasant, well-educated man who tried to talk me out of my pessimism.[171]

Two deaths here last night.[172] Earlier this week another death.[173] But they would have died a natural death anywhere.

Thursday [March 4, 1943]. Earlier this week some said with the greatest conviction: the English and Americans have landed in Romania. Via Turkey, of course. Yesterday evening's newspapers [arrived] this morning. No truth to the rumor at all, of course. Rzhev [west-northwest of Moscow] *has* been vacated. The Russian offensive seems to have lost some of its force. But people here don't notice that. In any case, speculations about the length of the war have diminished somewhat.

170. The Jewish festival of Purim fell on March 20, 1943.
171. David is probably referring to the Polish-Jewish refugee Josef Fleminger. He was deported to Theresienstadt in September 1943 and very likely survived.
172. The two men who died were the diamond cutter Daniël Pront (1867–1943) and the tailor Joseph Werkdam (1892–1943).
173. David is referring to the shoemaker Mozes de Metz (1902–43).

People are resigned and don't look for the end. Just what I wrote to Mother yesterday. Accept what comes our way, whether it be misery or the end. Don't long for what isn't there.

German Wehrmacht girls have arrived to be leaders in the women's barrack. Not a single man is allowed to enter now. Even Süsskind wasn't allowed through. There's one good-looking girl among them, the first of that kind. Her mouth is a bit too strong. But I doubt I'll become good friends with her.

Father has a job now. With the administration of the [shoe] repair shop. He's becoming as bureaucratic as a peacock.

Was writing this afternoon. Wrote a good letter, in which I forgot to say something [I wanted to say]. Even though I had thought about it all night.

Slept very little. A window was closed and now my voice is ruined. Therefore gave no lessons this morning.

Paul Meissler's birthday, we gave him a roll of mints.

Parcels from Kapsenberg, Geerling.[174] Also Grewel, from whom I got a parcel today as well.[175] Besides these, parcels from Samson. We contemplated our bread supply with concern. Yesterday we traded a jar of jam for a can of anchovies, knowing that we would become very thirsty but taking the chance all the same.

The world is so touchingly small: yesterday I met yet another relative of Bernhard's.[176] Not related by blood to the first. Now once again the best friend of the Kleins. He had lived with them all his life. And suddenly saw them again in Westerbork.

Roll call in the cold this evening. A motionless, frozen sunset. There was a problem. The first row had to count themselves. Some groups didn't do it properly. Then: do it again. Whoever made a mistake got slapped with an exercise book, administered by the *Oberscharführer* in person. If things really went badly, the first row had to squat. In some places it looked just like a group photo. The first time a whole group had to go down. But four rows were allowed to get up again fairly soon. Remarkable rationality of these punishments. The first rows are getting to be ever more unpopular here. Just as in a movie theater.

---

174. The Amsterdam jewelry manufacturer Lindenaar & Kapsenberg was Jacques Koker's employer. Geerling was a silversmith in the company. Lindenaar & Kapsenberg supported the Koker family throughout their internment in Vught, either by sending packages directly or by helping Karel, Tini, and Fré in obtaining food for packages.

175. See the entry on Israel (Ies) Grewel in the appendix. Grewel was murdered in Sobibor.

176. David may be referring to Barend de Vries.

A minor joke during the roll call: people passed a penny from hand to hand.

I often think the *Oberscharführer* is a wild animal, one that walks through us as through a forest. It shows itself only infrequently. And we know, but don't know exactly, how dangerous it is, because it remains unknown to us.

Friday [March 5, 1943]. A new transport arrived this morning. We shall see.

I forgot to note that there's a nephew of Grandfather's here who looks like him and speaks the way he does: quite ill-tempered.[177]

Yesterday Meissler to a German [Jew] who looks like an elderly professor: "I wonder why this old ox is still walking around." And the old ox: "I refuse to have you call me an old ox." Meissler: "Well, sir, in that case you are an old ass." Whereupon the old ass fell silent.

Something nice during yesterday's roll call. While [William] Tell was walking along, counting, *Oberscharführer* entered a barrack (ours; we were very worried).[178] Dresel came back and scurried around like a small dog unable to find its master. People here really enjoy that kind of thing. Everybody laughs.

This morning we counted ourselves as an exercise. It was a wonder to behold. In the letters we have written we've said a lot about the samples of Nettie's cooking. Let's hope something comes of it. To Mother I wrote: parcels are technical aids to life. But letters are life itself. I also wrote: if we didn't adapt ourselves so much to the world, we would accept the world in a more perfect sense. To surrender ourselves passively to reality kills both the experience of reality (we ourselves become the reality) and the ability to make demands on reality. We must be attentive friends, not unresisting cozealots, nor impetuous idealists.

I was assigned another class today. The children thought it was terrible. I regretted it as well. Now I have to teach language, literature, and history to grade six and to the HBS class.[179] Had an enjoyable conversation with Mrs. Speier, who has definite charms.[180]

---

177. According to Max Koker, David is referring to either Aron or Jacob Worms. Neither survived the Holocaust.

178. David is referring to Hauptscharführer Franz Ettlinger.

179. HBS stands for Hogereburgerschool (Higher Burgher School). Its graduates were given admission to a limited number of university courses.

180. The manager Marie Anna Speier-Legerman (1906–43) was murdered in Sobibor.

Members of the new transport say: Orel has fallen (some mistakenly say Smolensk), the Swedish envoy [is] back, also the German, but he has become Swedish.[181] H[ungarian?] units back from the eastern front, German units from Africa.

Stopped by an *Unterscharführer,* who reproached me for not walking on the center path.

Saturday [March 6, 1943]. The women are now under the orders of the ladies with the caps, who don't seem to be easygoing and who, people are saying, come from Birkenau.[182] The good soap has been taken away (will go to the babies, they say), replaced by a clay-based product, other things too. They're not allowed to keep anything. Twice a day they'll be allowed access to their foodstuffs, I believe. One of them gave Aptroot's wife two pieces of soap. Otherwise it will be taken away, she said. The children were nervous wrecks yesterday. Everything gets taken away. My God, what are they turning us into?

A part of the parcels will be confiscated and distributed [among those who didn't get parcels]. I worry about my rye bread. . . .[183] That's the worst thing that can happen to me. I'm thinking about Nettie a lot. I wondered whether I might wish she were here. How it would be during visiting hour. I wondered how it would be if I were in Amsterdam and I were paying a visit to her, the way we had agreed. Her image has vanished somewhat into the imaginary, just as used to happen in the past.

I heard the Oostjoden sing very beautiful *zemirot* yesterday evening.[184] Everybody was silent and almost everybody covered his head. There is so much Jewish in the people. But it is what it is, and it doesn't permit itself to be moved.

Nemeth is a thoughtful man.[185] Ferber is probably above average. But Nemeth is quite something. He dictated a beautiful Zionist song to me. Here I sense precisely what the value of Zionism is and is not.

181. This entry may refer to a rumor of a deterioration in Swedish-German diplomatic relations.

182. Given the highly secretive nature of the mass gassings of Jews in Auschwitz-Birkenau, which had begun in the spring of 1942, it is remarkable that SS headquarters transferred guards from that camp to Vught. There is evidence that in September 1943 SS man Joachim Perthes talked to Vught inmates Gerda Süsskind and Henny Glazer about the gassings in Auschwitz-Birkenau. See De Jong, *Een sterfgeval te Auswitz,* 15, 31.

183. Karel, Fré, and Nettie hid their letters to David in loaves of rye bread.

184. *Zemirot* are songs of praise sung on Sabbath eve.

185. See the entry on Leizer Nemet in the appendix. He was murdered in Sobibor.

The Oostjoden have a right to it, so to speak. We don't.[186] I'm going to ask the Oostjoden to allow me to *benchin* some time.[187]

Yesterday's roll call conducted by the *Oberscharführer.* The French aristocrat type. When he speaks he keeps his hands behind his back, smiles, and turns in all directions without moving his boots. He leans forwards and sideways from his boots. Taunting impression. He has the reputation of being very good. He began by abusing us, saying our beds looked *schweinemässig* [fit for pigs]. Shouting. Lustily. To his question: *Verstanden* [understood]? we had to answer: *"Jawohl"* [yes]. After five times *"verstanden"* it was all right. After that he came into the barrack. Yelled *"Achtung"* [your attention] four times. In between he kept saying, in a very friendly way, *"Hinsetzen"* [sit down], and then at once, gruffly: *"Achtung."* I was just going to the stove with a saucepan of broth. I had to stand at attention, with the saucepan between two fingers.

Last night in a rancorous mood, with that understandable vagueness of thought while sleeping and at the same time with a rare clarity of feeling: the life of all these people is worth nothing, only mine. And that this is individuality. Here you reach that point: this morning I looked around at everybody and remembered what I had thought. It did not strike me as mistaken. Only with Ferber did I hesitate. He has a big influence on me. I'm writing this in the dormitory, so he won't see me writing on Saturday. He has eyes as free and open as the heavens.

This morning I became conscious of why I'm writing my diary. A thought that I'm already quite unable to grasp but is irrefutably true: this diary reaches beyond the end of the war! I could be reading from it to Nettie, with an image available to me, an image full of remarkable things, full of the most astonishing as well as incomprehensible facts. Reading from it to Nettie is a big, heavy thought, charged with tenderness.

---

186. Zionism was carried by the enthusiasm of the Jews from eastern Europe, while the great majority of western European Jews had remained indifferent to the idea of establishing a Jewish state in Palestine.

187. In a narrow sense the Yiddish term *benchin* refers to the Hebrew prayer Birkat Hamazon (Blessing on Nourishment), which is said following a meal that includes bread or matzoh. The prayer consists of four blessings followed by a series of short prayers and, on holidays, additional prayers appropriate to the occasion. The meaning of *benchin* is elevated when it is said in the company of at least three adult men, and when ten or more men say it together the saying of the Birkat Hamazon acquires the significance of a short religious service. Many Jews use the term *benchin* when they refer to any prayer.

To make the image available to Karel, great objectivity falls within the range of the normal. Artistic whole, not an image of what I've lived through. Only of what I've seen.

Got a parcel this evening. A great load off my mind concerning the rye bread. It goes through unexamined. But otherwise it was a black day; instead of the wooden posts with barbed wire big concrete posts have been installed. Even down the middle of the grounds. The German chicks want a complete separation of men and women. It seems a man kissed his wife today. The good-looking but very cruel girl, who bloodied a small boy's nose this morning, saw it. Today the man was singled out during the roll call conducted by the *Oberscharführer*. Red hair and glasses. A resounding punch in the face. His glasses fell off. He picked them up and received a well-aimed kick. The *Oberscharführer* went on quipping to Süsskind and Dresel, said something about *Schweinereien* [smutty business]. By that he probably meant the kiss. These days Dresel usually winks before he gives his orders, which does dispose me favorably to him.

Something terrible this afternoon that profoundly depressed me. The men had to take the barbed wire down. To get out of that job I went over to the children. They had a matinee performance. Everything arranged exceptionally nicely. Something like an amphitheater had been built. A poignant sight. The children with their hands in their laps. And their eyes very still and attentive, the way you often see in newspaper photos. A comedian and a puppet show. The [good-looking] girl with the gray cap entered. Left again. Moments later: a roll call. The children obediently went outside. In rows of five, so narrow, those rows. And so there they stood, five minutes short of two hours. There's never a roll call otherwise. Submitting children to military drill is worse than abusing them. When I saw those children stand there this afternoon, for such a long time, such a long time, on their special day, to which they had looked forward so much, I saw *for the first time* what others have been claiming to see for a long time already, how far we have gone. I could hardly stand it. And yet: a grievous joy: because now [I] am experiencing reality here for the first time, even though by way of grief and indignation, for God's sake. I sense this as a victory and a capitulation at the same time. As a victory. To see it at last; I can't accept it as normal anymore. And yet not the ideal objective experience as *unadulterated reality*. But seen and felt through an ethical and emotional medium. I wasn't aware of this. Perhaps it's the only possible experience. And the other, the objective, is only what we experience through the emotional or, better said, what we imagine to be behind it.

Over at the women's they've torn up photos.

I'm starting to enjoy teaching. Spoke about the Sabbath this morning. Very nicely, keeping religion at a distance. Ended with Elijah—story by Perets and me.[188]

After that almost got into a quarrel with Aardewerk,[189] who talked this afternoon like a real *Jecke* [German Jew] about "praying": because of the distancing mentioned above.[190] Enjoyable, but nevertheless I'll try to loosen my ties to it.

Father threw out his back this evening. Engelander is full of concern about him.[191] Doesn't want him to end up on the sickness report. I still have to write about Engelander.

Sunday [March 7, 1943]. Great disappointment. An order that roll call will be at the same time as on other days. I don't care about getting up early or late, but about Sunday, which needs to be pleasantly distinguished from other days. Sunday is a solar day, Saturday a day for staying inside and talking with the Oostjoden.

But then the big surprise that made everything all right. Not the fact as such. But for me there was great joy in something I'll describe. Upon conclusion of roll call, the *Unterscharführer* turned around and said: "Gentlemen(!), I want to impart a small item to you. (He pronounces some words in the same peculiar way Tenhaeff does).[192] This morning is work time . . . Understood?" Everybody (not really all in

188. Isaac Leib Peretz (1852–1915) was one of the most important Yiddish writers. His story "The Magician's Visit" has become a staple of Passover literature. In this story the prophet Elijah, in the guise of a traveling magician, visits a poor couple who cannot provide for the Seder meal.

189. See the entry on Samuel Aardewerk in the appendix. Aardewerk was murdered in Sobibor.

190. The term *Jecke* refers to a German Jew who behaves in an overly formalistic manner. The etymology of the term, which became popular in Palestine in the 1930s, is unclear. Many believe that the term *Jecke* derives from the German *Jacke* (jacket), indicating that German-Jewish males in Palestine continued to wear jackets and ties that were inappropriately formal for the circumstances in which they found themselves. The linguist Dov Sadan postulated that the word derives from the cross-breeding of the Low German word *Jeck,* which means "fool," with the Yiddish *Jekl,* which means "Little Jacob" and which was an insulting way to refer to any Jewish male. David would have picked up the word in the Zionist movement. Sadan, "Alter Terakh," 142.

191. David is referring to Jacques Engelander. See the entry on the Engelander family in the appendix.

192. Nicolaas Bernardus Tenhaeff (1885–1943) was a professor of medieval and modern history at the University of Amsterdam at the time that David studied there.

unison): *"J'wohl!"* [yes]. And then: "Moreover, I'll allow you to visit your womenfolk this afternoon." People didn't know what to answer, they say things like *"j'wohl"* and *"danke"* [thanks], or clapped. The *Unter-scharführer* laughed a bit and shouted: "From two until five." Again *"danke"* and *j'wohl."* And he: "Did you understand: three full hours. From two until five." The man was a bit moved himself. And took so much pleasure in telling us, that he almost didn't want to let us go. After dismissal Süsskind reached for his hand in a formal way and kept on shaking it for a long time.

Let me put it this way: this has somewhat restored my faith in humanity. The last few days, I've known what it is to despair of people. I've thought at night about the theory that every human being lives at the expense of others. And how something like that leads to the completely unnatural and arbitrary aspects of what we see around here: it makes it possible for people to issue prohibitions to or yell at others. I thought: that's what military service does to people. The officers here don't know anything other than that in their working lives (so not among friends, of course, but in their working lives) in a group called by a certain name, they have to be in a relationship of reproach and abuse. And this morning it occurred to me that the desire for mutual harmony, being as one in feeling an emotion together, is something at least as important in human existence. Occasionally the Jews themselves do sense that: when they help each other with something. But mostly life is made up of quarrels, orders, and reproaches.

Monday [March 8, 1943]. I still have to record a dream from the night before last. I was reading to a few people, I don't know who, from my diary, told them about this time. Then Nettie came in. She was very beautiful. Her face differed a bit from what it really is. She also walked differently, swaying, not as sturdily as customary.

There are 32 sick children (among approximately 150) because of Saturday's roll call.

Visitors yesterday afternoon. On a sandlot. Just like the queen's birthday. People along the edges, in the sand. Picnicking. Along the road to the sandlot [are] the prisoners. Sitting on the ground, their backs against the barrack, sleeping in the sun. Some with their heads sagging on the knees of others. Smoking a cigarette, lazy and blissful. Strolling over the grounds. Until we are tired and our throats dry from the dust.

Something else about the celebration of the Sabbath. Mrs. de Wild said kiddush [blessing to sanctify the Sabbath's meal] in the children's barrack, said the prayer of praise, and blessed the children.[193] There were a lot of tears shed. By the roughest boys. The children and ladies were more than enthusiastic about my Oneg Shabbat.[194] In any case, the ladies are very fond of me.

Today I became senior teacher. I am now in charge of the room with seven grades, pupils and teaching. In praise of bureaucracy. Everybody comes to me to get permission to do whatever has come into their heads, children are sent to me and get a terrible scolding, I intervene if the teachers can't manage, call teachers' meetings, am held responsible by an active Mrs. Gerzons,[195] a married cousin of Bennie Meiers's, for things that are not my responsibility.

Rumors: the nursing staff here have to go to Berlin. Women with S [penal cases] out of here. Children in Westerbork belonging to parents who are here are coming here. Homeless children as well(!) Engelander's kid.[196] Engelander is a small fellow, 33 years of age, mustache, shows off his small stature demonstratively. Likes to be the center of attention. Talks, boasts, fantasizes about his adventures. Can't be trusted in that respect but is very kindhearted and amiably dependable. Last week, as he was sitting there drying his kid's diapers, and somebody joked about that, he said: "My boy, I've got only two things left at this moment, my wife and my child." And now that child is ill, seriously ill. Temperature 39 [102.2°F]. Half paralyzed, with bones showing through his skin. Hasn't eaten in 20 days. On Süsskind's request, the German officers parted with a bottle of table cream (we live in a magical, touching world). Süsskind phones Amsterdam (for the first time) to get hold of an intravenous feeding machine. He doesn't want the child to be sent to [a hospital] in Den Bosch, for fear that it will be sent through, that it will be sent to Westerbork together with Jackie and his wife.[197] That concern does [make me] feel good.

193. David is referring to Sarlieni de Wilde-Asscher. See entry on de Wilde-Asscher in the appendix. She was murdered in Sobibor.

194. Oneg Shabbat (Joy of Sabbath) is an informal and preferably congenial gathering on Sabbath eve.

195. David is referring to Josephine Anna Gersons-van der Hove. See the entry on Gersons-van der Hove in the appendix. She was murdered in Sobibor.

196. David is referring to Robert Engelander. See the entry on the Engelander family in the appendix.

197. By "Jackie and his wife" David means Jacob (Jacques) and Betty Engelander.

During roll call this morning: one man too many. "Better one too many than one too few": the *Unterscharführer* [Rudolf]. This man means a lot to me. To express it conceptually: that someone in a uniform like that can remain the way he is, to state it another way: to know there's good somewhere, in a strange world a heart that's related to ours and yet strange.

As in other places, I find myself in an exceptional position here. I don't know whether I've already written this, but I thought: if a person can say in all seriousness that certain rules don't apply to him, if he can say that without ulterior motives, then they don't apply to him. And it's the same way for the consciousness of the people, which determines what the rules are. This evening Krieker told me to go to bed. I was working. "People don't want any exceptions," he said. And I: "There are exceptions that people will accept." He agreed with me, and so I was able to keep on writing.

There's another way in which the German of the orders is Dutchified. *Augen gerade aus* [eyes straight ahead] becomes: *Augen gerade draus* [eyes straight out of your head]. The *Oberscharführer* actually has a peculiar way of giving orders, which sounds like *ololay aus*.[198] And then *aus* as an exhalation.

I often speak with Dr. Knoche. There's something about him I don't care for. Physically. What he says is true and often subtle. For example: "You keep the children enthralled, although you are neither a pedagogue nor a friend of children." But the remarkable thing is: he's not persuasive, even when he speaks the truth. There are pieces of metal you pick up only to be startled by how light they are. That's also how it is with the things he says. They make you feel bored and empty. Less bored than empty.

Sang yesterday evening. Folk songs. People were engaged and yet not satisfied. Like me hearing Knoche's words. In any case, my voice is deteriorating because of the roll calls and the business of being senior teacher.

It was actually a gorgeous day today. Warm. In the afternoon people were stretched out against the foot of the wall like laborers [during their break].

Wednesday, March 10 [1943]. I'm writing again today. Had no time yesterday because lots of things were happening. A bad day: HBS

---

198. The order is, in proper German, *"Alle austreten,"* or "Everybody dismissed."

class, where I was unable to maintain order and made the children sit still and be silent for a quarter hour. Also at odds with Mrs. Gerzons, [and] with the women teachers because I intervened in their lessons for the sake of keeping order. On the verge of tears; later recovered a bit. The problem is that I [do] these things too thoroughly. My nerves are jangling after a day like that. I can't see a child talking without telling it to stop. Call children to order, who're not listening to one lesson or another, etc. I worry about too many things. The others take it easier. But when I'm busy working I'm under a stress that I'm unaware of when I'm writing this. The scaredy-cat barrack leader is telling me to go to bed.

Thursday [March 11, 1943]. Our very good friend Aptroot left for Westerbork this morning. Once again we're a little bit more alone. Or quite alone: because Max had to go to the boys' barrack. Even worse. This evening I heard that the diamond workers are being separated from the rest of us. So Father and I are apart. I'll see whether there's anything to be done.

I've joined the vaudeville group led by Dixon (Simon Dekker).[199] Short little fellow, who has something voluptuous in his movements; when he sings or hears music. Then he moves his body in such a way as to suggest a woman's body. Add to this that he's a bit ugly, small, so that I get a grubby, sensual feeling when I see him. Something of all those half-naked women still clings to him. You sense it when you see him. His eyes still see them . . . And yet he's a calm, friendly, ordinary man. It's only because of his lifelong profession.

A great success this evening while performing with the official ensemble. Things were moving well! We sang: "Od lo nutka" (with translation) was evidently too long for the women. "The Fisherman," "Auprès de ma blonde."

Friday [March 12, 1943]. This morning many women complimented me. One who knew what she was talking about asked me whether I've had lessons. By the way, the reaction of the women to the different acts is curious. First, they laugh excessively at jokes, they explode, all at the same time. Repeat the punch line, clap their hands in enjoyment. Some inmates have less success with them than others.

199. See the entry on Simon Dekker in the appendix. Dekker's stage name was Dixon. He died in Bergen-Belsen.

Conjurers, for example. The sense that they're being fooled probably predominates among them. As I'm writing this: Kharkov retaken [by the Germans]. We won't be out of this place for quite a while. There *is* an offensive at Rostov(?). Their whole attitude has something sensuous: they swing along with every tune. That news about Kharkov turns out not to be true yet.

The women had to stand for three hours, before the move. An inferno [of activity] in their barrack. Lugging backpacks back and forth. Screaming. Weeping. Two women [acquaintances] saw each other for the first time: faced each other in petrified hysteria. I tried to take charge of the situation, but my shouting did not make them quiet down. So I hauled packs instead. Also to see the girl. I believe her name is Mona or something, she introduced herself to me but I forgot it. You should actually put a couple of eunuchs among the women, a man in any case, to be in charge of them.

Bernhard de Vries has to leave. Having reported that he suffered from several ailments, he allowed himself to be frightened by threats from Dr. Swaab and said that his wife was mildly diabetic. It doesn't seem to have worked. He himself is well over 55, but he was registered as a diamond worker. This afternoon, when a group of people, he among them, came to pick up the ladies' luggage, some loud-mouthed woman or other came up to him and said: "Mr. De Vries, you don't need to come, your wife's in the Westerbork barrack." He didn't get it at once. When it sank in, he stood still and became as immobile as a corpse. I quickly walked away. Later I heard that he said farewell with a speech: "Don't forget me, keep thinking of me." He embraced Meissler and kissed him. Later I went to him in the separate barrack, took a letter with me that he had addressed to Süsskind on my instigation. Took it to Süsskind but accomplished nothing. He wrote a note [to De Vries] and I wrote on it: *chazak we emeth* [strength and truth].[200] People are impressed by him in particular.

I'm too tired to go to sleep.

Saturday [March 13, 1943]. I've noticed I don't have socks and pajamas with me. Yesterday evening people were so tired that except

200. In wishing De Vries on his departure *chazak we emeth* (strength and truth) David created a wordplay on *chazak we emats* (strength and courage), which was the slogan of the Jewish Youth Federation, and *chessed we emeth* (love and truth), which, according to Psalm 25:10, describes as the quality of all the paths of God to "those who keep his covenant and testimonies." According to Psalm 89:15, *chessed we emeth* "shall go before thee [God]."

for three men the entire cleaning detail went to bed. I'm not exactly sure why, but I've offered to help. Officiousness, showing off, but also the wish to really exhaust myself for once. A conversation afterwards. Meissler said how he decided, the day after Hitler's accession to power, to go to Holland and did in fact leave two weeks later. Krieker thought he had spotted a Zionist tendency in me because of "Od lo nutka." "Better a day laborer's existence in Palestine than an ample existence here and the knowledge that our children may have to go through this again." He also said: "I am religious. God's ways are unfathomable, everything that's happening to us has meaning, even if it's done by humans." He kept on talking and I asked him: "Do you believe in guilt?" He didn't. A pleasant, naive, wonderful man, genuinely kindhearted. I didn't know there are people who theologize without being in the profession. A few days ago I was lying in bed and heard two guys (one of them Stibbe,[201] who's gone now), talk with each other. After they had spoken first about the prospects ahead and then about Meissler, one asked: "Do you believe in God?" "No," the other said. "Why not?" "If God existed he would have created a good world. And we who are experiencing all this know it isn't." In conversation with Krieker yesterday evening Wegloop said something similar.[202]

Sunday [March 14, 1943]. After performing for the ladies three times I understand something better, and also from what Mother told me. Where the men are concerned sexual matters are very much secondary. In fact, they tell each other that in a tone of scientific seriousness. Meissler and Krieker said so, and others as well. Among the women sexual matters are *the* conversation topic, Mother said. And when you witness an entire roomful of swaying, singing, laughing girls and women, totally under the control of a few men on stage who can make them do whatever they want, then you feel the sexual side as all-governing. But as something you aren't part of, even though you're the object (yes indeed, the object, *not the subject!*) of it, as if it were *one* sexual understanding of the women among themselves but aimed at the man. But aside from that and in self-defense: I don't expect anyone to believe it. All the same it's true.

201. David is referring to the textile worker Philip Stibbe (1922–43), who was murdered in Auschwitz.
202. David may be referring to either Mozes Wegloop (1899–1944) or Hijman Wegloop (1926–44). Both died in German captivity.

The last few days I haven't had time to keep my diary up-to-date. Teaching takes all my time and strength. Right now I'm happy doing it once again. Also know, now, how to deal with Mrs. Gerzons. On the Sabbath told the first tale about the shofar.[203] The children were keenly interested. Hebrew songs led by the pious, boring Aardewerk, who is cautious to a fault. I'm very popular with the children; when I walk by, for example on my way to visiting the women this afternoon, they call out: "Hi, Mr. Koker!" Girls on my arm, all from school. In any case there are a few pretty girls here who're available. I'm friendly with one of them, but friendlier would be even better and that's for the future. With another I exchange amicable glances and that's enough. Naomi Kohn is here and becomes friends with everyone, or at least makes an effort.[204] With Mother too. She was weeping when I left. She was able to tell me the following about Nettie. She was in *shul* when she heard about me. Was really upset and dejected. Loes had a "chat" with her.[205] I don't think she would have liked that much. She left on the Monday. She's in domestic service now, Naomi says.[206] I was very touched and will try to find out more. My departure drew a good deal of attention. People said that I was the first. Now they're leaving. They wanted to send me books. Naomi said: "I felt it was particularly bad for you, because I thought you wouldn't be able to adapt at all." And I said a few moments later: "So far, except for a few weak, sentimental moments, I haven't felt unhappy here." And that's the truth.

The women's behavior is extraordinary. I play to the whole room, lead them to store up pleasure during the song, compel them to hold it in, and allow them to explode in one great outburst of mirth at the refrain, which they sing along with me, laughing. Bending the

203. The shofar is the ram's horn that is blown on Rosh Hashanah, the Jewish New Year. All male Jews are obliged to hear the shofar that day. One of the best-known folk tales about the shofar is set in Renaissance Spain after the expulsion of the Jews. In order to remain, many Jews had converted to Christianity, but these *conversos* continued to practice their religion in secret. Because one cannot blow the shofar silently, these secret Jews, or Marranos (meaning "pigs" in Spanish), could not fulfill their obligation of hearing the shofar on Rosh Hashanah. One Marrano, Don Fernando Aguilar, was a court composer who found a solution to the problem by including a shofar in a musical performance given on Jewish New Year at the court. Hiding the shofar in public, Aguilar allowed himself and other crypto-Jews to fulfill his New Year's obligation. In 1943 the tale of Aguilar's shofar would have had a particular poignancy.
204. Naomi Kohn survived the war and moved to Israel.
205. David is referring to Louise Asscher (1920–1999). See entry on her in the appendix.
206. This is code for "she's in hiding now."

audience to my will like this is enormously strenuous and the energy
that you expend on it flows over to everything else. These days I play
the part of *het loze vissertje* [the crafty fisherman]. Turning to the left
I'm the fisherman, turning to the right I'm the farmer's wife. The
fisherman, his rod over his shoulder, pointing to his leather boots,
the farmer's wife with her hands on her waist, imitating his ponderous gait and his leather boots with irony and amusement, singing
excitedly.

Made the acquaintance of Martin Roman, pianist for Marek Weber
and Nelson.[207] At first a bit curt and arrogant, later quite friendly.
Spoke about the Oostjoden, about eastern Jewish food, eastern Jewish atmosphere, and about *Jeckes*. He's obviously a blowhard, but not
an unfriendly one.

There's a conjurer here who contributes to the cabaret. Specialty:
card tricks. Nobody stops wanting to figure out how he does it. People almost don't dare to hold the cards that he puts in their hands.
Every moment there's a different card on top. And the card you're
looking for is in the middle [of the deck]. People don't even get annoyed anymore.

Monday [March 15, 1943]. Performed yesterday evening. The *Oberscharführer* with a dame. In contrast with the German woman, who was
there yesterday and who applauded, he just sat there, barely laughing,
watching very attentively. Now and then he spoke out loud with Süsskind and Roman. Süsskind and Roman translated everything with
a smile and omitted everything they thought would not please Mister *Oberscharführer*. Turning with him to where he was looking. Constantly smiling. A pair of courtiers par excellence. Afterwards a big
discussion with Fisch, leader of the barrack I've gone into recently.[208]
An Oostjood with sharp features and unbelievably heavy and deep
wrinkles. Nice man. When someone's talking during roll call, he says:
"Don't keep people from their work!"[209]

He was in a rage yesterday. "Better to be dead than sucking up
like this to these people." Talked about the performance at the *Kommandantur*, the camp commandant's headquarters. An aversion to it.
For my own part, I just keep my mouth shut. Admire their hatred and

---

207. See the entry on Martin Roman in the appendix.
208. David is referring to the German-Jewish refugee Julius Fisch (b. 1899). He may
have survived the war.
209. David is writing sarcastically.

anger. For them it's not just chatter. As for me, I can't agree to the [charges of] depravity, [I] extenuate and soften. I say: "Military discipline, they've undergone the same thing themselves, [they're] not sadists" (I really do believe that) or: "I can't make sense of that man." And I have a strong tendency to want to put myself out.

Sang a German song last night. In a certain sense I'm strongly drawn to the *Kommandantur*, partly out of curiosity, partly out of assertiveness, because I want to associate with anyone who's highly placed, regardless of his quality. An ambition of the lowest kind. And without the means to make it effective. And other things accompany it: attitude to authority, etc. And what's bad: I know this so well and am trying to kill it. I wanted to know if this crude pushiness occurs more often among people of my kind. Otherwise I live as much as possible by the rules I've set for myself. But reluctantly. The matter has been resolved. I've left the cabaret company. Dixon kept quibbling.[210] At one point the Hebrew song was shortened, then it disappeared altogether. Today: "Mr. Koker, you won't be singing tonight." Whereupon I approached him later and told him [I was quitting?]. Now my evenings are my own and I won't need to neglect my diary anymore. And concerning the unworthy behavior I was writing about I want to add this: I find in myself a tendency to keep making excuses for the Germans. Surely that's a weakness and an unwillingness to accept reality.

But this evening something deeply moving. Honey cake for Father, a letter from Karel. With a very beautiful poem about Russia. In his positiveness he has strength and simplicity, so that he can say whatever he wants. He has substance. He knows what poems he has to write. I only experience something "musical," but I am so directionless, so lacking in knowledge. The two verses I've begun are still unfinished. I can't do it, and not because of lack of talent but because of lack of strength. Frederika is in touch with Lydia [Nettie David] and gets along very well with her. Perhaps Karel is half-aware what this means to me. Lydia is continuing with her [Russian] studies.

My nerves are deteriorating. Sometimes I have to weep. Not because I'm homesick, but because I'm moved. Tenderness towards others, a few times pity for others, often self-pity. A feeling of tenderness about small things I see. Often I think: I'm going to exhaust my capacity for love here. The emotions shared with others.

210. David is referring here to Simon Dekker.

Spring today. Hot and uncomfortable. The sand is dusty. The children in the large room, dozy and noisy in a sleepy way. Spring is a bad time for me. Very downcast. Also fatigue and the quarrel with Dixon. I'm over that now.

A lecture this evening by Knoche about the Jews and the Carolingians, very well attended. Very successful. Also crammed with information, which people find interesting.

Friday [March 19, 1943]. It annoys me terribly that I'm neglecting this diary so badly, but it really is lack of time. The bad thing is that I'm losing the style [of diary writing] in this way, the attention to details and to perspectives. I want to try to work at it regularly in the evening.

This afternoon I had a conversation with Drukker, a boy of eighteen who in many ways is remarkably grown-up.[211] Strongly self-conscious, which is a source of suffering to him. He feels here, he says, as though anesthetized. From the very first day, he says, he has been standing around with open, empty eyes and mouth hanging open. He has a girlfriend in Amsterdam, for whom he longs with all his heart.

Maxi and I each got a letter from Frederika. Life became bright and sunny when I heard that Nettie was in touch with her. I really love her a lot, Frederika says. That is: an appreciation. This will improve the relationship between Nettie and me, if not, define it. I am that dependent. But I've never denied that dependence. And always looked forward to this moment: Frederika's love for Nettie (Lydia!). Also because Frederika can shape much in Nettie that couldn't be shaped to this point. The comparisons between Nettie and the others will probably come to an end now. True, I'm not worthy of her. But that's the way I am. I've been working on a letter to Nettie for a couple of days, in which I tell her honestly how far away she has come to seem.[212] But there's also a lot of nice things about our relationship

211. David is referring to Sylvain (Syl) Drukker. See the entry on the Drukker family in the appendix. Syl Drukker died in Bergen-Belsen shortly after the liberation of that camp.

212. This letter survives. In this letter David assures Nettie that he has adapted all too well to life in the camp. "I immediately accept everything as normal. That's why I don't experience things sufficiently. They don't surprise me enough. You must believe me: from the second day on everything was quite normal: the German detachments, being together with so many people, the strange food, taking care of the most essential daily matters, etc. I didn't notice the passage from one kind of life to the other: I search my memory in vain for the moment that I saw this new situation for the first time. We always used to say: 'Nothing can happen to me.' But nothing has really happened to me. Because even the

in it, and I call her sweetheart, although that's a big and heavy word. What's to become of us? In the letter I've posed this as something of a problem. I'm afraid that the letter is a bit confused. But this contact Frederika-Nettie is everything to me. It has made my tired, listless day as bright as the weather around here.

Had a conversation with Dr. Knoche this week. Accurate but lightweight. I said: "We Jews only live, the goyim experience. They're centripetal, we centrifugal. In our contact with reality we strive for a kind of mastery, as it were." And he: "That's why our image is the Messiah and theirs the suspended Christ." An example of a change of styles in conversation. There is a Dr. Eckstein here, a German philosopher.[213] He and Knoche used to be friends, but now they're quite angry at each other. He's a short little fellow with a round head, open mouth, parted hair, who always keeps his head down and his eyes sharply staring at nothing in particular, so that you see a lot of the white [of his eyes] and he slightly resembles a detective or a soothsayer. Knoche says: "If I say A, he says B, even if he was planning to say A." Earlier this week Knoche was reading the book of Isaiah. Eckstein joined him and said: "I stopped reading the Prophets long ago. They've had their day. I've seen only fire, sword (according to Jul.!![?]). A bloodbath of peoples. The prophets of today are the political economists, starting with Proudhon and Lassalle."[214] And this in the most severe tone possible, glaring sharply through his spectacles. He speaks like someone in a Thomas Mann novel.[215]

Witticisms: Someone from Berlin said about Süsskind: "He's too high and mighty to walk."

strangest and most awful things become normal and agreeable. In a word: untragic. That's one of the things from which I suffer here: that I merely live this life and don't experience it. I write a lot about this in my diary and hope to let you read it. Because my diary is for you and for the others. I've dreamed that I read from it to you and Karel. For each of you I intend something different with it. For you it has to be the record of *my* experiences and thoughts, for Karel a record of experiences and thoughts in general." David writes that his whole life is now focused on Vught, and that life before Vught has become an abstraction. "I think of you every day. But you've become an abstraction too, something I think of because my thoughts know the way there. No living figure attracts my thoughts to it." Letter, David Koker to Nettie David, March 1943, collection 244 (Vught), file 1657 (Koker), NIOD archive, Amsterdam.

213. David is referring to the German-Jewish refugee Kurt Eckstein (1896–1943), who was murdered in Sobibor.

214. Pierre-Joseph Proudhon (1809–65) and Ferdinand Lassalle (1825–64) were revolutionary Socialists.

215. David very much admired Mann's style, both ponderous and precise, and its capacity to carry an incredible range of thought and emotion.

Someone late one evening: "Delicious, a week Friday." Someone else: "What happens then?" "Then they'll give us cabbage soup."

Saturday [March 20, 1943]. An officer has arrived, commandant from Auschwitz, so they say.[216] He seems to have taken charge of a reorganization of affairs: absolute separation of men and women. He didn't believe in it himself, or so nurse Soesan assured me. Nurse Soesan is a plain and pleasant girl of twenty or so, who is in the top leadership here and seems to have taken a shine to me.[217] Our identity cards were recalled. A big disaster for all who send parcels or letters. But we do have our own school barrack, which the ladies have nicely outfitted this morning and left unused. Late this morning we were called to the *Unterscharführer*'s and got permission for a return [of our cards?] and for new ones. "You can do what you want, but don't get caught." A friendly fellow, who can laugh very heartily. I wrote to Nettie about him for reassurance or an attempt in that direction in view of her parents.[218]

Roll call this evening, the *Unterscharführer:* "Everything all right?" "Yes." "Eyes straight ahead! Dismissed." Such moments are worth a lot to me.

Finished a stanza this afternoon:

> Until late evening you can hear them singing.
> They sing until the bitter end is here.
> Till then their songs will never lose their ringing
> for even when the last man disappears
> their voices live on in the voice that's springing,
> by which we're bathed in daylight pure and clear.

I'm very pleased with this, I hope to send it to Karel. Agency. I re-read my letter to Nettie, I do believe it's good. The essential mental

216. David is probably referring to Untersturmführer (second lieutenant) Otto Reinicke. In Auschwitz Reinicke had been in charge of warehouses.

217. See the entry on Eveline Susan in the appendix.

218. In the letter to Nettie mentioned in the entry of March 19 David responds to the news that her parents have been arrested. He expresses both shock and a measure of optimism. "Here in Vught we say: 'It's tolerable here, and it may be possible that this is the treatment the Jews receive in all the camps, strict, but not in the manner of a concentration camp.'" David's optimism was misplaced: Sobibor was not like Vught. By the time David had written this letter, both Siegfried David (1882–1943) and his wife, Berta David-Grunberg (1882–1943), had been killed in Sobibor. Letter, David Koker to Nettie David, March 1943, collection 244 (diaries), file 1657 (Koker), NIOD archive, Amsterdam.

contact with her is lacking, but that is just as much lacking with Karel and Frederika. I often have the sense here that I have less depth, less capacity for experience, than others. In my case all experience is stronger [when] unconscious. I have a toughness that is unbelievable but that gets in the way of a lot of good things. I love the weaker personalities, which are stronger from the point of view of *human* potential.

Spring

(March 21, 1943–June 19, 1943)

In 1943 spring came, as in the years before, on March 21. Yet the March equinox did not bring respite to the Dutch Jews. Deportations had continued, and by March 21 the number of them deported to the east had reached 50,000. Beginning March 2, trains leaving Westerbork traveled to a new destination that did not appear on any map in a Dutch atlas. It was the Polish hamlet of Sobibor. By the first day of spring 3,174 Dutch Jews had arrived in that place—to be killed the same day. In Vught, however, the Germans had other concerns.

Sunday [March 21, 1943]. Inspection for lice this morning. I submit to it passively, crack jokes, and am surprised that I don't feel humiliated. And I think of C v B, who didn't want to be lined up.[219] The action was prompted by the *Untersturmbannführer,* who gave a big speech to the administration yesterday about the dangers of vermin.[220] And that no one needed to be ashamed, because he had lice himself when he was at the eastern front, in spite of washing daily. The women are getting their soap back. The storing of clothes under the beds is improper. When someone speaks in that way he gets my full appreciation. People here say: "He's good and surely he . . ." This is a somewhat abstract attempt to justify their friendly mood.

---

219. This is a reference to a passage in the autobiographical stream-of-consciousness novel *Eva* by the Dutch-Jewish author Carry van Bruggen, who was born Carolina Lea de Haan (and who was Jacob Israël de Haan's sister). In it the protagonist confesses how she dreads the prospect of having to undergo a physical examination: undressing in front of another human being, or for that matter to be ordered to do anything, like being lined up at a ceremonial occasion, or having to obey orders during physical exercise classes. Carry van Bruggen, "Eva," in *Verhalend proza*, 445.

220. David was mistaken: the SS rank of *Untersturmbannführer* did not exist. He was probably referring to an *Untersturmführer* (second lieutenant), because there was no SS officer with the rank of *Sturmbannführer* (major) in Vught.

Knoche told us several interesting stories about the excellent relations that still existed between German soldiers and their [French and Belgian] hosts in the last war. In response to a remark of mine, that it wouldn't be that easy these days, he said, quite accurately, that you notice it here too, that real affection for officers who conduct themselves correctly. That's indeed perfectly true, I'm always very pleased with things like that.

The day before yesterday I also received a parcel of books. A Hebrew grammar. Now that we're getting the quiet school barrack, I should have time to have a good crack at studying Hebrew. Then my diary won't be so badly neglected either.

Within the prevailing circumstances, the same gap exists here between happiness and unhappiness as elsewhere. You can look forward to something really basic that you wouldn't even bother with in Amsterdam but that represents the highest stage of happiness here.

Because of all the commotion recently, I lack the precise focus on the facts that I've had in my diary up to this point. That's because at the outset my diary was not just a reflection on life but life itself. Now life has (really) differentiated itself into important and everyday, i.e., life here has become ever more normal. I hope that time will become more bearable when we have the new school. But time isn't everything.

Tuesday [March 23, 1943]. And now I'm spending a second day in the white, sunny hospital barrack, outside the windows a gorgeous sky, a dark pine tree sways in the fresh, golden air, and large patches of sunlight fall on our blankets. It is quieter here than elsewhere, of course, but that means it's still pretty noisy. In the first place, everything is naturally a bit primitive: up to a certain point people nurse themselves, and besides, anyone who feels a bit out of sorts shows up here. A lot of diarrhea sufferers like myself. On Sunday my eyes already hurt a lot. Men and women were on the drill grounds together, in the dusty heat. We were sitting close to each other. I felt impotent and empty. I felt great pity for my family and a vague and distant pity for the people around us. In the evening my eyes hurt so much, and my head felt so big and hot, that I took my temperature. Underarm 38.2 [100.8°F]. Father manufactured one of his bouts of despair and said dejectedly: now I have to cope with this too. Frederikstadt looked after me extraordinarily well, although even his friendliness has something businesslike.[221] Not the distance, that he doesn't have, but the busyness. I lay there quite lonely in that big ward, on the third level. Have I already written that the evening before I went to the dormitory when the nasal Jo Duizend was reading the Megillah [the Book of Esther] out loud?

Next morning 37.9 [100.2°F], taken rectally. Then after considerable trouble, before roll call I was taken to the hospital barrack on a stretcher. Blankets covering me. A curious experience. I thought: "What is movement?" and at the same time understood how pointless the question was. Except for a bowl of oatmeal they gave me by mistake at seven a.m. yesterday, ate nothing until ten this morning. Yesterday morning real, painful hunger, gradually dulling in the course of the day, and in the evening actually a feeling of numbness.

Worked almost all day on a letter to my friends.[222] It became nearly as long as the day itself. In the evening after lights-out became aware that one of the Bonewit brothers is family by marriage as well as a friend of Nico's [Presser].[223] If you want to call a member of the nursing staff, you shout: brother. As a result I've been a bit ignored here, because so far I have only twice been able, when I really needed them, to bring myself to address these guys as brother. Sometimes I shout hey, or hello, or signal when they're looking in my direction, but that's not very efficient. On the other hand: you get treated with a lot of patience and kindness. That makes me feel good. Then again: the Vught bureaucracy rules here as well, this time in health-related ways. For example, when I asked for something to eat this morning they calmly said no, even though the doctor had approved. There is a strong connection between bureaucracy and laziness. I could write an essay about bureaucracy here. And how it is that it is brought about by powerlessness, not power. And how it is linked to sadism. The passage is imperceptible. The doctor who's in charge here is a

---

221. See the entry on Israel Alexander (Roland) Frederikstadt in the appendix. He died in Flossenbürg.

222. A (censored) letter written in German on official concentration-camp stationary and addressed to Fré Samson survives. In it David writes to his friends how much he enjoys the packages and the "treats" (i.e., the letters enclosed within). Yet he counsels his friends to wrap them better. He asks for four nail- and toothbrushes (obviously one for each of the Kokers), two combs, and "his brown suit; preferably with the plus-four pants, but this suit only if you include enough knee socks." Letter, David Koker to Fré Samson, March 26, 1943, collection 244 (Vught), file 1657 (Koker), NIOD archive, Amsterdam .

223. David is referring to Isaac Bonewit (1893–1943). In Amsterdam Bonewit had operated an old age home, and in Vught he became a nurse in the camp hospital. Bonewit was murdered in Sobibor.

very nice man.[224] Not a strong figure, as a result there are constantly quarrels among the staff. But something exceptionally human. Treats his patients like children. Strokes their hair, etc. Will sit and talk with them for a long time.

There's a certain Nikkelsberg here.[225] He's 41. Friend of De Haan[226] and Roland Frederikstadt, with whom he carries on a very frank correspondence.[227] Is here with pleurisy. Has traveled all over the world as dancer.[228] Talks like a dancer, moves imperceptibly from one topic to the next, just as a dancer takes advantage of the coincidental points of contact or correspondences in his movements to make changes in them. Phrases his sentences with long flourishes, draws them out using his voice and his hands. Tells everything and everything at once! Talks only about himself and has a kind of nervous egocentrism that I've never encountered before. Manages to cope well in the camp but is going stir-crazy in this barrack. And makes this point in languorous sentences, in a drawling voice. Knoche was here this afternoon and commented on it. I was lying in bed next to Mossel from Oudemanshuispoort.[229]

Rumors about a change of regime in Germany. Visitors from Berlin were here today. The canteen for the prisoners was torn down. Our meals were better. All tailors had to go into the industry barracks. Knoche said quite rightly: "It's the same rotten business as in the Wilhelmine period.[230] Nothing has changed in that." He said this very convincingly. Nikkelsberg is talking with great howls of laughter about [the comedian Theo] Belinfante, who performed in evening dress in a concentration camp. And I'm annoyed with myself because from the very start I thought it was wrong and foolish but didn't really condemn it.

224. David is referring to the German-Jewish refugee Hugo Levy (1907–44), who was murdered in Auschwitz.

225. See the entry on Gerrit Nikkelsberg in the appendix. Nikkelsberg was murdered in Auschwitz.

226. The reference is to Jacob Israël de Haan (1881–1924). See "David Koker and His Diary," 45–7.

227. Nikkelsberg was a homosexual, and so, as we have seen, was De Haan. There are some indications in the diary that Frederikstadt was also attracted to men.

228. Nikkelsberg was well known as a tap dancer. He was the life and dance partner of Johannes Marinus Cornelis Bouman (aka Jack Bow), who introduced tap dancing to the Netherlands. They were known as Bow and Nicholson.

229. David is referring to David Alexander Antonius Mossel. See the entry on him in the appendix.

230. It is not clear what Knoche was referring to when he alluded to the corruption of Germany in the reign of Emperor Wilhelm II.

Two letters yesterday: one very nice one from Karel together with
Tini. Tini wrote very nicely and sweetly. Karel is very concerned to
help. I've been able to respond to that. Also a rather bland letter
from Frederika that was well intentioned. And an irritating letter
from Truusje in which she asks me to draw courage from the memory
of our relationship.[231] I'll do that little thing. And I must have the will
to live. Says she. This repeated several times and underlined. And,
would you believe it, all this based on the fact that my letter was so
upbeat and that I seemed to have the will to live. Like everything she
writes. Redundant, rhetorical, and wordy. I'm pretending I haven't
got her letter yet. It's remarkable that my being here has changed
nothing about my judgment of people and my dislikes. That's because where these are concerned life also goes calmly on its way.

Things have been getting tense here lately. People are fed up with
the bureaucracy, the rudeness, the favoritism practiced by the administration. There's a lot of talk now about the German mentality.
Against this, I contribute temperate comments and encounter a lot
of reasonableness. This is tied to the attitude that people normally
assume towards the [Jewish] Germans personally, of whom there really
are very good specimens here. Dresel is the one they love to hate.
Among his numerous nicknames he has one that's very hostile: *Dr.
Esel* [Dr. Donkey]. People have come to see Süsskind as he really is:
a big, blustery fellow, with little substance, who can flatter the Germans [the SS personnel] and play a role along the lines of a section
head in a department store but is unable to adopt a principled attitude towards them. Moreover: he seems to have been caught near
the women's barracks at 1:30 a.m. He does indeed seem to have several girlfriends over there. And people are ready to tell a lot of not
altogether untrue stories about it. And everybody knows that. And
Süsskind knows that everybody knows. The other day, when someone
said: "That's not decent," he said: "They also say that about me."

As I'm writing this there's great indignation here and with reason: cabaret this evening in the administration barrack, for clerical
staff, their ladies and invited guests. Add to this that Süsskind doesn't
seem to have much influence with the Germans anymore. There also
seems to be a big fight within the OD and a number of them seem

231. David is referring to Truus van Amerongen. The letter survives, and David appears
to have been rather harsh in his judgment of it. Letter, Geertruide (Truus) van Amerongen
to David Koker, March 1943, collection 244 (diaries), file 1657 (Koker), NIOD archive,
Amsterdam.

to have quit. Spring and the situation in Russia probably have something to do with this.

This afternoon the head nurse visited the administration [bar-
rack] and saw how the gentlemen there took the meat from the pots
intended for our barrack. The bastards, people say, shaking their
heads. And they're right, even if it probably wasn't the leaders. At
bottom it is a fact that a couple of people spoil things for the people
of integrity who are the majority there.

Last week they caught an OD man with his wife in the coal storage. And something seems to have happened with letters that were
being smuggled out of the camp. Süsskind had people searched and
reported the writers.

Sunday March 27, 1943 [In fact, March 27 was a Saturday]. Hospital.

[Sunday,] March 28, 1943. For copying: Later I'll return to a few
things that actually should come *before* this. Moreover, the letter to
Mother should precede this. The man next to me died this morning.[232] The difference between the two states wasn't great. He lay
there for days with a yellow, rigid face. With eyes that protruded as
if he were really angry inside about something. And breathing very
heavily at regular intervals. This morning the doctor was doing his
rounds when a couple of people called him to that bed. Silence and
a confused stir at the same time. He lay with his head on one shoulder. No longer had that appearance of goaded anger. Everything had
gone limp. His eyes were half-covered by his eyelids and his mouth,
which previously had stood so painfully and rigidly open, was care-
lessly relaxed. Only his skin was so stretched that you could trace his
entire skeleton. There's a strange man with a toothbrush mustache
from the administration here, a dandy with his hair plastered down,
whose pajama-clad body looks like a young girl's, who is so pious that
he wears his *tfillin* in bed and reads a *tfille* [prayer] for hours on end.
He was just being shaved and had to say Shema[233] with the soap still
on his face. Together with a hunchbacked little fellow who butchered
the Hebrew language. A strange procession, Father and Barber at the

232. The man who died was the leather merchant Herman Prins (1870–1943).
233. The Shema is a prayer to be recited in the morning and in the evening. The name
of the prayer derives from its first word, *shema*, which means "hear." The first sentence of
the Shema, "Shema Yisrael Adonai Eloheinu Adonai Echad" (Hear, O Israel: the Lord is
our God, the Lord is One), affirms the monotheistic character of Judaism.

rear. Later his wife showed up. You could hear her screaming even before she came in through the door.

On Wednesday, when I felt a bit better, I asked the doctor to allow me to get out of bed. I wanted to go to the school, to the new barrack. Partly because I love the work, partly because of fear that in my absence the reorganization would push me to the margin. This morning all diamond workers had to line up. No one knew why. People said: Amsterdam, Hanau.[234] Father also stood in line, white-faced, smiled at me helplessly. In the end it became clear that it was only about the surrender of diamonds.[235]

Something much worse this afternoon, and I was caught up in it in two ways. Suddenly: Everybody [had to] line up, the service sections also, even the administration. I was just on my way to school, the others were already there, and because I always obey every order I went calmly to the drill grounds. Endless bickering about the rows, etc. When everybody was standing there, various trade groups [had to] fall out. People nodded to each other and whispered: transport to Poland. My heart was in a vise. I thought: I'm almost reconciled to this, but I don't have any certainty yet. Of course I tried to marshal arguments against the proposition that it was a transport. "Teachers fall out!" I was the only one to fall out, because it later appeared the others hadn't shown up. I had to go back again. "We've got enough teachers." This was actually because of the halting way in which I identified myself. But to excuse myself: I was unable to figure out quickly whether it was good or bad to move out of line. In any case, the people who stayed behind were registered: the leading figures were among them. Me too. I was the very last, because I was still trying to find an excuse to get out of it. In the meantime we had already heard that it was about an assignment of four weeks of work at Moerdijk, which many did not believe, but I and others did.[236] The reasons this busi-

234. The inmates thought that the diamond workers might be sent back to Amsterdam to be put to work because it had become clear that the attempt to create diamond workshops in Vught had failed. Alternatively they might be transferred to Hanau, the center of the German jewelry industry, located near Frankfurt.

235. The Germans believed that the diamond workers had hidden diamonds and put pressure on them to surrender them.

236. David was admitted to the sick bay on March 22, and on Wednesday, March 25, he sought to be released. It was a very inauspicious day to be considered a healthy, young Jew in Vught. On that day the SS identified the five hundred Jewish inmates who were to be sent the next day to a new satellite camp near the coastal village of Moerdijk, in the estuary of the Waal and Meuse rivers, to do heavy physical labor. Moerdijk controls access to Rotterdam from the south, and close to Moerdijk are important road and railway bridges. In May 1940 the German airborne attack on Moerdijk proved crucial in the conquest of

ness caused me a lot of distress were: the bad week I had just had, for which everybody pitied me (hospital, school) and which I compared with my stay here in general, second, my lack of resolution had once again been responsible [for my fate], third, this probably meant that I was definitively out of the school. Fourth, I still feel very shaky physically. I took advantage of that. I've been to the hospital several times. But the first time all Levie said was: "Yes, my boy, you've had rotten luck," and the second time my temperature wasn't high enough.[237] People have been working hard to get me free, Verduin, Lehmann, Sister Susan.[238] The ladies lamented over me. When I returned to the hospital one of the brothers asked me for a cigarette. In return I asked him to get my temperature up. Help from Sister Susan.

Bal masqué [?]—This evening a bullet came through the window here. We didn't see the bullet, but we do see a small hole.

Monday, March 29 [1943]. *The Crime of Sylvestre Bonnard:* Early in the book: Even in a diary it's very difficult to keep the literal truth in mind.[239]

Tuesday, March 30 [1943]. So now I'm lying here in the lengthy unfolding of a disease that is the result of the most disparate causes and that seems to be inevitable in every respect. A protracted cold, physical exhaustion, spring, Moerdijk, etc., need for free time, etc. I had a very bad night on Friday. Temperature 39.6 [103.2°F] this morning, but have improved quite a bit in the course of the day and today had one of the easiest days so far. Wrote lots of poetry. Finally finished the second poem.

> The morning wind tells of a spring to follow
> and from the plain rise vapors clear and damp
> the light falls in a sunny grace that hallows
> over the reddish houses of our camp.

the Netherlands. In the middle of March 1943 the Germans decided to fortify Moerdijk. When David realized that he risked being sent to Moerdijk, he had himself readmitted to the sick bay. If David had been sent to Mocrdijk, it is unlikely that he would have been able to continue recording in his diary, and even if he had been able to do so, it is unlikely that the diary would have been saved. The Jewish prisoners remained in Moerdijk until October, when they were replaced by non-Jewish prisoners from the *Schutzhaftlager* in Vught. On November 15, 1943, the Moerdijk Jews were deported to Auschwitz.

237. David is referring to Dr. Hugo Levy.

238. The reference is to Eveline Susan.

239. Anatole France's *The Crime of Sylvestre Bonnard* (1881) takes the form of a diary written by an elderly scholar and bibliophile. It is not clear which passage David had in mind.

But on the other side prisoners tend the land
and push their barrows along straight-laid paths
or diligently rake the meager sand
and shiver in their long striped prison garb.

It is as if the spring wind leaves them cold
as if they hide inside their shadow's cowl
so too when sun's hues are a thousandfold
as if a storm and rain could better howl
around the camp where midst barbed wire and bars
their life continues its infernal paths.[240]

This morning the weather was so gray that the last lines did not seem inappropriate to me. Rain wept down the windows in great streaks. In the poem the climate changes [are] obvious, but I think justified. Now that April is at hand and people focus strongly on the weather you really notice how changeable the month is. The situation here is becoming ever more awkward. For my part I think it's due to the change from internment camp to labor camp, nothing more.[241] But people are becoming very depressed. Roll call every morning at 6:30, I hear, in rows of ten, next to the prisoners who are sometimes seen

240. David was able to send this poem to Karel. On June 12, 1943, Karel mentioned the poem in a letter to David. "You ask for criticism. In the first place: *write down all lines which you come up with.* Second, write poems. Write concentration-camp poems that are as flippant, unscrupulously serious, and biased as the frivolous songs you used to write. In a way I consider the poem about the prisoners on the other side to be your best. Nevertheless you're capable of much more. Why don't you write a letter in verse? In the work of a poet one can read all the possibilities of one's epoch. Great poetic possibilities have opened because the Netherlands is now in the middle of war and in a struggle for liberty, and especially for you, who are so connected to bourgeois reality. I hope you understand what I mean. You can become the Dutch poet of the concentration camps and the persecutions of the Jews, provided you don't limit yourself, like worker-poets used to do, by concepts." Letter, Karel van het Reve to David Koker, June 12, 1943, collection 244 (diaries), file 1657 (Koker), NIOD archive, Amsterdam.

241. This is the first time that David recorded the change of status of the Vught camp. When he arrived in early February, the camp was officially classified as an *Auffangslager,* or reception camp. Obviously the influx of skilled diamond workers and furriers and rumors about the creation of large diamond and furrier workshops suggested that Vught would become the site of industrial production, and that the *Auffangslager* would be reclassified as an *Arbeitslager,* or labor camp. Yet eighteen days later David wrote that "during the past month they haven't been speaking of an *Auffangslager* anymore but of a *Durchgangslager* [transit camp]. All of us have explanations for that, and they would be very reassuring if we believed them, only we don't believe them." If Vught were to become an *Arbeitslager,* the Jews there might have some hope to remain. As a *Durchgangslager* it was just a gateway to an unknown fate in the east.

receiving blows. Everyone works in the workshops, except for the diamond workers (and what's to become of them?) in day and night shifts. Several camp services, among them education, will also be excluded. Last night someone took a punch (he told the first-aid man[242] that he didn't know who hit him) and lay unconscious for a couple of hours. His glasses were broken and the skin around one eye a bit damaged. The first-aid man said he had to get up and that even boric acid was too much for this case. This is a lad of about twenty years with a very small head, who speaks with an exaggerated drawl, but then suddenly gets in a state and, still drawling, starts to scream in a way that has surely never been heard in a hospital before. Then Dr. Levie makes a very helpless impression and nods, as though he just wants everything to make sense. People call the first-aid man dumb Heinie or Henni. On the other hand, the staff physician, a relatively high-ranking officer for this location, is a very conscientious and serious man, from whom I've never heard an improper word.[243] There *is* this: every week a small fortune in medications arrives here, sent by the Jewish Council. They're taken in trust by the Germans. And Levie has to keep asking for them from Henny, who is very sparing in his use of them. If the man who died recently had been able to get more of certain medications he might have been saved. This morning Blüth was here. I asked him to greet people for me, and he asked about my position here in a very friendly way and said that my cousin was working under him.[244] He enters like a man of authority and is addressed by the *Oberscharführer* as a man of authority. I didn't recognize him immediately, didn't notice the Star of David and thought he was a high-ranking German civil servant. The *Oberscharführer* speaks to him with a hint of deference. That makes a big impression on people. I tried to explore that impression and said: "Wouldn't he be a much more suitable commandant?" People agreed fervently. The thought

---

242. This is an *SS-Sanitäter*.

243. David is referring here to *Lagerarzt* (camp physician) SS-Untersturmführer Dr. Georg Meyer. Born in Vienna in 1917, Meyer joined the SS in 1940. In 1942 he served as a doctor in Auschwitz, and in 1943 he became camp physician in Vught. Arthur Lehmann, the chief of the Internal Administration, characterized Meyer in his postwar memoir as a lazy man who showed no interest in the health of the inmates. After nine months Meyer was transferred to Stutthof concentration camp. After the war he established a medical practice in Vienna. See Klee, *Das Personenlexikon zum Dritten Reich*, 407; Arthur Lehmann, "Das Lager Vught (16.1.43–20.3.1944)," collection 250d (camps and prisons), file 663, NIOD archive, Amsterdam, 11.

244. David is referring to Roza (Rootje) Koker, who survived the war and moved to Israel. See the entry on Roza Koker in the appendix.

that this man would soon be leaving through the gate gave rise to a
lot of jokes that indicated his good luck is admired rather than envied. To some extent I shared that feeling.

A person can get some reading done here, even if all the books
here are in translation. First I read the disappointing *Tarabas* by [Jo-
seph] Roth, next *Sylvestre Bonnard* by Anatole France, now [Oscar]
Wilde's *Fairy Tales* in German. I'm also doing Hebrew.

Strange tales here yesterday about the SS. An officer who asked a
man named Moskou to step forward and cracked mild jokes about
his name.[245] Or a Dutch SS private who pulls a Jewish fellow out of a
row and says: "Aren't you Ome Brammie [Uncle Abe]? My sister was
in service with your family."

Now that I'm lying here so far from this life I can experience it
more undilutedly and therefore it is harder to accept. I'm also homesick now and then, and I'm very happy about that. Because in the
feverish, half-numb life here, up until now, there was no room for
tenderness that did not contain a large dose of pity. And to remember something with nostalgia is a much more objective tenderness. I
thought today about the Amsterdam canals, about the tender haze
that sometimes hangs over them, penetrated by golden sunlight. God
grant that I preserve this, then poems will come of it.

Tuesday [Wednesday, March 31, 1943].[246] Weather heavy enough last
night to frighten people. As if I had summoned it with my poem. Yesterday gave someone a letter for Engelander [in Westerbork]. Try to
calculate when they'll get it. Three parcels yesterday, from N[ico] and
L[ea] and the G[eerlings]. Today a parcel from Frederika. The day
before yesterday as well. No letter. I'm becoming half-worried about,
half angry with Nettie. Quite often she has the kind of indifference
that she doesn't realize is indifference. She has a complete absence
of initiative where human gestures are concerned. I don't say this out
of bitterness, more to reconcile myself to the fact by reducing it to a
formula.

A great fright this morning. A transport to Westerbork this afternoon.[247] All punishment cases (women and men on the other side),
sick people, and people over the age of 55. The school alone seems

245. David is referring to the furrier Samuel Jas Moscou (1914–93). Both Moscou and
his wife, Branca Moscou-Stodel, survived the war and moved to the United States.
246. In fact, the reference to that day's transport to Westerbork suggests that David was
mistaken and that this entry dates from Wednesday, March 31, 1943.
247. This transport included 282 inmates, among whom were 20 children.

to have lost more than five women, among others the sweet and as teacher very suitable Miss Frank. Also the singer Martha Glazer.[248] Dr. Lek, a specialist in sexually transmitted diseases, with a beard and that remarkable aura all old physicians have.[249] I wrote a letter at top speed. And that messed up the whole day, so did the bad news from Amsterdam.[250] I tried to work on a poem, to read Wilde, but I slept away the larger part of the day. Did not feel very refreshed.

I've got another pack of cigarettes and distribute them to people here and there. I myself smoke about five cigarettes from each pack. From the black [market]. There's a man lying here to whom I gave one once and who asked me for one afterwards. That pleased me, so I offered him one several times without prompting. Yesterday, when I offered him a cigarette he said: "I haven't received a parcel yet." I waved it off and said: "It doesn't matter." And he: "If you maybe had some bread for me." (Earlier he had asked me for something on his bread and I had given him a sizable hunk of cheese.) I answered negatively with a little joke and felt as though I had been defrauded. A few moments later he offered to buy the pack from me. This I also refused in a friendly tone. But he doesn't ask me for favors anymore, probably because of my body language. I find this really terrible. He now asks others in the same pleasant and reasonable tone.

Stories: Uprising in Munich, pamphlets, newspapers. 51,000 dead in Berlin. No fewer than four defensive lines breached in Tunisia.[251] None of it is likely to be true. It does appear from the newspaper that the Germans are retreating in Tunisia and that the English are over Berlin just about every night. The Population Registry has been blown up by a number of men in police uniform, who disarmed the guards.[252] It seems that many ladies have got out of labor duty. I was

248. David was mistaken: neither Sariena Frank-Palm nor Martha Glazer-Cohen were included in this transport. See their entries in the appendix.

249. The well-known urologist Willem Lek (1882–1958), his wife, Eva Lek-van Leuwen, and their three daughters survived the war.

250. David might be referring to the fact that Siegfried David and Berta David Grunberg, Nettie's parents, had been deported to Poland. He did not know that they had been murdered on March 13, 1943, in Sobibor. Yet he knew that the deportation of a sixty-year-old man and a sixty-year-old woman was not a good thing. Letter, Frederik Spits to David Koker, March 18, 1943, collection 244 (diaries), file 1657 (Koker), NIOD archive, Amsterdam.

251. In fact the news about severe German losses in Tunisia was true.

252. The *gemeentelijke bevolkingsregisters* (municipal population registries) were key tools in the German effort to make the Netherlands "Jew-free." The Municipal Population Registry of Amsterdam was located in the former concert hall of the Municipal Zoo. On the night of March 27, 1943, a group of resisters organized by the artists Gerrit van der Veen (1902–44) and Willem Arondéus (1894–1943) conducted a raid on the Population Registry with the aim of blowing it up. They were only partly successful: in the fire that followed,

startled: Flip Monnikendam is on the other side.[253] He whistled at
Maxi.

A few days ago someone was laughing during roll call. The *Unterscharführer:* "Do you want to go to bed without dinner? Then don't
laugh." "Not about myself, certainly not about myself."

Two guys returned sick from Moerdijk and were put in the hospital
on the other side by mistake; they're coming here but they haven't
arrived yet. One of their wives was crying. "Why are you crying?" Saat-
hof asked. She said why and he said these men are definitely coming
here and that she didn't need to cry.

Friday [April 2, 1943]. I failed to write yesterday not because of ap-
athy, but because I wanted to get some distance from some of the
things I had to write about, so I decided to hold off. A few new things
have now been added. The two guys who went from Moerdijk to the
other side still haven't come back. Nikkelsberg knows who they are
but remains studiously silent, in the proud awareness of being the
only one who knows their names.

Today I'm allowed to eat everything again. But upset. A new transport has arrived and is now occupying our beautiful new school barrack. Yesterday a note from Max. *Leckerbissen,* goodies [letters to be
smuggled out of Vught to friends in Amsterdam]. As it happens I
had been busy and could send quite a bit. I wrote on it: not for the
V[an] A[merongen]s, because I wanted to express myself calmly and
not add anything I didn't want to say.[254] What happened was actually
nothing pleasant and it bothered me almost to the point of tears all
day. From now on we're allowed to receive only one parcel per week.
Above all else the increasing isolation torments me. And [thinking
of] the goodies that they, and now Lydia too, will send during the
time they don't know yet [of the new policy]. But fortunately Max
provides the solution. There are children here who whine all day
long for a drop of water, or a bowl of soup (if someone jokes about

some 15 percent of the files were destroyed. Because a duplicate of the archive existed in
The Hague, the raid did not empty the trains to Sobibor and Auschwitz. Yet it did convince
a number of Netherlanders who had been bystanders until then to get involved in the
effort to rescue Jews by offering them hiding places. See De Jong, *Het Koninkrijk der Nederlanden,* 6:712–36.

253. See the entry on Philip Monnikendam in the appendix. Monnikendam was murdered in Sobibor.

254. David is alluding to his continuing irritation with the letter from Truus van
Amerongen.

that, which often happens, they take it very seriously) or wail about a tummy ache. They sometimes repeat the same sentence 10 to 20 times with the same nagging intonation. People become angry, but they also forgive readily. The children are so deeply unhappy. . . . I've managed to complete some verse fragments here in the hospital. I think eventually I'll turn them into complete verses, but just to be safe I'll write down a few things:

> We have to sleep here in our underwear
> and lie down on bare mattresses of straw
> and those still lacking covers, which are rare,
> use coats to help themselves keep warm.

> Inside this room of low walls painted white
> and with its small bulbs burning near the ceiling
> the powerless nighttime hours pass slowly by
> and yet my heart is changed, I have the feeling.

It continues by saying how in the deepest misery all the numbness of life here gives way and unexpected tender memories hesitantly reappear. How, under the hazy winter sky, I walked with Nettie along the canals:

> I'd thought I would be with her in the spring
> above the green canals of my hometown
> already that soft mist is hanging once again.
> The water, smooth, with blurred reflections, flows
> on through the chilly darkness of the bridges.
> The sun lies spread out over every story
> and higher still the white sky brightly flashes
> its early as yet hesitating glory.

One or two lines should precede this:

> The two of us together shared this winter,
> . . . I loved her in my town, and my town in her

That should become a long verse: the snow, too, and the lemonade and snow at Frederika's. Maybe conversations with Karel, my own verses for sure, and the passionate desire to see everybody again.

Yesterday somebody here went crazy. One of the patients, who up
to this point was very calm. Now he lies inside, ranting and raving.
You hear it through the door from time to time. And always when
the door is opened. He keeps calling out Shemot.[255] Threatens the
brothers with a bottle. Screams: "Someone's being murdered here. I
want to use only a gold bedpan. You've been going with my wife." He
wept when his wife and daughter showed up, pressed them to him.
But keeps on shouting when they're here. And talks gibberish. Calls
people to his side and then hits them in the face. Uses his voice as
if it were a large piece of something he wants to get rid of. Day and
night he's got two sturdy guys at his bedside. The great Overste himself also stands guard. And life goes on as usual. He lies raving in the
clinic, the doctors are doing research, the administrators are working
on their lists and don't look around. Dr. Ricardo is in the dentist's
chair, sitting there with his *kippah* on the back of his head, softly saying *ma'ariv* [evening prayer] to himself.[256] And the man lies there
raging. A gold bedpan. I had to think of Pa Samson's dream that his
father was king and made him a present of a yacht.[257] And thought
about how primitively constructed this [barrack?] is. And ask myself
whether I would say that. I suspect that [madness] would be more
complicated in my case. Witness how gloomy I get when I am drunk.
I'm not particularly shocked. Only in the dark do I become cynical.
Yesterday evening I wrote these fragments of poetry:

> Today one of our number went insane
> that all of us aren't driven past that border
> by misery is healthy yet our shame
> we're so good at adapting to each order.

> I hear his screams quite clearly through closed doors
> he cries *shema* and so I am commended
> softly complains about his son in Poland
> and what for us perhaps still is in store.

Then came a stanza about the visit from his wife and daughter, as I
had imagined it, but that didn't square with what really happened,

---

255. Shemot is the plural of Shema, the Jewish prayer that begins with the words
"Shema Yisrael" (Hear, O Israel).
256. See the entry on Eljakim Ricardo in the appendix. He died in Auschwitz.
257. David is referring to Frits Samson, Fré's father.

so that has to be changed: then something about how he speaks with
the last of his voice. And it ends cynically, perhaps wrongly so, but I
couldn't do it any other way:

> "For madmen have no place here in this camp,"
> "Your yea be yea here and your amen amen,"
> It's not our job to talk as if we're crazy
> and if an *offizier* here says: *Verstanden*
> then you're to answer as one man *Jawohl*
> . . .
> When you come to this *Lager*, it's to work
> this hackneyed phrase we've heard a thousandfold
> and if you should go mad you keep it dark
> obeying orders helps you to grow old.

This morning I got a letter from Father.[258] Very cheerful, but at the
end: he feels paralyzed by Mother's absence. Every life has its beauty
and also its sorrow—Something more from the poem:

> and in the songs that I once learned from them
> and sometimes sing in powerless recollection
> I hunger for simplicity and peace
> in what is one heartwarming retrospection.

And perhaps this is the conclusion for a sonnet:

> My memory refuses to dismiss
> all that was dear to me—it is retained
> perhaps, too, scores of years will ease the pain
> of loss, humiliation such as this
> though here it has become forever plain
> how paltry and how sick at heart life is.

All of this will provide points of contact when I'm out of here. A
number of poems should emerge from this. But I'm afraid of the outside. That's why I've been able to stay here so long. That I go outside
briefly is the result of necessity, but also because I see I have to get
through this.

---

258. David was not allowed to receive a visit by Jacques Koker.

We have to surrender our winter coats. I don't have a raincoat. And April promises to be a severe month. And the roll calls these days are so strict and offensive, and this evening we heard: parcels are blocked for fourteen days. Punishment, because we always flush food down the can. I forgot to write that the man who went out of his mind called a German officer who was in the barrack all kinds of names this afternoon. As a matter of fact, the pretty Wehrmacht girl who was counting the children here yesterday evening, asked: "He won't attack me, will he? Is he particularly disturbed by seeing German uniforms?" And walked very quickly through the room. She's a very fearful girl, I think, in spite of her resolute manner, and people say that she always runs when she goes through the camp at night. That makes me partial to her. Last week, on the one day that I was in school, a truant made a scene when I caught up with him. She happened to turn up just then. I had to explain it to her, and she addressed the boy in such a quietly menacing way that I had to feel sorry for him. Later during roll call she asked him whether he had been behaving himself.—I really long to see Mother. The parcel blockage led me to think: it's a nonsensical wish at this time to want to stay in contact with people of whom you know they'll survive the war in any case. And after the war either my time will have run out or I'll have a very happy time with them. To have the courage to write off this present time as a dead loss.

The parcels are temptations. If we didn't get them we wouldn't long for them, for treats [i.e., letters].

Saturday [April 3, 1943].[259] I think I'll have to withdraw completely into our family circle, even though it has become so loose here. No longer hope for the empathy of Nettie or the others. Simply live life here, with a silent recollection of them and in the hope of seeing them again. On the other hand, contact with them ought to keep that hope alive. And in the end, the hope to be in their company again is, at the same time, the hope to get out of this alive. Perhaps I should try to forget them anyway, to distance myself from all hope for the future, to live for the day, within my family here.—And yet: I'm so worried, so fearful whether Nettie and I will see each other again someday, or whether, after the war, I'll still fit into what I've built up with Karel and the others. I'm even afraid that everything is irrevocable, that my life from now on will travel along unknown

259. On April 3, 1943, Vught contained 4,513 Jews, including 950 children younger than sixteen years.

paths and that I won't see any of them again. At this moment it's from Mother that I expect hope and vision. I've just written her something of a despairing letter. My downcast feeling is the result of the parcel seizure. And why. Because of that event and because it is right now that I expect treats, especially from Nettie. Maybe it's still possible to hold the parcels back. Nikkelsberg said: "You all still have a wonderful future before you." I'm willing to let anybody comfort me. I think vaguely and hesitantly of a life with Nettie, after the war. She'll need peace and quiet too. Maybe in the small village where Mother wants to go. I'm thinking of something idyllic. Maybe everything is not so irretrievable, but still I'm fearful and desperate. In this place, you can't withdraw from life into quiet and reflection without paying a price. When I came here, I lost past and future, memory and hope. Now, in the hospital here, I've lost the present, and past and future have returned, tenderly but also frighteningly.

Has the foregoing said clearly enough how distraught I've actually been for the last few days? The sun has entered. The barrack on the other side is fiery red. It looks like the house opposite our farm in Mook.[260] But I haven't noticed anything. The day began gray and I didn't see how brilliantly it cleared up. Only now have I noticed it. Because a couple of hours ago I got . . . a parcel from Nettie. I was dumbstruck and for a moment unable to breathe. And what a parcel. With a cake from a very expensive store, a jar of applesauce, two loaves of rye bread, two sausages, one challah, one pack of cigarettes. That's just like Nettie. In my austere existence, this comes like heavenly luxury. That's the way she lives, too. Even in the most constrained circumstances, she creates something of abundance in her life. I said that to her once. And it's a rich abundance. I've often noticed how middle-class conventions are completely real, meaningful, and gratifying to her. That's because of the way she's been brought up. Not for nothing have I called her princess in this letter [I'm sending].[261] There's a letter in the parcel. It is so sunny and happy that

260. In the summer of 1941 David and Karel went camping in the large forest and heath area near the village of Mook, located south of Nijmegen along the Maas River.

261. David often referred to Nettie as "the princess." This custom had a double literary origin. The given name on Nettie's forged papers was Lydia. David was a great admirer of Kurt Tucholsky's semiautobiographical novel *Castle Gripsholm* (1931). Kurt's girlfriend is a secretary with the name Lydia. Because Kurt's friends Karlchen and Jakopp referred to every woman the friends date as "the princess," Lydia also became known as such. But, as Kurt wrote, once Lydia became the princess, "no other woman would ever be accorded the title again." Tucholsky, *Castle Gripsholm*, 18. In addition, Nettie came from the German

I suddenly noticed the day, which was also full of sun. Her contact with the others is evidently very affectionate. I wrote to her that the only happiness conceivable to me that's greater than this contact is to be reunited with them. She's reading with unprecedented fervor. Talks with Frederika about the most profound things. Corresponds regularly with Tini. I'll find a changed, broadened Nettie. My reticence, the inability to relax will have to give way. Or she'll become like the others and I'll have difficulty getting close to her, and she will constantly send me signals to come closer. No parcel blockage, no lack of treats will rob me of this joy.—Significant that she finds Truus disappointing, that pleases me on Nettie's behalf. Of course Truus is somewhat back in the picture again. This week I wrote on an envelope: it's becoming current business, and I also wrote to Nettie: don't talk too much about me in the past tense. Truus and perhaps also Leo [Seeligmann] (but not so affectedly of course) doubtlessly speak in such a vein. A bit like Annie Mozes.[262] Yesterday I received a parcel from Leo, put together with so much love that it already touched me even then. But only today did I realize how much was behind it. A large jar of cooked white long grain rice, but it had been smashed. I could have cried. Tried to eat it all the same, against the protests of my colleagues, but in the end didn't dare.—Behind me lies a handsome dark guy, Caranza, aged 21 but seems older. I give him something now and then, because he's so cheerful (without exactly being witty), can laugh so heartily, and gives me a kind of respectful and yet half-jovial friendship.[263] This affection for me, just for myself, always makes me feel really good. Also in Leo's parcel: luscious homemade cookies, really tasty children's cookies, two eggs, rye bread, a small jar of jam. He's devoted to me in a way that almost can't be measured. And that often pains me, just as I always have feelings of guilt about the Van A[merongen]s and especially about Fred Spitz.[264] I wrote that to Nettie as well, and I imagine she'll understand.

They've built a kind of circus tent here and all the little measles patients are in it. They whine a bit, all day long. I'll be leaving here tomorrow, I was already pronounced cured this morning, but the doc-

town of Cleve. Well versed in literary history, David had read *La princesse de Clèves*, a French novel published in 1678.

262. Annie Mozes was an acquaintance of the Koker family's.

263. David is referring to Barend Caransa. See the entry on Caransa in the appendix. He was murdered in Sobibor.

264. See the entry on Frederik Spitz in the appendix.

tor forgot to say what to do with me next. An exchange of glances with Mossel: also going today, fear of going outside. A joke of Caranza's, friend of Pais[265]: on the streetcar on his way to the station [to be transported], he called out: "Driver, next stop." But the driver kept on going. Under his influence I've been working on a sort of humor with a note of heartiness towards people, which makes me feel warm inside.

Sent a quarter of Nettie's cake to Mother and said some very nice things about her in a letter. The deranged man who is lying inside shapes very long, fluent, complete sentences, delivered without hesitation, a litany. He mixes pomposities and banalities.

Sunday [April 4, 1943]. Suddenly a bout of fever yesterday evening. Probably because of the excitement about Nettie's parcel and letter. And through it all, the screams of the crazy man. A German officer came here last week. "Are you German? In that case Pr[ince] B[ernhard] is someone else entirely." again. Began rhythmically: "*Boruch* etc. Jesus Christ." And the same thing yesterday evening. At that time he mostly whistled "Santa Lucia"[266]: "Now 'neath the silver moon . . ." —And I with my fevered head and my fear of becoming really sick now. And then suddenly, while the singing, whistling, and screaming went on, between ten and eleven: the report. Someone's been shot by the SS. I in a state of terror. Wide awake. They carried him in and he screamed against the background provided by the madman, who of course kept on going merrily. A high-pitched and frightened wailing. I thought: what would it be like on a battlefield? A shot in the thigh and some of the bone shattered. As it is, it can be healed, but the question is whether that's possible with the means available here. He arrived a few days ago, had joined the OD and was at once put on guard duty at night. Was sent on an errand, lost his way, challenged: three shots. The first one hit him, flames came from his thigh. The other shots passed over his head. A soldier yelled don't shoot, but it was too late. Saathoff and the *Untersturmführer* came at once to get information. Later the commandant himself.[267] The young man was in the same room as the madman. Meanwhile the bullet had been removed from his leg with pocket scissors and so on, during which he quite naturally

---

265. David is referring to Abraham (Bram) Pais. See the entry on Pais in the appendix.

266. A traditional Neapolitan song in which a boatman invites people for a ride so they can see the city's shore from the water, "Santa Lucia" was made famous by a gramophone recording made in 1916 by the opera singer Enrico Caruso.

267. Hauptsturmführer Karl Walter Chmielewski.

made a terrible racket. The madman called the commandant names. The latter had tried to speak with him. He comes from Hamburg and said so. "That's not possible," the madman said, "because that's where I was born." We heard a train go by. He said: "Do you hear that train, our queen's coming back on it." Began to whistle "Whom Netherlands' Blood"[268] and shouted: "Just shoot me."

Monday [April 5, 1943]. A few small facts: spoke with moon-face, whom I once criticized in *Vulpes* and whose name I don't recall.[269] He's among the students.[270] He said to me in passing that Schaef was among the students too and that Mackay was on the other side.[271] That hit me hard. On the other hand I put on a very cheerful face to show I didn't feel humiliated.

Last week Father was commandeered into chopping red cabbage in the kitchen from six to nine. All the ladies complimented him on the quality of his work. I laughed myself silly, as they say. We're going to be deloused and will have to cross the street stark naked. The prisoners already had to go. Out of bed again. Left the hospital with fear gripping my heart. A surprise: there are pale green leaves on the shrubs and it smells like foliage; no wonder, if you consider how many sunny days I've watched through the window. I've had it good in the hospital and enjoyed a lot of sympathy and privileges there.

Wednesday [April 7, 1943]. I'll do a quick sketch of the main events and postpone for a moment the continuation of the history of the madman and the wounded man.

268. "Wien Neêrlands bloed" (Whom Netherlands' Blood) was the Dutch national anthem from 1817 to 1932, when it was replaced by the current "Wilhelmus." Written by the poet Hendrik Tollens, the song celebrates the bond between the Dutch and the House of Orange. The second line, which states that Dutch blood is "free of alien stains," has become unacceptable in Dutch multicultural society.
269. David is most likely referring to Herman Bernard van der Heijde. *Vulpes* was the student newspaper of the Vossius Gymnasium, the secondary school David attended. David wrote an article in *Vulpes* attacking jazz music. Van der Heijde, who was an active jazz musician, responded sharply. He accused David of arrogance and ignorance. David replied that he took full responsibility for his judgment. See Verrips, *Denkbeelden*, 89f–90.
270. In February 1943 Dutch resisters shot the Dutch Nazi Hermannus Reydon and shot and killed the Nazi collaborator Lieutenant General Hendrik Alexander Seyffardt. As a reprisal, the Germans arrested 600 students and 1,200 sons of prominent Netherlanders. They were brought to Vught, where they were housed in a special section of the camp. After a stay of three weeks 180 of them were dispatched as forced labor to Germany. The rest were released.
271. There is no record of Piet Schaef. See the entry on Jan Mackay in the appendix.

The roll calls are dreadful. Next to the prisoners, in rows of ten, a lot of German officers. They say that one of them was in Amersfoort. Without overcoats in the cold. But the delousing by means of gas isn't going ahead, seeing it didn't work with the prisoners.

Had a long conversation with Dr. Ricardo and with Fränkel about the water here.[272] They posited several sinister hypotheses, with a lot of reservations to be sure, but if they turn out to be correct, it would indicate that a large number of us will be done for if we stay here for a long time.

This morning I was ill in bed, I'll write about that in greater detail. A man entered and asked where the sick people were. I put my head under the blankets, fearing trouble. One man said: "Here." "Then I have a cup of hot chocolate for you," said the gentleman, who turned out to be Sealtiel from The Hague and who is certainly not unknown to us.[273] Together with someone else he had made some hot chocolate for the patients. He emphasized that he himself had only supplied the sugar, "so that people won't think that everything comes from me." Such things always make me feel good.—So many treats [smuggled letters] from my side that I don't have enough paper left for the letters I'm allowed to write.

Tale of the raging man and the wounded man. Sequel.

He banged his fist on the table and said: "Just shoot me. Bang, bang. You think we're afraid of you, but you're afraid of us. We're not afraid of your bullets." When he left he was whistling "Whom Netherlands' Blood," that evening also "God Save the King." It was the same evening, I think, that he became completely normal again. He apologized to all the caregivers for what he [it is now] Thursday [April 8, 1943] had done to each of them individually: "I spat in your face," etc. "Three days I've been completely out of my mind, have eaten nothing. Please call my wife and daughter and give me something to still my hunger." Spoke very intelligently that evening, but the next morning things were bad again. In the meantime a whole lot of officers and soldiers came to see the wounded man. I was wide awake. Everything in me was affected by fright and fever, so I wrote a lot of lines of poetry:

272. David is referring to Fritz Israel Fränkel. See the entry on Fränkel in the appendix. He died in Dörnhau.
273. David is referring to Emanuel Sealtiel (1894–1943), who was the sexton of the Portuguese Israelite synagogue in The Hague. He was murdered in Sobibor.

> In former times you did not place a rifle
> into the hands of . . .
> . . . perhaps not in God's heaven
> but keep it in your heart faithful comrades
> . . .
> and like the heavens above knows of no mercy
> . . . stay mindful of this fierce old saying
> the mills of the gods grind slowly

This experience was unbelievably impressive. I lay in the dusky room. The caregivers kept walking in and out, inside the two men were screaming, and I kept reaching for my paper to try to catch some of the lines that passed through my head. The Germans have given the wounded man one of their splints. I don't know how it's going with him.

I wish I could arrange all this properly!

I'm thinking about how it will be between Nettie and me after the war. Up to this point our relationship was like a fruit that hadn't ripened yet, a summer's day that is a bit too windy, like the wind itself the way it is in the spring, fresh, because it's always tangible, even a bit painful. Maybe it will stay that way. And maybe that will be the element that preserves it.

In the hospital B. recounted how [Officer] Blonk from the Marnixstraat office, who was supposed to arrest him and his sister and who managed to fix it so they got free again, sends them a weekly parcel under a ps[eudonym] now that they are here . . . NSB member from the outset.[274]

Yesterday Mrs. De Wilde said a woman had foretold that she would be home again within four weeks.[275] Another had foretold that she would go to Poland. I was really startled, because part of me believes in these things. The more so because the [second?] woman had said some very true things about Mrs. De Wilde. Not until I was in bed yesterday evening did something reassuring occur to me. Humans can know about the past: fine. But about the future? I very clearly saw it isn't possible. Nevertheless it does haunt me.

The school, which in the meantime has shrunk to half its size, was requisitioned in its entirety for new transports. We had to clear ev-

---

274. NSB stands for Nationaal-Socialistische Beweging (National Socialist Movement), the Dutch Nazi Party that Anton Mussert and Cornelis van Geelkerken established in 1931.
275. The reference is to Sarlieni de Wilde-Asscher.

erything out. There's a man here, a gifted musician, but the biggest fool I've ever seen, [who] lets himself be tricked into playing the buffoon, gives singing lessons—during which the children laugh their heads off—and manages to fall off a bench. This afternoon he led the teachers' singing lesson, and we all sang very enthusiastically and out of tune. The small children were glad to say good-bye to school. We danced a hora.[276] Mrs. Gerzons tried to make everybody laugh and made a spectacle of herself. Yet it's all awful.

How can I forget to write about it: the day I got out of the hospital I had to attend roll call without an overcoat. My lips became cold. As if they were being cut. One moment two ice-cold knives. I said to Roland [Frederikstadt]: I'm going to keel over. Things went white before my eyes. I was losing my balance. At that moment the roll call ended. Home between two other people. There I got into bed and let Roland nurse me. At night he sleeps next to me. The night before I never got to sleep at all. That night I slept well and the next day I was completely better. Didn't have to go to roll call, courtesy of Meissler. He came to bring me a jar of rice. The day before I had mostly huddled near the stove in school. Leaning back, eyes closed. And in the afternoon slept for an hour and a half on two wooden benches placed side by side, with a briefcase under my head. Maxi was feeling awfully down; he had missed me so much during those two weeks, he said.

This disordered account will have to be edited thoroughly later.

On the occasion of my request for luxurious parcels I thought: isn't it nonsense to want to live a happy life here? But who knows how long this will last. In the hospital Belinfante said with a smiling certainty: in June we'll be back home! I was very moved.

Sometimes I'm in despair and terror for my life. And now there's the great disappointment of the weather. Spring began beautifully. Catkins and pale green on the trees. And now: an icy, nasty wind that sometimes literally blows us over during roll call.

Sunday [April 11, 1943].[277] I haven't written for such a long time because I felt so utterly wretched this week. Every morning after roll

---

276. The hora is a circle dance that originated in the Balkans and that Romanian Jews brought to Palestine in the late nineteenth century. In the 1920s it became a popular dance in the Zionist settlements and, as a result, important also to Zionist youth everywhere.

277. On April 9, 1943, Vught contained 5,183 Jews, including 1,058 children younger than sixteen years.

call I lay in bed and slept, and this gained me just enough energy so that I could drag myself to evening roll call. Ate nothing except toast and some oatmeal, which I managed to warm up on the stove with great difficulty. You have to defend your saucepan against countless people who claim to have seniority rights. I let people in ahead of me against the promise that they will defend my right to succeed them, a promise that only a few fulfill. You have to stand around for so long that at the end you become quite dizzy. My days this week have been a dead loss. At about three in the afternoon a visit to Mother, who looks me over with great concern and promptly cooks something for me. And the interest taken by the ladies! That's how every day went. Been properly sick, as they say. Couldn't eat anything because of diarrhea and should have eaten a lot to restore my strength.

Yesterday I took the plunge and, together with Roland, made a large pot of soup. In it: a bag of three-week-old ends of bread, a package of brown-bean powder, soup flavoring, oatmeal, fat, onion. Afterwards ate a large bowl of oatmeal. Diarrhea last night and this morning, but back to health this morning and able to take charge in the children's barrack. Because our school has given up the ghost.

Also immersed myself in speculations about the future last week. Fears of Poland. People say: "I'm not afraid of Poland. It'll probably be the same as here, and we'll probably return from both alive." All the same, very nervous and somber. At every roll call I see FM.[278] He walks very upright, but also with difficulty in his wooden shoes. Yesterday evening he seemed very downcast to me.

Last week transports from the provinces arrived here. A lot of very old people, small farmers and wives, who know very well what awaits them. But accept it very cheerfully.[279]

Got a letter that eleven friends had written together. It had wandered around for a month. It's just like a Mozart divertimento (with which it had in common the vacuity of what they all wrote and the friendliness.)

---

278. David is referring to Philip [Flip] Monnikendam.

279. On March 29 the Higher SS and Police Leader Hanns Rauter decreed that, with the exception of the Westerbork, Vught, Barneveld, and Doetinchem camps, the provinces of Groningen, Friesland, Drenthe, Overijssel, Gelderland, Zeeland, North Brabant, and Limburg were to be emptied of Jews. All Jews living in those provinces were to be interned in Vught by April 10. Later that month, also the Jews living outside of Amsterdam in the remaining provinces of Utrecht, North Holland, and South Holland were also taken to Vught. As a result, the size of the Jewish section of the camp almost doubled to 8,681 (April 30). Of these, 1,774 were children up to sixteen years.

Saturday, April 17 [1943].[280] That I'm writing again only now is not because of sluggishness or disinclination but because of *the* event of the last few days, delousing. Our clothes were fumigated with prussic acid or something like that.[281] Not that a small moth didn't fly out when we got them back, but okay: we're considered exceptionally clean now. We had to undress completely, right to the buff, and had to leave all our clothes behind. Weren't allowed to take anything with us. No foodstuffs either. It so happens that some people from the provinces had just come in, supplied with big loaves of rye bread, cheeses, and sausages, etc., which until now had caused great envy. Now they were faced with the necessity of sharing all of it. By coincidence there were a few tables outside, and there you could eat whatever was available. I ate a lot of bread with big lumps of creamery butter, at least a quarter of a pound. Anyway, you could have as much bread as you wanted. Somewhere someone must have opened a bottle of Samos wine. People ate big pieces of smoked meat with their hands. I didn't take much, because I couldn't find it in my heart to beg (to bum, as they say here), although I have done it fearfully, quickly, and almost surreptitiously, and even more because the entire wild blowout disgusted me. Even though on that sunny day there was also something quite wonderful about it.

So we left the dormitory (where I had spent the entire morning on my bed) behind us, all our clothes and possessions hung on makeshift clotheslines, undressed completely, had our armpit and pubic hair removed, most of it, anyway, had to rub those areas with Lysol, which really stung, and then had to put on old Dutch army garb over our naked bodies. The old prisoners' clothes, many of them still car-

280. On April 16, 1943, Vught held 7,041 Jews; this number included 1,152 children younger than sixteen years.
281. Delousing in Vught was done with the use of the cyanide-based pesticide Zyklon-B(*lausäure*) (prussic acid). Produced under license of IG Farben by Degesch (Deutsche Gesellschaft für Schädlingsbekämpfung) and marketed in the German-occupied Netherlands by Heli (Heerdt und Linger GmbH), this pesticide came in the form of small absorbent pellets that were soaked with hydrogen cyanide, a stabilizer and a warning odorant, and packed in a tin. The product could be used in various ways. David described a delousing procedure in which the inmates of a barrack would be told to leave all their belongings, including their clothes, in the barrack. After they had left, the windows of the barrack would be sealed, and someone protected by a gas mask would empty the contents of one or more tins of Zyklon-B in every room. This person would leave the barrack and seal the door. After twenty-four hours, when the poison had killed all the vermin, the worker would open the door, enter the barrack wearing a gas mask, and open all the windows to allow for cross ventilation. After a few hours it would be safe for the inmates to return. In Auschwitz, Zyklon-B was also used to kill human beings in specially built gas chambers.

rying the number and the red, yellow, black, or purple triangle.[282] Because I'm very vain I looked for a nice jacket for a long time, even took off one I was already wearing, and in the end made my appearance in a very smart jacket. The pants were too wide and too short; we didn't have puttees.[283] We walked around sockless in wooden shoes, which really hurt. Many of the tunics were missing their buttons. If we had a bit of luck and owned a piece of string, we could use that to tie them shut. But a lot of men didn't have a piece of string, or needed it to hold their pants up, so that their jackets hung open around their naked bodies. Some jackets that did have buttons hadn't been done up, because their wearers were so fat that their bellies hung over their pants and they couldn't button their jackets. There were a lot of old men and they hobbled along in their wooden shoes with bare legs, cold and hurting from the Lysol. It was a comic rather than a tragic procession. In general the old people are too bewildered by everything that's happening to be able to react to it in a human way. The procession marched to an empty barrack, which contained nothing except a number of beds with straw pallets and there, in the cold and draft, these barracks are open to the elements, we were supposed somehow to manage. The old men were put on pallets. We had nothing to cover them with. If you were lucky, there might be another straw pallet! That's how we lived for a few days, with a bit of bread and one warm meal daily, which arrived at the strangest times, without any coverings at night. There were some who lay on the metal coils at night, without a blanket, in their military garb. I was lucky because I had been able to supply Roland, who had a temperature of 40 [104°F], with a pallet I was able to share. The first night we pressed against each other in order to get warm. Slept in each other's arms. I have to smile, thinking of the physical revulsion I feel for him. In the

282. Many of the *Häftlinge* in Vught had been prisoners of the Amersfoort camp. In this camp, the inmates did not get the striped camp clothing that had become standard in the concentration-camp system in Germany, but old uniforms of the Dutch army. On these uniforms were attached colored badges following a standard code: a red triangle for political prisoners, a green one for so-called habitual criminals, a black one for so-called asocial types, a purple triangle for Jehovah's Witnesses, and either a double yellow triangle in the configuration of a Star of David or a yellow triangle combined with a red, green, or black triangle for Jews. When the prisoners from Amersfoort were transferred to Vught, they quickly received striped uniforms. The old army uniforms were stored to be made available as need arose.

283. A puttee (from the Hindi word for "cloth band") was a cloth strip that was a part of the military uniform of privates in the Dutch army. Wound tightly around the lower leg from the ankle to the knee, it was supposed to give support.

middle of the night I got up, went to the dining room, where in the meantime the stove had been placed and stoked to a red heat, and found a large group on pallets and benches around the stove. They sat very quietly, now and then they quarreled a bit about a place near the fire. But that was all. The stove door stood open, the glow of the fire lay red and hot on our faces. My skin did get hot; I waited for it to penetrate and make me warm, but when the heat became unbearable and I had to abandon the hope of getting rid of the damp cold, I went back into the dormitory. There Syl Drukker had taken my place next to Roland. I lay down in the middle between their legs, and this way we warmed each other enough to be able to get a couple hours' really good sleep.

I spent the next few days in bed next to Roland, even though a glorious sun shone through the window and the trees were decked in a beautiful pale green, but what I had seen of the misery of people in their bits of uniform, their half-naked bodies, crouching outside with their eating bowls or inside resting their heads on their arms at the dusty tables, trying to get some sleep [was too much for me]. Now and then we had to go to roll call. Then we took our wooden shoes in our hands, but the old men hobbled along on their painful feet, carrying canes, like a strange kind of war-wounded soldiers, or prisoners of war from some short story. Or Brueghel's farmers or pictures from *Uilenspiegel*.[284] A man with a large red head, a [illegible]. Somebody said: "Nach Frankreich zogen zwei Grenadier'."[285]

And I pressed myself against Roland in that dusty bed all day, with a straw pallet or two covering me, trying to lie as still as possible so as to ignore that I was in bed but not sick, and that I was hungry. No washing in the morning, because we hadn't been allowed to bring any soap along, and with that rough outfit on my naked, shaved body.

Wild rumors in the meantime: the prisoners are beating the dust out of our blankets and tossing our luggage into the street. Thieving, of course. Everybody over there barefoot or in wooden shoes: [it was] perfectly calm. Our relationship with the prisoners has changed.

284. David is referring to the bold wood engravings following the principles of the so-called Nieuwe Kunst (the Dutch branch of Art Nouveau) made by the well-known artist Albert Pieter Hahn Jr. for an edition of Charles de Koster's *De legende en de heldhaftige, vrolijke en roemrijke daden van Uilenspiegel*.

285. This is the first line of a poem by the German-Jewish poet Heinrich Heine (1797–1856). In "The Two Grenadiers," Heine describes the return of two broken-spirited French soldiers from Russian imprisonment after Napoleon's failed attempt to defeat Russia in 1812/13.

Their (German) barrack leaders lord it over us a lot.[286] They threw
a critically ill man, who was lying on his bed in his military outfit,
out of the barrack because he had to report for roll call: "*We* have
to go even when we're sick." One of them punched our great leader
Süsskind because he had reported the thefts. There are days when
the only association you can make with the word "prisoner" is: thieving. I wouldn't be able to write verses about them the way I used to.
And yet that is wrong, because what the ordinary prisoners exhibit in
the way of perseverance, strength, and cheerfulness continues to be
unbelievable. But things are rendered abominable by the behavior
of their German leaders, from whom they actually suffer a lot themselves. Instinctively, however, we've become a bit wary of all of them.
It's an uncomfortable change, especially for me in view of my verses.
Uncomfortable especially because of the aspect of unreasonableness
[on our part], which I recognize clearly enough.

Huddling together that way in the quarantine barrack we had but
one wish, and life's possibilities did not seem to extend any further:
to go back to our own barrack and to sleep in that comfortable third-
level bunk. The somber thoughts that you get when you spend the
livelong day on a bare bed in a weird, ripped outfit.

What already began earlier won't let go of me these days, so fierce
has it become: fear of Poland, fear of death. After all, during the
past month they haven't been speaking of an *Auffangslager* [recep-
tion camp] anymore but of a *Durchgangslager* [transit camp]. All of
us have explanations for that, and they would be very reassuring if
we believed them, only we don't believe them. And so we keep talking to each other about it and so I keep being startled when I hear
that word *Durchgangslager* during the roll calls. As a matter of fact,
people are firmly convinced that somehow and somewhere they'll get
through this alive. Although they aren't wild optimists. I allow them
to console me. In moments of terror I'm a pathetic child. When I
write letters to friends or receive their letters I sometimes think it's all
for nothing. Because contact now makes sense only if the old direct
contact can be resumed in the future. And can it? Sometimes I think:
certainly. Sometimes: maybe not.

Last week I was returning from roll call: the trees were very bright
and the sun was golden and cool. I thought: now to have the certainty

286. David is referring here to the non-Jewish *Kapos* in the protective custody section of
Vught.

of getting through this alive. And I felt what that happiness would be, without actually possessing it. The evening before yesterday and yesterday evening (while I'm writing it has become Monday [April 19, 1943]) I had conversations with the students who are being held hostage here. I stood there as a student among students. It was after eight; the guards turn a blind eye to breaking the eight o'clock curfew. The evenings are now filled with an orange sun. It turns dark slowly, and our little group imperceptibly comes to be standing in the twilight, hastened by the pine trees, which are tall and full. It's a great pleasure to be speaking with the goyim once again. They don't understand our worries at all, and for that very reason they've retained a great freedom, an objectivity and a reasonableness that I find very salutary; they live an agreeable life here but long terribly to get out. There you see *our* lack of understanding, because why wouldn't a person wait calmly until his day has come, if he knows he'll make it through? Roland and I only half understand it. They see very clearly the dangerous prospects that we face but are of the opinion that it won't be that bad. They're exactly the same types who hang around the university coffee shop. But right now I'm very pleased with that.

By now it's Tuesday [April 20, 1943]. I'm writing to my friends about those students. Hugo really likes to write.[287] It doesn't promise to be a cheerful letter.[288] There's a lot in it about the stupor that alone makes life possible here: stupor through work or through nothingness. And how spiritual possibilities stand in opposition to life here. I also write openly about my fear of the future. And finally I write about how much I value them all and about my relationship with Nettie. It has become a somewhat bitter letter. Also something of a farewell.

The blocking of parcels has ended and right away we get very ample parcels from Nico. Containing a treasure trove of bread (challah, rye bread, cake), butter, sugar, candy, cigarettes, fruit syrup, remoulade (with greetings attached from Margot and Leo [Seeligmann]), matzos, etc. Max and I have great festive meals. And that sudden passage from poverty to what for us is riches, and excess, caused me a very bad night yesterday. Actually threw up in the morning and completely liquid stools. We speak about our stools as about our record

---

287. The forged identity card that David had obtained and never used carried his picture but described him as Hugo van der Brugge, born on December 8, 1920 in Leiden. David used the name Hugo to sign the letters that were smuggled out.

288. This letter does not survive.

of service, only with more reticence. Beneath me a man was groaning constantly. I asked myself if I should pity him (you'd have thought he was dying) or feel aversion because of his playacting. Likely both.

I read *Niels Lyhne* about which I made a few notes.[289] Rilke borrowed an awful lot from it.[290] But not that tremendous seriousness which in fact leads to excesses now and then.

This afternoon spoke with Mother for a very long time. The women have now been deloused as well. A couple of old women died as a result. Also several small children.[291] I don't know whether the lice suffered much inconvenience. In any case Süsskind stood there and watched. Mother put a brave face on it, however. And she's clever. She is org[anizing] something at the moment. The warehouse. A band of trustworthy people. Yet there's bad stuff. A lot of theft. It's difficult to stay out of that. Shameless! Not for the satisfaction of need, just greed and lust for power. Mother has a grim strength, that's why I have the courage to say certain things to her. She asked me about my relationship with Father. And I spoke bluntly. And about my mood. And I told her what it was. She believes we'll make it through alive. But is afraid we'll retain something from it psychologically.

Blüth was here today, to form a Jewish Council. Roland and I had an interview with him, but for the time being we'll very probably stay out of it.

289. Niels Lyhne (1880) is a bildungsroman by the Danish author Jens Peter Jacobsen (1847–85). The protagonist is a melancholy, idealistic, and ultimately existentialist poet who confronts "the bleak arbitrariness of life." Going through his life without a belief in God, he ultimately dies "the difficult death." Jacobsen, *Niels Lyhne*, 176, 187.

290. David knew of Rilke's dependency on Jacobsen because he cherished Rilke's *Briefe an einen jungen Dichter* (*Letters to a Young Poet*). On April 5, 1903, Rilke wrote to the nineteen-year-old Franz Xaver Kappus that only two books were indispensable: the Bible and Jacobsen's *Niels Lyhne*. "A whole world will envelop you, the happiness, the abundance, the inconceivable vastness of a world." He predicted that Jacobsen's prose would "go through the whole fabric of your becoming, as one of the most important threads of your experiences, disappointments, and joys." On April 23 he wrote that "the more often one reads [*Niels Lyhne*], the more everything seems to be contained within it, from life's most imperceptible fragrances to the full, enormous taste of its heaviest fruits." Rilke's only novel, *The Notebooks of Malte Laurids Brigge*, was very much inspired by *Niels Lyhne*. Rilke, *Letters to a Young Poet*, 16–17, 19–20.

291. Between April 13, when the delousing procedures began, and April 20, when David recorded the death of old women and small children, the following inmates of Vught who fit those categories died: April 16, 78-year-old Hanna Tof-Woudstra, one-year-old Louis Eleazar Schavrien, and one-year-old Adele Vera-Kool; April 17, six-month-old Rosalie Zilverberg; April 19, 75-year-old Hester Berg-Muller, 73-year-old Carolina Isaac, and one-year-old Adelheid R. Poppers; April 20, 74-year-old Rosalia Staal-Forster, two-year-old David Levy, and one-year-old Sophia van Emden.

The last few days the camp has been in a Pesach [Passover] mood.[292] Aardewerk and Duizend busy and fat and important. The pious live from the fruits of the field now,[293] mostly sent by the Jewish Council, the SS are adding ten potatoes per day. It remains to be seen whether the food supply will last them to the end [of Pesach]! At first Father didn't participate, offered a sentimental motive, does participate now, offers a sentimental motive. And yet it's nice, the care they're taking. They eat off white tablecloths, from new bowls and pans. They also held a Seder. The first evening I was in the boys' barrack, but an unpleasant *rebbetje* [rabbi] there was explaining everything word for word, so that the boys ran off en masse. In our barrack, where I heard the second part that first evening, and where I lay listening from my sickbed the second evening, there was more than one unpleasant rabbi (Aardewerk, Duizend), but because of the presence of Nemeth, who sang a number of beautiful melodies, the proceedings gained something light and cheerful. White tablecloths, bottles of sparkling mineral water, candles, a platter (with almost no ingredients, by the way) and everybody with great devotion. Shining eyes and tired, red faces, like at home. I constantly notice how little I associate with home, because only someone's remark got me to think about it and I promptly forgot it again. Father led a part in his barrack and spoke, using many citations. He also, taking the meaning of the word Seder as his point of departure, said we are all members of the OD.[294] I myself [supplied?] some of the ingredients for the Seder in a feverish and rather affected excitement.

One of these days, it will be a year since I started speaking to Nettie again. I composed a long letter to her.[295] Strange, it's so very much in one rush yet strikes me as a bit literary. I notice how distant she has become to me, because I presented myself to her very concretely. How we walked together that first afternoon and how it went later. I write about the landscape and the weather, through which we always

292. The first night of Pesach, which occurs on the fifteenth day of the Hebrew month Nisan, was on April 19, 1943. David must have written this entry just after the second Seder had ended.

293. Bread was an important food in Vught. Because observant Jews would not eat bread during the Pesach festival, and because ritually acceptable unleavened bread was not available, they relied on potatoes, fruits, and so on.

294. The Hebrew word *Seder* means "order," and OD refers to Ordedienst, literally "order service."

295. This letter does not survive.

passed and I connect that with the nature of our togetherness. I mean everything very seriously. I didn't know I could write this way.

Saturday [April 24, 1943].[296] The last few days I've been washing little, naked children in the morning and have therefore been excused from roll call. During the day I write file cards in the administration barrack, all day long. Am with the big shots now. Every now and then a small transport of very respectable people from the provinces. A lot of them have been baptized or possess a baptismal certificate. There's a priest and a Protestant minister here. Someone handed in a letter from a German lady, who as "an important National Socialist" was convinced that the Jews "had done a lot of evil" but wanted to make an exception for the so-and-so family. This family should be given the opportunity to work for G[ermany]. The decision: Moerdijk. Someone else submitted an NSB membership card for the year 1940.[297] I write file cards all day long, around me the atmosphere is that of a Jewish Council office. Jokes, laughing, flirting, Mrs. Gerzons sways and wriggles, caressed by the pleasantries. Women are terribly primitive when a group of men admire them and flirt with them. In that case they're unimaginative little children. Writing cards is totally deadening. You don't sense how cold you get in the unheated room. You write very slowly, as if you were painting, card after card, without knowing what you're writing. B, a very untrustworthy man with a prim and proper look about him so that it's doubly obvious he

296. On April 23, 1943, Vught held 7,410 Jews; this number included 1,215 children younger than sixteen years.

297. Initially the Dutch Nazi Party, the Nationaal-Socialistische Beweging (NSB), welcomed Jewish members. While the Dutch Nazi leader Anton Mussert understood the anti-Semitism of the German Nazis, he believed that the situation in the Netherlands was different and that most Jews were fully part of the Dutch nation. Fewer than a hundred Jews became members of the NSB. As Nazi Germany became more powerful many in the NSB began to adopt the Nazi attitude toward Jews. From 1938 onward Jews were unable to join the NSB, but those who were already members could remain. Mussert, however, remained skeptical of anti-Semitism. After the German occupation of the Netherlands the NSB fell in line with the Germans and adopted an explicitly anti-Semitic line. In 1941 the remaining Jews had to leave the movement. When the deportations began, Mussert tried to protect these former members of the NSB. He created a list of sixty-four Jews who had been members of the NSB and who should be exempt from deportation. Most refused the honor, but Simcha Selina Ancona, Abraham Spetter, and Paul Drukker accepted Mussert's protection. From February to May 1943 these Jews and the well-known artist Jo Spier and his family, who were also protected by Mussert, lived interned in a villa in the town of Doetinchem. In April the so-called Mussert Jews were interned in Westerbork, and from there they were sent to Theresienstadt. The Spier family survived. Ms. Ancona, Mr. Spetter, and Mr. Drukker died in German captivity. See Van der Heijden, *Joodse NSB'ers.*

doesn't dare look anyone in the eyes, walks around like a corporal and flirts with the ladies.

The last while it hasn't been possible for people here to be fully themselves anymore. Having a regular activity helps, for otherwise you feel like a hunted animal. You don't dare stay in the barrack: I *literally* haven't had a chance yet to open my *Pelgrimstocht*. [*Pilgrim's Journey*].[298] There's now an *Unterscharführer* here who is specially charged with monitoring us, because pint-sized Rudolf has been promoted and is now with the prisoners. The new one has people carrying beds or luggage and hits them with a piece of wood. People call him Eylie [Commotion], and although it doesn't hurt, all that kicking and hitting is very annoying. History of Eng[elander?] and me and the window.

Mother has been promoted. She's now leader of the repair shop. We dined with her this past week. Very tasty and pleasant.

Sunday [April 25, 1943]. Tremendous scenes yesterday. People assigned to Moerdijk. All of life at breakneck speed. Men who had been assigned were weeping. Grim excitement. One said: "I'm married and have two kids." A seventeen-year-old presented himself in his stead. Later it turned out he was single. One said: "My wife has just arrived here, I haven't seen her in nine months." Later it turned out she was his fiancée. Süsskind in a delirium of rage, in the rain in his voluminous gray coat, among the crying and begging people. (Naschalske with an attack of nerves.[299]) Suddenly he was standing all alone. "Whoever is a coward will perish. You're cowards. A people of cowards. And that is why you *will* perish. You'll see! You're finished."

298. *Pelgrimstocht der menschheid* (*Pilgrim's Journey of Humanity*) was a fine, multiauthor history of the world published in 1937. It was one of David's prized possessions. He did not take it with him on the night of his arrest. Karel and Frederika tried to salvage some of David's possessions in the days that followed the arrest, but overlooked the book. David must have inquired about it in a letter that does not exist anymore because on March 15 Karel wrote David that "sadly" the book remained in the house. He either returned to obtain it or bought another copy, or he obtained it from David's friend Frederik Spits. On March 18 Frederik wrote David that Karel and Frederika had collected all the books that David had requested, but that some of them were his own copies. By April 25 David was in possession of a copy of the book, but it appears that he proved unable to confirm arrival to Karel: on May 14 the latter asked David in a letter if he had received the copy. Letter, Karel van het Reve to David Koker, March 15, 1943; letter, Frederik Spits to David Koker, March 18, 1943; letter, Karel van het Reve to David Koker, May 14, 1943, collection 244 (diaries), file 1657 (Koker), NIOD archive, Amsterdam.

299. He is referring to the German-Jewish tailor Siegbert Naschelski (1901–43). Naschelski was murdered in Sobibor.

Disappeared through the door. I was moved to tears. I tried to assess whether I was being sentimental or not. But Süsskind with all his hollowness, his self-seeking, has something special from time to time. I wouldn't dare say it to my fellow inmates, but at that point he was a bit like a prophet. And he prophesied misfortune. Like a prophet sent to another people. Am I overexcited?

The last few weeks there's been a lot of pressure and agitation in our camp. The place is dirty, people are worked up. Quarrels. Swearing, fights. Everything the result of the delousing and the move. In our barrack a man who had pushed himself into a leading position was unmasked as a usurper this evening. Confusion everywhere. There's scum in this barrack. TD [Technische Dienst, Technical Service] who quarrel all day with the jolly pickpockets as they call them and who are rather conspicuous now during Passover. The TD threatens others with knives, has plans to play the harmonica during prayers, seems to have put the lights out of commission during the Seder. In the morning, when they're allowed to sleep in and are lying in bed, they sing loudly, well aware that there are sick people around.

Verduyn spoke today in a meeting of teachers and child-care workers. These work badly together. True: there is a group of us who wash the children starting at half past six, and that is so fatiguing that I have to sit down at eight thirty. Yet we're received with a lot of disdain and irritation. That's happening partly because Aardewerk and Duizend, and others, for example, walk around looking bored. I had someone ask today whether he [it is not clear to whom David is referring] couldn't do something, because he said that we couldn't understand how much those children's bodies repelled him.

Most to blame is Frankenhuis, a remarkable combination of ambition, nastiness, egotism, and immaturity.[300] Verduyn's talk was an early indication that, while the camp's mood is wild and poisonous, a lot of things have begun to settle down this week.

Wednesday [April 28, 1943]. I'm tired of recording facts. It's always the same thing. Entire issues. We're excused from roll call because we helped with the children in the morning. The child-care workers wanted to get rid of us. We're represented by the self-serving Frankenhuis, who hangs around the kitchen all day long and irritates everybody. Suddenly we're no longer excused [from roll call] and are

300. Eduard Frankenhuis (1904–43) was murdered in Sobibor.

woken up at half past four for the roll call at six. A big fat fellow with glasses, the voice of a lion (he really does snort like the M[etro] G[oldwyn Mayer] lion), who probably used to own a very small tobacco store, shouts: "Gentlemen, get out of bed." I have a running quarrel with him and am acquiring some skill in this activity.

I have nothing to do and don't get a moment's rest, because there's nowhere safe to sit down. This morning I was in the warehouse with M[other], who made coffee and soup for me. At least there I can feel a bit safe. Father is completely helpless. And today he's sick as well. This I can say: since I came out of the hospital I haven't been able to get back into the swing of things and yet that's already a month ago. I measure the time here until I entered the hospital. The rest is: the few days after that, and life must now resume its course. The advantage is that I retrieved myself in the hospital and haven't lost myself entirely since, the way I did before. But now it has become difficult.

Every morning I go and wash children. A labor that proceeds mechanically. The children are very dear to me. But I can't find any quiet and steady work. Spend my day in going to Mother, schmoozing extensively with Max (who in the meantime is in quarantine, which is most unpleasant), preparing food on the stove, etc., etc. Incomprehensible how quickly and how slowly a day like that passes. You can measure the time by anything. That's why everything partakes of an exhausting emptiness. No time for my diary, no energy. Not a verse, although in a rare moment of softness marvelous melodies go through my head. Which are, however, not meant to become verses. Sometimes you notice that from their aberrant meter.

It is now Sunday [May 2, 1943].[301] This week we had the history of [SS-Scharführer Menne] S[aathoff], who chased us from the empty barrack where we made picture frames and cooked. We're so driven. We can hardly find time to do something for ourselves. In the free moments I manage to save by deliberate effort I finish reading *Niels Lyhne,* which gradually comes to seem rather clumsy, but in its primitiveness and its unformed, I would almost say, wisdom, leaves a big impression.

This morning people were ordered to haul rocks and were hit while doing it.

301. On April 30, 1943, Vught contained 8,681 Jews, including 1,774 children younger than sixteen years.

I spoke with Kurt, a tailor from Berlin, who has gone through three years of penitentiary and five years of concentration camp.[302] He worked in the crematorium at Sachsenhausen and had fifty assignments per day.[303] He told me how as an ordinary prisoner he was hunted, under, on, and over tables and wardrobes, hours on end, constantly fleeing for his life. "I don't give a damn about my life anymore." At night they had to roll in the mud and in the morning they had to present themselves in their wet garb. "You don't feel pity any longer; if you see your buddies starving next to you, you don't give them a slice of bread." (I already have something of that selfishness here, I even take a cynical pleasure in it. Although it's somewhat different.) "But now things are different: you have to change your ways, because you're in a camp with women and children." He's really very good to the children and steals food for them. When he appears in the children's area, the children rush up to him and shout: "Kurt." When a new transport arrives and he happens to be in the registration hall, he says: "All right, children, that's something for me!" He seems to have relations with the girls here. Story of Süsskind. "In two months the war will be over." The people in his barrack think he's a pain in the neck. He's very handsome, very tall and solid. His zebra outfit is spotless, and he wears his white beret rakishly. His skin is bronzed and his light blue eyes are very beautiful and reflective. Huge cheekbones, so high that his eyes become smaller. Sunburnt under the eyes. He laughs with his eyes when he's speaking, his mouth is too busy with talking. He pulls his lips up high and you see his flawless teeth. He walks within a storm of words, seems not to listen to what others say, doesn't laugh about himself but while speaking makes a lot of laughing sounds, as if he's tossing out his words because that's his duty, but while doing it is also trying to do something else as a kind of decoration, a little work of art. Or like a jazz musician who throws a variation into the mix from time to time.

302. David is probably referring to the German-Jewish refugee Kurt Adrian.

303. Until 1940, those who died in Sachsenhausen were cremated in Berlin crematoria or buried in the Oranienburg cemetery. In 1940 the SS commissioned the construction of a small crematorium with one oil-fired oven supplied by the firm Heinrich Kori. In September 1941, when the camp became the execution place for Soviet prisoners of war, the SS obtained four mobile oil-fired crematorium ovens that were able to deal with the average "supply" of over one hundred corpses per day. At the same time the SS began with the construction of a new crematorium to contain those four ovens. The building was completed in 1942 and known as Station Z. Because of oil shortages, the four ovens were decommissioned in 1943 and replaced by coke-fired ovens. Station Z had an incineration capacity of six hundred corpses per day. See Morsch, *Murder and Mass Murder,* 28ff.

We're in the reg[istration] barrack, Roland [Frederikstadt], Barber, Fried[länder],[304] Max Fried[länder],[305] van Praag[306] and Roman[307]
are working on a humorous magazine for the Germans. R[einecke]
and E[ttlinger] are spinning tales about each other's past. Roman
is supposed to compose dubious verses about this, Van Praag is assigned to do the drawings.[308]

On May 1 some children walked around with red pieces of cloth.
That day I also thought of K[arel].[309] Van Praag and Roman are extremely popular with the Germans. They know, they must know for
the magazine, who has been sleeping with which female prison guard.
Things aren't going badly for the plump one. They are going badly
for the good-looking one, even though she's changed her hair.

It's Monday morning [May 3, 1943], about half past six. This morning, just as on other mornings, not to roll call but walking along the
laneway to the children. Panoramic views through the barbed wire.
Roads in green, gold, yellow and behind them clouds, red morning
sky. It is May 3, and I realize that we've already been here almost three
months. I mention it to Syl [Drukker], who thinks about the same
things I do but reaches the opposite conclusion; I'm glad about it.
That time didn't exist. He's sad he hasn't seen the people in Amsterdam for three months. As adult as he is in many ways: he's in love, eighteen years old. Although he does get the occasional letter and talks
about that. And wants to be questioned but says nothing. I sometimes
talk with him, but what really animates me he ignores, I won't say without understanding it. He doesn't reach the point of understanding.

I also talked a lot with Alfred Spitz.[310] He's awkward and heavy in
his thinking, every word he says emerges laboriously. He lives his life

304. David is referring to Adolf Friedländer, head of the OD. See the entry on the
Friedländer family in the appendix.

305. Max Friedländer was the son of Adolf Friedländer.

306. The decorator and ad draftsman Hartog van Praag (1907–43) was killed in
Sobibor.

307. David is referring to the musician Martin Roman. See the entry on Martin Roman
in the appendix.

308. This was most likely the *Illustrierte Kameradschaftszeitung* of the SS garrison in
Vught.

309. The first of May has been an important date in the international workers' movement since the 1890s. In the Netherlands it was known as De Dag van den Arbeid (Labor
Day), and on that day the Social Democratic and Communist parties would hold meetings.
Karel van het Reve grew up in a Communist household and, in the 1930s, was involved with
the Communist youth movement.

310. See the entry on Alfred Spitz in the appendix. Spitz died in Dachau.

here arduously, without saying a thing. "It can't go on this way," that's all you sometimes hear from him. "You know," he says to me, "if you do have to be in a camp, it's better to be put in one run by the Germans, they've got a lot of experience with that kind of thing."

In the children's barrack we eat a proffered slice of bread. Because food has come to be central in our lives. If we're offered something we take it, and if not offered anything we take it for sure.

Because of the strike in Amsterdam (at least, we hope that's the reason),[311] Father, Mother, and Max still don't have parcels, while I already got mine on Friday evening. Hungry all day. I'm trying to trade three cigarettes for bread.

You become selfish, even towards your own family. I regard myself with a lot of pleasure but also with cynicism. Sometimes I treat the children with bitterness, yet the friendliest treatment hides a bit of sadism and lust for power. I feel it indescribably clearly. I love them a lot and make a lot of effort for them, and yet . . . I don't feel bad when I deny them something or give them an order. A kind of feeling of being in charge.

It's Tuesday [May 4, 1943]. Father and Max got their parcels yesterday evening. Roland said I was yellow with misery. And yes, I *was* hungry. And then even more all those feelings that cluster around an awareness of hunger. And also despair about the vanished parcels. For I don't part with anything easily; it becomes ever less easy all the time. I give hardly anything away anymore. Just to Roland. And that's more

311. On April 29, 1943, the Wehrmacht commander in the Netherlands, General Friedrich Christiansen, announced that all members of the former Dutch army, some three hundred thousand men in total, would be interned in prisoner-of-war camps. This decision proved to be the proverbial straw that broke the camel's back. The Dutch had accepted earlier restrictions and a continuous decline in living standards and, after the violent suppression of a strike in support of the Jews (February 1941), had witnessed without much protest the liquidation of the Dutch-Jewish community. Christiansen's proclamation triggered spontaneous strikes all over the country. Fearing a national uprising that could inspire the Belgians and the French and cause an Anglo-American invasion, the Germans responded harshly. Shootings of protesters in the streets led to ninety-five deaths, and mass arrests of thousands were followed by quick trials before summary court-martials and the execution of eighty people. Some nine hundred workers were brought to Vught. The April-May strikes meant that a general attitude of accommodation, which had ruled Dutch-German relations for the first three years of the occupation, was now seen by a large part of the population as immoral. The strikes meant that this middle road was closed. Resistance became now an increasingly popular option, and this triggered increasing repression. As non-Jewish Netherlanders needed hiding places, the number of people opening their homes for the hunted increased dramatically. But for the great majority of the Jews this change of attitude proved too late. See De Jong, *Het Koninkrijk der Nederlanden*, 6:799ff.

from a sense of duty. Just as I do everything from a sense of duty, even the greatest self-denial. Of which I have in any case been capable even here. I can part with something, keeping nothing for myself, but it's because of a feeling that the presence of another compels me to do it. I also sense a certain pride in myself during good times, because of the abundance of food I have. More and more I believe that both abundance and its absence need to exist. Such strange thoughts come to you here when you think of nothing but food all day long. Mother's parcel hasn't arrived. Something like that I find appalling.

Sunday, May 9 [1943][312] —This past week there has been great excitement about the strike in the country. The reports were fairly trustworthy and gave us that impression from the start. Only there hasn't been any fighting in Amsterdam, as people said here. And beyond that, the strike hasn't spread to other countries. Which I also didn't believe from the outset. All day long large groups of hostages and strikers were brought here, some of them women. And I don't know whether it's true that a number were executed here. Some of the women were initially placed among the Jewish women, and there was one girl who cried terribly when the groups had to be separated. "Don't cry," the Jewish women said, "you'll find nice people over there as well." There were NSB women among them too. They have one Jewish barrack leader. An enchanted world. Barber had to take their watches and rings away. R[einecke] had one NSB member haul garbage. The strike has been very violent. Thursday a transport [of people] from Amsterdam who talked about it. A huge fright: The UB [*universiteitsbibliotheek*, university library] is in ruins! But these people don't seem to know where the UB is.[313] More about that transport. How I'm feeling will appear from the accompanying fragment from a letter to Mother. On Mrs. Lehmann's advice, I submitted it to Lehmann. Next morning: was called by Lehmann and put to work registering [people]. Extraordinarily friendly, even when he caught me in a copying error. Strokes my hair in a paternal way. People do such things much more readily here than on the outside, and by the same token react to it more willingly and appreciatively. In any case people can be very gentle to each other here. And how often doesn't it feature in my

312. On May 7, 1943, Vught held 8,684 Jews; this number included 1,776 children younger than sixteen years.
313. In fact, the library of the University of Amsterdam was not touched during the strikes.

diary: poignancy, affection, etc.? The tone of my letters has also become more heartfelt. Now and then still choking in abstraction, but yet with more courage to deal with the commonplace, i.e., with things that are meaningful in their essence but conventional and compromised through overuse. What I really want from Lehmann, however, I haven't managed to fix up yet. All the same, through repeatedly showing my face in the administration, it has become possible for me to sit in a corner every now and then and work. But what I want is something that's officially better tolerated. Van Praag reinforces me in this by his example. Although his case is different. He's now working daily at the *Kom*[*mandatur*]. Together with R[oman], he's working on the first illustrated soldiers' paper in the Netherlands.[314] Ettlinger and Reinecke are his friends. Ettlinger is the good one, Reinecke the intelligent one. They come when they please, leave when they please, because "they don't always feel inspired." Reinecke is a playboy with artistic ability. An SD secretary enters.[315] "If you please, young lady. Draw this young lady." Everyone comes up to admire the drawing. Van Praag draws like a real dilettante, in fact. They're the kind of drawings in which you yourself have to reconstruct the likeness from the available material. But people consider it exceptional. "And now, my dear young lady, autograph it and wish the readers of the soldiers' paper all the best." That's roughly the style. There's an SD official who allows himself to be interrogated by Roman as though this were normal. Also a secretary who proudly claims to spend time only with

314. This was to the *Illustrierte Kameradschaftszeitung*.

315. SD stands for Sicherheitsdienst (Security Service). Established in 1931 as an intelligence service within the SS, the SD became responsible after 1933 for gathering information on society, churches, universities, the economy, and groups that were considered hostile to the regime, and Jews. From the late 1930s the SD also provided regular reports on the mood of the population. Organizationally the SD had been united since 1939 with the Sicherheitspolizei (*SiPo*, or security police)—which in turn combined the Gestapo and the Kriminalpolizei (*KriPo*, or criminal police)—in the Reichssicherheitshauptamt (Reich Security Main Office). In the occupied Netherlands the few hundred members of the security police, which coordinated the so-called Final Solution of the Jewish question, and the men and women of the SD fell under SS-Brigadeführer Wilhelm Harster. While formally the two organizations remained distinct, members of both organizations carried the SD emblem on their uniforms. The SD had little business in Vught, but the security police oversaw the Jewish section of Vught, and hence one must assume that the woman belonged to the security police. One of the most notorious members of the Dutch branch of this organization was Gertrud Slottke, the secretary in the Jewish department in the security police headquarters in The Hague, who managed the files of Jews exempt from deportation—and decided when and how those exemptions were to lapse. In 1943 she was forty years old, and it is unlikely that she was the secretary David refers to. See In 't Veld, "Jahresbericht 1942," 277ff.

higher officers. In any case, they talk only about women there, and with the greatest candor imaginable. Last week Ettlinger, Reinecke, Roman, and Van Praag were chasing each other and trying to smear stencil ink on each other's faces. They don't much care for the *Unterscharführer* who beats us. His name is Polk and they call him Polak.[316] I try to picture all this, but it's the most disturbing as well as the most corrupt scene one can imagine.

I used to know beggars only from books, but now I know what they are. They're prisoners who stick their heads around the door and say in a faltering manner: "Guys, can you spare anything to eat?" And when people here say "no," and that happens often out of fear or because they can't be bothered, the prisoners wait until they see someone else and ask him the same thing. Wary and patient. Last week the children gave them things and were punished for it. We have roll call together with the prisoners these days and can see what tricks the Germans have taught them.

Roll call is a kind of religious ceremony and, like all ceremonies, an empty form that people see through very clearly. If any are missing, some have to be fetched, if there are too many, some have to be sent back, and if there's no time to do either, calmly report the official number to Reinecke or Ettlinger, who nod graciously in acknowledgment of the trouble you've taken. First a time of silence, during which the numbers are compared with the official report, and then suddenly liberation: "Caaaaaps off!!" A loud, dull smack, and the prisoners, who at "caaa . . ." have put their hands on their berets, slap their caps on their thighs in unison. The harder the better, so long as it's at the same moment. The strikers screw things up, they don't know yet how it's done, so that the smack is a bit uneven: a little drum roll. And Saathoff follows, using roughly the same timbre, "boo." And the Jews laugh. Van Praag does a good Saathoff imitation. He's timid and nervous. Can't keep his hands still. Curls his tongue between his lips before he says anything, shifts his eyes back and forth and recoils when he wants to hit someone.

I must say I almost never get annoyed by the internal affairs in this camp. The charges against the people working in the kitchen, who're always stealing (indeed, I wouldn't know how that could be otherwise), the whining about the administration, etc., etc., I hardly notice

316. Polak, meaning in Dutch someone who comes from Poland, is a common Jewish family name in the Netherlands. Reinecke et al. showed their contempt for Polk by pronouncing his name as Polak.

them. But I can become furious about the behavior of the OD and its leader F[riedländer]. There's a special gang here, the SB [Special Brigade], who act particularly arrogantly, beg for food when the new transports arrive, and with their attitude of silent authority hold back the people who are already here.

They come in during the middle of school time (we've been giving some lessons in the barrack again these last few days), then start talking loudly and threaten to report anyone who says anything about it. They're really keen to report people. There's a fellow, with restless eyes, thin lips which he always keeps shut, a long, meditative face, black hair that's already graying, receding over the temples, who ostentatiously says little, is always accompanied by another man whom you don't notice because that arrogant face draws all the attention. The whole business makes the same cowardly impression as the gang from Schalkhaar.[317] Outside power takes them to a certain limit, and beyond that they're allowed to do the work themselves.

I still need to say this: I can't recall the face of anyone in Amsterdam, sometimes I really make an effort but then have to remind myself: how far away from me they are! A lot of people complain about that. And not long ago: I was half-awake and suddenly saw Truusje in a characteristic pose: she was standing on a table, giving a speech, and I saw her very clearly. I thought with cheerful malice: now I'll certainly be able to conjure up Nettie. And I did see her: all of her, standing by herself in the light, gesticulating excitedly and laughing heartily. I felt very happy, but it was for just a moment and she was gone almost at once. Since then I haven't seen her again.

This morning (Monday [May 10, 1943]) I asked Alfred Spitz (and I was thinking of Nettie): "Do you think that, if you survive this business, you'll be able to pick up your life again together with those who

317. The so-called Schalkhaar police took its name after the village of Schalkhaar. Before the German occupation the Dutch police had been highly decentralized. In order to create an efficient tool to control the population, the senior official charged with police matters, Rauter, set out to create a centralized police organization. He also sought to create ideologically reliable units within the police organization. In some former military barracks in Schalkhaar, Dutch policemen sympathetic to National Socialism received special training and then were stationed in the major cities: one battalion in Amsterdam, two companies in The Hague, and one company each in Rotterdam and Eindhoven. Under direct control of the German Ordnungspolizei, the policemen trained in Schalkhaar were invariably assigned to the rounding up of Jews. The Schalkhaar police dressed in black (*zwart* in Dutch) uniforms. Hence they were often referred to as the *zwarte politie*. Huizing and Aartsma, *De zwarte politie;* Kelder, *De Schalkhaarders.*

are dear to you (he's engaged) and to commit yourself anew to the work that's dear to you?" He said: "No." I asked him about his fiancée. He said: "There's just one possibility of reunion: Poland."

This last week we've been living in one great abiding fear. In fact, almost in a certainty. I'm preparing myself for deportation. A few days ago: woken at 4 a.m. To listen to an important announcement. I was petrified with fear. My heart was beating laboriously, was almost frozen. People to the dining hall. There's a transport to Westerbork. Old and sick people.[318] You can say your farewells now. People went back and dressed. I lay down and after perhaps 15 minutes went to see Mother. We breakfast in the grubby morning light and sit at the table in silence. Later to the school barrack. Children there are dragging small parcels of bedding. Because—this is a shock—the big families, with more than three children, have to leave too. The day is dull, rain weeps along the windows. And the young trees are jerking in the wind. It's cold where we are in the school. Someone's reading to the children. We make sure that the children are quiet. They don't have to pay attention. They're too deeply miserable to make noise. They rest with their heads on their hands. Once in a while one of them gets up, [wants to go] outside or to the dormitory, and you stop them. Then he says: "I have to go to Westerbork," as if that explains everything. Then you let him go. I kept walking back and forth. My hands behind my back. And in the end I spoke. It was very quiet. I didn't speak very well, but it was satisfying all the same. And Verduyn complimented me. Later that day they came for the families with three children, they need 1,500 people. And now Drukker and Spitz are saying, and I don't think they're wrong: "They're going to empty this place. This will become an Aryan labor camp." That sounds plausible. I want an important job. I'm going to see Lehmann tomorrow.

Thursday [May 13, 1943]. I did see Lehmann the day after. Made an appointment for yesterday evening. More about that and other things later. First the transport to Westerbork. All day long my head was so heavy and so tired. In the afternoon they lined up. Old people, supported between young ones, who often went only for [blank], all of them bowed down under luggage, loaded on their backs and shoulders, but also blankets in their arms, as if they were moving from one barrack to another and not to Poland. Parents with their

---

318. Two transports with a total of 1,280 people left for Westerbork on May 8 and 9.

children around them, and solicitous for their children and their luggage, which is also for the children, after all. The parents and children don't know it, but the others do. They are so timid in their distress. Grim, but not forcefully grim. They don't say anything, not because they can't spare the energy to speak but because they can't give voice any longer. The parents have been a curse to their children. They've dragged them here. And now the children have become a curse to the parents: they're dragging them along to Poland. And this is all so wretched that there's nothing more to be said. They stood there on the drill grounds, 1,500 of them, but they seemed like a smaller group. The sky was very dark, and large, torn clouds sailed past. Those unable to walk were pushed along in wheelbarrows, their legs hanging down. The light was treacherous and changeable. The white patches on their luggage and bedding had a ghostly hue. Later that afternoon a shower of rain fell that was as sharp as hail, and there was a raw wind. They stood there for two hours and then were taken away.

Early to bed that evening. And at nine thirty: everybody out of bed! General roll call. The sick have to come too, except for the very seriously ill. They're allowed to stay in the dining hall. My thought processes were like a sheet of glass. The smallest movement would have cracked it. I felt icy cold. My heart was beating as I had never felt it beat before. Transport to Poland, I think and we all think. And once outside: we stand and stand. At the outset the Germans stick around, but after a while they go to the women's camp, and then two sick people are carried out with a whole crew of children surrounding them. At first people wait in frozen anticipation, later they relax a bit, begin to talk nervously and volubly. And still later, when the rumor does the rounds that they are looking for 78 people who have made themselves scarce, the talking turns into exuberant joking. I myself utter one pleasantry after another. I say: "You mustn't think I'm drunk. Nor that I'm talking this much because I'm nervous."

When we got back to the barrack, people made themselves comfortable, sat at the tables, started eating and drinking, like the end of Yom Kippur.

And since then the fear of being transported hasn't left us. And when I look at the camp now I think, just as I did at the outset: it's not for us they made it this attractive. And I've got support for all those dark thoughts. It even causes me to have them. Every time I hear that word *Durchgangslager* I go cold. In the morning, when I'm at roll call, standing there at the edge of the grounds, I'm glad not to hear that dreadful word. Anyway, the fear of Poland is just one thing. There is also fear of Moerdijk, for which people are constantly being drafted whenever a transport of sick people and so on returns. On days like that people warn each other to avoid doing certain things in particular: don't walk slowly with your hands in your pockets, don't talk too much while walking, don't walk through the bed of sand outside the door when you go around the corner (because people have already been nabbed for that), and above all don't go to the women's camp. I don't keep to that last warning. Mother was ill for a few days and my days were very empty. Something drives me towards her, is it a habit that I go there every afternoon, with all the risks attached to it? In all fixed habits there is, after all, something that's alive, even if you aren't aware of it. And this isn't even a fixed habit, it's something I experience an urge to do every afternoon. But not an urge arising out of tenderness, rather out of a need whose character I'm unable to determine. Partly of a moral character, but also to give everyday life a fixed point. I always get something nice to eat when I'm with her, and we talk very pleasantly, but on those days of panic I'm rigid and feel a bit hunted. Now that I've started the ball rolling with Lehmann, Mother makes a big deal of my merits. I have to recite my verses to admiring women, and I become ever more the ladies' pet. The pet poet. Mother yesterday: "Mrs. Jakubowski, may I introduce my son?" Mrs. Jakubowski is a lady who has lived in China, tawny, but very largely painted in matte colors, with bleached hair, and chirping like a cheerful bird.[319] "My son writes poems even here," Mother says in a tone of proud satisfaction. "Do recite them for Mrs. Jakubowski." I think of *Woutertje Pieterse*.[320] "Oh, I do so appreciate poetry, you must know that I'm an artist myself. I have always associated with artists." And I recite a poem for her, and she closes her eyes, shakes her head like a horse and says: "I didn't know Dutch could sound like this." And when she's heard everything: "Oh, you must suffer terribly. Oh, how well I understand it" (everything in an immigrant's Dutch). "I've experienced everything that same way. Just so, Mrs. Koker, we are

319. David is referring to the German-Jewish refugee Hertha Jakubowski-Gotthilf. She survived the war.

320. The reference is to Multatuli [pen name of Eduard Douwes Dekker (1820–1887)] *Woutertje Pieterse*, one of the most important works of nineteenth-century Dutch literature. In this humorous bildungsroman, the young Wouter has to write poems in school. The devout spinster Miss Laps recognizes his talent for poetry and asks him to create a religious poem for her uncle on the occasion of his birthday. See Multatuli, *Woutertje Pieterse*, 79.

kindred souls." And then a paean of praise: "When you leave this place, you will have grown and then your talent will open the way for you. You know, Mrs. Koker, he's not strong. I mean in spirit." Mother protests. "But people who are so delicate, so subtle, etc., etc." And yet she's not stupid. Suddenly: "But I've seen you before. At Fritz H's. You know, Mrs. Koker, I never forget anything. Everything that's in this head, stays here. When I was taken away Fritz said, 'one of my disciples has been carried off.' A highly talented young man, who was interested in me(!!!), and now I care for nothing anymore."

This morning I registered a new (though not very interesting) transport from Amsterdam, and she appeared before me with a mug of the tasty bean soup that's being served up here today. And why is Mother doing this? I've wanted to write about this for some time. You have to make friends with everybody here. And to keep them as friends. And Mother is particularly good at it. She knows people here are generally not particularly refined and therefore doesn't recoil from any device, no matter how crude it may seem in my eyes. Does small favors for people, stays on good terms with the people in food services, with the women in the administration, deals with them all in a rather ostentatiously polite way. If she introduces her children, she praises them to the skies, so that people become embarrassed, but she gets what she wants. Father has a rather clumsy style of flattery that gives me the willies. It also costs cigarettes. I can't do it. Not because I object to it morally, although it does irritate me, but because I can't hit the right note. As I see it, every act of flattery is simply too obvious. That's because I overestimate the refinement of others, although from Mother's results it's clear that I'm mistaken. But it still gets in the way of acting effectively.

Monday [May 17, 1943].[321] The last few days there are so many facts worth noting that I should actually take on someone to help me. There are the big general roll calls in the evenings. First the practices of the labor units. Everyone in his own group. We are with the small teachers' unit. Behind the post office. Music has its own unit. The musicians don't have to do anything. We do, but there's nothing for us to do. Because we taught for a couple of days in the youths' barrack; I was the leader and gave singing lessons with a sore throat, and then the barrack went into quarantine again. Ours was closed up at

321. On May 14, 1943, the Jews in Vught numbered 7,874, including 1,703 children younger than sixteen years.

the same time, and Spitz, Fraenkel, and I fled from it, afraid to be locked up for ten days, afraid also of being hassled by the barrack leader, Fisch, who has it in for teachers, so to speak, because they're not doing anything. For a while he made me very nervous. This is no way to live, in fact. Once again I'm writing registration cards for Barber, who really should be hanged, the expression is not all that inappropriate.[322] Barber comes and stands behind you and says: "Are you done yet, Mr. Koker?" so you become totally worked up. He has a peculiar, coarse way of drawing someone's attention to mistakes, has something untrustworthy in his gaze, and is completely incompetent. If you've sorted something, he messes it up again and then reproaches you vehemently because things aren't as they should be. The day before yesterday I laughed in his face. I was that nervous. But he doesn't notice. But okay, you're glad if you're allowed to work for Barber. Moreover, I have the permission of the administration barrack leader to come and work there on my diary, verses, or whatever I want. But I don't want to make too much use of it. Anyway, this Neumann is a remarkable fellow. A face that mostly looks severe, like an animal with a snout, contemplative behind an enormous hooked nose that is red at the edges, so tightly does the skin stretch over the bone. Everything he says is both intended and unintended, but he always expresses things in a very literary way, like Dr. Behrends in *The Magic Mountain*.[323] Sometimes it's time for cleaning, and then he says: "Mr. Koker, I'll show you the royal road out," and opens the door with

322. The popular Dutch proverb "Barbertje moet hangen" (Little Barbara must hang) describes a situation in which a scapegoat must suffer punishment even after proven innocent. The (incidentally incorrect) saying derives from one of the great masterworks of Dutch literature: Multatuli's *Max Havelaar* (1860). In a parable that precedes the narrative a certain Lothario stands accused of having murdered and pickled Little Barbara. The judge sentences him to death twice, once for the murder and once for the pickling. Lothario not only maintains his innocence but also claims that he always took care of Little Barbara. The judge then adds a third death sentence, for vanity. Next Little Barbara enters the court, alive and well, and proclaims that Lothario is a kind and noble man. "You hear, my lord, she says I am a good man," Lothario tells the judge. The judge responds by canceling the first two death sentences, but because Lothario has declared himself to be a good man, he confirms the third death sentence. "He must hang," the judge declares, and adds: "He is guilty of vanity. Recorder, cite in the preamble the judgment of Lessing's Patriarch." In Lessing's play *Nathan the Wise* the Christian Patriarch of Jerusalem insists that a Jew who saved a Christian girl and raised her as his daughter must die for having seduced a child to apostasy. To all pleas for justice and mercy, the Patriarch responds, "The Jew must burn." See Multatuli, *Max Havelaar*, 18; Lessing, *Nathan the Wise*, 98–9.

323. In Thomas Mann's *The Magic Mountain* (1924), Hofrat Behrens is the effusive chief physician of the International Sanatorium Berghof. Nicknamed Rhadamanthys (after a wise Greek king who became judge in the underworld) by the patients, Behrens delights in long, jovial monologues. See Mann, *The Magic Mountain*, 1:60–62.

an elegant gesture. But in any case he doesn't mean it maliciously, because this week he said to Father: "I know your son, I threw him politely out the door this morning, but he's a good lad. If all the others were as polite as he is, . . . always sits so quietly in the corner." Last week we happened to be using the toilets at the same time. By way of paying him a compliment, I say the washroom is a good place for meeting agreeable people, provided it's kept clean and proper. And he: bent over, hooked nose to the fore, hooked pipe in his mouth, a satyr, is obviously flattered and says that this is a place for getting together and that they sit here side by side, talking for hours, but that a few people who are less liked are absolutely not part of this. Now and then he really startles you: when he shouts at someone at the top of his lungs. He really gets into the right posture for it, and he enjoys every term of abuse he utters.

This, roughly, is the life of a teacher in Vught. To which you have to add the hours that you're wandering around, but it's not a blissful drifting, because in appearance and manner you have to imply that you're out on business, and you're constantly afraid of being stopped and taken along to carry rocks, a task that doesn't see the SS men who accompany the workers exhibit their most easygoing side. A task during which someone was shot in the chest yesterday—he later died of his wounds—because he was relieving himself in a place that may have been approved by one soldier but not the one who shot him. So people really don't need to envy me my freedom or to reproach me for it, although that does happen.

The sun isn't shining, [but] the weather is delightful, the scent of the pine trees blows over this way and makes you feel wonderful and nostalgic at the same time. I didn't know that a smell like that could conjure up so many associations: to Karel, to Nettie (I don't hear anything from her these days). But I don't feel anything of what's around me, except maybe during the short noon hour. But I'm so tired then. . . . We're woken at four. We get up a bit later than that, but it really takes a toll on our sleep. And in the evening I never have the opportunity to go to sleep early. And yet . . . it's summer and I need to notice it for just one moment each day in order to know it! Add to this, of course, that in spite of everything we really are *outside* here. If I had the time, the quiet, and the stimulation to write poetry, I would now be writing my first nature poems. The most wonderful lines enter my mind. That is to say, enter is not the word, that's the way it used to be: now it's more a matter of calling them up. For example:

The evening air so pure and intimate
A sky that's hazed in whiteness by the sun,
and trees with foliage in great profusion,
with glittering flecks of silver from the sun.

Sunday [May 23, 1943].[324] A week full of turmoil behind us. [A week] of idleness and nevertheless a lack of free time. In the first place, the weekly disappointment over the failure of treats to appear. (This morning once again something very gratifying, Mother extracted it. It's just as I thought.) Next the idleness, the fear that you will be assigned to work you aren't capable of. Yet another word about the labor unit. Its formation is accompanied by major hitches. The first time a great rush job by the SS. It was Saathoff's birthday, the painter among us should have made a sign: "A thundering *Heil* to the birthday boy."

This evening they were very happy and really hurried us during the formation of the unit, during which one man fell and the gentlemen cleaned his clock, just as if they were rubbing his face with snow.

As a matter of fact, often there are punishment roll calls too, I don't know how long we stand there. But the sunshine is beautiful, and I don't mind.

Something amusing: the children are in quarantine. Therefore no school. Some of the men's barracks are also in quarantine. Then I quickly change barracks, I'll explain why later. But for a punishment roll call everybody has to line up. Even the people in the quarantined barracks. Duty is duty. The bureaucratic dogmatism of everything that happens here is really the new thing I've come to know. Everything elementary and self-evident turns into dogma here, and the dogmas often work at cross-purposes without canceling each other out. At the start of the week: Moerdijk. Everybody has to line up. The first evening we all stood around without anything happening. Two prisoners are missing. Finally they're located, sleeping in our warehouse. Flogging. I didn't watch. They had to count the strokes out loud themselves, voices becoming ever weaker. The sun was hot and the sky bloodred. Next day at noon roll call again. Another one was missing. Suddenly [the roll call] dismissed. They had found him. He had hanged himself. But the succeeding days it really was Moerdijk.

324. On May 21, 1943, Vught held 8,143 Jews, including 1,731 children younger than sixteen years.

First the list was called up. Did not fear it. But then came what we did fear.

We're standing in a row. Saathoff sees [Fritz] Fr[änkel], is impressed by his build and says: "You, how old are you?" He: "42," and summarizes some of his good points. "On your way [to Moerdijk]." Me too. I was kicked because I held my fingers down when he asked who did not work with diamonds. My first kick. Even though it hadn't landed hard, I felt the spot all day long. As it happened, the previous day I had worked for a personnel selection by Philips, together with Spitz.[325] That way had come into contact with Lehmann. It was most remarkable. I represented the two of us, far more than Spitz, and I also had to be ready for Lehmann's outbursts. Later he came around,

325. In December 1942 Dr. Walter Schieber of the German Ministry of Armaments and War Production contacted the chief administrator of the concentration camps, SS-Obergruppenführer (lieutenant general) Oswald Pohl, with the proposal that the new concentration camp in Vught might be made useful for the German war effort by becoming a production site for the Philips Electronics Corporation, headquartered in nearby Eindhoven. Pohl agreed and contacted the German overseer of Philips, Dr. Ludwig Nolte, who in turn approached the de facto head of the company, Frederik Jacques (Frits) Philips. Initially unwilling to use the labor of concentration-camp inmates, Philips changed his mind when he considered how a Philips workshop could provide them with protection, and on February 19, 1943, Philips officials Rutger Egbert Laman Trip and Carel Braakman visited the camp to review the situation. Three days later they established the so-called Philips Kommando (Philips Detachment). Initially it consisted of only non-Jewish *Häftlinge*, who assembled radio sets. These prisoners did not have to participate in the daily roll calls and obtained extra food provided by the factory: the so-called *Philiprak* (Phili hash) or *Philipsprak* (Philips hash). On May 8, the day of the first large transport of Jews leaving the camp, the Jewish engineer Alfred Spitz was admitted to the Philips Kommando. The *Häftling* Hein van Wijk realized that the Philips Kommando could provide protection for the Jews, and on May 15, Van Wijk organized a meeting with Braakman and Spitz. The three men agreed to push Philips to create a large Jewish section in the Philips Kommando, and Spitz asked his friend David Koker to help him identify candidates. Frits Philips hesitated, however. He feared the many problems that would ensue. Philips had, incidentally, a good record at the time of protecting Jewish employees at the factory, who had been brought together in a special department assigned important work for the German war effort. The heartrending scenes accompanying the departure on June 6 and 7 of two transports with almost three thousand Jews, including some thirteen hundred children, changed the dynamics. Realizing that all Jews were in danger of losing their lives, Van Wijk and his fellow prisoners Abraham de Wit and Dirk Wissink persuaded Braakman to absorb a large group of Jews into the Philips Kommando. Braakman approached Frits Philips, who finally authorized the inclusion of Jews. Now they had to convince Chmielewski, the Commandant of Vught. Braakman proposed to Chmielewski that the Philips Kommando should also produce radio tubes. Chmielewski contacted Berlin and received approval, but the question arose as to who would make the tubes. Braakman told Chmielewski that the psychotechnical office of Philips, which oversaw the testing of potential employees, had decided that Jews were particularly suited to making radio tubes. When Chmielewski responded that he could not make Jews available, Braakman countered that in that case he would not be able to produce the radio tubes. After some haggling the two agreed on a contingent of two hundred Jews. See Blanken, *History of Philips Electronics*, 256ff.; Klein and Van de Kamp, *Het Philips-Kommando*.

and we had the opportunity to laud his marvelous understanding and above all his succinctness, which allows him to say everything relevant in a couple of sentences. He has a kindheartedness that shows itself from time to time, doesn't radiate, isn't active, shows itself occasionally in a calm smile (like water) that you suddenly become aware of, or in a glance.

Lehmann took charge of me that morning and pleaded my case to Saathoff, who made a solitary exception and released me from the list. After a couple of days I thanked him, didn't know whether it was a sensible thing to do, and was surprised by the fact that he seemed to appreciate it. Now and then I walk over to the administration barrack, negotiate with the authorities there, and check something on a list. So I am an official personage, can debate very ably about the orders of the *Arbeitseinsatzführer* [work-assignment leader], and actually have nothing to do. Sat in on letter censorship, which is unbelievably mind-numbing work. But one with a fine official function. The day before yesterday, Tuesday, then went to Philips at last. Said honestly that, before I arrived in the camp, I had never done administrative work, and am now allocated to Philips with another one of the seven people who showed up. Does it offer some protection against Westerbork? The Philips man believes it does and is irritated by Spitz, who thinks not. If Spitz can say that things will go wrong with Vught, he won't let the opportunity slip by. He takes a certain satanic pleasure in pointing to our somber prospects. And not just as an empty phrase he doesn't really believe. Sometimes he has other pessimistic insights, for example that great masses of deportees will remain in Poland and Russia, which you can talk him out of only if you persist long enough. He means everything he says. Last week: an immense anxiety: the age limit has been lowered to 50 years, and there's something the matter with the diamond exemption. I went half-crying to Assau.[326] And he: "Maybe it'll be all right; don't count on it." I had someone call Mother. She was merry, almost cheerful. Glad it's us and not you. And she means it. I couldn't speak for fear of breaking down in tears. Had to take deep breaths now and then so as not to choke. Later that day [I was] calmer. It'll probably be a question of who you know. And Max: "What do you think?" I: "I think things will sort themselves out all right, but I can't imagine how." Remarkable. I immediately imag-

---

326. David is referring to Philip Assou. See the entry on Assou in the appendix. He died in Dörnhau.

ined how everything would be. How I would hear it. I think: then I'll
faint (it's terrible when you always picture yourself that way). How I
would send along our parcels and everything we have. (Last week,
in response to letters, we really got a lot; they were genuinely enthusiastic that they could send things to us.) How I would write a long
letter to Nettie. I'm in the same circumstances now as she is.[327] This
business of constantly seeing yourself is a form of mental obstinacy.
One more extremism.

The business has indeed sorted itself out, and Father and Mother,
who were at the top of the list, have been taken off it. Anyway, I think
we'll all go soon. Am fully prepared for it. For that reason I'm so
happy that I've been receiving treats the last little while. Perhaps from
Nettie this week. Hilde Seelig has come here.[328] Nettie spent several
more evenings in our home. And she got my portrait from Mrs. Blu-
menthal.[329] In fact I've often asked myself what might have happened
to it. I was able to work up some emotion yesterday by thinking that
she had the portrait in her care.[330] The parcels this week exhibited a
touching concern. I've written a curious letter. Karel asked me to send
some verses.[331] He must know I'm completely barren. In the evening
I think: "I'm going for a walk. Something is bound to come to me."
And that does happen. But working it out doesn't. Lines aplenty: during the time that I heard nothing from anyone:

> For all the things we placed reliance on
> were merely creatures of a single day
> and friendship that soon grew pale and wan
> should meeting suffer even brief delay
> a woman too, a love that's been and gone
> and god knows what she's thinking of today.

327. David may be referring to the fact that both were separated from their parents.
328. David is referring to the German-Jewish refugee Hildegard Elfriede Seelig-
Blumenfeld (1915–44), who was a neighbor of the Kokers'. Seelig-Blumenfeld was murdered in Auschwitz.
329. David is likely referring to Ernestine Blumenthal-Kempner (1868–1943) or her
daughter Margot (1905–43). The mother was killed in Auschwitz, and her daughter in
Sobibor.
330. In a letter written in March, Nettie told David that she had obtained from the
apartment a framed photo of David. Letter, Nettie David to David Koker, March 1943, collection 244 (diaries), file 1657 (Koker), NIOD archive, Amsterdam.
331. Karel wrote on May 14, "We didn't write for a long time because everyone put fear
in us. In the future I'll send you a weekly letter through this route. Send poems and write
how your days unfold, and what Max and your parents are doing, etc." Letter, Karel van
het Reve to David Koker, May 14, 1943, collection 244 (diaries), file 1657 (Koker), NIOD
archive, Amsterdam.

But still not the poetry I'd like to write. Which sometimes appears clearly before my eyes, so to speak. Curious, too, is that my memory for lines I've thought up leaves me in the lurch. This and the lack of energy (and shortage of opportunity) to work them out turns this into a horrible malaise. Yet something will come of it. The loss of memory is a general feature here. There are people who suddenly can't remember the names of people they meet daily. Everybody complains about being unable to recall faces. I, too, am absolutely incapable of it. I try to conjure up Nettie's face before me, see a vague contour, and a color, which in terms of the atmosphere and the feelings it awakens comes very close, so close, in fact, that I seem to sense her body warmth, but which then, as perceived image, vanishes instantly. Loss of memory, too, is part of the stupor of this life. Thoughts keep going around in the same circle. Our receptiveness lies open and shrinks and hardens at the surface. Because life has become a nothingness, a void. And our thinking, our entire internal life is no longer driven by anything [external], keeps going only through its own momentum.

Last week, it was beautiful weather again, volunteers were requested for Vught, i.e., for a kind of gardener's work at the commandant's place. I suddenly had a great desire to go outside the gate, see people, and work among flowers and in the sunshine. I became conscious of this in a flash. Aside from the practical advantages. That evening while we were in bed: "Gentlemen, please listen for a moment. The following gentlemen have to come in." In deadly silence the names are read out. Lampie: "Am I among them too?"[332] After that people wandered around, calmly and openly. Conversation with Bosman about Jaap Mei[j]er.[333]

Friday, May 24 [actually May 28] [1943].[334] Every morning there is a rotating work detachment for Den Bosch, the so-called *Genesungs-Kompanie* [Healing Company], in which we're cured of our Jewish aversion to work by means of twelve hours of hard labor, cursing, running along a sandy road, fifty deep knee bends, etc. Nobody wants to be part of it. The art of avoiding work is becoming ever more refined.

332. David is referring to the diamond worker Simon Lampie (1885–1943), who was informed that day of his transfer to Westerbork. Lampie was murdered in Sobibor.

333. David is referring to the Rotterdam industrialist Maurits Bosman (1895–1943). Bosman was murdered in Sobibor.

334. On May 28, 1943, Vught numbered 7,073 Jews, including 1,456 children younger than sixteen years.

They're still going easy on me, but I suddenly realized that volunteer-ing for the lighter work of the Vught detachment might get me sev-eral days' worth of exemption from Den Bosch. So I registered. Went with five men, a lot of bread, butter, and sausage. Guarded by two SS guys, who allowed us to walk slowly, for my taste a bit too slowly, led us along detours in order to prolong the beautiful walk, and let us lie down in the woods. We went along a pleasant forest road. There were still drops of rain on the trees. Came past a spring that flowed vigor-ously, probably because of the loop of the Reusel River, and finally ended up on a heath, and that was the most beautiful place I've ever seen. The moist, glistening dark overgrowth beyond it, a low white wall of mist, bushes looming above, and a tall pine forest on the ho-rizon. And above all this the sun, between streaks of mist and bits of cloud. The day hasn't been fully unwrapped yet, I thought. It's still half in its husk. And the red light, reflected, broken, scattered, by and against all the mist. A Van Gogh painting in its pure straight lines and circles. (Maxi puts his hand on my shoulder. Reinecke was standing behind me, he said, wanted to startle me because he thought I was sleeping, saw that I was . . . writing, and went away . . .). These lines say it well:

> and up there spinning wildly was the sun,
> with radiating broken shafts of light.
> And in the garden too and in the house.

I started to pull weeds from flower beds that had been much ne-glected. A genial, warm sun shone. I felt my body. As I had imagined it. A wide view and "a heaven frosted by the sun." And over the whole plain and under the huge sky, a cuckoo, calling as decidedly, as simply as a church bell. You become aware how small the sound is in itself, but that it reaches us all the same, because there's nothing to hold it back. In the camp we also hear the cuckoo, but muffled and lonely in the woods. But there's no empty space here either. And the house, an old farmstead, and the commandant's garden, stand between the sky and the land. If you go through a hedge you see meadows below, with cows and slender, nimble horses in them, and in the distance, half in the mist, Saint John's Cathedral in Den Bosch.[335] And you retrace

---

335. Saint John's Basilica in 's-Hertogenbosch is one of the finest examples of Gothic architecture in the Netherlands. It rises above the city like an ark. In 1941 a beautifully produced book containing one hundred superb photos by Martien Coppens had brought renewed attention to the church. See Van Goirle, *Gedachten in Steen.*

your steps and look in the garden, which meanwhile has become burning hot, for the flower bed you were working in. The mild scent of the hawthorn drifts through the warm air. You halt, look at the dreamy water and the gnats dancing over it, and at the columbines growing on the steep slope of the garden down to the stream. And all of this is part not of an exuberant joy but rather a steady, modest happiness.

The SS guys who came along were quite decent. One of them knew me, he knew from where but evidently didn't want to say it. He was embarrassed; hit a big, heavyset guy in the face. Later that day we came under the supervision of a *stormman* [Dutch Nazi paramilitary]. I had my first conversation with a National Socialist. Wanted to compel him to be reasonable, the way I had imagined it, but the attempt failed utterly. It *was* interesting. Ended up with Jewish exploitation etc. And with two times twenty up and down.[336] Wasn't allowed to come back because I did things poorly. He was right in saying: "Unwillingness." But not consciously, and I couldn't do anything to change it. In any case: a gorgeous day, in spite of everything. I almost had tears in my eyes when I walked through the village and saw living rooms. How far we've gone. And on the way back the people. Many vacationers, whose faces show sympathy when we pass by, with our [yellow] stars and our SS men following us. Holiday activity around the IJzeren Man recreation park.[337]

I'm giving teaching a rest for now. These days I have the library in my care. Roman has promised to give me cover. Have become something of a client to him, carry his stuff when we're going in the same direction, and he really likes to feel himself to be a bit of a patron. He's unquestionably a very powerful man around here, and as such requires one or more courtiers. Around him hovers a somewhat corrupt atmosphere, but the curious thing is that he himself is relatively untouched by it, because in a certain sense and in his own way he's very active. But it still sticks to him, you start feeling as if you were in an over-warm and humid space. Of course this does also affect the relationship, which is most offensive and humiliating. Anyway, the kind of work that's available in the library, where I'm like the fifth wheel, doesn't suit me at all. I do still have the reservation by Philips as a fallback, of course, and I seem to have been put in the library to give

336. This was a form of punishment in which one hit the ground and immediately got up again.
337. The IJzeren Man (Iron Man) recreation park remained open throughout the war.

me the opportunity to do some of my own projects. That's happening. This diary will, I hope, once again become a daily record, which is bound to strengthen the realism of the entries. Aside from this I'm reading Thomas Mann's *K[önigliche] H[oheit]* [*Royal Highness*].[338] We're living in a friendly concentration camp here! And every day an assignment from the copy of Homer belonging to H. Asser, who has gone to Moerdijk in the meantime.[339] But the verses that I'm waiting for haven't shown up yet. A letter from Roland [Frederikstadt] in Amersfoort, which makes me surmise bad things.[340] Yesterday I went to roll call late: the [protective custody] prisoners' Philips Kommando was passing by. Alarmed shouts: "David, David." Jan Mackay, who disappeared months ago.

Very impressed by my fifteen weeks [in the camp], which astonish everyone, in fact, and which I just can't resist being proud of. "When I came here fifteen weeks ago," or, "I've been here fifteen weeks now," etc., in any case very touched by Jan Mackay, to whom I'll write a letter.

A few nights ago: a loud bang, red flames outside. When I come to consider it calmly, I think: a bomb. Probably more will drop. And near us. Or even on us. A half-cynical feeling. It turned out to be two airplanes that went down in flames. Great panic among the women.

Thursday [June 3, 1943]. First the story of the rocks. The men hear that the women have to line up. They've all gone out the gate. Nervousness. Later it turns out to be true: they have to carry rocks, two stones each by hand, seven times along a route that takes ten minutes each way. Despondency among the men. Not even anger now, profound sadness. The women went on strike at a certain point, refused to go on. Ettlinger threatens them. No effect. At his wits' end, he

338. *Royal Highness* was Thomas Mann's second novel (and the first to be translated into English). The story concerns a midsize German grand duchy ruled by a family in decline; the fairy-tale plot focuses on the education of Prince Karl Heinrich and his romance and ultimate marriage with Imma Spoelmann, the daughter of an American millionaire who has taken up residence in the grand duchy and whose fortune promises to bail out the dynasty and the country. See Mann, *Royal Highness.*
339. David is referring to Henri Abraham Asscher. See the entry on Asscher in the appendix. He died in transit to Theresienstadt.
340. Between May and July 1943 the Vught camp operated a subcamp in the compound of the former police transit camp in Amersfoort, which had been closed in January 1943. Some seventy inmates from Vught and six hundred from Westerbork worked on the construction of a shooting range. After the completion of this work, those men were sent back to Vught and Westerbork.

shoots into the ground and later says to Süsskind that he didn't know what else to do.

But the worst was yet to come.[341] The women had assumed a very cheerful front, but when they entered the gate the orchestra was lined up on both sides, playing under the direction of WD.[342] The musicians suddenly found themselves face-to-face with the women. People therefore were under the impression that the orchestra was there for important visitors, for whom the rock carrying had also been put into motion. The women couldn't hold themselves in any longer, and there seems to have been a lot of crying. And the men dropped their sheet music on the ground, but had to keep playing. Afterwards Reinecke was in the women's barracks. Apologies. The next evening again. But this time the orchestra is playing popular songs. And the women are on their guard and sing along. And someone says: "Hey, they're still singing: stop!" And the orchestra stops.

People have put me in the library so I could work on my own projects. But it's the way it was in school when we read surreptitiously under our desks. I've finally finished Thomas Mann. The book's not altogether convincing. But that way it keeps a fairy-tale aspect that works in a very special manner because it does have so much that's realistic. By the way, it's written in the same style in which Imma Spoelman speaks.[343] At the moment I'm reading Schopenhauer, *Über Schriftstellerei und Stil* [*On Authorship and Style*].[344] But all the same it's an empty business, a whole day like that. Now assisted by Gerzons,[345] which robs me of even more quiet time. And working on my own projects? I don't even manage to get to my diary, let alone my poetry. I'm aware now that my letters aren't getting through.

341. With this sentence David continues his diary in one of the purple-covered exercise books that had been supplied to the school in the camp. This exercise book contains his entries from June 3 to July 27, 1943.

342. David is referring to Willem Drukker. See the entry on the Drukker family in the appendix. Drukker was killed in Sachsenhausen.

343. "This dainty creature in her red-gold gown was merely a wielder of words; she knew no more of life than those words, she played with the most serious and most awful of them as with colored stones, and was puzzled when she made people angry by their use." Mann, *Royal Highness,* 219–20.

344. It is remarkable that David made no comment on Schopenhauer's discussion of authorship. It suggests the way that life in the camp had pushed all more literary concerns to the background. David might have related to Schopenhauer if the latter had discussed the importance of writing as a means of emotional, spiritual, and even physical survival. But at no point in his essay does Schopenhauer consider the position of the writer facing the abyss. See Schopenhauer, *Parerga and Paralipomena,* 2:501–53.

345. David is referring to Josephine Anna Gersons-van der Hove, who was in charge of the school.

Had sweet letters from Nettie and Tini, which contained that information.[346] They write to me regularly now. I wrote a very nice letter to them, in which I complain about this stupefying blow. My letters are better than my diary. That's why it's such a disaster when they go missing. I was talking with Mother last week about how we're changing, how rigid we've become, how hard also in our attitudes and in our judgment of other people. Joyless too. Which is not to say, however, that we feel unhappy. Unhappiness is also too human an emotion [to describe what we feel]. Our feelings are like skin that has been stretched very tight—you get that with wounds sometimes—and then becomes insensitive and oversensitive at the same time. Then feelings don't have any color, as it were. When something happens that once would have simply made us happy, now we're deeply moved, so that sometimes tears come to our eyes. And if there's something disagreeable or threatening, we don't feel sorry for ourselves, but it's just as if we were paralyzed. All emotional life becomes something preeminently physical. And an enormous amount, agreeable *and* disagreeable, goes by without your reacting to it— . . . . . (About the intentional summoning of feelings through photos and through thinking of certain people) . . . I often think: you have here the highest degree of consciousness and of unconsciousness. The nuances between them, which used to make life so rich and full of possibilities, are absent. In the same way, asking for photos was intentional. I look at them and I know they are yours. And I do feel happy about that. But to associate them with the real thing, that I can't do. The incapacity to experience matters—memories as well as present circumstances—is something about which all kinds of people complain in many different ways. People often, as recently as yesterday, say to me, for example, that they seem so far away from their fiancées, that the relationship has become something theoretical, i.e., has become a concept, *that it still produces major impulses,* but ones different from the spontaneous feelings of the past. People vitrify here, as it were. They hold on to everything they used to have, but it is as if they were objects in a museum. Yesterday evening I consoled someone who was complaining to me about his distress. He had received a letter from his girlfriend; he let me read it, and it seemed flat and brittle. He felt the same way. I said: "To despair of you two would be to despair of

346. This is probably Tini's letter of May 14, in which she mentions that she had not heard from David for a long time.

myself. It's nonsense to ask for any kind of happiness from this period. The only thing that matters is to conserve all your possibilities. You can allow all your feelings to freeze; when this has ended you can thaw them out and then they'll live again. . . ."

Lately this line has been running through my head: "Wer spricht von Siegen? Überstehn ist alles."[347] Everything, certainly the contact with our friends, is actually nothing more than maintaining past relationships, in principle, with an eye to resuming those relationships after the war in their original form. Our whole life in here is, in fact, formalistic. Our relationship to people: a form from which the living, experiential content has been stripped. Don't worry: as long as the form maintains itself it is fine. In the future everything will fill up again. Then guesses about the reasons we become so hard and tight. Efforts to keep in shape physically. Keeping up appearances before other people, etc. And all of this is beneficial. Because to remain awake, to experience, not just to endure this life but to live it actively, would be a proud, exalted attitude, but difficult, too difficult, would probably even destroy your health. Hibernation is better, even though I often think: this period is wasted on us. It could be a time full of experiences. But now so little reaches our awareness. It's possible, of course, that everything will be stored in our unconscious mind and will manifest itself after the war. To activate that unconscious experience must be the task of this diary. . . .

Wednesday, June 9 [1943].[348] Have regained a degree of serenity. Last week I went over to Mother's, with my squeaky book-laden cart that everybody laughs at, pulling it along on a rope. In the course of our conversation she says: "Don't tell anyone, but there's going to be another transport." I'm crushed. My heart is cold. But it won't be for a while yet. And after all, there's something I know and she doesn't: Father and Mother were on the list last time but were taken off it.[349] But on Saturday official figures said: "The worst days of the camp are

---

347. "Who speaks of victory? Survival is everything." Rainer Maria Rilke, "Requiem— Für Wolf Graf von Kalckreuth," in Rilke, *Gesammelte Werke*, 2:343.

348. On June 4, 1943, Vught contained 7,088 Jews, including 1,456 children younger than sixteen years.

349. David is referring to the transport of 1,253 inmates that left Vught for Westerbork on May 23. Almost all those on that transport were shipped to Sobibor on May 25, to be killed upon arrival on May 28. As he recorded in his diary entry of May 23, through his relationship with Lehmann David had been able to remove both himself and his parents from that transport.

upon us." People guess, but those who know won't say. I've never seen
a secret kept so perfectly. It's a scary feeling to walk among people
who know what's going to happen to us all and won't tell us. The day
wears on. Nobody does anything, people are waiting. It's one of those
days we pass over because it's a preparation for something else and
people need to get ready for that. Like the day before graduation.
No sense of urgency, because people won't get to know beforehand
anyway. Boredom, rather. People are talking with each other, solely
because they can't cope with the total emptiness of this day. A dry silence. I walk back and forth all day long, running errands that are un-
necessary and quite pointless. Am tired. Almost can't move forward,
as though an elastic band were holding me back. Gradually what's
going to happen leaks out. Nobody knows who heard it first. But in
the end people are convinced, although no one has made an official announcement: all the children have to leave.[350] First people say:
without their parents; later that's left open. Suddenly it confronts us
as a certainty. People see it as an actual fact, but they still don't believe
it, just as people can occasionally see something real without fully
accepting its reality. Fortunately, between the reality and the people
lies the fact that it hasn't been officially acknowledged yet. People
are shocked to the core. I am too, but also relieved with respect to
Father and Mother. In any case these days I'm in no condition to experience fully the things that are happening, because I am myself too
much in danger, as are my parents. So I sleep very deeply that night,
even though in the evening the message is read to us in the form of a
proclamation.[351] People reacted to it with a wailing I won't soon hear

350. In the beginning of June the SS informed Süsskind and Lehmann that the children were to leave for a special *Kinderlager* (children's camp) at an undetermined location.
Mothers would be allowed to accompany the children and remain with them for a few
days to ensure that they were in good hands. Neither Süsskind nor Lehmann believed the
Germans and proposed creating at some distance from Vught, a subcamp for the children.
Blüth set out to buy barracks. The SS did not want to hear about it. See De Moei, *Joodse
kinderen*, 71.
351. In the evening of Saturday, June 5, the barrack leaders read to the inmates of each
barrack a proclamation signed by Süsskind and Lehmann. All children up to sixteen years
of age would have to leave the camp: those younger than three would have to leave the next
day, accompanied by their mothers, while children between four and sixteen would have
to leave on Monday, June 7. Families were ripped apart without the possibility of farewell
since many of the fathers were employed at the Moerdijk subcamp. Lehmann proposed
sending buses to Moerdijk to make it possible for the fathers to say good-bye, but the SS refused this. In their proclamation Süsskind and Lehmann wrote that the SS would maintain
the strictest order. They added that they had some hope that the children might remain in

again. I myself was half crying when I told W[illem] D[rukker], but that may well have been over-excitement. On that evening, and on previous evenings, visitors were allowed, which had already caused a certain amount of disquiet. As a consequence the women heard the announcement in our barrack. The document was read out by a barrack leader, B[illegible], who had to stop repeatedly because he was weeping throughout. The next day the summonses and then a crowd of people begging to go along. People are jostling each other in the secretariat. Shouting, threatening, weeping, anything to get out of here. A very strange sensation. And some people were unable to get out of here, because they were barred from leaving by factory work, etc. Then we were confined to our barracks. I went out anyway. Asked at the secretariat whether they needed me. But asking didn't get me anywhere. Under these circumstance it really is undignified to be begging for work. Watching the children leave.[352] "I'm allowed to go today," or "I can't go till tomorrow." A complete lack of awareness. And the men at the side of the road, screaming, until their voices are worn to shreds. Saar van der Hal that day: "Not impossible that your parents will get called up as well."[353] I go to Mother. She very grim. Completely ready. I less afraid. Actually [lost some of my fear] in the course of the day. Was more afraid the day before, when I didn't know yet what was wrong.

the Netherlands and that, if this were to occur, their parents might return to Vught. Nevertheless, "in view of the terrible situation, we order for the whole Jewish camp an eight-day period of mourning and forbid all entertainment until Saturday, June 12, five o'clock in the afternoon." For the full text of the proclamation, see D. Koker, *Dagboek geschreven in Vught*, 128n.

352. The transport consisted of 1,593 persons, among whom were 806 children. The train left Vught late in the evening. By morning it had reached Westerbork. The journalist Philip Mechanicus witnessed the arrival of the train. "At about half past four in the morning a transport with 1,750 Jews arrived in cattle trucks. Except for a hundred men, they were all wretched women with their infants and older children. Wives and families of the men who had been sent to work at Moerdijk to dig earthworks and had been given an assurance by the German authorities that their wives would not be deported to the east. The women are in fact going on next Tuesday's transport to the east. They arrived thin as rakes and worn out after a ten-hour journey. They spoke vehemently about their despicable treatment at Vught, the exhaustion and humiliation of it all." The next day he noted that all children were to leave Vught. "Only as a result of protesting have a large number of mothers managed to go with their children. But, in spite of this, young children are being sent alone. Vught is certainly one of the bitterest chapters in the persecution of the Jews in Holland." A few days later all those who had arrived from Vught were deported to Sobibor. Mechanicus, *Year of Fear*, 37–8.

353. Sara van der Hal-van Adelsbergen (1909–78) and her husband, Dr. Isidoor van Hal (1907–86), survived the war. See the diary entry for November 20, 1943.

The next day: a second transport.[354] Call-ups especially for the diamond trade. In the morning van der Hal. Father and Mother had a summons the day before, but it was withdrawn again. Before that day she wasn't afraid. That morning there were some loud comments about our case. Orders left and right. Ages much lower than Father's and Mother's. But not them. Just as I'm unofficially exempt from doing jobs, they're exempt as well. Both on the basis of nothing at all. But justified and very sensible nevertheless.

Thursday, June 11 [June 10], 1943.[355] Helped out on the second evening. A kind of hard-nosed OD was formed. I had lined up too. All single men aged 21 to 40, one of the first requirements—but Friedländer allowed me to leave the lineup.[356] Spent the first evening with Syl Drukker, who [was?] in the orchestra room. A strange sight, young men sleeping on mattresses, wearing their shoes, amid the quasi-artistic decoration of the barrack, the musical instruments, and the bright-yellow glow of the footlights. Others are seated at the tables, talking. Right off it struck me as having the character of a military barracks with this factual basis: these people won't be personally affected. This is how I picture the barracks of the *zwarte politie* [black police] in Amsterdam.[357] The second day I made work for myself, i.e., I proposed it and had them assign it to me. The result was rejected: people thought it was superfluous. In any case it gave me the opportunity (and distinction) of going outside and getting into the children's barracks, and to observe their desolation and melancholy. Walked around for a long time that evening without doing anything. Finally

354. On Monday, June 7, a transport of 1,356 people left Vught, including 502 children. In Westerbork Mechanicus also witnessed the arrival of this transport. "In the middle of the night the second transport came from Vught, about 1300 people, men, women and children. Tired and worn out, filthy and ailing, some of them were simply transferred, amid snarling and shouting, beating and pummeling, from the dirty cattle and goods wagons they had come in to the dirty cattle and goods wagons that would take them to the east. The quota had to be complete." Mechanicus, *Year of Fear*, 40.

355. On June 11, 1943, Vught held 4,158 Jews; this number included 190 children younger than sixteen years.

356. Adolf Friedländer was in charge of the Ordedienst.

357. The reference is to the Schalkhaar police. The so-called Green Police (*Grüne Polizei* in German, *Groene Politie* in Dutch) were Germans who were members of the *Ordnungspolizei*. Their name derived from the green color of their uniforms. In the occupied Netherlands the three thousand green policemen were the "fist" of the German occupation: they played a key role in the mass arrests of Jews in February 1941 and were also central in the *razzias* of 1942 and 1943. See Kelder, *De Schalkhaarders*, 36–7.

succeeded in finding a red armband.[358] Then to the gate. The air very
mild. The first day it rained very hard. But now the field is very peaceful. At the gate a small band of agitated people. Then you see people
approaching across the field, very small, you don't know who they
are, but even from a distance you can see they're carrying luggage.
Head over that way to lend a hand. All your feelings are subdued on
an evening like that, except the one that leads you to help people.
That feeling remains. At the gate, people are lugging their possessions, trying either to get through without a summons or to postpone
the moment of departure as long as possible. Waiting for someone
or other who "will do something for them." When a group like that
becomes too large Ettlinger starts yelling or the commandant does,
and they drive them out the gate. The way you chase someone out
of the house. . . . In any case a lot of shouting over there. More from
worry that [the operation] isn't going to succeed than anything else.
Because after the proclamation there was a lot of sympathy from [the
SS]. The commandant: "We didn't want this!" Ettlinger something
similar. Children are his soft spot, after all. Bubi shows up with bread,
butter, and sugar for Th. B. and tries to help, etc.[359]

Saturday, June 12 [1943]. I relived that evening at the gate in a
dream. A hellish dream, but nothing more than a dream. People approaching across the field in small groups, enlisted men and officers
watching from the balcony, half-interested, half-indifferent, officers
and enlisted men who roam through the crowd, shout occasionally
and beyond that hang around the female guards like flies and can't
keep their hands to themselves. And now and then the shrill voice of
a female guard, making an ugly gash in the sky. A bustling enterprise,
there in that narrow gate, luggage that we hand on, people that we
allow to pass through, officers who hurry us along. The commandant,
who stands there watching like the lord and master of it all and who,
every once in a while, intervenes quite unexpectedly. And everything
under a wonderfully clear sky, the evening is not yet ready to depart.
When everybody's gone, we go to eat and to discuss the matter: the
close of Yom Kippur. All the time I expected to see Father and Mother
approach across the field. Instead of them: young people . . . , in excellent shape. . . . Ettlinger reached into the filing cabinet, pulled out

358. Inmates involved in the preparation of a transport had to wear a red armband when
approaching the gate. Without it, they ran the risk of being included in the transport.
359. Bubi was the nickname of a fat-faced SS man.

a bunch of cards, and now these people have to leave. The diamond group is being called up as well, and before others. . . . Ettlinger orders me to go into the barracks and announce that everyone who fails to show up will go into the prison camp. Didn't do it. You sense: a crappy job, all of this, but I feel hard and grim that evening, and I want to sample everything to the bitter end. Sample it while keeping my mouth shut.

Rumors spread by highly official sources that those who remain here now will stay. And that it will become a real industrial camp, less of a concentration camp. Shorter hours of work. In any case, the industrialization has created a strange situation. There are a lot of noninterned Aryans walking through the camp, noninterned Jews too. At night in bed Spitz and I often discuss the strange situation here. Spitz is uncommonly clever. He used an expression that I used early on: enchanted world. And the strange part: I love this community, precisely because of its paradoxical being. A few days ago I reached the following conclusions: everything the Germans put their hand to becomes dogma. And all the anomalies here are [the result of] dogmas that collide but in no way cancel each other out. For the Germans, collectively and individually, it is the case that they want to do everything in the best and most correct way possible. Collectively: they want to give the Jews, although they regard them as their mortal enemies, the most perfect treatment possible. In the rigorous manner and according to the norms characteristic of them, but still: within the guidelines, faultless. Individually: they do feel some sympathy for the people, although they only occasionally show it, such as during the children's transport.

The orchestra is complete now. The first performances have taken place, but I didn't attend them, because Mother was in quarantine. We tried very hard to keep her out of quarantine. She was out, but then had to be quarantined with all the others. We did our best, and that's the most important thing. That's what it was all about, as Mrs. Gerzons rightly said. There's a concert hall now, with wings and nicely executed music stands, and on everything the initials of the great Martin Roman, whose portrait, more or less recognizable, hangs on all the official walls. Up to this point he seems to have been a largely unknown nightclub celebrity, but here he plays the role of the world-famous accompanist of Marek Weber. Although it seems he was just a replacement for a couple of days when someone else was sick. Programs are handed out, invitations are sent out, people act secretively and carry on intrigues. Roman rules like a kind of king of music. One of the first evenings Bubi, animated by evil impulses, good intentions, and confusion, gave a speech and in it said that this camp was of no great importance for the SS, for they could enter and leave whenever they wanted. But it was important for the Jews, "because you're staying here and can't leave." The entire hall laughed. He laughed along heartily. "That's why everyone has to give money for the flowers coming into the camp. That's in your interest and especially in the interest of your wives and children" (they were still here at the time). In fact, odd little flower beds *have* been laid out with geraniums, in themselves very beautiful, and this project is ongoing. But again systematized to death, just as enjoyment of the cabaret has been completely killed by the chic music hall and the self-important entourage. In a certain sense, say I, the Germans do want us to feel happy here. Not out of amiability, it seems to me, but out of that wish to be faultless that animates them with respect to everything.

A big change has come into our lives. Or rather: as a result of the recent transports we've become conscious of the fact that we are a kind of camp aristocracy and now conduct ourselves as such. One major thing: we've managed to get hold of plates. I am so pleased about them. Every time I have them in front of me. I'm actually very meticulous about eating. Want to remove platters, papers, boxes from the table before I start eating, the room set up as tidily as possible, etc. That often leads to conflict with Max, first of all because he doesn't have the same sense of order in these things, and second, and this proceeds from the first, that he wolfs everything down. I'd much rather eat by myself. I know no greater pleasure than to be very frugal with my things and arrange exactly when I'll eat what. And it is a sin if the precious contents of our parcels are not enjoyed slowly and deliberately. On the other hand, I have a strong tendency to parsimony, and I've become greedy. Our parcels enable us to live in style. Last week we had absolutely too much bread. Spitz, Max, and I sit for a long time at our special table, eat from large supplies without care, and are better off than at home, so to speak. Feel ourselves to be a kind of camp aristocracy. He (Spitz) with his work at Philips, where he seems to be able to continue his own private studies, and I with my exemption from duties.

Tuesday, June 15 [1943]. A couple of beautiful Pentecost days behind us. Friday. Days of genuine happiness. The insights I wrote down above took form during those days. Sun, sleeping outside in the morning after getting up and having watched a wide-awake sun shine in through the windows. You used to call that getting up early. No hurrying out to roll call, you get up because you're awake, you dress, have a nice shave, eat calmly after roll call, but not surreptitiously the way you used to, and then go to sleep in the sun. In the afternoon I pay a visit to Mother. I look forward to these visits, but once I'm there I grow bad tempered and silent. Father's presence and the way he argues weigh on me. The second time we actually had an open quarrel. Got a letter from Mother (attached) [360] and answered rather firmly. The honesty of my answer evidently satisfied her.

In the evening a soccer match, in which Reinecke joined, and one of the Jews bodychecked him so hard that he fell over a fence. Also a boxing match, which was very good to see. All these things get people mightily confused. "What's gotten into them?" they ask, mistrusting the benevolence. But that's not fair. Alfred and I often talk about it during the Pentecost roll calls under a delicate sky. He and I watch Ettlinger and Reinecke go by and decide in a mood of softness that we actually have nothing against them. In any case I like the camp a lot these days. I'm a bit sorry not to have been here from the very beginning. Add to this the expectation that it won't last that much longer, which puts me in a light and cheerful mood. Karel writes: the end of the war seems generally to be in the air, one way or another, something that's exceptionally encouraging coming from him, and that has changed me completely for a week now. There is also Tini's prediction, to which I cling: you'll never go to Poland. Also the sense of increased safety I derive from my Philips *Sperre* makes me feel better. It also means I don't get irritated by my life of leisure in the library. In which I'm sitting, by the way, reading calmly: *And Quiet Flows the Don*,[361] Dostoevsky, Tolstoy, Schopenhauer. And writing: because I've resumed working on my poetry. They're going to have cultural evenings here. And I'm supposed to produce some verses. That seems like fun. Last week we all went to the concert. A real happening. A lot of light and glitter and feasting. The program didn't interest me much, but I topped up my feelings of interest and pleasure in what was offered with all my other feelings of good cheer.

360. Despite David's note that he had attached the letter to his diary, this letter does not survive.

361. A novel by Mikhail Sholokhov (1905–84).

And that way it went just fine. The whole first row was occupied by gray-green uniforms.

The nature of this diary: it describes the facts. But in the objective sense. It doesn't suggest I live among these circumstances. The personal is not permitted here.

Saturday, June 19 [1943].[362] Yesterday evening and the evening before some prisoners were flogged. Among them *Kapo* Kurt of the *Lagerreinigung* [camp sanitary unit], the good-looking *Kapo*.[363] After that I saw Reinecke assault a prisoner with unbelievable fervor, jumping on him, putting his whole body into each blow. A slim, fit figure.

I began this poem:

> So seated at my peaceful windowpane
> I write the verse that ends my useless day
> the sky weeps down its final drops of rain
> the wind flings squalls that strike in chance array
> the window's eardrums in its violent train.
> Its sense is spare and airy as the sound
> of gusts of wind and of rain.
> My poem then? God knows what it may mean:
> for unexpressed remains what's most profound.

The opening lines could go differently:

> I write
> the sky
> the wind flings round and steely drops that spray
> the window's eardrums time and time again.

---

362. On June 18, 1943, there were 4,277 Jews in Vught, including 212 children younger than sixteen years.

363. David is referring to Kurt Adrian.

Summer

(June 29, 1943–September 1, 1943)

By the first day of the summer of 1943, over 81,000 Jews had been deported from the Netherlands. During the spring of 1943, twelve trains had left for Sobibor carrying over 21,000 Jews, and one had carried almost 300 privileged Jews to Theresienstadt. In one year, the Germans had reduced the Jewish community to two-fifths of its original size. Vught also had declined in size. In the beginning of May the camp had over 8,600 Jewish inmates. Seven weeks later half of them had been sent to Sobibor.

Tuesday, June 29 [1943].[364] Reinecke and Ettlinger, dressed in overalls, are hunting. Female guard †?[365] Oh, shock and shame, I haven't written in ten days. I'll have to summarize briefly: on an evil day the order came to empty the storehouse. Everybody in a panic of dissipation. Everything was stolen in full view of Saathoff, who paid no attention to what was happening. Somebody walks out carrying a box. People jump him and tear it open. Contents scattered. The floor of the hallway is white, covered with oats, people with sanctimonious faces everywhere, with their hands at the level of their midriffs and bulging shirts. A disgusting performance in which shame, shyness, and greed contend in my mind and in full view of Saathoff I drag away several boxes of tomato juice, which, like all foodstuffs, are returned the next day. I did share in other people's booty: fondants, oatmeal, woolen clothes that were in the attic.

This evening: a prisoner [is introduced] with a drum roll, dressed as a woman, the clothes of a woman draped over his flat-chested, narrow-hipped body, wearing a wig, revolting.[366]

---

364. On June 25, 1943, Vught held 4,276 Jews, among them 207 children younger than sixteen years.

365. It is unclear if Reinecke and Ettlinger were chasing after the female guard. David identified her in his text with a cross sign followed by a question mark.

366. This prisoner had made an attempt to escape in women's clothes.

Saturday, July 3 [1943].[367] Right now it's impossible for me to write at length about the events of the last two weeks. So a summary. Instead of in the storeroom worked in the *Effektenkamer*, sorting out dirty, shitty laundry.[368] The stench nauseated me. Not bad for a poet and philosopher. Together with the almighty Lehmann, whom I love with a sentimental Vught-inspired love, I'm working for the [Ph]ilips Meeting.[369] I viewed the Philips workplace with him. Were guided around like distinguished visitors.

I'm starting work Monday. And the humble work means a big comedown for me, of course. In the meantime I made a reservation for Mother [to work at the Philips workshop], which has led to conflict in the women's camp. Conversations with Drukker, who falls ever more into a childish impotence, a consequence of the fact that he's never been able to obtain a firm footing here, which in itself used to be a strength but now has changed into its opposite.[370] That's the conclusion Alfred and I have come to. We also concluded that the toughness I exhibit is a synthesis of strength and weakness.

Sunday, July 4 [1943]. Yesterday I found a very sweet letter from Nettie, who prepares our parcels with unbelievable diligence. Our parcels are famous here, and everybody is aware of the luxurious way in which we live. Everybody also admires the friendship shown to us. Nikkelsberg composes resounding poems in French that greatly touch me. He's in ecstasy when he reads them out loud and says: "That's great, eh? Do you sense how great it is?"[371] And repeats a passage. His poems and Karel's upbeat messages stimulated me to write this week. But I had absolutely no opportunity. Last Sunday I pictured myself calmly bringing my diary up-to-date and writing verses. But not a chance: barracks to be cleaned out. I managed to get out of it in the morning through a conversation with Lehmann, but in the afternoon no chance. A day completely wasted.

367. On July 2, 1943, Vught held 4,276 Jews, including 206 children younger than sixteen years.
368. The *Effektenkammer* was the room where the internees' clothes were stored.
369. A group of Jewish inmates involved in the negotiations to have Jews admitted to the Philips workshop.
370. David is referring to Willem Drukker, not Syl Drukker.
371. David obtained many of these poems and had them smuggled out to Karel van het Reve, who preserved them with the diary. One of them, dedicated to David, ends as follows: "Remain just what you are, and poet too by right, / Remain the tender friend, remain the man of dreams. / So act that all your thoughts can set your soul alight: / The unreal rivals true great happiness it seems." Translation by John Irons.

Last week at night: a stream of airplanes to which there seemed to be no end. An air-raid warning in the distance that was followed by a long tone, exactly a quarter of an hour in length: the highest state of alarm. It was the night the invasion was announced.[372] Alfred to me in the middle of the night: "I have a lot of faith in your premonitions: is this really the beginning of the end?" And I: "Not at all." And to Van Leer: "This seems so much like the invasion that I'm immediately as skeptical about this particular instance as I am with respect to the concept of invasion itself."[373]

Van Leer has turned out to be a lot better than expected, by the way. A good comrade, with a fine sense of humor and a sound, sharp, and fair sense of judgment. Our friend Mossel appears to be a fool, and we think that Mussel is too rude a nickname for him. He has a watch with three bands of numbers. The outside one, says Van Leer, is to measure the speed of ships. Useful to have that here in Vught, says Van Leer: "He thinks he'll go to Poland by ship." His actual name is Professor Pipi. Materia medica.[374]

But all of this is catching up on what I should have written down right away. Here's the big news: last week: evening roll call. The commandant in attendance, which is an exceptionally bad sign. Although sometimes it is only to flog a couple of prisoners. This evening he's there for us. All industry groups are dismissed. Also half Aryans, etc. The others are registered. Max among them, although he could easily have lined up with some group or other. But we Kokers don't have the courage for that. We marched off. Father in a state. "They won't send my dear boy to Poland, will they?" This bookish, sentimental means of expression comes naturally to him. That evening we feared the worst. Even though all sorts of prominent people had been standing in line. The rest of the week there were official and unofficial reassurances. Lehmann extremely irritated by the pessimism. The slogan of the *Kommandantur:* "There will be no more transports from this camp." The Moerdijk group returns. I sound out Lehmann about this. He's angry because people are worrying about that. On the contrary, the official announcement is now: the prisoners are leaving,

---

372. It is not clear to which invasion David is referring. The invasion of Sicily did not occur until the night of July 9, 1943.

373. The chemist Isaac Simon van Leer (1915–45) was deported to Auschwitz in June 1944 and died in Wüstegiersdorf camp shortly before the end of the war.

374. The German word *pipi* translates into English as "pee." Mossel was interested in urine.

and the Jews will do all the work in the camp. No prisoner's uniforms (people have been worrying about that all week).

Last week sat at a table facing Dr. Rosenthal of the Jewish Council.[375] Someone gives him a request for parcels. He, grinning sardonically: "Oh, never mind. No answer required, mister." And I: "Why not? Won't there be any more parcels?" He: "Oh, there may well be more, but (grin widening) 1,600 people will leave here tomorrow." Quiet for a moment. He looks like a comedian. In a boastful tone: "Everybody who's not working in industry. All the children, the whole Moerdijk group, the whole registration list." We still don't believe it. He seems to be saying it with too much pleasure. I calmly finish my hot meal (my predilection for finishing things doesn't let me leave it), go on my way, and get confirmation of the message from Wolff.[376] Over to Spitz, who gets to work with exaggeratedly energetic gestures. And who truly goes and does great things. Really takes the job onto himself. Like Atlas carrying the world on his shoulders. Puts Max on the reserved list. Feel a bit relieved. That evening the call-up comes through. Alfred and I worked on the Philips side of the operation all day. We're up until one, one thirty. There's a call-up for Max. The following morning Mother comes over right away. Every time we believe anew that it's irrevocable. But this time completely. So I have little hope. I ask someone who's willing to go voluntarily whether he'll trade places. Together with Mother cool my heels waiting to speak with Lehmann. He says come back at eleven and nudges me encouragingly. Back in line at eleven, a good deal more reassured. Half the camp is prepared to go voluntarily. Rumors: trades are taking place, trades aren't taking place. In the meantime some of the people who're on my list of recommendations turn out definitely to be skilled craftsmen. Afterwards I think I must have been crazy to believe that everything will go exactly as it ought to. . . . I'm very close to crying. Max is very grim, has packed everything, but also wept up a storm. We can already see him going by himself: a small, determined boy on his way to Poland. We do believe he'll make it. The most recent Philips list has not been accepted. We get a priority note from Otto Wolff. Cool our heels again for hours. The secretary of the prisoners' camp kicks and punches people out of his way. People don't retaliate, just as they wouldn't if he belonged to the SS. Süss-

375. David is referring to the physician A. Roosendaal.
376. The German-Jewish refugee Otto Wolff seems to have survived.

kind screams an order to clear the room. People stop working. He wrestles with men and women. Confronting one of them, he takes off his jacket. Lehmann calmly keeps on working. Finally I'm able to ask him via his wife. He shakes his head. Half an hour later I ask again. Negative once more. Wolff says: "Just wait." And we wait. Partly because we can't leave. And Mrs. Lehmann comes towards us and says: "Give me the summons for a moment." Motions us to come along with her and then says: "You can go, it's been fixed." We ask her to repeat this. I congratulate everybody, go to the barrack, throw myself on my bed and immediately fall asleep. Mrs. Lehmann seems to have made a very strong plea, but Lehmann was thinking about the matter in any case, and if Max hadn't been released that morning, it probably would have happened that afternoon.

Other than that, worked in the afternoon on behalf of the Drukkers, who have to leave because of the unfortunate coincidence of the Barneveld list.[377] Willem Drukker exhibits an unbelievable degree of laxity and resignation. Apparently there's nothing to be done. They're gone in the realization that it was bad faith. I believed that too, but now I know better. It was not possible, in fact. No fiddles took place that day. And that people favored their friends is perhaps indefensible, but it certainly can't be challenged.

Wednesday, July 7 [1943]. Quiet days. The absence of rumors is already enough for happiness. It is true that the mood is very pessimistic. Seventy percent of the people believe we'll be gone in two weeks. Reinecke said something about the people who aren't craftsmen. In itself that would already be bad enough, but now it's inspiring every possible hypothesis.

I still miss young Drukker a lot. He gave me a certain courage to act decisively, and on the other hand, his devotion really strengthened me. I don't feel friendship for him so much as a strong solidarity cre-

---

377. There were two country houses in Barneveld that served, together with the Villa Bouchina in Doetinchem, as internment camps for seven hundred "deserving Jews" protected by Karel Johan Frederiks, the senior Dutch civil servant in charge of the Ministry of the Interior, and, indirectly, by General Commissioner for Special Projects Fritz Schmidt. Frederiks had been able to make a list of Jews to be exempted from deportation by exploiting the rivalry between Hanns Albin Rauter, general commissioner of the security forces and the highest SS officer in the Netherlands, and Schmidt, who represented the Nazi Party in the Netherlands and who sought to limit the influence of the SS. Schmidt died in an accident on June 20, 1943, and this marked the beginning of the end of the Barneveld list.

ated by the circumstances. Also affection and above all solicitousness. In comparison with him I feel wiser, older, more experienced, but less strong.

Philips continues to keep me waiting. With every day that passes I lose out on a bowl of delicious food.[378] The good midday meal is never the chief association I make when I think about the matter, but it *is* a very important secondary consideration. That's what this place turns you into! Mother is going there next week. Max too. That's not bad. Yesterday received letters from Karel and Nettie. They've gone missing. Here the contents. Nettie: she is so happy to be in a milieu in which people talk about me. That gives her mental support. A very nice letter. Her care for us is really touching. My love for her is becoming like my love for all my friends, male and female. Where will it lead? It *is* remarkable.

That reminds me: that I have a sweetheart here in the camp, whom I find extraordinarily attractive physically. A girl of 18 with the appearance of a 23-year-old.[379] I had noticed her quite a while ago, and many times,

> I noted the brief glance of rapt attention
> She gave me as I was about to pass.

Mother introduced us to each other at the concert a while ago. I don't know what she had in mind. Probably nothing. But she may have intended something. Since that time we smile sweetly at each other.

> So don't be sad and frightened, my young lass.
> We've sized each other up, no false intention
> And both of us know what that signifies.

Mother: "A nice girl, but just a bit hysterical. She can't do without a man." Actually, that's what she says herself. This is our Vught cynicism, Mother's, the girl's, and mine. I enjoy playing along with the sensual game. Even though you notice little of the sexual side here, to what extent your tastes are physical becomes clear when your eye

---

378. This is the meal known as *Philiprak* or *Philipsprak*.

379. David is referring to Hannelore (Hannie) Hess. See the entry on the Hess family in the appendix.

happens to spot a shapely figure. That's all we need. We're just like the prisoners. The young lady is on the Philips reserve list. Very likely we'll talk at greater length there. I think: a woman should leave me my freedom, right? Something like that strikes me as acceptable. On the other hand: perhaps this is all Vught prisoner impudence, and in Amsterdam I'll know calm and faithful happiness again. Perhaps this will later turn out to be one of the most characteristic passages of my diary.

Little news in Karel's letter. A good joke. It's becoming quiet around him. No lads, no Jews. It seems we still had ration coupons. Cor has a poet friend.[380] The sonnets will go to Strasbourg. The text of "Ännchen von Tharau."[381]

Blüth and Cohen are here today.[382] The nervous camp is already making the most somber prognoses with the greatest sense of certainty. Yesterday evening Lehmann asked me to get Mrs. N[eumann] something with Philips. Good to be asked to perform a service. So long as I'm not at work yet I'll probably be in the secretariat. No more sorting of dirty laundry. Nor peeling potatoes like yesterday. Assigned to it because of working in the clothes storage room. The second time in my life. Once for the commandant of North Brabant. Now from 7 to 12, 1:15 to 6:45. Harassed by a louche 17-year-old *Kapo* (Hollander), who in his own way had a certain unspoiled quality. Joined by a larger part of corruption, of course. By the way, on such an occasion you get a demonstration that there's no other possible way of managing the prisoners. Although harassed and threatened by an SS man, yet in quiet moments the *Kapos* try to do something, secretly give away bread and hot food. But out of pure fear they also hit people in the face, and they're almost always yelling. In the course of just one day it becomes clear that the whole prisoner society is much rawer than our group. In any case, I knew about it from the hours of conversation I had with Flip Monnikendam at the time of the second Westerbork transport, when he had to leave.

It's a very long time ago now, but I want to write for a moment about the optimistic, flippant impression he made. Just as though

380. Cor Israël was Tini Israël's brother. In 1943 he was sent to Strasbourg as a forced laborer. There he met Alfred Kossmann (1922–95). In 1941 Kossmann published a volume of poetry and after the war became a well-known poet and novelist. In 1980 he received the prestigious Constantijn Huygens Prize for his contribution to Dutch literature.
381. "Annie of Tharau" is a German folk song of the seventeenth century.
382. David is referring to Dr. David Cohen, cochairman of the Jewish Council.

his thinking and feeling were separated from reality by a glass wall. No worries about the future. "Too bad I have to leave here, this place has been good to me. And what happens next . . ." A smile and an unfinished gesture.[383]

> It was as if a glass wall came to stand
> between himself and all reality
> . . .
> a laugh and certain movement of his hand
> . . . that day
> as agile as the birds up in the sky
> his rapid words, his laugh that did not stay.

Just called by Blüth to meet him. [illegible] in Amsterdam are moving. A terrible fright. A few stories about T,[384] talking to Philips people: "You can listen to it better on the 80-meter band." To the tailors: "At night, don't turn the English station up so high that everyone outside can hear it." Meeting of industry group leaders: "If you do half of what I say, I'll be satisfied. And don't think I've been so friendly lately because Germany has already lost the war. . . ." A friendly fellow, paternal towards the guys who work under him. One who perceives the catastrophe but suffers as a result. And doesn't hide it.—People are preparing themselves for a transport. On the basis of nothing, actually. This afternoon Jewish Council meeting. The last transport began the same way. Cohen is here. People think that's a bad sign. In fact, nothing seems to be the matter.

Sunday, July 11 [1943].[385] Yesterday the long-awaited transport from Westerbork. Fifty-six men all told. Among them Werner Snoek, who had interesting news about all the folks in Westerbork.[386] Also a letter from Syl Drukker.—Spoke with Cohen for half an hour. He'll propose me for Palestine documents.[387] They're in fashion at this moment.—

---

383. After his arrival in Westerbork Philip (Flip) Monnikendam was included in a transport to Sobibor. He was murdered on May 28, 1943.

384. David is referring to SS-Untersturmführer Karl Friedrich Titho.

385. On July 9, 1943, Vught held 2,778 Jews, including 34 children younger than sixteen years.

386. The German-Jewish refugee Werner Snoek (1917–43) was killed in Auschwitz.

387. During the British Mandate of Palestine, Jews could enter Palestine as legal immigrants if they had a Palestine Certificate. When in September 1939 war broke out, the British government feared that the German intelligence services would use the certificates to

Meanwhile Mother has started working for Philips. I'm still waiting for the result. I'm best friends with Lehmann. Asked me to intercede for Mrs. Neumann at Philips. The world is a strange place and especially here in Vught. Long ago they established a Jewish Council here. It had grown to be a big department, which existed because it served to shield a number of people who worked there *and* by virtue of the fact that the Germans showed no interest in it. After the last transport, only one man is left of the entire flourishing enterprise. It was located in an empty room with curious constructions of benches and tables. Signs hung from the ceiling above the tables: Legal Department, Financial Department, Censorship. Saathoff came in and said: "What's all this? We don't need this. This is a labor camp." As for me, I always find such comments very appealing. There had just been a JC meeting (with Cohen), and Saathoff sat down in one of the stuffed chairs that had been very nicely arranged there. And sat there, holding forth: the Netherlands declared war on Germany, the Jews are to blame for the war.[388] The queen left on May 11 at nine in the evening.[389] We have to work and pay. He's never seen a Jew who worked. Germany will win the war. Camps in Poland are labor camps.

smuggle agents into British territory and ceased to recognize the validity of the certificates of Jews from Germany and German-occupied territories. Yet the certificates continued to promise a way out of Nazi Europe. In 1942 the Germans began to identify Dutch holders of the certificate with the aim of exchanging them for German nationals interned in Palestine. When these Jews were exempted from deportations it became clear that the certificates might offer real protection. The authorities in Palestine learned about this through the Swiss and decided to issue a list with the names of people eligible for new certificates. This list reached the Netherlands on May 21, 1943. Since the Jewish Council decided which Jews were to be exempt from deportation, and since a Palestine Certificate had become a de facto exemption, Dr. Cohen had influence on whose names would be proposed. In the end, 1,297 people received certificates. David was not among them. Of the 1,297 "Palestinians," 1,100 were interned in Bergen-Belsen. Of those, 222 left that camp on June 29, 1944. They traveled by train to Istanbul, and on July 10, 1944, they reached Haifa. While the train with the 222 "Palestinians" crossed the Balkans on its way to Istanbul, another train with 499 traveled from Vught to Auschwitz. David was one of those 499 deportees. See Presser, *Destruction of the Dutch Jews*, 293ff; Oppenheim, *Chosen People*.

388. Germany invaded the neutral Netherlands in the early morning of May 10, 1940. In a meeting between the German ambassador and the Dutch foreign minister, the former justified the attack by referring to an upcoming invasion by the Allies. He did not mention the word "war." In response, the Dutch foreign minister told him that, "in view of the outrageous German attack on the Netherlands . . . a state of war has arisen between the Kingdom and Germany." As for Jewish responsibility for the war: this was Nazi claptrap.

389. When the queen and the government left the Netherlands on May 13, 1940, to create a government-in-exile in London, the majority of the Dutch felt betrayed. Nazi propaganda portrayed the departure as an abandonment of a position of responsibility: the Dutch deserved better rulers. As the war progressed, Dutch public opinion changed, and the action of the queen and government found understanding.

Conditions comparable with those of the prisoners here. (SS people have said that the Jews in Poland earn money, that there's a canteen where you can get more things than in the SS canteen). Alfred and I say: "Maybe we'll be overcome by amazement if we should ever get there." I do believe that. After all, the English radio station tells such exaggerated tales about Vught, that the tales about Poland will probably turn out to be of the same caliber.[390] Saathoff also said that the Jews were badly scared when that bomb was dropped here a while ago. Martin R[oman] the apple polisher: "They crapped their pants." Rolf L. begins to quarrel with him about this while Saathoff is still there. Saathoff gets up to leave. Roman gives L. a little push as a kind of joke, and in response L. slaps his face hard. The whole camp applauds that.

Thursday, July 15 [1943]. In some respects we're living here in a society that is harsh in a sympathetic way. The *Lagerälteste* [senior inmate] of the prisoners, the bull-necked one, is in bed with five knife wounds. The prisoners say the *Kapos* very probably did it. The *Kapos* say he must have knifed himself to show the Germans how tough he is. In any case he's in the bunker now for homosexual activities.

A *Kapo* with whom I've had a lot of dealings lately is Ome Piet [Uncle Pete], the gatekeeper in the industrial area.[391] Yesterday a prisoner said: "He's a homosexual, priest, and madman." A big, sunburned old fellow with glasses, who bellows at everybody and makes jokes while he bellows. He hurries out of his guardhouse and yells:

390. David's observation must be understood in the context of both the atrocity propaganda from World War I and the particular disinformation about Vught current in 1943. The most notorious symbol of the war atrocities is the gruesome but false account of the *Kadaververwertungsanstalt* (corpse utilization establishment) that the Germans were reportedly operating behind the front lines, making soap from corpses. The story of the *Kadaververwertungsanstalt* was the centerpiece of Arthur Ponsonby's best-selling *Falsehood in War-Time* (1928) and triggered widespread indignation and resentment. As a result, during World War II reports of German atrocities were commonly viewed as exaggerations. In February 1943 an article appeared in the underground newspaper *De Oranjekrant* entitled "'t Martelkamp te Vught" (Torture Camp in Vught). "Vught! The most degrading acts, the most sadistic cruelties are now connected to the reputation of that village." It described the camp as a "sea of tears and blood" and the "mire of the most perfidious tortures." Arriving Jews were kicked and bayoneted to death. "Every day prisoners collapse as corpses. . . . Every day crack the shots of the execution squads." And so on. Vught was not a holiday camp, but it had little in common with the description of the place in this article, which became the source of a news item on the BBC. Taking his own experience as a point of departure, David could make the reasonable assumption that the stories about the camps in the East might be exaggerated too. See Ponsonby, *Falsehood in War-Time;* Read, *Atrocity Propaganda;* Lipstadt, *Beyond Belief;* Rijksinstituut voor Oorlogsdocumentatie, *Het Woord als Wapen,* 181–83.
391. David is referring to Piet van der Toren.

"Just a moment! You're going to be photographed!" Or: "Hey, don't be in such a rush, it'll soon be peacetime." A call is heard: "*Rijks-duitsers* withdraw."[392] He: "So what am I? I'm a German national, I'm Dutch, I'm nothing." There are days he's nervous. Then you have to be careful with him. Then he roars and he rages. You have to accept him the way you accept an animal.

More and more our parcels are being prepared by Nettie. They're perfect. Mother has been asking for more without my knowledge, and in that way she seems to have irritated the people in Amsterdam a bit. Me a whole lot, in any case. Alfred: "I'd rather go hungry than ask for anything." I feel the same way. And certainly when they show this kind of care. Life together with my family isn't all that easy. It keeps me from pursuing a style and insights of my own.

The small transport from Westerbork is here. There was a letter for me from Syl Drukker.[393]

We had to take a bath one evening a few days ago. It was like a painting by Sluyters.[394] A beautiful and chaste scene. Unexpectedly beautiful, about fifty of us in the splashing water. Mosquitoes, because of the dampness. Jumping and laughing in the warm soapy water. Haven't experienced this in five months here. Alfred was completely beside himself. I said: "I'd be happy to sit in this shower for a couple of hours, to talk philosophy."

Yesterday the meal was really good, boiled peeled potatoes, cucumber and leaf lettuce, and meat gravy. Einhorn, the king of the concentration camp,[395] talked about a protest action in The Hague.[396] Today the food was as good as it has ever been. Just with gravy.

Timekeeper since Monday [at Philips], secretary on top of that, in fact. Nothing much to do in either function. But it may become pleasant. Because people do strange things around here. They put someone in a position and then suddenly remove him from it again.

---

392. The Dutch noun *Rijksduitser* (Reich German) referred to a German who was a citizen of the German Reich. A *Volksduitser* (ethnic German) was an ethnic German who was a citizen of another country.

393. Syl Drukker had been sent to Westerbork on July 2, 1943.

394. Jan Sluijters (1881–1957) was an important Dutch painter of the interwar period. In 1941 the Stedelijk Museum (Municipal Museum) in Amsterdam hosted a large retrospective exhibition of his works.

395. David is referring to the banker Burech (Bolo) Einhorn. See the entry on Einhorn in the appendix. He had been wealthy and thanks to bribes was able to live a life of relative comfort in Vught. Hence inmates referred to him as the king of Vught. Einhorn died in Mauthausen a few days after the end of the war.

396. It is not clear to which protest action Einhorn might have referred.

Monday, July 19 [1943].[397] I spent the week keeping time. Philips meals good. We have too much bread. And so we are drunk on bread. After a long workday, which has been systematized in every conceivable way and is nevertheless completely empty, it's a madhouse in the dormitory at night. Fighting with Max Cahen, who is partly to blame for this idiocy.[398] Actively and passively. Passively: because he, a somewhat older man, still walks around with a stiff collar, bow tie, and a nice suit, leaves the camp practically whenever he pleases, is a bit deaf, and has potatoes brought to him in bed.[399] Actively because he's a good-natured life-of-the-party type who likes to use affectedly crude language. And all that with his rather helpless bespectacled face. At night we lie there gabbing until all hours. A kind of prisoner mentality, which is, of course, encouraged by our association with those people. Compared with them we're ambitious. In our case, someone with intelligence and status will try to get a job, which will give him the chance to work himself to death through sheer excellence. In their case, the important thing is to be in a place where you can get as much to eat as possible, do as little work as possible, and, if it can be managed, meet girls and have the means to secure a hold over them. An example of that in the Philips group is our Piet, an impresario, a man of fashion, who hands out the food and openly gives his girlfriend double and triple portions. She has been prematurely put to work on his insistence. Those who are in charge, and who are inclined to be friendly to the girlfriend, can also get more. But if they were not to be friendly there would be the open blackmail threat of in the future no extra ladle, etc. There's another prisoner: Black Jack, a burglar from Amsterdam, who has something going with a dolled-up creature, the daughter of Metzelaar, but who also has another in reserve for use in the camp. . . .

These two sweethearts plus one more make common cause and make Mother's life a bit hard.

I'm busy with a kind of statistical study of the enterprise, in which I'm painfully handicapped by my ineptness and sloppiness. Met the leader of the administration here, an uncommonly intelligent and educated man, whom I immediately recognized in his prisoner's

397. On July 16, 1943, Vught had 2,808 Jews, including 34 children younger than sixteen years.

398. See the entry on Max Cahen in the appendix.

399. Max Cahen was employed as a purchaser for the camp and hence often left the camp, accompanied by a guard.

garb.[400] An exceptional pleasure to speak with him on any subject at all. There are occasional oases like that here. Otherwise the prisoners generally have something lazy and casual and animal-like about them. They hang around in a corner, sing and hum sentimental songs. When a German approaches, they get up, sometimes fleeing through a window, and return ten minutes later to pick up their songs where they left off. We, too, have something of this congenial, anticipatory quality now. Also because for us, just as for them, there is nothing more we can do to increase our safety. It is in any case a continuation of what has existed to this point. For quite some time now, Alfred and I have been speaking in paradoxes, especially when it concerns the condition and security of this camp, and so on. Whoever can say the most elegantly skeptical things has won the game. Moreover, a casual style like that has developed in all areas of discourse. People will notice it in this diary as well. And my letters to Amsterdam seem to be highly appreciated. Last week I mentioned the typical wisdom of stupid women—I couldn't think of a better way of saying it. Although these last months I have been expressing myself with difficulty (physical difficulty, with badly flowing sentences), I have little trouble with mental expression, to use a phrase, have an unbelievable freedom in images and comparisons. That, too, is connected with that strange, flippant quality which is part of our lives and makes this camp seem festive to us all day long, that permits us to play a wilful game with circumstances of which we do know that *in reality* they are exceptionally foul. But it bathes everything in a full, rich light, no one is ashamed of what they do. All of life is thoughtless, aimless, but with respect to all mad antics, purposeful.

The women took a bath, and Reinecke operated the taps. We could have done that too. Because, after all, why not?

By the way, you can also learn other things from the prisoners. There was a leader of the measuring department here, a fellow named Vrins, a tall, handsome guy, fit looking in his blue and white clothes. Being a reserve officer, he still had all his hair.[401] I had noticed him earlier. It's the evening roll call. A prisoner is missing. Erich [Beck], our *Kapo,* is called.[402] So is [Albert B.] Hendriks, our good SS man.

---

400. David is referring to Jan Hendrik (Hein) van Wijk. See the entry on van Wijk in the appendix.

401. See the entry on Theodor Vrins in the appendix. Prisoners of war did not get their heads shaved.

402. See the entry on Erich Beck in the appendix.

Alfred says: "I'll be hanged if it isn't Vrins. And maybe he'll make it. . . . If he's gone, they won't find him."[403] They went out to look for him with *Rijksd[uitse]* OD, dogs, just about every group they could think of. Vrins seems to have said: "Better luck next time." That same week he asked someone for a pair of shoes, that morning he had [his hair] nicely cut, went to the dentist and hasn't been seen since. It's amazing how easily the Germans resigned themselves to it, which did not keep them from making us stand around until midnight. I thought [it would be] until eleven or all night, but was wrong. We sat, lay all over the field, masking the red tips of our cigarettes with our hands. Lineup time and again, shaking awake those who'd gone to sleep whenever the rumor went around that Reinecke or Saathoff was approaching.

Most of the time nothing was happening. The last half hour we stood calmly, because of Saathoff's promise that we'd be allowed to go home if we showed orderly behavior. When your longing is so great, the barrack is a home, something more homelike is unthinkable.—I didn't have as much of a grip on myself as I normally do under similar circumstances. Was very tired and went to bed without eating.

The small transport that has been under discussion for so long has gone now. Rather more than 300 people. They're "special lists." Everyone who has one or more Portuguese grandparents, Aryan ancestors, baptized, mixed married, etc.[404] (Dr. Eul has gone home).[405] Beyond that a roll call to top it up. The strange thing about these transports is the relationship between categories and numbers. I continue to believe that the numbers are dictated by The Hague and Berlin and the (arbitrary) categories by the *Kommandantur.* These fictitious categories have only their names in common with the categories established by the German authorities. If these accord a special right to Jews with four Portuguese grandparents, then it is extended here to everyone who has a bit of Portuguese blood, for the purpose of reaching the required number in an authorized manner. A story did the rounds here, purveyed by Lehmann with a great deal of conviction and seriousness, that all of them, even if they were only a frac-

403. Vrins had tried to cross the North Sea to England in March 1943. He escaped from Vught on July 14.

404. The transport of 317 people left on July 16.

405. It is unclear who Dr. Eul was. It may be that Eul was a nickname. *EuL* was the acronym of the German department *Ernährung und Landwirtschaft* (Nutrition and Agriculture) in The Hague. Dr. Eul must have been an employee who fell afoul of the law.

tion Portuguese, would go to Portugal.[406] Of course they've all been sent on, except those with four [Portuguese grandparents], which it wasn't even necessary to prove. Actually the commandant let them go without eagerness, and Reinecke took people off the train at the last moment, gave cigarettes to R. L., who had to leave, said to others: "It's against my will, but there's no other way."[407] Alfred says: "If Reinecke returns to Poland, I'm going with him." We like him a lot these days. And he looks after us well, that must be said. R.L. went with wife and child. L[illegible], Bril (the boxer), let their children go by themselves.[408] Kan and his three children.[409] On the basis of

406. In the census of 1941, 4,303 people registered themselves as Portuguese Jews. These Jews were known to have descended from so-called Marranos, Christianized Jews. These Marranos had returned to the faith of their ancestors after their departure from the Iberian Peninsula. In 1941 the Marrano element in the genealogy of the Portuguese Jews became the basis of the argument that Portuguese Jews had probably very few racially Jewish ancestors, and because in the Netherlands, Portuguese Jews had generally not married German and Polish Jews, their allegedly largely non-Jewish background would have been preserved. Believing that a reclassification as non-Jews appeared possible, prominent Portuguese Jews commissioned a number of ethnological studies. One, prepared by the University of Amsterdam in July 1943, concluded on the basis of skull measurements that Portuguese Jews "cannot by any stretch of the imagination be classified as Jews and . . . show strong affinities with western Mediterranean races." For some time the Germans were willing to consider this argument. In June 1943 Portuguese Jews with at least seven Portuguese-Jewish great-grandparents received a special exemption. At that time most Portuguese Jews had already been murdered in Auschwitz or Sobibor. A total of 273 of them remained. In February 1944 the Germans rounded them up, sent them to Westerbork, and submitted them to a visual inspection. Judged to be "a subhuman race," all of them ended up in Auschwitz, where they were gassed. Presser, *Destruction of Dutch Jews*, 305–11.

407. David is referring to Rolf Walter Levie. See the entry on Levie in the appendix. He died in Auschwitz.

408. The well-known boxer Barend (Ben) Bril (1912–2003), his wife, Celia (Sara) Bril-Blits (1915–2003), and their son, Abraham Benjamin (Albert) Bril (b. 1937), were interned in Vught on April 16, 1943. Albert was taken to Westerbork on July 16, 1943; his father and mother, seeking to be reunited with their son, followed at the first possible opportunity, on September 11, 1943. The family was protected from deportation to Auschwitz because of Ben's reputation—he was given the task of organizing boxing matches—and because of Celia's American connection: she had lived in the United States as a girl and claimed that she was an American citizen. On the strength of this claim, though fictitious, the Germans sent the Bril family to Bergen-Belsen on February 1, 1944. They remained there until January 21, 1945, when they were included in a transport of 136 Jews with Central and South American passports and sent to Switzerland. They arrived in Switzerland on January 25 and were sent on to Marseilles for transport to the United States. When it became clear that Celia was not in fact an American citizen, the Bril family was interned in a refugee camp in Algeria. They were repatriated to the Netherlands in August 1945.

409. The prominent textile manufacturer Willi Kan (1898–1944), his wife, Susannah Kan-van Minde (1904–1944), and their three children, Daniel (1932–1944), Raphael (1934–1944), and Betsie (1934–1944), were interned in Vught on February 20, 1943. The children left for Westerbork on July 16. Their parents stayed behind, to join them in Westerbork on September 11, 1943. See also note 478.

promises, to be sure, but we know how much *they* are worth, ought to know it, anyway. This is unbelievable. There was a lynch mood in the women's camp, with respect to the various ladies [who let their children go]. Lehmann seems to have prayed with L[illegible]'s child before it left. Something that greatly affected me. I believe he'd be capable of sending L[illegible] away under a pretext.

The night before yesterday we couldn't sleep, no matter how much we talked and horsed around once we were in bed. The blankets and sheets were clammy. Mosquitoes. We lay there panting on top of our bedclothes. Got up at 10:30, went to eat something. In pajamas with big boxes in the dining room. Cracked jokes until we went to bed paralyzed [with fatigue] and fell asleep at once.—The *Kapos* seem to be out of step. Apparently the princely life they've lived here so far was not part of the plan, as I thought it was until now.

Bubi allowed a couple of prisoners whom the *Kapos* had maltreated to flog them. They get it on with Aryan women, but in the middle of the night they're dragged from their beds together with the women who are in there with them. Yesterday evening they had punishment drill. Jumping like frogs and rolling in the sand. The poor *Kapos*. This morning their red badges were mostly gone and they were wearing the colors they were allotted. A lot of green, professional criminals. But Kurt is wearing a green patch, too.[410] All kinds of rumors: there are supposed to have been complaints in The Hague. But people have been saying that for a long time. It was said a couple of days ago that the *Kapos* are not allowed to hit people anymore.

Monday [Wednesday], July 21 [1943]. Because this is a camp with glass walls, if someone gets beaten then Vught knows it that evening and the whole country the next day. This camp is totally Dutch. People seem to have been really serious about establishing a brothel here (just as in Mauthausen and other places), but they didn't dare to go through with it.[411] The *Kapos* have to stay together in one barrack and

410. David is referring to the colored triangular patches that prisoners had to wear on their uniforms. Political prisoners and resistance fighters were issued red patches, convicted criminals green patches, black marketers black patches, and Jews yellow patches (no pink patches denoting homosexuals were issued in Vught). David was rightly surprised, because Kurt Adrian was a political prisoner, and as such he would have worn a red patch.

411. Concerned about the low productivity of concentration-camp inmates, Himmler decided that "industriously laboring prisoners" ought to be given access to camp brothels. The first such brothel was constructed in Mauthausen (June 1942). Other brothels came into operation in Gusen (fall 1942), Auschwitz (June 1943), and Buchenwald (July

can go to bed with each other there or knife each other to death, something they also like to do. It'll undoubtedly be a cage full of wild animals, because there are two parties among them, a decent one under Sep[412] (a Jewish-looking Communist) and its opposite. In the decent one is our Erich, of course, although he has also shown up with a green patch on occasion.

It has happened. We, who have been calling the prisoners "pajamas," or sometimes even "zebras," for such a long time, are wearing striped uniforms ourselves. A rumor had been going around for quite a while. And, of course, all that time it was also contradicted. And as it happened, the rumor was always asserted and denied whenever a transport was going to take place. So, by way of joking about it, we took the news about the uniforms as a bad sign. A joke that typifies the mood here. And a line of argument, characteristic of the situation: the uniforms are the best exemption. During the roll call comes the command: "*Häftlinge stillgestanden*"[prisoners stand at attention]. Alfred and I are very pleased with that, because we don't care for the position of civilian internee.[413] And Van Leer is completely wrong when he says: "They're shouting: '*Sämtliche*' [everyone]. But okay. Yesterday evening: fifteen minutes after roll call, we have to line up. We know what this is all about, tuck our possessions into our beds, and, after hanging up our jackets, find our way to the roll-call area. Everyone to the *Effektenkamer*. Meanwhile a short, orderly column of *Unterscharführers* which marches slowly to our barrack. And the smart ones among us say: they're going to empty our beds. A deadly, deadly, deadly fear. Diary. Treats.[414] Sick with tension. This could put me on the wrong side of the barbed wire. But maybe it won't be so bad. The *Unterscharführers* remain standing there. After a short while a slow procession of horses pulling flatbeds. Calm as if on stage. Blankets, sheets, clothes fall from the windows. I think: everything will be removed at one go;

1943). In Vught a construction crew began with the transformation of a barrack into a brothel. However, it was never brought into operation. See Alakus, Kniefacz, and Vorberg, *Sex-Zwangsarbeit*, 125ff.; No. 469 [Albertus Santegoeds], *De hel op de Vughtse heide*, 118–19.

    412. David is referring to the German Communist Sep Jozef Kaufman. He served as a *Kapo*.

    413. Alfred Spitz and David believed that Jewish civilian inmates had no status in the camp system, but that those who were officially registered in the protective custody section of Vught, the so-called *Häftlinge*, were protected from deportation to Poland. Hence they welcomed any assimilation into the regular prisoner population, even if this meant that they would have to wear striped prisoner uniforms.

    414. This refers to the secret letters he had received from Karel, Tini, Fré, and Nettie. Their discovery might have had dire consequences for him.

there's no personal danger. Meanwhile the first group of men strip to the buff. Disappear into the *Effektenkamer* and return in zebra suits, nice and bright. A bit strange. They look like sick people who've gotten out of bed for the first time. Lehmann: so small, thin, old, and clownish. Later he was given some nice overalls. The lines of men are crowding forward or are preoccupied by the appearance of the German carts. I no longer think about the garb. No more fear, either. Just regret about the diary. All has been for nothing. Saathoff shoots into the air twice. Running in a gasping frenzy. Strip completely. A handkerchief, socks, shoes, belt, and a few more things. A strange exhibition, because we put on our belts. An all-too-modernistic painting. If it didn't go the way it was supposed to, a renewed sound of slapping. The new clothes in a big pile. Meet Th[eo] Enklaar, who touched me deeply through his spontaneous devotion.[415] A good jacket and shirt, but the pants were too long. When I emerged the stripes made me dizzy. Later: back to the barrack. A scene of appalling devastation: blankets, sheets, broken jars of food, wrecked boxes on the floor. Some beds completely stripped. On my bed I found my small boxes and a letter from Karel. I sat up and heard myself say: "It's all still here, it's all still here." Lost relatively little. But many were robbed of everything. Not just clothes. In one evening we've become dirt poor. But our family seems to be above these accidents, as it were. Our luck keeps on being uncommonly good.

> So seated at my twilight windowpane
> I write the verse that ends my useless day
> the wind flings round and steely drops that spray
> the window's eardrums time and time again.
>
> My sense is spare and dismal as the sound
> of sudden gusts of wind and splashing rain
> my poem then? God knows what it may mean—
> for unexpressed remains what's most profound.
>
> And yet: it is the tenderness maybe
> with which I sometimes wait and think of lines
> that stops this place from suffocating me.

415. The *Häftling* Theodor Enklaar was the *Kapo* of the storeroom of camp uniforms.

And down the drainpipes I hear water seep
and write the verse that in the silence cries
when in weak moments I can sometimes weep.

Reinecke cycles past, says to W.: "You're looking good." Has a good
laugh and shouts to the crowd: "And yet you still won't believe you're
staying here." If that's the first association he makes and he also expresses it at once, he must harbor a remarkable concern and care
for us. Anyway, Alfred and I are filled with a sort of fondness for him,
which [is] part affectation but also based in reality.

Slept deeply that night, woke up drenched with sweat. In my un-
derwear, among my possessions, books, boxes, papers. In my pigsty,
as we say. "Others have a dovecote two stories up, I have a pigsty," we
say. The following evening, numbers were handed out, a 90-minute
process that the camp leadership screwed up in the most inept way possible.[416] They started counting, and as a result of their fatigue people
evidently had a fine instinct for what was essential and what wasn't, so
that, in fact, they refused to obey. Reinecke showed up when everything was supposed to be finished and nothing had been started yet.
Proposed we get some exercise, whereupon P[417] made us play a game
of "get down, get up" that lasted about 20 minutes. Also included was
rolling around and jumping like frogs. This last he himself demonstrated very nicely. Said to Van West: "You're looking at me as if you'd
like to hurt me. Here's my revolver. Go ahead and shoot. My heart's
right here." In the end they agreed that he would shoot in the air.
No success, because the safety was on. Slapped him, with the words:
"Give it back to me." To the panting, dusty throng: "You numskulls,
you could have been in your barracks a long time ago." The air was
thundercloud black with dust. It was getting dark. The Germans were
friendly and reasonable. Like people who know they're in the right.
As they were that evening. And by far the most competent of anyone there. Süsskind also had to lie on the ground for a bit. Which
he promptly did, smiling and with many jokes and hesitations after
he was already lying down. One of ours shouted: "Mr. Lehmann."
Whereupon P[annicke], more in amusement than entirely on principle: "What's that? Mr. Lehmann? Prisoner Lehmann, please."

    416. David's registration number was 15,169. He received a slip to be sown onto his uni-
form. In Vught numbers were not tattooed on the arm; that was an Auschwitz specialty.
    417. David is referring to SS-Oberscharführer Kurt Pannicke.

Tuesday, July 27 [1943]. We have some miserable days behind us. Especially the women. But we men as well. Broken, by the escape-time roll call, the clothing exchange, and the exercise evening. Added to it: earlier morning roll call: up at four. For practical purposes that means a quarter to five. But all day long that glassy feel of sleepiness stays with us. And now we have the dog days too.

The women, who were ordered to turn in all their clothes but refused, had to stay in all Sunday with closed windows. Showed up at Philips the next day. Upset. Had hung around and sat at tables half-naked; it must have been a disgustingly sticky business. The reason was that they had thrown things over the fence when they thought they would be subjected to a body search. Reinecke gave them a terrible dressing-down. They're now subject to the FKL,[418] which also makes them very nervous. The gate is closed and they now have to pass through the concentration camp to get to their barracks. Anyway, the whole business of the clothes is much worse for them. Sanders gave a speech yesterday, in which he cheered them up.[419] Right afterwards the daily production of the capacitor factory jumped.[420] The question of the production and the intrigues surrounding it is interesting. Mother and Silb[er]mann seem to favor high production.[421] Less because of opportunistic considerations than because of uncompromising seriousness. The prisoners are very apprehensive about the work performance of the Jews. Fear higher demands will be made of them as a result. So make oblique remarks if someone picks up two tabletops instead of one. In particular they're afraid that screwdrivers on the radio assembly line will make the work go more quickly. On the other hand, there are production intrigues among the Jews themselves. In these matters Alfred assumes a pithy point of view. Is very talented politically. You can have an excellent discussion of these matters with Van Wijk. I read him sections from my diary and gave him some verses. In any case, the former really pleased him. Gave me an interesting statement of his thoughts about what I've called vitrification, and we both have called exposure of the nerves.

418. FKL stands for *Frauenkonzentrationslager* (women's concentration camp)

419. David is referring to the businessman Combrecht Bernard (Gerard) Sanders. See the entry on Sanders in the appendix. He died in Langenbielau camp.

420. A capacitor is a common electronic component. The Philips workshop in Vught produced capacitors, transformers, radio tubes, electric shavers, and dyno-torches.

421. David is referring to the Polish-Jewish engineer Arnold Silbermann. See the entry on Silbermann in the appendix. He died in Langenbielau.

Someone with the same analytical interest in the concentration-camp
phenomenon that I have. And who up to this point has also experienced this camp, especially Philips. Also a conversation with him
about the prisoners' idleness. I'm also beginning to make my peace
with it. Talk all day long with everybody here. Either as part of my
duty (with Van Wijk, Sanders, Lehmann), or mostly emerging from
it. With the same people. Vegetate, vegetate. And outside, a fierce
light. The girls taking the soldering course next to me are working at
an easy pace, or huddle together when the power is off again.[422]

[Friday] August 6 [1943]. I haven't written for a long time, although
I'm my own boss here for twelve hours per day, more or less. But who
am I, and what's to be said of me? I'm drawing graphs assigned to me
by Van Wijk. And am not his slave, but my own. Yesterday evening
conversation with Alfred. About the ultimate. Also about Tini.[423] And
discover what she means to me. How being away from that atmosphere has stripped from me the varnish that was so beneficial. How
my nerves are exposed again. How I do everything in an extreme way,
walk around tense and tortured. Act as if I were crazy, as Alfred says,
and don't have a word to spare for Mother. And still make mistakes.
And don't do all that much. But dead tired in the evening. At noon
we eat in a stinking wooden shed. But I lie in the meadow. Anyway,
the weather's been unsettled the last few days. Meanwhile I've been
in the hospital for a couple of days. The runs. Enteritis, as we say.
And I hadn't been there for half an hour before the same thoughts
of four months ago [came to me]. Thoughts of Nettie, of walks with
her through Amsterdam. Went to the hospital in a procession. "The
sky looks doleful, rain is on the way. . . ." etc.

The women here receive good news with the joyfulness worthy of
a family event. I feel ever more unsuited for any kind of work. Above
all I'm too full of rage, too neurotic.

422. With this sentence David ended his entries in the exercise book in which he had
kept his diary from June 3, 1943. Remarkably, although the exercise book contained another nine pages, David did not use them. Considering the fact that David never wasted any
paper, one must assume that he found an opportunity on July 27, or in the days that followed, to have this exercise book, and the earlier parts of the diary written on loose sheets
of paper, smuggled to Karel.
423. It is not clear if David is referring to Karel's girlfriend, Tini Israël, or to his fellow
inmate Albertina (Tini) Lansberg, who appears frequently in his diary from September
1943 onward. See the entry on the Lansberg family in the appendix.

Last week another prisoner was gone. Another Philips worker. People had to stand until 10:30, on roll call (I was sick in bed), one group had to get down and get up, and the whole crowd had to sing patriotic songs. Yesterday evening we were supposed to return at seven. Probably to lug bricks. Because of the rain it was canceled. Now it'll probably be this evening. Neumann.

Now Süsskind is in the [Philips] concern too. Teitelbaum was called, but Van Wijk gave him an earful.[424] With the help of [Laman] Trip, the women got new overalls, that is to say, those who were not appropriately dressed. Don't say: "That he had already gotten some." B[raakman] managed to make the case. He also managed, again backed up by T[rip], to secure the return of fountain pens and mechanical pencils.[425]

[Saturday] August 7 [1943]. Yesterday evening lineup at seven. Should have been the evening before but canceled because of rain. Big processions of work detachments. But only a few chosen. And we the only Jewish detachment. And the last. The SS man at the gate: "Bad luck, guys." Through the gate to the open field in the woods, houses there, nice and red under the pine trees. Quiet and mysterious. I've always been interested in the houses and the area behind the *Kommandantur.* An amiable *Kapo,* who took a very businesslike view of things. While keeping a straight face, shovel a shallow layer of sand on the wagon, and then the wagon leaves. Saw the pint-sized Rudolf for the first time [since he left us]. And right away: "You're organizing [things], but in the wrong way." Five wagons (with two horses each) and eight shovels (for 35 men, at first 2). The joke: this is work therapy. And it doesn't even have any objectives. So we wait calmly, hands on our backs, leaning against a tree. And talk. And laugh. And now and then, when someone has shoveled ten spades full of sand, take the shovel from him. Or from pure sporting spirit take hold of one of the unused shovels. One prisoner: "I'm part of the keep-the-horses-calm detachment." Another: "These horses are just like prisoners, enjoying the sweet mild air." Some of us are actually working fairly hard. Under the leadership of Sanders, who can't

424. David is referring to the German-Jewish refugee Jacob Teitelbaum. It appears that he survived the war.

425. Rutger Egbert Laman Trip and Carel Braakman were Philips executives.

help himself, here or at Philips. Wants to boost production there on his own, which leads to discussions with Alfred. He brings all of the Twente industriousness with him.[426] Therefore lectures the personnel, but also pushes a wagon around in the evening. *Chillul Hashem* [blasphemy].[427]

When we were lined up, the prisoners behind us: "Look how serious the Jews are looking." There is a Philips construction detachment: prisoners and Jews. The *Kapo* doesn't let anyone take any of his Jews away from him, says Oster, the labor service leader. [Friedrich] Meyerhof[f], the *Oberscharführer* at Moerdijk, tells the prisoners to take the Jews as a model. Our industrious, all-too-earnest people. Something's going to happen when our radio assembly line, girls included, gets under way! The hands of the male prisoners on the radio assembly line are beginning to shake. Our girls, who at present are making Philora machines, work quickly without requiring external incentives.[428] And that is Sanders's assembly line: he wants to speed things up here, which in itself is reasonable enough. In any case: the lazy life of the prisoners is probably finished now. Right now the Philips prisoners' group gets blamed for everything. "The laziest, most overfed, most anti-German detachment" (Tito). They've had to carry rocks for the last two Sundays in a row, together with the hostages. Max went with them yesterday. To the hostages ([SS man Arthur] Gross [Grosz]): "We'll teach you to listen to the BBC and to say we'll be gone in two weeks." Moreover, a week ago the two radio assembly lines were forced to crawl (on their elbows; strange-looking caterpillars) and roll on the ground, because they had been singing. Dialectic: the best detachment and for that reason the most exposed.

A conversation with Mother and Alfred about women's suitability for modern work. Work is not a determining factor for their personality, as it is for men. Therefore they can do this assembly-line work and it leaves them untouched. Dialectic.

Reinecke is in a bad mood these days. Every evening there are long roll calls. One evening for one thing, another evening for something

426. Twente was the center of the Dutch textile industry. The entrepreneurs in the area were known to be ambitious.

427. *Chillul Hashem* means "desecration of God's name." Jews use the term when they witness an act or behavior that brings disrepute to one's faith in God, to the teachings of the Torah, or to Jewish tradition. The biblical source is Leviticus 22:32.

428. Philora was the brand name of a low-pressure sodium lamp used for street lighting. Philips produced this lamp from 1935 onward. From 1940 to 1945, when blackout conditions prevailed, Philora lamps were used in factory production halls.

else. And: K. of the accommodation office: "When the diplomats get sick, things go badly." Also Father Christmas [the nickname of an SS man] in this vein: "We live in expectation of the dawn of the thousand-year Reich."

[Tuesday] August 10 [1943]. Slept badly last night. Max is feeling terrible since he has joined our excellent Philips Kommando. We Kokers are too ambitious for jobs like cleaner (and simple timekeeper). Add to this that he's a bad prisoner and can't very well do nothing. He began to study electricity and soldering. And was summoned by S[anders] to spend the whole day walking between the work benches and machines and picking up the litter. This was in response to a remark by L[aman] T[rip] that the floor was "rather dirty." He doesn't have to do anything else. No more running messages, which we liked to have him do in order to distract him. (That's how deep I've already sunk, he says.) You're getting the work of a full-time janitor, S[anders] says tactfully. Also at lunchtime. When the others are eating. Max was crying on his bed, desperately unhappy. Is thinking of leaving the group. "I'm not a slave," and "in this way you become completely numbed." "Is that a job for a boy like me?" A puddle of misery. He is, of course, both right and wrong. And S[anders] wrong. But the situation will probably stay as it is. With all his faults, S[anders] is otherwise goodness and generosity personified. And trustworthy. I like him a lot. But: he is the [personification of the] Algemeen Nederlands Werkgeversverbond.[429] [General Association of Netherlands Employers], Twente version, and a [typical] prov[incial] Jewish association.

People said some time ago that the *Kapos* would be restored to their power if they would reveal who passed on the English news stories. But it's been made difficult for them because practically all radios have been confiscated, so that people hear relatively little. Only on Sunday: a sudden rumor that ran around the barrack for ten minutes and then evidently exited through the window: meetings concerning a new German government. In any case the Germans seem to be very irritable. S[üsskind] is in disgrace. Said no longer to be welcome in the *Kommandantur*. In any case they've slapped him around a bit (for the first time). Extra rations have been held back for approximately a

429. David refers to a national association of employers he identifies as the Algemeen Nederlands Werkgeversverbond (General Dutch Employer Organization). Such an organization did not exist. He probably meant to refer to the Verbond van Nederlandse Werkgevers (Association of Dutch Employers).

week. There have been attempts to make us work on Sunday. But on the other hand: everything, it seems, is tackled with a kind of impotence and lack of persistence.

Slowly but surely even the most criminal of *Kapos* has gotten his red badge back. And nothing much can be seen of a restoration of power.

The last few days I've felt a kind of nostalgia that's stronger than ever before. Engaged in long deliberations with Van Leer about what the return [to Amsterdam] would be like. Considered every moment. Strange thought, to be able to head only to someone else's house.[430] That's what our thoughts are like these days. But the last miles are the longest. And the spasms of unease. Felt a wave of that in the evening a few days ago. Letters from Amsterdam that left me feeling dissatisfied. Nettie was looking after Karel's work [reporting war news?]. Out of pure cussedness I beat Roland Frederikstadt with a belt. And hit him where it hurt. Just now Gross was here. He's replacing Tito at the moment, and he smashed a lot of jars of jam. Alfred and I spoke about Poland and are afraid of difficulties after the war. Because of the disorganization that will exist in Poland.[431]

Wednesday, August 11 [1943]. Yesterday evening a long conversation with Alfred. He lives entirely within the framework of this camp, eats everything [that's served to him], in a spirit of malevolent irony. I talked with him about myself, about my conscious disinclination to happiness. Remarkable to have a conversation here that touches on the most basic things. We also talked about the camp, the dreadful thing of which is that it so treacherously imitates real life and happiness.

Max got a letter today from Dannie and was a bit unhappy about that.[432] Not long ago a police officer was caught smuggling thirty letters out of the camp. Many measures against writing clandestine letters. Yesterday at roll call three outside workers were, after an appropriate speech, shaved bald and undressed.[433] For the same offense

430. David knew that, on orders of the Germans, the Dutch moving firm Puls had emptied the family apartment on Biesboschstraat.
431. It appears that they are thinking about the problem of repatriation of displaced persons. In fact, this became a major concern for the Allied leaders in 1943. In November that year they established the United Nations Relief and Rehabilitation Administration to deal with this.
432. Dannie Andriessen was a friend of Max's and remains so today.
433. Civilians employed by the companies that operated workshops in the camp, and architects, contractors, and workmen involved in construction could enter and leave the camp using special passes. They were forbidden to act as messengers or couriers for the prisoners, and they were not allowed to speak about conditions in the camp to others.

[as the police officer's]. People say that the letters taken from the officer went missing moments after their seizure.

At Moerdijk two prisoners and two SS men seem to have taken to their heels. A roll call that lasted sixteen hours, and no food for 24 hours.

A *Kapo* had done something wrong and the commandant ordered him to hop to the camp. Thought no one was looking and hopped into the FKL. Got 150 on his ass and now lies in the hospital. Very likely on his stomach.

This afternoon we accepted ten girls; Smit [executive at Philips] did not want members of the same family at any one assembly line. In contrast to the policy followed up to now. Because of gossip in the women's camp: Spitz and Sanders are appointing their friends. The gentlemen from Philips not only have a charitable attitude to us but also the arrogance that comes with it. We're only Jews. And live by the grace of our enemies and our benefactors. There's also been criticism that women have been talking with their husbands. Philips is unbelievably censorious. The clothing manufacturers interfere far less with their employees, for good and ill. Anyway, the prisoners are treated with much more humanity and dignity. We've lost every right to be treated as valuable workers. Everything that's done for us and doesn't come from the Germans is supposed to be a bonus.[434]

This morning Father asked an *Unterscharführer* whom he had served breakfast: "Would you like anything else?" "Yes, peace," was the answer.

Thursday, August 12 [1943]. There's going to be a PDL here.[435] For some time there have been rumors that Amersfoort would come here. Additional fences are already being put up.[436]

---

434. David repeats his accusation that the Philips management did not care about the Jewish workers in their workshop in his entry of November 20, 1943.

435. PDL stands for *polizeiliches Durchgangslager* (police transit camp).

436. The first police transit camp, established and operated by the German security police in the Netherlands, was located in Amersfoort. Its purpose was to relieve the pressure on the jails, which were overflowing with men and women arrested by the security police. Amersfoort closed in January 1943, and its prisoners had been sent to Vught. Beginning with the strikes in May 1943 German oppression of the Dutch population became harsher, and the jails were overflowing once again. The security police not only brought Amersfoort back into operation but also designated, in August, a part of the *Judendurchgangslager* (Jewish transit camp) in Vught as a *polizeiliches Durchgangslager*. Because of the deportations between May 23 and July 16 the number of inmates in the *Judendurchgangslager* had dropped from over eight thousand to a little over twenty-six hundred, and the Germans did not want to see empty barracks.

Yesterday evening there was a sudden move. In just over two hours, one barrack emptied and another occupied. The Philips Kommando looked with amazed eyes. Everyone had to have worked hard.

The women had to stand at roll call for a long time. People were being sought for Breda, work in the Hero plant. But this morning it seems the work will be done here.[437]

This morning a conversation with Jan, the cleaner of the radio assembly line, a cheerful, hearty old gent.[438] According to a foreign newspaper, he says, the queen's face shows lines of suffering around the mouth. "Yes," he says, "and what about our women here in occupied territory? And what about your mother?" I gave him a cigarette.

My graphs are finished. It was a hard slog, but I was praised for their neatness. . . . [Albert B.] Hendriks, our good SS man, has opened the hunt on parcels. Eating in the shed is a shambles. The Jews push and scream and try to get double portions. Hendriks beat people with a branch, the manager [?] with the Christmas tree, says Steg[e]m[an].[439] And this morning he made someone stand in the corner. A few days ago he drew his revolver and said to P[iet] E[ngels]: "Do I dare?"[440] Fresh rumors about a military dictatorship.

[Friday] August 13 [1943].[441] They're now in the process of putting a fence around a number of barracks. With a gate. They evidently don't know what to do with this camp.[442] Yesterday evening we were confined to quarters. Big transports from prisons, Amersfoort. One man gave them something to eat and is now black and blue.

Yesterday morning a cheerful scene. Yesterday morning: horse and cart, surrounded by prisoners. One wearing a top hat. A white wooden coffin covered with branches. It was unloaded. Opened. A

437. Established in 1914, the Hero plant in Breda, located twenty-one miles from Vught, was (and remains) one of the largest producers of canned fruits and vegetables in the Netherlands.

438. David is referring to the Communist non-Jewish prisoner Johannes (Jan) de Kleyn, who had been imprisoned first in Amersfoort and later ended up in Dachau.

439. David is referring to the non-Jewish prisoner Willem Zweer Stegeman. He was released in March 1944.

440. The non-Jewish inmate Peter (Piet) Engels was the *Kapo* of the cleaning crew. Like De Kleyn, he had been in Amersfoort before his imprisonment in Vught and ended up in Dachau.

441. On August 13, 1943, Vught numbered 2,627 Jews; this included 18 children younger than sixteen years.

442. David witnessed the creation of a special compound for the police transit camp within the Jewish transit camp.

prisoner wearing only a jacket; the rest of his body, which was shaking with laughter, was inadequately covered with feathers. He was hosed down with a powerful jet of water. Jumped up and used the hose to soak our group.

Monday, August 16 [1943]. Meanwhile, we've had to shell beans, first the women in the evening and then the men as well. For Hero, whose executives came to have a look. We're very angry. But as in point of fact angry people tend to do, we sang very hard: "The working class can kiss my ass . . ." Van Leer was fit to be tied. The next evening and also Sunday afternoon we were shelling in the kitchen, and finished our allotment an hour early. And were pretty proud of ourselves. Reinecke, who has returned, seems to have picked a quarrel about this work, in the evening and on Sunday. Held back external detachments so they could do the shelling instead of others. We almost had visitors on Sunday and a women's basketball game. But for technical reasons it didn't take place. We like Reinecke a lot. Tito's back, too. And started in about the head scarves. This is how it is. The women have to wear head scarves. Their hair is not supposed to protrude. And if the commandant sees any women without head scarves, he'll shave their heads. This is rabbinical morality, but against it stands this: it seems there really will be a brothel in [block] 1b. We're all joking about it. The essence: it'll be compulsory. And the SS is going to compel us. The *Kapos* don't seem to be going. Because they say: they're doing this to distract us from the FKL. And now we'll show them. Last week at roll call. Saathoff: children leave. A nice new vaulting horse. And five *Kapos* stretched over it. Old punishment going back to Dachau.[443] We were arranged in a square. They had to count the lashes themselves. Some of them (a homosexual, who had done it with Dutch guys, as was said with emphasis) in a weepy voice, others firm and strong. Neumann stood there as though standing by a grave. Had earlier defended the proceedings. Lehmann was also extraordinarily moved. Ettlinger struck skillfully. So did Titho. Great commotion among the *Kapos*. Piet at the gate: "I can't bear to watch it. That is what they call culture." Piet is both wildly crazy and reasonable. Not long ago he drove a couple of guys into the barbed wire with a group of screaming women looking on and said in explanation that he was

443. The disciplinary and punishment system practiced in all the German concentration camps was developed in early 1934 by the second Commandant of Dachau, SS-Brigadeführer Theodor Eicke.

not a villain and had never betrayed anyone but that people like this spoiled things for everybody else, who as a result had to stand at roll call for such and such a long time, etc. The way the women reported was also wrong, but he let them go through, "the poor things." This mixture of wildness, reasonableness, and sentimentality is characteristic of Hezensiert.[444] Hurkmans has refused to flog people.[445] The *Kapos* have agreed among themselves not to beat any more Dutchmen. We're becoming ever more like prisoners (and also increasingly *heftelingen* in revenge).[446] The secretariats have already been coordinated. *Kapos* are now in charge of the hospital.

Monday, August 23 [1943].[447] The previous was a summary, written at one sitting. And now we're not allowed to receive any more parcels. Yesterday I was cold and rigid with misery. Fear of hunger, but desperate because of the loss of contact. And the bitter feeling that the people in Amsterdam are standing there with empty and powerless hands. Yesterday still relatively optimistic concerning the possibilities of getting nourishment. After an experiment this morning I felt hungry. W. was full of plans and wept: "We won't let them wreck the arrangement we've built up here." He entered the gate and a moment later we both looked back, smiled, and felt very moved. Yesterday I also had contact with someone else.

[Thursday] August 26 [1943]. The remainder is gone.[448] Have carried on bravely. If you have children parcels are allowed. A few days ago I did without parcels as an experiment. Was hungry. The next day

444. Some prisoners believed Hezensiert was the camp's name because censored letters carried the stamp "Poststelle K. L. He Zensiert," short for *Poststelle Konzentrationslager Herzogenbusch zensiert* (censored at the Herzogenbusch Concentration Camp Post Office).

445. David is referring to the non-Jewish prisoner Johannes (Jan) Hurkmans. A former inmate of Amersfoort, Hurkmans became senior inmate of the concentration camp section of Vught in July 1943. While Hurkmans had a bad reputation in Amersfoort, he behaved himself in Vught—probably realizing that he would be held accountable after the war.

446. David exhibits some wordplay in this sentence. He used the German noun *Häftlinge* when he observed that the Jewish inmates were becoming more like prisoners, and then coined the noun *Heftelingen,* which in Dutch is pronounced identically to the German *Häftlinge* but which refers to the Dutch adjective and adverb *heftig,* which means "violent" or "fierce."

447. On August 20, 1943, Vught held 2,662 Jews; this number included 18 children younger than sixteen years.

448. With this sentence David continued his diary in a new exercise book. On October 10, 1943, this exercise book was full.

it went more easily. Gave away bread and felt disagreeably benevolent. Anyway: it seems that we'll get our parcels again in the future. The consoling S[aathoff?] has expressed himself in this spirit. Last week I also spoke with Süsskind. In his earthiness, primitiveness, and brutishness he nevertheless has something grand. Showed snapshots of his child. "Beautiful child," we say. He slaps his thighs and says: "We make only beautiful children." He's also the man to tell us about Paris and how much he used to spend there. Also the big business deals he scored there and how after a day of seeing models and a night of boozing he suddenly saw the model with his mind's eye. Without thinking or even wanting to. He shuts his eyes tight, raises his arms, and smiles beatifically. Indicates a moment later how heavyset he used to be: "A Prussian lieutenant general, my dear young lady." Or how he stood talking with Reinecke at 11:30. Beautifully acted. He stands there in an intoxication of words and expansive gestures. He's bragging, but from a position of strength.

Out of the old-clothes bin I recovered H. A.'s photo album.[449] And now also successive letters from E. to H. They are of a simplicity and a purity you can only imagine, can't conceive as belonging to a real human being. She's an adult woman, because all the girlishness in her has subsided, but expectancy and transparency are the qualities that stay with her, alongside the ones that now exist within the marriage itself and are no longer directed towards it from outside. You also learn from it the strength (which may be rooted in narrow-mindedness. But okay.) and seriousness of the Zionist milieu. It has the same expectant and tense attitude with respect to something that is actually possessed already. And also that giving quality, that unrestricted effusiveness. And the images were of a simplicity and clarity that moved me. Apart from that, you shouldn't value love so absolutely. Once again that's clear.

We call the capacitor factory "libido." We say: "Where's Sanders?" He's at libido. And that's where Mrs. N.B., among others, is at home. Husband at Moerdijk. And she's on the go all day long with a prisoner. We call him Mr. Naccent, because of his accent.[450] Anyway, he

449. David is referring to Henri Asscher, who was married to Esther Asscher-Pinkhof; both had been inmates in Vught until July 2.

450. Mrs. N.B. was most likely Frieda Noach-Brommet (1921–2003). She was married to Amsel Salomon Noach (1915–45). It appears that Mr. Naccent, later referred to as Mr. Aksent, was the accountant Barend Stokvis (1905–45), who was married to Alida Stokvis-Koningswinter.

looks like a Buddhist priest, but she likes something aesthetic, she says. By the way, she herself is, as Van Wijk says, one of our Lord's masterpieces. And very friendly and easygoing. Too easygoing, they say, but all the same, anything but riffraff. Also quite sweet. I enjoy talking with her. But Van Wijk (who studied theology) and Sanders (Algemeen Werkgevers Verbond [General Association of Employers] and N[ederlands-] I[sraëlitische] H[oofdsynagoge] [Netherlands Israelite Main Synagogue]) don't approve of her. Pick at her soul, as Mother puts it, in long conversations. And Mr. N. returns. There's weeping in the morning as a result.

Silbermann angry, because walking around and weeping don't produce capacitors. But S[anders] highly concerned, says that this morning is an exceptional event. Not so exceptional, it seems to me. But okay. And she's allowed to cry in a corner with N[accent]. She seems to want to get divorced for his sake. And he declines the offer.

Thanks, there already is a Mrs. N[accent]! And so he stands there, with that long-suffering bored face that men wear under these circumstances, waiting until she's finished. But that lasts all morning. For she has been grievously wronged. And S[anders] looks on as though he were watching an egg being laid. That's the way men have always stood there. They feel really on the spot. So much on the spot that they can all too easily see the damage they have done.

[Monday] August 30 [1943].[451] Nervousness this week: on the other side [in the workshop] you can see a gallows. Just finished. Since four in the morning. The commandant was back from Berlin. Probably it's to get the whole business completely in order. But who knows. In any case it's a chilling sight to see a dark wooden thing like that, with a twisted white cord, before you in the half-light. And so nicely and functionally constructed, like the whole camp, in fact. Mrs. N. B. and N[accent] aren't seeing each other any more.

Whether Mr. N has actually returned I don't know. And then the story of the SOBU.[452] They would come here as families. And the work

451. On August 27, 1943, Vught contained a total of 2,718 Jews, including 35 children younger than sixteen years.

452. SOBU was an acronym for Speciaal Ontwikkelingsbureau (Special Development Office). Philips established SOBU in 1941 in order to shield Jewish employees—initially from being laid off, and from July 1942 onward from being deported. Philips pretended that the SOBU was a special operation of great importance to the German war effort. In early 1943 Philips tried to organize a transport to take the SOBU Jews to the Dutch colony of Curaçao via neutral Spain, but this plan came to naught in July 1943. Subsequently some

barrack had been completely renovated. And then first they were coming and then they weren't. We had partly settled down in their beautiful work barrack but had to get out. They arrived with freshly pressed pants, and we doubted whether we would even be permitted to address them. And [Hans] Maarschalk [a Philips executive] held long orations about the schools and the family context.[453] And when he had left they all went into the baths, were issued striped uniforms, and lost everything even more thoroughly than we did. Food supplies too. This is all both sad and laughable. Especially because all they've managed to retain is their pretentiousness. And the blows and kicks that are the consequence of that pretentiousness ("we want to keep to ourselves as much as possible" "you think you're better than the others") and of their ineptness as novices. They keep S[üsskind?] waiting in a storage room. As if that's the way we do things here. Their leader is a lad of twenty. We report as Philips Jews. They as Philips SOBU. And everybody laughs. When we go to roll call in the evening, we're always last. Then have to run like a soccer team. On the corner stands L. De V., who kicks people as a joke. The trick is to pass behind him while he's kicking someone else. Slowly but surely we're coming to live at the human minimum. I have big holes in my socks and am very happy. I wrote a cheerfully cynical letter. The secretariat is being Aryanized except for two men. A detachment is going to Venlo Airfield, dangerous. PDL 300 men to Gilzen Rijen.[454] The women's secretariat has been moved to the Aryan women's camp.

[Wednesday] September 1 [1943]. Mrs. P. is in charge again.[455] So the interests of a thousand Jewish women are being looked after by this woman, who in the nature of things has no contact with the Jewish camp. Sanders and Spitz very, very enthusiastic about her charm, professionalism, and strength. She's done a lot for Philips. When she had to go to the FKL it was a blow, though many cheered. There,

SOBU Jews went into hiding. On August 18, 1943, the security police arrested the remaining SOBU Jews and their families—seventy-five adults and seventeen children. Initially they were kept separate from the Philips Kommando, but by the end of the fall the SOBU Jews had lost their special status. All of them were deported in June 1944. See Klein and Van de Kamp, *Het Philips-Kommando,* 75ff, 148ff.

453. Hans Maarschalk was the non-Jewish Philips manager who ran SOBU. He continued to look after the welfare of the SOBU Jews in Vught.

454. Gilze-Rijen was a military airfield between Breda and Tilburg in the southern Netherlands. The Germans expanded the facility for use by Luftwaffe night fighters.

455. David is referring to Hertha Poppert-Speier. See the entry on her in the appendix.

too, she's been able to work her way up from potato peeler to head of the secretariat. There are those who say that Süsskind created the women's secretariat just for her. In any case the women are being sacrificed in an *almost grandiose* fashion for the sake of this one woman. The remarkable thing is that Süsskind has gone seriously downhill since she left. Maybe it's because of the changes here (about which I hope to say more), but I guess also because of that. About a month ago, one time when she was marching to the kitchen with the others to go peel potatoes, they both looked down at their feet. A week ago I was at the post office. She and some other women came to pick up parcels. The two of them stood far apart, as if they were separated by a fence, and communicated with each other using signs and words. And kept smiling. Irony and memory. And now this magnificent gift. Indeed, almost grandiose.

The gallows seems to have been used yesterday evening. Two Poles. I don't understand this hatred of the Poles. A people, decayed and hollow, who are filled up with bits and pieces of the past. The rumor isn't true. But the gallows will be used for eleven Italian civilians in a couple of days, or so it seems.

Peeters, a new friend.[456] Recently I've been reading *Wallenstein*.[457] Powerful to a degree I've rarely seen. This isn't the only time history has been made into drama so perfectly. But this is a historical epic, lyrical even. And its poetic genius is as elemental as Homer's. I've found a new friendly and stimulating girl, with whom I enjoy talking. The slow, reserved type suits me. We prisoners like to talk to girls in all honor and decency. As far as that's concerned I'm like my colleagues. A guy from the pay office, who knows K. T. and T. well, says that for the sake of his peace of mind he wouldn't like to be in my position. But he does like to share my company. Mine and the girls'. And when I moved my table very close to the assembly line I thought of him with affection. This is all good and free from sin. Neither here nor in Eindhoven do they have a line that works as beautifully as ours. Hurrah! We're extremely proud of our output in the KL . . .[458] And

456. The non-Jewish lawyer Jacob (Jaap) Peters (1912–76) was an official in the Tilburg court. Arrested as a resister, he worked as a bookkeeper in the Philips Kommando. He survived his imprisonment in Vught and, subsequently, Dachau. After serving on the bench in Amsterdam became, in 1961, a justice of the supreme court of the Netherlands. He died in office.

457. David is referring to Friedrich Schiller's trilogy of dramas *Wallenstein's Camp, The Piccolomini,* and *Wallenstein's Death* (1799).

458. KL is an abbreviation of *Konzentrationslager* (concentration camp).

the Germans are also very satisfied. Today our parcels were released. I was just talking to Miss H. and looked worried.[459] Afraid of crying. D. has wanted to do a lot. Regards our total preservation as his work and his duty. Weeps when he speaks about that. Says with tears in his eyes that some time ago the commandant said to him about the Jewish girls: "You can give them bread. Makes no difference, marked for extermination here anyway." But that time has gone. And we're alive. And know we won't die. Not here and not in Poland. But maybe we're not doing as well as the people in Poland. Because we are in a KL, that can change any day, after all. I'm all but convinced that in many respects they're doing better. That we *are* in a KL we notice all too clearly during evening roll call. Last week there was a flogging just about every evening. Among others the first Jew, David Wolf,[460] who has now also lost his cushy job with the CDK.[461] Because of a clandestine letter. And soon after that a roll-call leader, barrack leader, and barrack secretary. Because of a falsified report.

Rolling in the sand two evenings ago. [SS-Oberscharführer Kurt] Pannecke seized two fellows by the chest and stabbed himself with pins twice over. March. Lie down. Hop. It was all very nice and sporty. Selected yesterday evening to dig [a hole]. Worked fairly hard. L. de V., probably a farmer's son, instructed us in shoveling. He said something admiring about the spade one of us had. As soon as these fellows are confronted with something from their own occupation, they become calm, reasonable, and almost sympathetic. The *Kapo* was the red Mr. S. Kupferschlag. Reached the barrack tired and angry. There quarreled with Meissler, who shouted at Father. Felt sorry for Father. Mother continues to be sick and will probably settle down soon. This evening we were deloused because of two typhus cases from Buchenwald. Theft and everything that followed it. The delousing went this way: Woken late in the evening. Our possessions left outside. Stuff was stolen and in any case there was no way of preventing it. To the bathhouse. Under the shower there, what for many meant: standing around the shower basin. Nice, heavy winter outfits. Then on to another barrack. I was lucky—one of four men in two beds, with two blankets. But got up with Max and Van Leer in order to tape barracks for gassing, and thereby earned a morning of extended sleep. Be-

459. David is referring to Hannie Hess.
460. David Wolf (1907–43) was murdered in Auschwitz.
461. The abbreviation CDK stands for Centraal Distributiekantoor, the Dutch name for the Zentrale Lebensmittelverteilung (Central Food Distribution Office) in the camp.

fore that we had gone to the barrack to see who was actually stealing things. We heard nothing. Taped quietly. And then back to sleep.

I see the Philips Kommando marching off in the morning, one man short of what I had estimated. Perhaps one is ill, I think. Then to bed and to the factory in the afternoon. Who was actually missing that morning other than ourselves? Lansberg.[462] But wasn't he taping? Consternation. His brother goes looking for him. Doesn't return. I feel misgivings. Alfred and I go into the camp together. Someone addresses us: "Are you working for Philips?" We think: news, and keep on walking. "Maybe you're looking for L[ansberg]? He has been gassed." [It is] as if someone had thrown water into our faces. We go on, although pointlessly. A crowd at the barrack. The Yugoslav to the brother whom we've met in the meantime: "Well, he's sleeping forever now. Tough luck for him. Haha." Not unpleasant to hear. To the secretariat. Suicide hypothesis. Alfred: "Incomprehensible that you can be in a barrack like that and no instinct warns you there's someone still lying there." Indeed, it is strange how relatively crude the human senses are in perceiving life that's close at hand. I think about this fairly often. In any case, the affair had another side, which for some, the secretariat and the commandant, was of paramount importance. The lad had been lying there from the previous evening on. So the morning and afternoon roll calls could only have been squared with a falsified report. Naturally this weighed more heavily than the loss of a human being. For those falsified reports Meissler got 25 strokes. And was sent to Venlo. With that transport to Venlo went pretty well all the prominent people from the early days. Hayn,[463] Wolff, for whom I did feel really sorry, that good man Verduin, etc.

We've experienced the flowering of the camp here, a kind of charitable Jewish Council camp, and that was also the heyday of these people. Now we're experiencing the decline. In short, these people are now targets for the SS because they've sinned against the form of the KL.[464] By the way they functioned and by their separatism.

I'll keep on writing for a while about a few other important things and will then turn to the momentous facts of the last half week. An

462. David is referring to Martin Victor Lansberg. See the entry on the Lansberg family in the appendix.

463. The German-Jewish refugee Herbert Emil Hayn (1909–44) owned an atelier that produced women's clothing. He was deported to Auschwitz in November 1943 and died there two months later.

464. This probably refers to the fact that in a "normal" concentration camp Jewish prisoners were forbidden to organize themselves in any manner.

evening of digging on an empty stomach, in a camp full of semi-dressed and sympathetic women. For a few days everyone in the barrack had to carry heavy roof tiles. Four at a time, and stay out of the flower bed as we carried the heavy and brittle tiles. There was an outside civilian in attendance who calmed us down and counseled us not to be nervous. Everything because of the tiles. On the other side fellows who loudly urged us on. Also someone who came after us with a bloodhound, much to the dismay of the civilian. The next Sunday we pushed heavy wheelbarrows from the brothel to the industry area at the rear. Brought in by H. The case of H. The ladies H. Almost broken. But it was wonderful being in the sun, shirtless and strong. "We'll become he-men this way," says Alfred, who's pushing with the rest of us. But on to business: lately we've felt ourselves to be safe and stable. Suddenly: Cohen and Blüth are here. Rumors: a transport, the camp to be shut down, with the exception of industry. Industry to be shut down, etc. We go to hear Cohen, who stands there taking notes for two hours, with an endless and astonishing patience. I feel a mild tinge of admiration when I see anyone listen to anyone else for more than three minutes here. He makes a curiously precise and mild impression. I hear: a general order from Himmler: all the Jews out of western Europe. Westerbork to be emptied. So Vught has to go as well. For the time being Escotex, Philips, and the diamond industry will stay.[465] But within the foreseeable future these, too, will go. He gives me an apple. Only gradually do I get an overview of things. Everything here has now become very unreal. Some special cases will go to other camps. The rest simply to Auschwitz. That seems very close now. People are picturing the situation there in a way that's very concrete and far from horrifying. I write a letter of farewell. A transport will be leaving. All day long discussions about replacements with De Wit and Smit[466] and Van Wijk. We've made a plan that meshes very precisely. But which doesn't go into effect. The selection for the transport takes place in a very interesting way. The commandant has

---

465. On September 29, 1943, the Germans were to have completed the official liquidation of the Jewish community in the Netherlands when they closed down the Jewish Council and deported its members and five thousand others carrying Jewish Council exemptions to Westerbork. The only Jews left in the Netherlands after that day were those interned in Westerbork, Vught, and a few smaller camps, Jews in hiding, a couple of hundred Portuguese Jews whose racial status was being investigated by the German lawyer Hans Georg Calmeyer, and Jews married to non-Jews.

466. David is referring to the non-Jewish prisoner Christiaan (Chris) Smit. See the entry on Christiaan Smit in the appendix.

been to Berlin, very probably to fight for us. Reinecke is also strongly
of the view that we should stay here. So he and Ettlinger go "sorting"
during evening roll call. Pull young guys out of the line who return
behind their backs. Everything proceeds in a cheerful, friendly, and
ironic way. The evening is bright and mild. In the distance you see
groups splitting up and reuniting. Where they [the SS guards] walk
in their green uniforms, the lines separate. People have to step aside
quickly to join the right group. The SS men don't understand why
people don't choose the right side with more spirit. "Hey you, show
some sense when you're walking." They select the people in the housing office and, with a few exceptions, send them back again. They let
the women who've been let go by the workshops line up together and
then ordered them to go stand with their old occupational groups.
They take both the Moerdijk group and the Philips construction detachment. Everyone and certainly those affected think: transport.
The diamond workers are taken from the other groups and put with
the Philips construction detachment. And the old Moerdijk-Philips
construction groups are suddenly told: "Be here tomorrow at eight
with your blanket and bowl. If even one of you is too late, you'll all go
on transport." This is repeated once and the words about the transport replaced by: "I'll hang you all." This evening, and not for the
first time, they are definitely sympathetic. I can't believe that Reinecke
isn't a mensch in one way or another. "Well, now we've done some
sorting, right? . . ." After that comes visiting time. The next evening
first visiting, then moving, then a roll call for the transport, from which
I remove the two Lansberg sisters[467] (which earns me the applause of
the Philips Kommando, both Jews and prisoners, Alfred's approving
irony, and the indignation of the secretariat). Then Reinecke has to
leave, to listen to Hitler's speech, he says.[468] These days I'm very close
to crying. I slouch in my chair, look sadly at the assembly line, and try
to keep the H[ess] girls, my last lovely refuge in this ugliness, from
going with the transport. I enjoy speaking with them, and abandon
all reflection. The only possible word for the situation is: disappointment. Disappointment because of what we achieved here for ourselves and what we created for others. The disappointment of others

467. Four Lansberg sisters were to work in Philips until June 1944: Helene-Marie, Albertine (Tini), Louise, and Eleonora. In this passage David is referring Helene-Marie and/or
Louise and/or Eleonora.
468. On September 10, 1943, Hitler gave a radio speech about the Italian "betrayal" in
ending the alliance with Germany.

because of us; they already thought we would be sitting down to eat with them. The disappointment of my parents, who will have to separate now, etc. Then suddenly the news. An order: the Philips group is staying. The reserves too. The administrator was here the day before.[469] We don't know what to make of it. But that afternoon all girls on the reserve list, and also a couple of men, were removed from the transport. With that, my accomplishment the previous evening with respect to the Lansberg girls is nullified, although it caused enough of a commotion, both positive and negative. (That evening I also wanted to get T. L. off the transport.[470]) We're in a strange position now. People envy us, the official circles take a hostile view of us because of their own impotence, which stands out so clearly in contrast, and furthermore because the officials don't know whether it wouldn't be better to take refuge among us. . . . The urgency is enormous. If what Spitz and I wanted had been carried out, the matter would have been firmly closed, but now Mrs. Poppert is sending [people for] three soldering courses in rapid succession, each under the strong protection of R[einecke?] and H. At the transport roll call these are counted among the employed. . . . And Reinecke personally checks with Spitz to get information about Mrs. Lehmann's chances. That, of course, is as good as an order. Or as bad. And we're unable to frame a position in response to Mrs. Poppert's machinations. There are going to be new projects: mounting radio tube receptacles, probably a radio assembly line, and certainly hand-powered flashlights. Some women were put to work a week ago, and Mrs. Poppert has protested loudly against these placements. She's going to report what's happening here. And people have indeed exposed themselves to criticism. Not through fraud but through tactlessness. This is what we do. Family members of those already working, young girls, finally women with husbands elsewhere. That nice young woman M[471] falls into the first category and has been put to work after a day's probationary course, because she had already learned soldering earlier. And so: at roll call Reinecke, with a note in his hand, summons Mrs. M and another lady, also reserved very recently and put to work at once, to come for-

469. David is probably referring to Ludwig Nolte, who was the German *Verwalter* (administrator) of the Philips factory in Eindhoven.
470. David is referring to Albertina (Tini) Lansberg. See the note on the Lansberg family in the appendix.
471. David is referring to the seamstress Gertrude Maykels-van Minden. She was sent to Westerbork on September 1943 and survived the war.

ward. Mrs. M has to go on transport, she just came from the work-shop, "and others have already been waiting for so long." The other lady has worked in the barrack and is allowed to stay. S[üsskind], standing there, points at a girl and asks how long she's been on the reserve list, and it is a long time, and he says: "Another case like that." I knew at once: nothing much to be done here. Gerard [Sanders] very optimistic. B. says, quite rightly: hands off. Süsskind deeply sorry, approaches Mrs. Poppert, who urges Süsskind to do everything possi-ble, "because it's really important to me." And when Mrs. M does go on transport, as was to be expected, she embraces her and weeps bit-ter tears. And so it goes. In the meantime our relations with Süsskind and Poppert have improved somewhat, but the price *is* high. Mr. M stays here.[472] Reinecke wouldn't allow him to leave. The farewells. We were at roll call. A wonderfully clear evening. Behind us the trans-port. She sat on her luggage and looked in another direction. Very attentive and nervous. People crouched near their bits of luggage. There is ever less of it. It was inspected and torn apart. Then the march off. So slow, that little procession. I stood there and watched it intently. Spitz cried. The analogy. I felt how still I stood there. We ran across Van Wijk. He felt guilty. He wanted to give us something. He's a typical Christian. One of the few whom people appreciate for their goodness. He made me take a loaf of rye bread for Maikels. When he gave it, it was easy to accept. "Although it's odd, of course, a loaf of rye bread instead of a wife," he said. Then he left and I didn't know what to do with the loaf. Spitz and I walked on. The order really does seem to have come. And is seriously meant. Applies to the diamond and Philips groups. The Escotex group is leaving. Yesterday evening a long conversation with Bied[er]m[ann] and Rosenberg,[473] who were extremely friendly. I want to try to become a better person, just a little bit. G[rosz]'s stories: to a German lady: "Sooner than you think [reference to the end of the war?]. You won't recognize Germany anymore." G[rosz] rants and makes an unpleasant impression. But during a roll call he does let a boy go to the back row. His letter. By the way, Reinecke has instructed E. B. to stay with the SOBU children. And if the commandant shows up, not to reveal himself. The Einhorn enterprise is bankrupt. Einhorn is king here. A heavyset man with a

472. David is referring to Gertrude Maykels's husband, Alexander Maykels. He was to remain in Vught until March 1944, when he was sent to Westerbork. He appears to have survived the war.
473. See the entry on Max Rosenberg in the appendix.

limp, a big head, and a pince-nez: like J[acob] I[sraël] de Haan. Strange, you might say hermetic pronouncements. With something of the rhetoric of eastern European poetry. Not so much intelligent as royal. Many depend on him. He has his people for that. He hasn't had to work. Not even at the time of the worst rush. He's in the accounts room now. But without an assignment. A couple of weeks ago the prison suits were inspected for alterations, such as pockets and things like that. He openly has a pocket cut into his jacket.[474] But no one does anything to him. Inspection for money. Out of the line. But money was seized. Many little people. He bears it like a defeated monarch. And his delicacies. "In this camp you have to live just for yourself," he says pensively. "You do live only according to that rule," I say to him. "You're right about that," he says contentedly. The Q family is having a hard time.[475]

[Illicit] letters found. One evening the father gets 20, another evening 40 strokes. Max gets 25. They're afraid they'll have to go. A transport of Jewish prisoners is going to leave.[476] Then Samuel will go too.[477] Spitz, who's the most capable person here, has been persona non grata from the outset. Wherever he goes his position is restructured out of existence. It has happened again. The radio assembly line ran well under his leadership and that of Kan (also inclined to push, but he was good to work with).[478] Kan is going on transport voluntarily, so they're inserting a Jewish prisoner. It is quite clear, but evidently hard to grasp except for Spitz and me, that Jews aren't interchangeable, and that in this camp the dividing line is between prisoners (among them also Jewish punishment cases) and Jewish internees, far more than between Jews and Aryans. You can say: it's a formality, but in this camp it is, in fact, the formal that is the essential.

474. Inmates were not allowed to have pockets in their uniform jackets. Einhorn had pockets made so he could warm his hands.

475. David is referring to Abraham and Max Querido.

476. Jewish *Schutzhäftlinge* (prisoners) had not, like other Jews, been interned just for transport to Poland, but had been arrested for an infraction of some regulation applying to Jews.

477. David is referring to the Jewish *Häftling* Henri Samuel. He was deported to Auschwitz in June 1944. It appears that he survived the war.

478. As the owner of a large textile mill in Oldenzaal, Willi Kan was an experienced manager, and he could have remained in the Philips group. Yet he and his wife, Susannah Kan-van Minde, chose to join the transport that left for Westerbork on September 9. They had allowed their three young children to leave by themselves on July 16. The Kan family was reunited in Westerbork, only to be deported to Theresienstadt and, from there, in October 1944, to Auschwitz. All the members of the Kan family were murdered upon their arrival at the camp. See also note 409.

A paradox, but also a simple truth. Spitz and I, at first I chiefly, but he has caught up to me, have gained a lot of talent in and also a lot of pleasure from this formal way of thinking. And know, too, how in real terms it actually means everything in the life here. The roll call, a purely formal affair, it may be said, but it governs everything, and especially Saathoff did it so beautifully. If, on logical grounds, you can alter something in the arrangement of the groups, you go ahead and do it. That they gave us striped suits was in order to make us into prisoners, and thereby to remove us from the transit camp. "Be glad you're prisoners" (Ettlinger). True, there was the inconsistency of leaving us with our hair and shoes, but this was on the basis of international law with respect to the treatment of interned civilians. For every beating permission seems to have to come from Berlin, to give another example. But they have ways of getting around such obstacles. But then again: very rule bound. The PDL is here. There's a big fence around it. The treatment of people is just the same inside as outside. Some of them still have their hair. For reasons so subtle that they themselves scarcely know them. All this attachment to formal principles makes me surmise good things concerning Poland. Although it must also be said, of course, that the greatest arbitrariness is being legitimized. Nothing happens in a KL without a formal motive. That means the business prompts cynicism. And in our existence as transit camp we're subject to the same formalities. I wrote earlier about the fictitious quality of the categories for the transports. Now a new one has joined them: the family connection. . . . Think of the children's transports of a while ago! But no: they need to send away a number of people. The number is the important thing, but they have to have a category available, no matter how senseless, in order to reach the chosen number. A brother and sister who worked for us had to go, because the word had come from the SD in The Hague that they were on a holding list in Westerbork. Now Westerbork will probably go in its entirety. But that makes no difference. Even a favor is an order. . . . It was the same thing with the pseudo-Barneveld list. It was clear to everybody what was going to happen. Et cetera, et cetera.

Otherwise good reports are coming in from Poland. It's only too bad that people really are working in the coal mines. But the work isn't all that heavy, many write.[479] Probably *Schwarzarbeit* [moonlight-

---

479. The Reich Security Main Office in Berlin, which coordinated the deportation and killing of the Jews, created a special project to deploy letters as camouflage. From time

ing] on a very broad basis. Gratifying, too, is that cases of punishment (at least to the extent that it concerns specifically Jewish offenses) seem to be canceled once people leave Dutch territory.[480] Anyway, the transports go to Braunschweig now, so that these days the punishment transports don't go to the *Vernichtungslagers* (extermination camps) any longer (a name like that, *Vernichtungslager,* is also remarkable for its legalizing tendency) but simply to the Polish labor camps.[481] The fact that so much mail is arriving in Amsterdam, in my view also points to an increase of that tendency to legalism, which of course becomes easier because they've been deporting Aryans on such a large scale. As far as that goes, those people who predicted the Aryans wouldn't fare any better than us Jews have unexpectedly and quite undeservedly turned out to be right. They've interned whole families here, even women with babies. In the accounts room I saw a 13-year-old hostage (in overalls) doing his arithmetic.[482] Ever more SS men are leaving this place. Titho, Saathoff, and Pannecke departed a couple of weeks ago. Things are a bit healthier, says Van L[eer]. In the mornings, when the labor detachments stood there, ready to go, they always came to see if they couldn't hit somebody. Since they left things have become very quiet. Only Bubi still gets very excited, and yesterday, on his own account, gave our dear barrack leader 40 good ones on the ass. A lot of Dutch SS here. There is one with a strange dog face, who really likes talking with the girls here. And who says he

---

to time, the Auschwitz SS forced inmates to write cards "home" to soothe the anxiety of those left behind and counter rumors of mass killings in the camps. According to Dieter Wisleceney's testimony in the Nuremberg trials, the so-called Briefaktion der RSHA (Letter Program of the Reich Security Main Office) was one of his boss Eichmann's inventions. "He had thought out a special system of post cards and letters, whereby he believed he could mislead the public. The Jews brought to Auschwitz or to other extermination camps were forced, prior to being murdered, to write post cards. These post cards—there were always several for each person—were then mailed at long intervals, in order to make it appear as though these persons were still alive." A few thousand Auschwitz inmates worked in the Jawischowitz (Jawiszowice) coal mines. International Military Tribunal, *Trial of the Major War Criminals,* 5:11.

480. David was well informed. Jews who had gone into hiding or who had committed other offenses and who had been caught were designated as so-called punishment cases and interned in special barracks. This distinction did not matter anymore once they boarded the train to Sobibor or Auschwitz: at their place of arrival they were treated like the other deportees.

481. David's use of the term *Vernichtungslager* in his diary.

482. Among those interned in Vught were the family members of Dutch military officers, public servants, police administrators, and others who had refused to obey German orders and who had gone into hiding. The official reason for their incarceration was known as *Sippenhaft* (kin liability)

feels so much at ease among the Jews. Because he was born on the Foeliedwarsstraat.[483] And so it was a happy time this morning in the measuring establishment (it's now Sunday, September 19 [1943]).[484] The commandant's radio was tuned to L[ondon] and played hot jazz. Jews and prisoners are gathered around it and happily keep time with their knees. And a female prisoner dances with a male prisoner, and next to the radio stands a crazy SS man, looking slightly envious and swaying along with the music. The warm sun shines through the windows, and all are contented and cheerful. Sunday morning in a concentration camp.

There's the other young fellow, a picture in the Nutcracker with his stubby nose and his face like a half-moon.[485] He comes into the accounts room and shouts: "You must all leave here as doctors and lawyers." One of them came a few days ago to ask whether he could listen to English radio. Of course that was not allowed. "Do you listen to the English radio station?" a German SS man asked. "Never," the man at final quality control said: "I've got four children in Poland, I'm on the wait list myself, what am I supposed to do with the English radio station?" "But can you get it?" "That I can." "Up to this point, wherever I asked, they said 'no.' Stupid idiots. But if you listen to anything, keep it to yourself. That's more prudent." He had never hit or kicked anyone arbitrarily. "Anybody will tell you that." He was not with the SS from his own volition. There are more like that. A. is one of the most likable.[486] And he takes seriously that things are going badly, without camouflaging it. "I'm going east, to build a new life." Wieland is another downright congenial SS man, who a few days ago took real pains over my request to release [from transport] the husband of one of the women working with us. But he does believe that H[itler] and M[ussolini] will put themselves at the head of an army and that everything will then be all right.[487]

483. Foeliedwarsstraat was located in the old Jewish quarter in Amsterdam.

484. On September 17, 1943, Vught held 2,084 Jews; this included 19 children younger than sixteen years.

485. For many centuries German wood-carvers have produced nutcrackers in the form of soldiers with chubby faces. Such nutcrackers were the protagonists in Ernst Theodor Amadeus (E.T.A.) Hoffmann's story *The Nutcracker and the Mouse King* (1816), the source of Pyotr Ilich Tchaikovsky's *Nutcracker* ballet.

486. David is probably referring to *Arbeitseinsatzführer* (Work Assignment Leader) Franz Auer.

487. Mussolini was removed from power on July 24 and arrested that same day and interned in a mountaintop hotel. Liberated by the Germans on September 12, he was flown first to Bavaria and then to Hitler's headquarters in East Prussia. On September 23 Mussolini proclaimed, under strong German pressure, the Italian Social Republic.

Ettlinger to M[ax] Q[uerido]: "You have to remember this: in the KLs it's the *Kapos* who have murdered Jews, never the SS." In the corner of the industrial courtyard here there is a wide view out over the fields that makes you happy and sad. So distant, so free. A creek flows close to us, then the fence and then the fields, where the yellow wheat used to be that's now been harvested, exposing farmhouses to view. Those are the fields and the sky and the woods of vacation time. You don't feel as far and as disconnected from it as you'd think.

Fall

(September 24, 1943–December 16, 1943)

By the first day of the fall of 1943 over 94,000 Jews had been deported from the Netherlands. But, compared to the spring, the frequency of the transports had declined: over the summer only nine transports had left Westerbork: four to Sobibor carrying a little over 9,000 Jews, four to Auschwitz carrying a little under 4,000 Jews, and one train carrying 305 Jews to Theresienstadt.

[Friday] September 24 [1943].[488] Yesterday a long period of tension came to an end. Never again will Lydia's hand be on our parcels. Cohen had made inquiries about her. Everything all right. But now I've received nothing for almost two weeks. Then a parcel blockage. More of this later. At roughly the same time as the report that there were parcels for us, but that we wouldn't be getting them. So this delightful news made the other news seem unimportant. And yesterday evening [someone showed] beautiful city views of Amsterdam, which made many people sad but put me in a good mood. Very nice inscriptions. The identifications were actually rather vague. If I return to Amsterdam, I'll feel right at home there. And now that I don't live in Amsterdam it is a foreign city and Vught is in a certain sense my "home sweet home."

We didn't think that the emptying of western Europe [of Jews] would take place as slowly as it has so far. It is true that three transports of 300 people each have now departed.[489] They've left Philips untouched, although with gnashing teeth as far as the secretariat is concerned. Because the secretariat is inspired by the well-known Vught fairness, which teaches that all people are equal and that

488. On September 24, 1943, Vught contained 1,784 Jews; this included 19 children younger than sixteen years.
489. David is referring to the transports to Westerbork of September 11 (327 people), September 16 (318 people), and September 20 (300 people).

therefore you should not protect all the Philips people and leave the rest on the outside, looking in, but you should keep some people here from every group. Furthermore, Vught fairness teaches that the older people who are here should be sent on, because they should have been gone long ago. . . . So they're going to start taking people from the reserve lists, they say. If we're not careful, that is. But we are careful. And with a hundred girls, some of them not even on the reserve list as yet, we're going to install radio vacuum tubes. That's very exacting work, you need good hands and eyes. The inspection is very meticulous. Moreover, it's a Wehrmacht order. And people are actually a bit angry with us.

Escotex seems also to have secured an exemption for itself. The secretariat is very enthusiastic about this. And rightly so, of course. But now people don't think much of us anymore. This is linked to the novelty of the safeness of the clothing group. And also to the fact that the SS blames the Philips Kommando for everything that goes wrong. But then people forget that the *Jewish* Philips Kommando is the darling of the SS. Especially of the commandant and of Auer. So it probably won't work. Yesterday a semiofficial report from the secretariat. No more transports will be leaving Westerbork. So, Reinecke says, not from here either. The Venlo group won't come back for the time being. The ladies here were very happy and expressed it by being very boisterous. Today they're saying that it probably will come back. And also that a transport will be leaving on Monday. Anyway, the fact that the deportation is going slowly is probably linked to the military situation. Perhaps they're using part of the Polish camps to accommodate the supply and communication units, which will have to retreat a considerable distance now that the [eastern] front is pulling back. In any case, the gentlemen here are not particularly happy. The broom maker.[490] And the raids on foodstuffs, clothes, and so on. Hendriks removed a totally unfamiliar dressing gown from under my table. And the roll call that was used to announce that all our parcels were to be blocked, that until further notice we would have to stand for an hour in the evening, and wouldn't get any 15-minute breaks in our workday, which now amounts to 11 hours. "Because of your high productive capacity," Reinecke states. "Because you all work so hard," Hurkmans translates aptly. Anyway, Hurkmans is a splendid specimen. A tall, heavyset man, with a large red head that hangs down like

490. It is not clear to what David is referring.

a broken flower bud. Dark slits for eyes in it, and a language that is neither Dutch nor German. The pronunciation, the obscenities, and the "spirit" behind it are Dutch, many of his words are German. "And if in future you don't do that, everything will be confiscated. The block seniors have to make sure that everybody lines up quietly for roll call. You people open your traps when you should keep them shut, and keep them shut when you should open them. When you're at roll call, you don't smoke and you don't talk, you don't play with your nuts, you stare at the neck of the man in front of you and you keep your trap shut. Understood?" *"Jawohl,"* says the choir of prisoners. "You've got to understand that you're not here for your own enjoyment." By this time the gathering is cheering or shouting: "good for you, Jan," or "way to go!" And Jan really enjoys himself if no one's looking. Some evenings, when we stand there for an hour, he thinks it advisable to have one group crouch down, but people are glad to do it for him. Airplanes [overhead].

[Thursday] September 30 [1943]. Sunday afternoon, 9/26, we're lying on our beds, resting. Suddenly the doors are flung open. White faces. Screaming, voices that downplay the underlying emotion. Alfred is on his bed and says in a wild exaltation that he's got nothing to do with it. After a while I go to have a look. People are standing on benches, some speaking, others urging them to be quiet. A hideous sight. I quickly get back on my bed. Someone lies on his bed in a daze, smoking. After five minutes the denial.[491] If . . . In itself important enough. I encounter [Van] W[ijk]. We walk under a damp sky with wild clouds. He says: "The notary doesn't know anything." And that's confirmed from all sides that day. But people continue in an agitated state. In the end it is significant that something like that can be asserted. In the women's camp they're holding spiritualist seances. The next day Spitz and I have a conversation, and for a number of reasons we reach the conclusion that one way or another it's probably true. And we tap into a source of information from which something trickles through now and then. A fruitful hypothesis, which gets support from the report about the exchange that flew in one Sunday. Later it appeared there was some truth in it. For a couple of days Alfred and I live in a state of great excitement. [Van] W[ijk] says we're insane.

491. It is not known what the commotion was about. In a conversation, Max Koker suggested that it concerned a rumor about the end of the war or a rumor about an exchange of camp inmates for Germans interned by the Allies.

At the beginning we said: "Our stay in Vught will seem wretched to us when the High Holidays arrive." And now they're here. Sanders wants to speak. And Spitz becomes furious and says crude things.

Yesterday evening in Neumann's barrack. Everyone's wearing *kippot*. And an eastern Jewish cantor is praying. I join in valiantly. I missed Lehmann's speech. But I read it. And it was short and stern and good. With all his shortcomings, Lehmann continues to be an outstanding figure in my view. His hot temper and his lack of patience are against him. R[oland?] says that when he is dictating something to you and you ask him to repeat it, he stamps his foot. But, says R[oland?], whose uproarious laughter I so much like to hear, then you just laugh right in his face, and everything's all right again. The report. And the additions made by R. I heard Lehmann say the blessings. It really did touch me. They had a restrained strength, just like everything about him.

Aside from a sizable hangover, nothing much is left of our bout of ecstasy at the beginning of the week. Yesterday I said to the ladies of the assembly line: the war may go on for another 50 years. And we talked about how we would then be unusually good at making radios. They would fly along the line, increasing in number as in an animated cartoon. We'll all be old, and the SS will become good-natured from sheer old age. "There is," Van Leer said, "just one way out that's left to us, through the chimney of the crematorium." In the accounts room he has made V. nervous and afraid by saying there are wars that never come to an end. "But the Eighty Years' War," V. said, "it ended, didn't it?"[492] Van Leer: "There weren't any airplanes yet." In any case we are very downcast, to which hunger (the parcel blockade continues) and the reports from Amsterdam (which by now, October 2, seems to have been definitively emptied) make their contribution.[493] The consequences for our camp seem to be self-evident, although you never know. R[einecke] and St[okker] repeatedly said this week that no more transports would leave, but yesterday evening Jewish(!) prisoners were selected for the Venlo detachment, from which our people were supposed to be coming back.[494] The transport will probably leave on Monday. And then what? Then they'll finally have to begin focusing on industry in a fundamental way. Or it has to be this

---

492. Lasting from 1568 to 1648, the Eighty Years' War pitting the Dutch against the Spanish is remembered by the Dutch as their war of independence.

493. See note 465 accompanying David's entry of September 1, 1943.

494. SS-Hauptsturmführer August Stokker was in charge of the camp administration.

way, that industrial interests will finally begin to weigh against the desire by the extremists to be in control and against the rivalry with Westerbork. Anyway, the latter is the more dangerous. Because Westerbork wants to retain its old guard. And in general keep its camp intact as much as possible. No matter how, we'll go. In any event we'll go with the last train. Max Cahen came in a moment ago and he said that last Wednesday he had come to a locked door on Oude Schans with a sign "closed Thursdays" and thought he'd gone crazy . . .[495] Yesterday evening letters from Frederika. I have a great sense of isolation. She's like a voice speaking from the back of a room. And it's dark. All day long the harmonic completeness of those sentences remains in my head. Tini Lansberg, the beautiful girl about whom I wrote earlier, is working here now. I had a long conversation with her this morning. This camp has been one great round of pleasure for her. Where R. takes her arm, where you can sleep in late, eat a lot, and in the evening go to the cabaret with one escort or another. Her speech and movements are not provocative or challenging, but she moves, turns, approaches, and withdraws, in the performance of the supreme moment. Never before have I seen or spoken with someone with whom I have, you could almost say, such a complete physical intimacy from a distance. And this is not a joke. This is purely a complete physical life without awareness or guilt. I simultaneously feel enjoyment and anxiety. And all day long my nerves are wound up to the highest degree.

Have spoken with Jan, who is very angry with himself because he didn't reach the other side.[496] He could hit himself. And to think of all his comrades who did manage it. There's no honor in being here, he says. The big news was a couple of days ago (it's October 5 now): Chm., Gr. and the rest had a business.[497] One that did not, in fact, exist but issued receipts to associated agencies all the same. And made a lot of profit that way. There were supposed to be high-ranking visitors last week. The entire camp was in tiptop shape (especially the Jewish part had to be that way, the solicitous Reinecke said), but those high-ranking visitors never showed up. At least not in the camp. But they

---

495. Accompanied by a guard, Max Cahen was able to travel outside the camp to purchase equipment for the Philips Kommando. The Jewish Council warehouse that supplied the inmates in Vught and Westerbork was located at Oude Schans in the Jewish Quarter.

496. "The other side" is England.

497. David is referring to Commandant Chmielewski and his brother-in-law SS-Hauptscharführer Arthur Grosz, who was in charge of labor deployment.

did in the *Kommandantur.* And examined the books. And found a shortfall of 80,000 guilders. And photos as well, some say: the newspaper reporting the last party. The commandant stood at attention in the corridor and later was not allowed to leave his room. Gross was confined to barracks, went into the prison camp, and is supposed to have been taken out again by a Jewish prisoner. Also this story: Ettlinger arrested in Berlin (meanwhile he's back here 10/10). Another story: Ettlinger and Saathoff are returning. Met them: 10/9. And Reinecke is leaving. In spite of the spirochetes.[498] That's certainly not an improvement for us. The more so because the commandant, no matter what else people may say about him, has always worked hard to keep us here. Like everything else the months-old rumor that he would leave has been verified, just as all the claims made here always end up coming true in some form. People also say that Westerbork's commandant had registered a complaint that people [from Vught] had arrived there without being equipped for transport. Others say: there was a complaint from the commandant of Braunschweig.[499] Yet others say: there were [complaints] from [August] Stokker, the *Hauptsturmführer* [captain], who in the meantime has become the acting commandant and is supposed to have been promoted.[500] And yet others assert: it was not so much the looting as the private sale of supplies. Somehow I have the feeling that this business has been going on for a very long time and that many things have contributed to it.

Also on Sunday: our factory is awash in fear. The Venlo group is returning. Another transport will be leaving. I head into the camp. Neumann confirms [the rumor] under condition of strict secrecy. There are a few people with us whose husbands, fiancés, or sons are in Venlo and who were called in for assessment quite a long time ago. Of course they are now particularly worried. That evening: summoned. Also two young boys who are working with us. They were detained by Reinecke a while ago and apparently reported to the secretariat for transport. They're also summoning some of our reserves. And a couple of women who are now working for us so they can

498. Spirochetes cause, among other diseases, syphilis. Saathoff was known to have syphilis, hence this sentence expresses David's surprise that Saathoff was returning in spite of his syphilis. Telephone conversation with Max Koker, August 29, 2010.

499. It is not clear to what David is referring. In 1943 there was no concentration camp in Braunschweig. Yet it appears that, at least in the imaginations of David and his fellow inmates, "Braunschweig" played some significant role in the deportation of Dutch Jews.

500. August Stokker, who was in charge of the camp administration, was the deputy Commandant.

accompany their husbands. The secretariat pays no attention to our exemption, but they can't do that anyway if they want to keep families together. Something for which there's a lot to be said. They're unhappy with us because we want to maintain our group as integrally as possible. But there's a justification for that point of view, too: after all, a work group that remains intact is more productive than one from which people can be removed just like that. That's why, in the interest of us all, I'm also in favor of prohibiting Philips employees from leaving voluntarily to accompany someone. Hard, perhaps, but unavoidable for a sound and above all businesslike and not pro-Jewish policy. W. shares my opinion, B. doesn't.[501] On the other hand, you need to have the strength to sacrifice people if it can't be avoided. I'm slowly learning this. And now the fact is that someone or other has to go, and that it should be exclusively a matter of what is best for everybody.

October 10 [1943].[502] Sunday. An idyllic scene on production lines I and II. People are walking back and forth slowly or lie at their places, asleep. A few foremen are gathered in a circle, talking to each other. Somebody is writing a letter and quite a few are reading the newspaper. People are playing chess or are seated around a table, playing cards. The smooth pale blue sky outside is cold. High in the sky, the sun shines brightly and warmly, but the crisp cold lingers around. And inside it is noisy and pleasant.

The new commandant has made his entry.[503] His general regulations and insights are favorable, to say the least. Parcel blockage lifted, money and possessions returned to people from whom they had been confiscated (the money will be put in an account). Einhorn will have to stay here for a long time if he wants to use it up. The canteen cash belonging to the accounting room has been returned. . . . Much has happened and much changed. Also a statement that the

501. David is probably referring to the Austrian-Jewish refugee Sigmund Biedermann. See the entry on Sigmund Biedermann in the appendix.
502. On October 10, 1943, Vught held 1,770 Jews, including 19 children younger than sixteen years.
503. David is referring to Adam Grünewald (1902–45). In the 1920s Grünewald served as a volunteer in the German army. In 1934 he joined the SS and made a rapid career in the concentration-camp system. Vught was his first command. His tenure as commandant lasted only three months. After the so-called bunker tragedy (see p. 315), he was removed and tried before an SS court. In March 1944 he was convicted and sentenced to three and half years in prison. Pardoned by Himmler, he was demoted and sent to the eastern front. He died in action.

noon roll call is superfluous. The noon roll call is our biggest worry. Usually it comes out all right, but always with a lot of difficulty. He visited the factories, showed a lot of interest in all kinds of things that the previous commandant didn't concern himself about. To the gentlemen from Philips: not enough Jews are working here. They had to put more to work. This was prompted by the appearance of our factory and the complaint that the prisoner assembly lines have too much turnover. Earlier transports, he says, would not have needed to go if the issue had been properly addressed.[504] Whether that's right is another matter. But we're going to have our heads shaved. As it happens, he doesn't recognize the difference between imprisoned and civilian Jews. And in the interests of our staying here he thinks it's better if there are no differences. So the time has come to make my situation clear. He saw Jews at the Philips construction detachment leaning on their shovels. Asked the *Kapo* what was going on and got the answer that they were civilian Jews.[505] An answer, of course, that was meant to do us harm. Which it did at once, because the commandant said that he didn't distinguish among Jews and that they had to do the heaviest work. The *Kapo* added to this that they also get the least food and, besides, they get a good beating once in a while. I'm curious how this will now affect our deportation. Monday's transport, just about ready to leave, was canceled with the explanation: "No trains." Rumor: a transport has returned from Braunschweig. A "blissful cackling" (Van Wijk) along the assembly line. And women embracing their shabbily dressed husbands, fiancés, and sons. With his composition of the transport Lehmann had sought to forestall a general roll call. He had also summoned some of our people, which seems to have been grounds for Eindhoven [i.e., Philips] to phone. Because of that, last Sunday evening [there was] suddenly a general roll call, which, in fact, people could have avoided if they chose. Everyone who was with Philips and didn't want to go could get out of the transport. A number of others, guys and girls who looked young, had to leave. "How old? Where do you work?" What we say is now left to our bad faith. A remarkable story. Of course the secretariat keeps getting angrier and angrier because the Philips group messes up everything, and because they believe that they've never been able to influence its composition. A bad relationship like that leads to trouble.

504. With this sentence David had filled the exercise book in which he had kept his diary from August 28. The entries for the next three weeks are on loose sheets of paper.
505. David is referring to the non-Jewish *Schutzhäftling* Johannes Felix (b. 1903).

Call-ups which then have to be undone by the commandant. Talked a lot with Van Wijk about the estrangement between Eindhoven and the secretariat. A plan. This past week I've begun to work behind the scenes a bit, a role that suits me and that I detest, just as I detest so many things that suit me. Went to Lehmann yesterday. Sat and talked there for a long time. Candidly pointed out all the mistakes and tried to clarify the whole state of affairs. Lehmann extremely friendly and self-controlled, but stuck to his guns. The best people are now in Poland. The riffraff has stayed here and a large part of it is in the Philips Kommando, due to the lack of contact [with Philips]. Now that is absolutely not true. There's not much riffraff here, and what *is* here got here because of string pulling by civilians, prisoners, and *Kapos*. And you can't prevent that. The rest is a selection from the group sent to us by the camp administration. And it's possible to demonstrate grounds for all appointments (family, hauling rocks, recommendation, good marks), just as for nonappointments (bad marks, flirting with prisoners, and—for a while—because family members were already here . . . etc.). These constantly changing considerations should have been explained throughout. To an outsider the business does give a rather chaotic impression. There are various reasons why the contact hasn't been maintained. More a matter of impotence than of principle. In any case it is to weep: somehow this good opportunity for staying and living here has been totally spoiled. Now we are, in fact, dumped on by everybody. Quarrel Sanders-Biedermann.

[Thursday] October 14 [1943]. I don't know if anyone will notice, but I'm writing everything that follows with a shaved head. Sunday, Saathoff in the barrack. "All hair off." Felt hurt for a moment, but these things are so inescapable that without hesitating you just jump into the middle of them, laughing hard. So that is what we did. It *was* rather chilly. Spitz had them cut off his hair with tailor's scissors followed by some tidying with clippers. I waited all day. It's happened before that people were being shorn bald and that in the course of the day a countermanding order came. After all, we're civilian internees. The fact is: the previous commandant had seen us in our civilian clothing. That always protected us to some extent. Now the detachment is leaving. Or is about to leave, so that all contact with old acquaintances is coming to an end.[506] Saathoff is back. He's looking

---

506. It is not clear to what David is referring.

good and cheerful. Yet we were really startled. But we haven't noticed much change. Except that on the very first evening the roll call lasted twice as long, and cooking in the barracks has been prohibited again. So E. was working away at the stove and Jan Hurkmans came in. "You know you're not allowed to cook here?" "This is called frying, Mr. Hurkmans." We're ever closer to becoming prisoners, but in that case Jewish prisoners, who in principle don't get treated as well as the others. People are even saying that we're going to be in one barrack with the Jewish prisoners in the *Schutzhaftlager*. About a week ago I entered that forbidden terrain. I visited no. 16. They really live there. Read, study, smoke there in their big, clean room. We're put up in our pens, where it is filthy, noisy, and unfriendly. And where in the evenings people crawl onto their beds simply because there's nothing else to do. And then we have a bit of fun (so sad are we) or sing a song:

> There once was a Yehude,
> who lived inside a camp
> poor man, he'd *aggenebbish*[507] such bad luck, such bad luck.
> He lived there in a pigpen, top bunk in his block
> and the guard he shot him, sitting duck.
>
> Blindman Maupie[508] we are still not done for,
> blindman Maupie soon we're going home.
>
> The lime pit grew still fuller,
> the Jews were nearly gone
> and still the war went on and wouldn't end, wouldn't end
> the smoke it rose still higher, above the wood it rose
> and the guard he shot at what he chose.
>
> Blindman Maupie we are still not done for etc.

That's the kind of fun we're having these days. I'm feeling a bit less at home in this camp. I used to be part of things, interested in camp

507. *Aggenebish* is Jewish slang: *akh* means "alas!" and *nebbish* refers to a loser.

508. "Blind Maupie" or "Blindman Maupie" is the Jewish equivalent of Doubting Thomas. The expression is often accompanied by placing a finger under the eye and pulling the skin down lightly. Maupie (Dutch-Jewish slang for "Moses") was a famous Amsterdam street vendor who was known to be extremely skeptical.

business, in [Ph]ilips business, knowing it was an insincere attitude, so to speak, but adapting myself out of impotence. That's kind of coming to an end. I'm studying history again, reading a bit. Not because I'm animated, because in many respects I'm as listless as can be, but because real life is beginning to make itself felt again. I don't see it yet, but I feel it, as the outer layer of a flame, invisible yet hotter than the yellow flame itself.

Anyway, it's getting dicey here, as we say. The new commandant is very keen on discipline. We saw the old one leave earlier this week. His car was parked in the courtyard behind the gate. We all stretched and stood on tiptoe, that's the way we are, and Reinecke said: "Don't watch, that's none of your business." The new commandant made an appearance in the sick bay and said of someone: "He'll probably croak." "But he doesn't know it yet," said Dr. Levie. "You can just tell him he's going to croak." Reinecke and Stokker recoiled.

The parcels are now limited to 2 kilos [4.4 lbs.]. Camp staff, OD (now consisting of only ten men) into the Philips construction area. Dire threats against speaking during roll call. That's not much use, because it's hard to detect people before sunup and after sundown. In the morning we stand there in the dark, and in the evening in a twilight that's far advanced. That does give us some protection. No more singing or whistling while walking. Men and women separated in the industrial court. That's impossible [in our branch and] also in textiles. So it won't take effect. But what has taken effect is that during the lunch hour, when married and engaged couples used to get together, men and women are separated by the Fire Department.[509] We also don't eat in our barrack any longer but in the dining hall, which I left with my nerves completely shot the first time I used it. And a new *Unterscharführer* has shown up. He walks between the barracks and looks through the windows. Beyond that, [new] female guards now wander around at Philips. The previous one we had gotten on our side. She always ate her meager sandwiches from a paper bag and got some extra food from us. Her successor is a new broom, full of rancor moreover, that swept very clean, at least on day one. The relationship between the women and the guards is quite remarkable. Downright friendly with a number of them. Ilse, the children's nursemaid, seems already to have gotten into difficulties because of

509. Vught, like other concentration camps, had its own firefighters. They were selected inmates who could also be put into action as auxiliaries of the camp police.

"favoritism to Jews." "Oh, what a pretty child, I want to show her to Hauptscharführer Ettlinger."[510] Mostly they're rather lonely types who are very happy when the women treat them like human beings. Something they rarely do, by the way, or do only when it's in their interest. The women in the women's prison camp never do it. They hit them and swear at them. One of them is supposed to have reported not long ago that she couldn't complete the roll call because several women refused to get out of bed. . . . The guards' supervisor, a kind of sweet schoolteacher, had a hysterical fit. All this while, as we are hearing, the treatment in the German women's prisons is very harsh.

There's another issue altogether. I already wrote once about H. and his papers.[511]

He now wants to come to Philips, it seems, and that's not pleasant.

There's also something else. There's his daughter.[512] And all day long I think of her with great emotion. In the morning, when it's still too dark to work, and in the evening, when the women have also stopped working, we have long conversations. About very general things, in which I open up completely. Perhaps I don't attain the old adroit and systematic formulations, but certainly I talk about my area of knowledge with the same love. I've also talked about this with Alfred a lot. But that was probing, digging deep beneath the surface, and often painful. This is light, instructional, "horizontal," and very human in nature. I have the strength to be very open with her, about "personal" matters and about everything that inspires my thoughts and feelings. And she always knows exactly the right moment to give me the stimulus to keep on speaking, by means of some pleasant words, a sweet anticipatory or assenting gesture, or a friendly question. She doesn't let me get very close to her. Sometimes she tells me something about herself, but it isn't much, and she won't say what it means when I see her staring out of the window for a long time during work, or what she's thinking when she looks at me in a certain way. One of the good things that exist between me and her is that during a conversation I can instantly elicit a physical sign of attention from her, simply by *willing* it. Perhaps it's also that there's something in my voice that asks for an appearance of attention. And it is this

510. Only a few children were left. They were part of the SOBU group and had arrived in August 1943.

511. David is referring to the German-Jewish refugee Siegfried Hess. See the entry on the Hess family in the appendix.

512. Hannie Hess.

contact that creates this open relationship, so that's the most important thing. Sometimes she looks up at me, knowing, agreeing, and yet surprised. And then suddenly an image seems to slide between me and her, not of something else but of something that is very likely identical to what we are talking about and to everything that passes back and forth between us, but of another quality, of another material. Perhaps it's not even an image, but her eyes are suddenly seeing something else, more eternal, so to say. In love with her? It's because of that unknown, almost uncomprehended something that exists between us. That newness, not yet habitual. And also the wonderment each time we reveal something of ourselves to each other. Whereby I give more than she does. But although what I give may be bigger and more weighty, what she gives is in any event more precious. Just like anything from a girl. Last week she talked about her fiancé for the first time. In hindsight: of course she's engaged, people protect this kind of girl from the very start. And they also take the initiative in protecting themselves in this way. It was painful all the same. She didn't say it by accident, of course, but with sweet and inept cunning. But it's difficult for me to think of someone next to her and linked to her. To realize she isn't entirely present when we're talking with each other. That the best of her girlish wishes reside elsewhere. That does smart. And this too: somehow I had the illusion, along with everything else I was trying to impart, that I was also awakening new feelings in her. Perhaps that's true anyway. But then you don't notice it. Because fiancé is such a big, sensual word for such a little girl.

[Saturday] October 23 [1943].[513] Reinecke and Ettlinger are standing at the gate late in the evening. Erich after Otto: "Caps . . . off!"[514] And Otto: "Don't talk to me about it. I'm feeling much too jittery." The next day the gentlemen have departed. Erich is of the view that they may in fact get striped outfits. Or else maybe yellow and black (house-of-correction colors) (Reinecke in heavy-duty socks). To tell the truth, I actually feel sorry for Reinecke. A brute, a womanizer, and a charlatan. But all the same with a certain natural benevolence. That has been clearly apparent and emerges even from this diary. The postponed transport has gone after all. Martin Roman, who had

513. On October 22, 1943, Vught contained 1,496 Jews, including 19 children younger than sixteen years.
514. David is referring to Chief Kapo Erich Beck and Otto Reinecke.

written those rhymes in that scummy little paper, had to leave with it. Stokker was in Berlin with that paper. It seems to have been not without significance as a damning fact. . . . "That's the thanks I get," says the conceited Martin Roman, who in fact does provide a virtuoso farewell evening. Because the pose he adopts really matters to him a lot. And he plays beautifully. Biedermann wanted to do us a favor, calling up some of our reserves and giving us others in their place who have useful skills and/or have husbands or wives working with us. But it proved to be impossible. All the same, we were treated decently. At the last moment I almost pried two guys loose. It was their own fault that the attempt failed.

[Wednesday] October 27 [1943]. It rarely happens—people will have to grant me this—that I make big claims for myself. In a way I actually don't quite exist in this camp. This week and last I had a bit of a feeling that I really was here, and it didn't happen in the most agreeable manner. Severe stress, nerves shot, sleepless night, etc. Why? Well, everything you've stored up all those months, repressed as they say, comes to the surface at some point. I had figured [it would happen at the] end of the war. It has actually happened a bit earlier than that. In itself a gratifying sign. And then the immediate occasion: Miss H. H., Hannie, as I say with some difficulty, although from the very first day I insisted on using her first name, while she was still being more formal. The production line stopped, the Aryan women had to be deployed, more about that later, and she had nothing to do all day. And all day long I urgently and blindly sought her company. She gave it to me, but not always eagerly. But when we were talking it was with great mutual interest. At the outset I was for her a fellow who had an awful lot to offer, who had a lot upstairs. Gradually my conversation became cutting and self-accusing. And she: "From the first day I saw you, when as yet I didn't know you at all, I already knew how much immaturity you had in you, concealed behind all your knowledge, your argumentation. and your ideas." And when last week I was talking with her sister and asked her the next day what she had made of the conversation: "I didn't listen, but I did see one thing and it kept me thinking throughout: how adult you are in dealing with her and how much of a little boy with me."[515] And I: "But I don't open myself up to her and I do to you. I've revealed myself to you in all my confu-

---

515. David is referring to Ruth Hess. See the entry on the Hess family in the appendix.

sion and weakness." She gives me a searching look and then laughs briefly. And she's right. And what is she thinking? Spitz says: "She'll have a good laugh when she's alone." He says she's just like a pussycat. Actually, I said to A. G., with whom she has a lot in common, so to say, both physically and intellectually, and generally in the elements of her personality: "You, you're a pussycat." This morning I explained to Hannie what a pussycat is. It knows just about everything, has a lot of feelings towards and against its housemates, and it goes softly through the house, makes no noise, and gives no indications of its awareness. And sometimes bursts out angrily and without warning. And has a kind of warm, retiring nature.

When I was just starting to be in this very personal relationship with her, it gave me a very hard time. Regrets over forgotten Amsterdam, this blindly daring and irresponsible adventure, the ill-fated way in which I'm drawn to her, and her friendly, quietly reserved attitude. But the question is whether I didn't do everything for a thrill. Very likely even. I need this excitement and these difficulties. Actually, I'm more or less over them now.

[Thursday] October 28 [1943]. The relationship has stabilized somewhat. We know exactly what we mean to each other. I come to her looking for help just as to my other female friends. And she gives it to me, because she has much to give. I candidly told her everything. And what do I mean to her? Well, she just laughs a bit. And that's all right. But a good thing: I've discovered a new good acquaintance for later. One who'll keep. I'm over my nervous tension a bit. And now immediately have grounds for renewed stress. Without me Mr. Topel and spouse would have been occupying a small apartment in Poland long ago.[516] Instead he has become a timekeeper. My colleague in a certain sense. In fact, he has few people under him. And add to this that I still have some influence around here. More even than I used to. P. and S. explicitly put me in charge of personnel questions upon S[anders]'s departure.[517] Something, in fact, that already used to be the case. But De Wit: a cool, aristocratic, somewhat timid figure.[518] But a silent and

516. David is referring to Szaja Topel and Kaatje Topel-Boers. See the entry on the Topel family in the appendix.
517. David is referring to G. H. Peuscher and Combrecht Sanders. Peuscher was the Philips employee in charge of technical operations of the Philips Kommando.
518. The non-Jewish prisoner Abraham de Wit was the head of the Philips Kommando. See the entry on de Wit in the appendix.

tough autocrat, who knows only about the limits of things. And who thinks I exceed those limits. And so gives me a shove.

[Monday] November 1 [1943].[519] I don't know where I was, but there's a lot to tell.[520] The end of last week: hectic rumors. A transport will be leaving, the whole camp will be emptied. Escotex is going, etc. People also claimed to know more: H. is in Berlin. B. too. Actually, the former was still here that morning. Anyway, now he'll stay away for a couple of days. So it's true? Moreover this is an unreliable tale, one that does, sadly, contain an element of truth and, God knows, may even be true: the new commandant is far from keen on the Jews. Originally he thought there were only Jewish prisoners here, hence the shaving of heads and so on. The civilian Jews who are here should, [he thinks], have left a long time ago. That this didn't happen was, according to him, due to Chmielewski, together with H., pulling some strings. So he has been in The Hague (that's certainly true) to get rid of us. I do a bit of consoling, speak with Smit, who gives me definite assurances. The next day: a telegram from Berlin. The industry groups are barred from leaving. For all that, the situation is still hopeless, even though we can, with fear and trembling, stretch things out for quite a while. You have to have experienced days like that to be able to understand the unstable, nervous mood in which we live here. A few times already Hannie has asked me, with big, appealing eyes: "Is it true about the transport?" In a tone of voice that invites me to say: "Yes, it's true." And constantly the questions to and from each other: "Have you heard anything?" "Is there really a transport leaving?" And the endless exhaustion around the middle of the day, when people have been squandering time heedlessly, and mouths are dry and heads tired and confused from the many things they wanted to say but couldn't find the words for because they weren't conscious of them. Consolations, calculations, pleasantries, profanities, complaints. But people have only been kind of talking around the feeling of emptiness, and the outside of thought has become hardened by words. Within that circle everything has stopped moving and suffocates and ferments. That's what such days are like.

519. On October, 29, 1943, Vught held 1,496 Jews; this included 19 children younger than sixteen years.
520. With this sentence David began a new exercise book in which he was to keep his diary until November 11, 1943.

I've remembered now what I was writing about: the table issue. Relations between De Wit and myself have never been the greatest. De Wit is the very opposite of a schemer, but he has an iron will that [shapes] his character. Because of that and the silent and determined attitude which the others (especially the civilians) adopt here, everything gets shifted back and forth, things happen and you can't tell who set them into motion, as if everything were suspended from fine strings as in a marionette theater. You notice it from the movements, but it isn't clear who is pulling the strings. "Everything that happens here goes equally badly," Hannie said, and she's right.

So I moved my table. In itself improper, that goes without saying. In a fairly ungracious tone I was informed that it was not possible to have two timekeepers in one department, that I could do the additional work somewhere else (nota bene in a lonely, drafty corridor), or leave it for the other [timekeeper], who in any case had asked for more work. Walked away in anger and immediately spoke with Smit, who is very well disposed towards me. Spitz maintains neutrality in things like that. I immediately jump right on such matters and flog them as hard as I possibly can. Moved on Smit's authority and then had to see how, on De Wit's orders, my table had been moved during my absence. Mobilized Smit and Van Wijk, later also P[euscher] and achieved a great quarrel on a point of principle, during which De Wit turned the issue into a question of confidence, whereupon, of course, Smit had to abandon me, something I can hardly be angry about. A great consolation was: the sympathy and help from the Eindhoven people and the fact that I had pushed the business to the very end and in this way for once had done no violence to my nature. To pick a fight of that kind and to let myself go that way (I really was quite beside myself for a couple of days) may not be to my taste, but it is very much part of my character.

I sat in the corridor for one full day, hoping to be forcibly ejected from it by the commandant or the very large and strong prison leader. This plan did not work out, but De Wit comes to me a day later and says, as if he had thought of it himself, that he's discussed it once more, but that he does find it less than desirable, etc. So I have to move again, but it's not explained or, better said, should not be explained why he now adds that Topel will keep the work that he took over with the precise intention of occupying my work place. Good. I don't get back to my original place. I now sit in the place where Topel used to sit. He now huddles like a strange, shy, yet satisfied monkey in the back of the hall, where I once sat. This is also unexplained. My table now stands behind a kind of wall, so that I can't see anyone approach. So I'm writing this diary at another table.

A disagreeable experience at the beginning of last week. I'm writing a nice letter to Lydia. The guard comes by. She's very kind and very fearful. Looks over my shoulder and tells me that this is very dangerous. I speak very openly with her, which earns me strong and justified reproaches from Hannie. We talk about Jewish and Aryan women. She feels more at ease among our women. Just keep on writing. Between the afternoon inspection, etc. The relationship between the female guards and the Jewish women is one of the most remarkable features of this camp. In general it is simply good. Too good? We're so afraid, and fear has made us forget to hate everything that comes out of that corner. The Aryan women can do that so well. (The prisoners in the prison camp.) For me it keeps being a diversion and at the same time a source of self-reproach to talk with people like that. Anyway, conditions are changing significantly around here. The new commandant is an old-fashioned man. And his entire staff consists of old-fashioned fellows. So this is turning into a genuine concentration camp. No bouts of murder and torture, at least not yet. But definitely strict rules, dangerous inspections, and things like that.[521] If this book were to be divided into chapters, there would now be one with the title: things are getting dicier here by the day. With the exception of eight clergymen, the entire post office is now part of the Philips construction group. The ninth clergyman is Mr. H. The SS now goes through the parcels, rips off wrapping paper, slices into loaves of bread, etc. A dangerous situation. Recently there have been treats in my parcels. The Philips first-aid man was stopped carrying a clandestine parcel with a letter. A big investigation during the roll call in the evening twilight. They cracked one of his ribs when they beat him, and he's spitting blood. A big campaign against clandestine letters. The Philips driver was stopped at the gate. Auer kept on driving with the Philips stew.[522] But then Auer is an estimable man. At roll call a large-scale inspection for undershirts. People had to lift their shirts to show their bare bellies. How oppressive the situation has become

521. David is alluding to the uniform and very harsh regime developed by Theodor Eicke in Dachau and standard practice in German concentration camps since the late spring of 1934. Especially in the Jewish section of Vught, procedures had been more relaxed.

522. SS-Oberscharführer Franz Auer was the head of labor deployment in Vught.

is evident from the fact that suddenly a line of people was standing there to volunteer information, among them a big bunch of prisoners (!). The good times are pretty well gone. Women and men are no longer allowed even minimum contact. For that purpose all kinds of barriers are raised up and heavy punishments are threatened. A nasty doorman has been posted in our work barrack, so that no outsiders can get to our delectable women. Their own husbands are being kept away too. Furthermore, a second gentleman will come to look for sabotage and smoking on the assembly line. Because, so the commandant has told the Philips administration, our barrack worries him because of its marked heterogeneity. The fifth year of war, but things are becoming dicier.

People should not let me read their palms. The evening I got here I told my own future, and last week I told Süsskind's. The almighty one, who had a private toilet, at the outset a private secretary, who smoked emphatically when others had been forbidden to smoke and wanted to demonstrate his rights and his position in that way, who lived here generally as a kind of Grand Old Man (he protected the camp, but the camp was very serviceable to him, he could take his cut from all JC shipments, because in a way everything belonged to him), is hauling rocks at the moment.[523] I foretold it with a certainty that astonished me. On the other hand, his position was indefensible, especially after S[aathoff]'s return. After all, he was head of the "club" and S[aathoff] had no use for the "club." In any case, an important part of it is already in Poland. His greatness had been remarkably reduced. He wasn't able to hold his own anywhere. Lehmann and Jacob denied him entry to the secretariat, which was doubly bad because it was the only place he could still use for a rendezvous with Mrs. P.[524] Anyway, Lehmann had already told him that he didn't want Süsskind to chat with any woman at his desk, and Neumann has already said something to him about "his whore." "A misfortune for the entire camp, Mr. Koker, I tell you in all confidence." This is reasonable, because he says it in confidence to many people. And to everybody many times over. Biedermann not long ago: "I have a new orderly: Süsskind. He asks to be allowed to run errands for me." Then a speech by Süsskind which expresses an enormous fear. "You've made it this far. But I don't intend to put up with further disagreeable things for

---

523. Süsskind's fall did not end with his demotion. In November 1943 he was deported to Auschwitz.

524. David is referring to Hertha Poppert, who had a relationship with Süsskind.

your pleasure." Now he's lugging rocks for our sins. But whether we shall be saved because of it? That's another question.

My tale is becoming tedious, but it's almost at an end: just like the last time: E[ttlinger]: "Orders from Berlin, the whole outfit has to go. In very short order." Otherwise everything remains calm. I pass it on to Hannie as a rumor. That evening the men's camp knows nothing about it. Except for Lehmann and a few initiates. The women's camp seems to have been in a panic.

The next day the story becomes generally known. No new fabric is to be cut [at Escotex]. Someone makes a speech. The matter is very probably lost. People have to prepare themselves for that. And that is what they do. The enterprise stops working. People make sandwich bags and useful things of that kind. H., the administrator, has spoken about Auschwitz, where the industry will go in its entirety.[525] Stories of the kind that Reinecke told early on and which have a more or less sunny aspect. Jewish camp leadership. A lot of agriculture, the camp is largely self-supporting. Synthetic rubber factory. If you ask me, it sounds livable.[526] The only bad thing is the way the matter affects my family. But as far as this goes it's very bad. I can't talk about it at all with Mother. Becomes abusive as soon as she starts talking about it. I can't talk with Father in any case; the impression he makes is so helpless. That's always the way it is: you hurt people because you feel sorry for them. As far as I'm concerned: I talk a lot with Spitz and Roland, especially the latter. He's my friend. What binds me to him is his very special openheartedness and punctiliousness with respect to the services he can render you. He's the type who can't stand being by himself and therefore constantly seeks out others. He frightens me with his dependence. In the meantime, in spite of all the trouble we went to for him, he has moved to the capacitor night crew. Not a day passes without a letter on my table. His letters are hurried, there's so much on his mind. He can't impose form on this overflow of thoughts. And to think that this takes place at night.

Letters. I received one from Lydia. Max got one too. She writes an almost perfect Dutch. My days are changed, they are of a different, more delicate material, as it were. I had tears in my eyes when I read

525. David is referring to Siegfried Hess, who managed the Escotex branch. As he predicted, he was deported to Auschwitz two weeks later.
526. The elements that David mentions were indeed integral parts of the Auschwitz operation. He did not know about the core element: the killing installations. For a reconstruction of the causal connection between the Auschwitz farms, factories, and the crematoria, see Dwork and Van Pelt, *Auschwitz*.

them. And everything acquires new meaning: the one it used to have, but more complete and free. She quotes from a poem by Gorter that seems to have been written with her life in mind.[527] This uncertain wandering through emotional language is all hers. A letter like that makes all my nervousness and doubts vanish. But also: I'm going to Poland now. (The wager, the sex-crazed paradise). And that *is* hard to take. Yesterday (it's 11/6 by now) I was completely upset. And what comes before was written over several days. I thought I was sure to be going. If I have any trace of optimism in these circumstances, I exploit it in offering irresponsible encouragement to others, especially the girls. Yesterday I didn't feel this way at all, and given the way I am, I had to testify to our complete wretchedness. I stood at the stove with a small group of women. I said: "You have to prepare yourselves . . . for leaving with your families. Every family member will be notified separately." Hannie later said reproachfully: "You're getting a very bad reputation around here." I conceded the point. Actually I was already feeling ashamed. I mentioned a bet I had with Tini Lansberg. I: "We are going on transport." If not, she'll get a verse from me. She: "We're not going." If we do, she'll make me a nice embroidered handkerchief with a suitable motto. That's possible, she has enough peace of mind, because her *Sperre* will surely keep her in Westerbork. I entered into this bet fully convinced [I would win it]. Right after that I had, you might say like a bud [of hope], because in fact it's that kind of feeling, a small sense: it might still be possible. . . . Within half an hour this thought filled me almost completely, mixed, as it were, with that other definite feeling. I also felt a need to give it form and to justify it to my own mind. So: a bet with Max Rosenberg, who is a sensible person and therefore believes we will go.[528] I: "We won't go." He: "Yes, we will." Hannie contemplated me for a long time and said in a perplexed tone: "Do you know what you are?" I: "Well?" "You are" (a gesture with both hands) "such a little baby. People sometimes talk about the child hidden in the man, but you really don't need to fear that." That kept me happy all evening. I reported it to Alfred, who definitely considers Hannie to be someone who will always see the child hidden in the man. And I keep laughing about it, because she's such a little girl herself. It's a remarkable insight and conscious-

527. Herman Gorter (1864–1927) was a major Dutch impressionist poet and a committed Socialist.
528. See the entry on Max Rosenberg in the appendix.

ness. Now I also know precisely what she is to me. Know that this is a friendship I need. Stimulating because of the distance. And because of her friendly irony. And beyond this: a point I can focus on during our brief conversations.

[Sunday] November 7 [1943].[529] This at 2:30 a.m. Because I'm on night-watch duty. That was instituted a few weeks ago. On whose initiative I don't know. In any case, yesterday half the jam was gone. That's not because of the watch because it often happened before. The women also have night watch. Cook and bathe at that time just as we do. But there's also this: recently the scandals in the women's camp seem to have been increasing sharply again. That was always the way: when the camp was bigger, the OD applied its care very differentially, which offered opportunities to others. S[üsskind] also was full of personal concern and charged the OD in general not to watch too carefully. In itself this was not unsound, for it made the competition with the much bolder prisoners and above all the *Kapos* a lot easier. S[üsskind]'s buddies, all of them members of the leadership team, showed up there with particular eagerness. From this perspective, the period of the cabaret, which generally put people into a very sensual mood, seems to have been very favorable. The women's prison camp was notorious for its shocking conditions. Two prisoners are standing outside a barrack, raking or something like that. At a certain moment one says to the other: "Jan, keep watch for a moment," hops through a window and returns five minutes later looking pleased and says: "Thanks, that was that." The evening that we worked in the Jewish women's camp, others had to dig in the women's prison camp. The women there seem not to have kept the men from seeing arousing sights through the windows. Something, it seems, that people didn't care for. But at the moment it's a total sex-crazed paradise in the women's camp. As a matter of fact, you notice it in our factory. The raging condition of the somewhat older girls, but above all of the married women: a gynecologist said the other day: ovary madness. This is completely pernicious for the young boys, like Max. It's nerve-racking for everybody. The guard said that she and a couple of others try every evening to catch a few women who seek and undoubtedly also find enjoyment in the empty barrack 35 (the so-called Wester-

529. On November 5, 1943, Vught held 1,493 Jews, including 19 children younger than sixteen years.

bork barrack from the early days! Almost 9 months . . . I'm turning
into a pro). People know that they're in there: "We hear them, the
blankets (blankets? Yes, they bring them along) are still warm, but of
the ladies not a trace." Love breeds cunning. And all's fair in love, I believe. And people are here to have a good time, after all. Which does
not, by the way, keep the camp leadership from locking the doors in
the women's camp at 7:30 or 8:00 at night. But there are also windows.
They figured that out after a while, so they put a guard at the windows.
But when you consider that a guard is only human and in this case a
woman, and besides that I keep watch at our place, but that I've spent
more than an hour in the washroom, then you can understand that
even this measure need not pose insuperable obstacles.

I don't know whether we're staying here. The commandant, who
was going to come back yesterday with a committee in tow, or so people say, something that raises my hopes, has called to postpone his
arrival and won't get here until Monday. Beyond that, guard Suze,[530]
the well-informed one, says that Escotex is going and Philips is staying, because we have a Hermann Goering stamp here.[531] An institute hitherto unknown to me. Similar stories are doing the rounds
in well-informed circles. People also are saying something a bit more
cheerful: both enterprises will be staying here. But Escotex will start
making uniforms. But the commandant isn't back yet, so it's doubtful
whether stories like this have even a core of truth. So I don't know
if we're staying. But it is a fact that a couple of weeks ago we had the
feeling: with all these changes and escalations, it wouldn't be a huge
disaster [if we left]. To use a Vught expression: it's getting dicier all
the time. Since then, however, the sharp edges have been smoothed
down, the camp is beginning to breathe a bit more freely, people
look at each other in a contented and happy way, and quietly, with
a prudent calmness, people are once again beginning to do a bit
of whatever they like. And that's the way it should be. Because this
is a concentration camp at the end of 1943. We should never forget that. How long a concentration camp like this one can continue
we don't know. Strongly optimistic expectations dominate here, and
they are that much more valuable than earlier prognoses because

530. David is referring to the notorious guard Susanna (Suze) Sophia Maria Arts. She
was tried for war crimes and sentenced to fifteen years.

531. Reichsmarshall Hermann Goering was in charge of the Four-Year Plan and as such
of the war economy. The Philips workshop was part of the war economy and hence fell at
least formally under Goering's authority.

they assume a fairly short term. To this point, people were assuming three months at least. Now many keep saying: before the end of the year. Everything has become a bit more realistic. The conference in Moscow gave the impression of being the last of the war.[532] The fact is, of course, that you can't estimate the length of time anyway. Strategically speaking, there's a lot of work still to be done. But these things don't take place purely strategically, right on to the end, so it can't be calculated with any accuracy. Yesterday Kiev fell, the counterattacks at K[rivoy] Rog, which briefly held up the process, have collapsed, and we're all holding our breath for a moment. Sometimes when I see the mass of people here, a strange thought passes through my head: we don't deserve it [i.e., liberation]. Not true, because who deserves to be in a camp, but as an image it's instructive. There's little in this diary about my thoughts about the Jews, and yet they're dominant. But I prefer the facts.

It's getting cold. In one day it has become winter. For quite a long time already our days have been bounded by darkness. In the mornings we stood at roll call in pitch-darkness and watched the sky behind us change color from deep dark blue to a green and later a bright yellow plane. Still without sun. Too flat and tightly stretched for a sun. Too cool as well. But it was as if the light were trying its best. It tingled in your eyes, you couldn't keep it out, and in that way it was brighter than the sun, because you can't see the sun. Black and sharp against the sky the roofs of the kitchen, at first part of the darkness, then very much separate and massive. As though they had grown. When the roll call ended, it had just become light. Back in the evening. It's growing dark as we line up. The sun is gradually hiding itself behind the bathhouse. For a while we still stand in a warm and merciful light. The evening sky is like the morning sky, so utterly clear that you can't fathom its depth. But it doesn't have the almost unbearable glory of our morning sky, it's more matte and mild.

That's probably past. It's winter now. We lined up that morning, and all the low roofs were white. Behind them the sky was a dirty yellow. Some wet snow fell that day. The branches of the shrubs and the brown, ragged leaves, with little touches of white throughout. And across the frost-covered roll-call grounds, the slow, dark tracks along

532. The Third Moscow Conference was held from October 18 to November 11, 1943. Participants were Cordell Hull, Anthony Eden, and Vyacheslav Molotov, the US, British, and Soviet foreign ministers. They agreed to the Moscow Declaration that reaffirmed Allied commitment to Germany's unconditional surrender.

which the blocks of men come marching. And then in the course of the day a droopy December 5 mood. A slow rain falls outside the fogged-up windows. I think of lit shop windows in the early-twilight afternoons in Amsterdam. And of all the delicious things you're hoping to get. And of walks through the city, which is never more familiar and comforting than at that season. And never do you feel more at ease with yourself than at the beginning of winter. And never do you love another person more. But: will we get the cake or the rod?[533]

[Tuesday] November 9 [1943]. Suspense yesterday and today. The commandant was supposed to be back yesterday. Without being aware of it, I was particularly tense and nervous. I noticed that later. Along the assembly line people are working intently and with flushed heads. Guard Suze comes in and asks: "Why are you all so red?" Then, late in the evening, the tension is discharged in rumors and stories. A message comes from a usually reliable source: the commandant is back. Later it turns out that isn't true. But he's probably as much a stranger at the *Kommandantur* as he is here. Alfred and I say: "He hasn't answered any questions, won't touch a cake that the female guards have baked for him as a welcome present, has locked himself into his room. People see through the window that he's lying on the sofa, shaking. He's upset, but we don't know what about. Whether we're staying or whether we're going." Later it appeared that others passed this fiction on as the truth. The silly geese!

The tale that the commandant had allegedly returned at once triggered invented stories. Transport this coming Friday. Everybody unspeakably miserable. The story was not clearly outlined. It contained a lot of emotion and surmise where reality should have dominated. To put it another way: in its factuality it emerged only halfway from the mood and the tension that lingers in each of us and around us. I heard it only afterwards.

Today an almost unbearable suspense. The commandant still isn't back. But Rauter is here in the morning.[534] We get everything ready for his arrival. We place all coats, neatly aligned, on benches, backs facing forward, men's and women's jackets separated. All boxes lined up straight. Personal possessions neatly camouflaged. I organize

533. Dutch children who behave badly are threatened that at the festival of Saint Nicholas they will not get cake but the rod (and, in case they behave very badly, they are told that they will be taken away to Spain by Saint Nicholas's aides).
534. The Higher SS and Police Leader in the Netherlands, Hanns Rauter, had established the camp. His visit did not promise much good.

things diligently and with an extreme precision. I look at things more or less through German eyes. And everyone has a lot of fun. But when Rauter shows up he doesn't seem to be aware that he is actually in a Jewish section. Because he asks N. R. whether she's been here for a long time and perhaps because she had helped Jews. . . . Is it for this we arranged everything so neatly?

[Thursday] November 11 [1943]. That same day in the afternoon. I'm cold and dizzy. We don't know anything. We're not getting anything done but are dead tired. Bubi walks through our corridor, silently and with the ironic pride I really like in him. Spitz looks at him and is told: "You've got to work hard here." Spitz, who's playing dumb, asks: "Is there any information?" Bubi: "Isn't that enough?" And we [Spitz and I] shake hands and look into each other's eyes.

That evening: it seems Escotex is leaving. Diamonds and metals are staying. And so next day the problems start. Actually I don't really dare to talk with people. Feel a bit embarrassed. The girls on our assembly line are staying. But they're still so young. And have their fathers and mothers and sisters here and want to go with them. But they would rather have them join Philips. Van Wijk, Spitz, and I are in the office, at work on deployments and replacements. The old system: we don't take someone's husband. Then the wife leaves. Then we put another woman in her place. And then *her* husband stays. Meanwhile young assembly line girls come to inquire whether they've been approved to stay. And if they've been approved, whether others have been approved as well. Or, whether others can be considered. Especially sisters. Or mothers whose daughters have been approved. Whether they themselves can't be put to work. Or others who are on the diamonds list, for example, and who have come to do something for their children. Or girls who should have been called up for the vacuum tubes line but have been overlooked by mistake and who now have to leave and so are separated from others who have been called up. What's being torn apart here doesn't bear thinking of. We note down one or two very bad cases. Nothing can be done for most of them. Fairly soon there's a long lineup crowded into the corridor. Hendriks intervenes, the female guard intervenes, Erich is shouting.[535] The Philips people confront Van Wijk with an ultimatum. They won't enter the barrack until he stops doing this kind of work, which is none of his business. Smit: "Koker is capable enough

535. Hendriks is a member of the Landwacht (see note 502); Piet Erich is a *Kapo*.

to handle it." Add to this that B. has already gone to Br[aakman] and in a high-handed, hypercritical manner has insisted on keeping families together.[536] I'm dizzy and at my wits' end. Have difficulty controlling myself in dealing with several who have managed to push their way through and ask for the same thing as dozens before them. Everything seems to be lost. Our beautifully exact preferential lists are pointless. I tell everyone not to be under any illusions. And have no intention of doing anything else.

To all these matters I bring an *angry* but nevertheless *abstract* sense of responsibility. I *have* to do this, this is my job, it has to do with people, but it makes absolutely no difference who exactly is doing it. This way of dealing with things is much more exhausting than the direct and spontaneous way. Hannie says: "You care too much about these things. But you do look very tired." Evening roll call. Which I already feared.

Useful hints to make camp life more pleasant

At roll call make sure you don't chatter
If you can't help it, you'll learn it someday
And what you say won't really matter
As long as you jabber away.

Make sure that you don't keep in step,
Though it's tidier than if you schlep
Since by keeping in time you won't tread
on the heels of the person ahead.

When you come home, you must rush
And take two food bowls for your mush,
Otherwise, strange way of thinking,
Someone else has it for drinking.

If you would wash in hot water
Then it's quite clear that you ought to
Make sure the stove's open throughout
'Cause otherwise it won't go out.

536. Philips manager Carel Braakman did his best to keep the Philips Kommando together.

Furthermore you really ought to
Not put on extra new water,
Using more would just be heedless
And also for others quite needless.

In the canteen talk loudly to all around,
In the dorm that makes a wonderful sound,
For if you should let your fun fall flat,
People could go to sleep just like that.

In the dorm do not take off your shoes
A rhythmic clacking sound be sure to use,
For otherwise you cannot take as read
That people hear you're on your way to bed.

Furthermore listening in rich measure
to giggles and whispers gives great pleasure
Drop your shoes hard on the floor once or twice,
Otherwise others won't wake in a trice.

Cranking a flashlight is fine when it's late,
You must all realize this is just great,
Such a device makes a noise and gives light,
And it shines so well in faces at night.

If some hint has been left on the shelf,
I hope you'll think of it all by yourself
Just make sure on this you keep a good hold:
"I do what I like, the rest leaves me cold."[537]

---

537. This poem is typed on a sheet of paper that was glued on the inner cover of the exercise book that covers the period November 20 to December 22, 1943. John Irons, the poem's translator, observed that "in terms of rhythm, vocabulary, and content I have my doubts about its being Koker's work. It is not nearly as competent in terms of pulse as his poems normally are. An example: "Spreek in de eetzaal luid en krachtig / Dat klinkt in de slaapzaal prachtig" (In the canteen talk loudly to all around, / In the dorm that makes a wonderful sound). The first strophe has nine syllables, the second eight. That is very un-Kokeresque. Furthermore, he rarely uses an *aabb* rhyme scheme, normally choosing *abba* or *abab*—and sometimes mixing the two. The poem is not sardonic enough, and there is a lot more padding and cliché in the lines." In a letter Max Koker confirmed John Irons's observation. "This is not a poem by David." Letter, John Irons to Robert Jan van Pelt, May 20, 2010; letter, Max Koker to Robert Jan van Pelt, July 5, 2010.

[Saturday] November 20 [19]43.[538] A lot has happened. The tension of last week, tension due to anticipation and intensive labor, was discharged on Monday.[539] This time Spitz and I took part in the entire preparation. The camp lived and laughed on merrily, knowing that something was wrong but not knowing any details, and thus completely unconcerned. We spoke with people of whom we knew that they would be summoned for transport and who didn't expect it. We said nothing. Meanwhile, working with Van Wijk to fill the remaining open slots [on the Philips list], up to 400, with immediate family of our people, thus minimizing the personal calamities. But this is how it is. Philips has no interest in our personal fortunes. It's interested in the group. But the individuals in it are small and weak and insignificant. That's why the prisoners enjoy a very definite preference. To Philips, the female prisoners are typically individual cases. Our Jewish girls constitute a mass that matters only as a total entity.

In another context, M. is an interesting figure. My conversations with him.

Meanwhile a number of people through Auer have taken care to be protected at our expense, so that every morning we thought: who'll turn up on our lists today? I've observed all this in a state of nervous tension and with a constant, debilitating sense of failure. Because all day long [we get] inquiries from our assembly line girls on behalf of their sisters or brothers or from our women on behalf of their husbands. I've spent a couple of furiously busy days. Two small successes: Van der Hal and Spitz.[540] The last evening before the transport, Van Wijk was with us: we don't know what still has to be done. But on to the secretariat, to be present, in any event, for the conclusion of the piece. There, after the fog and darkness outside, there was a lot of light. An almost cozy atmosphere, the way it feels after a lot of work. Jacob and the Aryans at their usual work. L[ehmann], B[iedermann], R[osenberg] and JR, who were calmly putting the finishing touches to their transport. L[ehmann]: "I was about to send for you." They've called up three women who work with us (among those deployed in their stead are the two S. women. Inexcusable string pulling by AB)

538. On November 19, 1943, Vught numbered 697 Jews, including 19 children younger than sixteen years.

539. On Monday, November 15, 1943, a transport with 1,152 people left Vught for Auschwitz.

540. David is referring to Dr. Isidoor van der Hal (1907–86). His wife, Saar van der Hal-van Adelsbergen (1909–78), was a member of the Philips Kommando before November 15. By pulling Dr. van der Hal from the train David saved his life. He died a natural death at the age of seventy-nine.

Also called up old D., whom we let go with an easy conscience, at least at that moment. L[ehmann] calls for volunteers.[541] We refuse one volunteer's request after checking with his foreman. The others are accepted. We even find an additional one. Result: the three malicious summonses are undone, and a man's wife is taken on. Van Wijk is exceptionally enthusiastic; me too, just a bit. That changes at once when I meet H. K. at the same time that the man who has just been released gets all excited. After that in my barrack, old D., who keeps saying he never considered it at all. It turns out his wife received a summons, and he had taken pains to try to get her into our group. He didn't think of going with her, which by itself is an argument for dropping him. In these cases you confront a problem no matter what. When you've played at being providence for an evening, you go to bed with a moral hangover and great doubts. For a long time I hear the people in the dining hall, busily getting their luggage together. Now and then they walk into the dormitory to retrieve something. Barber was busy for a long time, cutting and buttering bread for his child. He had everything in good order.

The next morning the first transport team has to present itself at four. I hardly sleep at all that night, or only very shallowly. In the morning I hear the farewells. And very soon the rumor, which flies around wildly. Everything has been taken from them. We consider what this can mean. The instruction had been so definite: everyone could take all their belongings with them. We don't really believe [the rumor] but make all kinds of guesses that are very sound formally but, alas, ungrounded in reality. When we march off after roll call, the whole group is standing there in big, silent blocks. Not moving. Hair freshly cut off. Wooden shoes. Many without socks. And striped uniforms, of course. The old ones, which the prisoners took off the day before. Their small parcels of luggage, blankets, and boxes of food are lying neatly on the roll-call field. Around it Landwacht.[542] We look, upset by that immobile mass but a bit relieved because of the

541. David did not complete the sentence. This is very unusual. He had reached the end of the page and must have been interrupted.

542. The Landwacht Niederlande [literally Country Guard Netherlands] was established in 1940 by the Dutch national socialists as an auxiliary police force. This force participated in the rounding up of Communists and Jews. In 1943 the Waffen SS established a regiment of the same name for Dutch volunteers. This regiment was to serve as a territorial defence unit to defend the German-occupied Netherlands against allied attacks. David is referring to members of the Landwacht regiment who were stationed in former Dutch military barracks in Vught and who provided, when necessary, support to the SS batallion charged with guarding the concentration camp.

tidy way the luggage is piled up, and because the *Landwacht* men have said: "They'll get it back." The luggage lay there all morning, and they [*Landwacht* men] were busy all afternoon taking everything away and unpacking it. When the Germans weren't looking, a *Landwacht* man reached into a box of food and ate something hand to mouth. The secretariat dog came in carrying Barber's child's teddy bear in its mouth. The cattle cars were partly without doors, with barbed wire over the openings and there were, so people say, ten blankets in each car. Sixty people had to make do with that. A hole in the floor as toilet. The Philips people saw them leave. Their wooden shoes often too small. Some had two left shoes. After the change of clothes people were able to help in a few individual cases, with a sweater, a vest, or scarf. But in the big picture that makes no difference.

A few days later we were given bread porridge. That same day the story: they've gone to M[authausen?] We don't believe it. But we do just a little bit. For several days, the feeling: our concentration-camp existence has become very much for real. We're standing at the edge. Often I think that thought from the early days: at a certain point death, too, can be thought of as possible. And thus it is possible.

Our further reports from returned SS men are: reasonable food and drink en route (the marching rations were also sufficient), in Poland people wear striped uniforms too, it's like a holiday resort here in comparison, and people were waiting for them with whips. Gradually I begin to think less optimistically about Poland.

The case of H[ess?]. Lugging bricks. Palestine question. The ribbons. Nostalgia. The letter from S[üsskind?].

Among the many who went was Süsskind (meanwhile it's November 23. It's almost my birthday and I'm really looking forward to it.) Frau Poppert had been here with us to do something for "her man." I really pity him. R gave him a sweater, an undershirt, and a scarf. Poppert was very grateful. Later he got a very beautiful sweater back. The evening before, Süsskind had been given permission to say his farewells but was kept out by force by the prison-camp leader. He wrote a note from the railway station that I won't soon forget: "60 people in one boxcar. Everything looks very dreary. Be glad you're not part of it. R. has my lighter." He had not only the cigar lighter but also the fountain pen and the watch. Poppert noticed he was wearing both after saying he had surrendered them. Small things like this make everything even more ugly and maddening.

Another prominent person went away. I was talking with Hannie, a few days before the transport. Max Rosenberg comes in: "Your father is going along as manager." She was confused and agitated. For us [at Philips], of course, it was a reassurance. But heard later: he was made to sign something without reading it, which later turned out to be a waiver of his Theresienstadt papers. Probably it was on punishment and business grounds both. The day of the transport Hannie was in rough shape, but that seems to be completely over now.[543] I was able to see the transport through her eyes, as it were.

Because the transport was going directly [to Poland], a few people who otherwise would have been held up at Westerbork have been sent on. In a small number of cases the SD consented. They went separately to Westerbork. As a result of our interventions. Spitz's initiative. Perhaps a genuine political triumph. It would be agreeable to have played this game.

Received greetings from T[rudie] L[evit]. Remarkable. Mother received a birthday parcel with ribbons inside, and I'm saving them faithfully.

[Saturday] November 27 [1943].[544] It's my birthday. Terrible hangover as a result. Got nice letters and cards from Nettie, Karel, Frederika, and Tini. Also one from J[an Erik] R[omein], which especially touched me and made me feel ironic at the same time. Otherwise this promises, for very concrete reasons, to be one of the worst days. But first to continue the whole story.

A week ago Sunday there was no power and we had to haul rocks. A little piece of concentration camp [life] that, in itself, feels good. We went out through the gate, it was early and damp. Under the trees the grass had turned brown. Yellow and reddish in many places, due to the red morning sun that slithered along them. Such opulence, everything so cool and carefree. The first few moments I felt myself to be free. That soon came to an end, a constant back and forth. Guards on the sidelines, with dogs and canes. There were a lot of us, but the Jews were the particular target. I thought: the others are being harassed this way only because there are not enough Jews. Now and then some rocks fell off my pile. Once at a guard's feet.

543. Hannie's father had been deported in that transport.
544. On November 26, 1943, Vught contained 677 Jews, including 17 children younger than sixteen years.

On the other hand, many of the guards said that they were heartily sick of it.

On the way back made the acquaintance of a French guy. Miner, from the Lille area. I gave him my name and block number, and he showed up that afternoon to get some bread. Was allowed to talk with him for half an hour. He did his best in an intelligent way not to make things hard for me. I could follow his remarks very well. He mine too. We were talking about children [acting up] in a concentration camp. "Ah, ce n'est rien, un enfant veut la liberté. Et en outre: c'est innocent, n'est-ce pas." [Ah, it's nothing, a child wants freedom. And besides: it's innocent, right?] Something like that doesn't hit home in Dutch, but it does coming out of the mouth of a French miner. He has now departed for his own country. "Avec un convoi special" [With a special convoy] (because "transport" means "enthusiasm"). Being here is becoming ever more normal for us. Every day I begin to hate life here more. And [feel] a nostalgia now and then that's very strong. It's November now, if you look through the fogged windows you think of the streets of Amsterdam with the Saint Nicholas hustle and bustle. People are walking with their hats pulled low over their foreheads, the scarves and shawls peeking out of their coats, on the way home, with a slightly hurried pace, parcels under their arms. It's drizzling. A luxurious light shimmers through the gloom. It must be cold outside, but you picture everything from within the sphere of a warm room. In reality there's nothing. Nothing besides the fogged-up windows, black, damp trees, and the barracks on the other side. And the cold, inside and out. Winter in the KL. Of course there's also the tenderness. But that's only because of loss.

Our hair is growing back nicely. I've had the sides shaved. I'm beginning to resemble a normal human once again. Because it's normal, of course, that I'm wearing a striped uniform. "It's a joy looking at you guys," says Hannie.

We're also wearing long coats and caps now. If I turn up my collar and put the cap over one ear, I look really jaunty, so people say. So I like doing it. It's a pretty good uniform, I think. Sometimes I feel something of the high spirits that a uniform in any case carries along with it. Max discovered he had lice and was terribly unhappy. Last week I heard Beethoven's "Coriolanus" Overture and *Pierrot at the Lamppost.*[545] I almost had to cry.

---

545. *Pierrot aan de lantaarn* is a verse drama by the poet Martinus Nijhoff (1894–1953).

The mail we receive gives us a ration of affection that we some-times have to make do with for rather a long time. R. and the mail. I was almost through it.

Hannie said the other day: "What's with you, you're talking very differently from the way you usually do. Recently you've been so calm around me, and now you're suddenly so agitated." I: "I, too, had noticed that we were good together recently. Also that you had changed. Less forced. And now it's clear to me as well that I'm once again very agitated." She: "How come?" I: "Because I'm losing contact with Amsterdam a bit, and as a result I'm strongly drawn to you again. This is the reaction." She understands this. But we talk so often and so regularly that she has had to listen to reproaches from her sister and girlfriends about flirting with me (women guard each other's morality so shamelessly). Undoubtedly I'm presented in this context as a poor deluded fool. The day before my birthday she got up dur-ing the break and went to sit next to her sister. I later: "Was that a hint?" She denied it for a moment and then admitted it. Not that she pays attention to what the others say, or concedes their right to say it, but at that moment it was the only choice open to her. I did un-derstand that, but it really affected me. On these occasions I become aware how extremely thin-skinned I am. The morning of my birthday, then, very hard at work, ignoring her. During the break I stayed in my place. She came up to me and said: "I want to congratulate you. I shouted at you several times this morning but you didn't want to hear me." I explained to her how particularly painful it is suddenly to find yourself the object of women's gossip, even if you're mentioned only obliquely.

Once again we're very congenial and friendly together.

Mother and I had a lot of mail from Amsterdam. Two beautifully written letters from Nettie, who in my opinion is becoming more ma-ture each day. Not where depth is concerned, but when it comes to ways of expressing herself. We're going to be surprised when we see each other again. Also postcards from Karel and Tini.

Then on November 27 in the evening a parcel from Nettie, which had been prepared with great care and endearing dedication, so that things were achieved that are unbelievable these days. Fish, cake, cof-fee candy, grated chocolate, fondant. We've been living very austerely the last while and therefore this is quite astonishing. In my mind's eye I saw her and her typical taste for luxury. And also with the pa-tience to prepare something like this. My eyes filled when I ate what she had baked: raisin bread. I wrote her a letter. In the other parcel there was chicken. Sunday afternoon we ate chicken (roasted in butter, Roland's doing), cake, raisin bread, a kind of home-baked apple pie, challah with grated chocolate, and coffee with milk. Toast with sausage. Everything on a red handkerchief. Very respectable. But November 27 was my birthday, after all, and so . . . I looked forward to the day with some trepidation. Not for nothing was it unhappy. Two times running. This time the world has changed. Up to this point we took a very optimistic view of Poland: camps, perhaps even better than here, no concentration camps, after all, labor action. The weak won't survive it. But beyond that everything seems quite favorable. We have been misled in this by the relatively humane principles and especially by the strong formalism that apply here.

The morning of my birthday: Spitz reads an excerpt from a letter from Poland. Three people (his fiancée and her parents) are living with Moves [Dutch-Yiddish expression for "they are dead"]. And Moves's business is working overtime. And then a reference to letters from M. I read it over and over. Seldom have I seen anything set out so clearly in writing, and yet I seemed to have forgotten it as soon as I had read it. Our optimistic messages from Poland are not incorrect. They have simply been incomplete. A (probably relatively small) group is working and doing reasonably well. And the rest: wiped out. The world has changed.

Now we know where we're at. We: Spitz, Roland, Van Wijk, De Wit, M., H., and I. The others don't know anything. Don't suspect anything either. And if they say anything in that vein it's simply a manner of speaking. In all conversations in which people make guesses [about Poland] we're bound to keep a straight and noncommittal face.

But this too: the feeling I got after the transport: we're standing at the edge. In the middle of life. But we can't move a step, because before us is an absolute void. And this wouldn't be so important if another feeling hadn't settled in. I feel bigger and stronger with this knowledge. Disdain for one's own fate and for that of others is the necessary basis for every great style of life. In any case: in essence all great action rests on disdain, all poetry, for example, rests on the underestimation of its stimulus and content. I wrote about it to Amsterdam. I don't know whether they'll understand it. I'm well on the way here to becoming some kind of Nietzschean, without any rhetoric, by the way. Without being indifferent to it, I can make peace with doom. Above all I can reconcile myself to it when I see so much that's small and ugly go to ruin. That doesn't exclude pity. And it certainly doesn't exclude making an effort to hold on to life. But otherwise . . . The conversation with Mother and with Van Wijk about S[üsskind?]. I never thought this feeling would seem so real to a person. But it's one of freedom and power. And because of it, acting on behalf of people in whose doom you acquiesce becomes objective and functional. The evening before the transport Van Wijk and I were in the secretariat. The atmosphere there was tired and satisfied. And lots of light. And after we had put the last touches to Philips transport issues, Lehmann, Van Wijk, and I talked about the Philips point of view. Van Wijk quoted Nietzsche in a rough-and-ready German, and Lehmann agreed. A scene and a mood not soon to be forgotten.

At the moment the Philips building-site detachment is keeping us occupied. A real concentration camp detachment for Jews, and it keeps getting worse. Last week someone couldn't carry on any longer. "Finished off" on command.

Another case: wheelbarrows, filled high with sand, [a man] pushes them along a road with potholes, then is thrown into water, next is covered with sand, then sent out to look for mushrooms outside the chain-link fence surrounding the post office. The man in question didn't do that last task. He *is* still alive. Not a day goes by without the severest abuse. The *K[apos]*.

I often think: as far as I'm concerned they can kick those ugly runts to death in the Philips site. In a KZ there shouldn't be any tolerable place. For the time being it doesn't look as if this noble wish will be fulfilled, although people seem to be taking great pains to bring it about. But the workdays were very short for a while because roll calls still had to be held in the morning and the evening. These roll calls have now been canceled, so that we're in the industrial courtyard from seven to seven. Enter in darkness, leave in darkness. Mornings and evenings in the dark. At the gate, Piet's new gatehouse has a small warm light.

All the same, about a week ago I got whacked on the head in pitch-darkness by K., because I was out of step. [Sarcastically:] "We'd like to have your sharp eyes." So all day long we're safely inside the walls of the enterprise, and that way nothing much happens. A female guard walks around, but she eats the Philips stew and entertains herself with the ladies and a couple of shady-looking prisoners, while now and then Bochel comes to have a chat, and that does create a certain amount of stress for a moment. Actually, he leaves well enough alone. Grins, looks around, and disappears again. Very slowly. He's a philosopher, Unterscharführer Bochel. He knows the value of everything, gets excited about something only when it provides him with a diversion, and, without making an effort, dominates the situation through his stature, his wrinkled yellow face, his voice, and his slow gestures, also through his wild screaming. We've all adopted his: *"Pass mal bloß auf"* [Just watch your step] and then move the index finger in a half circle before our noses, like the pointer on some measuring instrument trying to find an equilibrium. A few days ago he had a conversation with Rosenberg. "You like it fine here among the women, don't you? Just watch your step. One of these days I'll catch you." Rosenberg: "Then you'll have to get up earlier, *Herr Unterscharführer.* You won't catch me." "Why won't I?" "I have a year of camp experience." Meanwhile H. comes in and says in his composed businesslike tone: "Rosenberg, you're such a big organizer. Can't you organize a hand-cranked flashlight for us?" Bochel: "He's too fine a gentleman for that. He won't organize anything for us. 'Mister' Rosenberg. The last of the prominent people." "That's why I stayed here, *Herr Unterscharführer.*" "What cheek. You're not going to say we sent Süsskind away because he organized things for us." "But you did think of him, didn't you, *Herr Unterscharführer.*" "Just watch your step. One of these days I'll catch you all the same." The conversation is carried on by Rosenberg with one hand in a pocket, using the other hand to respond with little pushes to the other man's confidential shoves.

Bochel is such a satisfying figure because he represents the type so purely. Which the others certainly do not. His boots extend over his knees, he takes laborious and irrevocable steps, and, simply because of his crooked shape, he always seems to be spying and peering.

To mention the laziness in dating this. The previous is from many days at the same time, and today it's December 14. I've been here more than ten months. What are they really planning for this place? A night crew is working on the prison now. They're building a nice wall around it, and it is said that Saathoff is becoming bunker commandant. He's back again. Active as always, with that heat in his eyes that's all the more alarming because his face is even more pale and wasted than it used to be. He must be close to death. Yet with all his fanaticism and bigotry he has something strangely timid. When I saw him for the first time I wrote, I think: he has a petrified tenderness. That must be it: perhaps it's death that appears right behind his eyes.

Even more than in the past, central in my thinking has become: the general attitude [we adopt] towards the Germans and everyone who belongs to their following.

None of them is innocent. But it's a difficult truth. You value human qualities, excuse a lot, and all of this simply out of weakness. In this the prisoners, especially the women, are better: they ignore the guards, no matter how good they are. T. [Margreet Tasselaar][546]: "When I play handball, I don't give the ball to someone on the opposite team just because she's not unsympathetic. In fact, if my best friend draws the wrong straw and lands on the other team, I find it annoying, but she doesn't get the ball. And if the guard says there'll be bed inspection this evening, that's just stupid. Because she's playing her hand and I mine. And she shouldn't expect me somehow to reward that kind of stupidity."

[Thursday] December 16 [1943].[547] We're already well into the month. There's little for me to do. I'm working in the shipping department for three assembly lines in the capacitor factory, and to that end I'm putting the heat on two small boys. Yesterday one of them let a cart loaded with boxes topple over. Boxes and packing material were blowing around in the neutral zone.[548] I ask the chief of the shipping department whether he might be an accountant. Great emotion: no, actually he's a teacher of classical languages. We talk about Pos and his lectures.[549] Strange disguises: a classicist and a historian-to-be with a strong literary bias are looking after shipping for the firm of Philips Inc. Yesterday morning I walked between barracks 41 and 42. The air we're walking through is mild and misty. The trees glisten. With every breath you take, you feel the world to be more spacious and yourself more free. The ground is hard. There are patches of slippery ice on the road, and icicles hang from the windowsills. Too bad it's almost completely built up around here. Because you think you'd be able to see everything right now. In spite of the mist, which blurs the sun to a small white disk. The way you also think you

546. David is referring to the non-Jewish prisoner Margarethe (Margreet) Tasselaar (1917–2001).

547. On December 10, 1943, Vught held 677 Jews; this number included 17 children younger than sixteen years.

548. The neutral zone was a strip of land along the fence. Guards had the right to shoot prisoners entering the neutral zone.

549. Hendrik Josephus Pos (1898–1955) was a professor of linguistics at the University of Amsterdam.

can know everything and do everything. Feeling pleased, you step along the ground with a slapping sound. Life isn't all that bad. Near the hospital is a small meadow, white with frost. A tiny hostage. He hasn't been walking all that long. And he doesn't do so with any great confidence. He stretches his little arms out and stumbles along the white, misty field like a small dark bird. In this perfect and clean cold we feel ourselves to be so real. And our presence in this enclosed piece of the world so unreal. And these mixed feelings themselves become reality again in that tiny hostage, who totters so uncertainly across the vaguely misted meadow.

Later there are a lot of them: tiny soldiers, but a dog barks and drives them away. They scream and cry for mama. Fat Felix, the block senior from 22, the punishment block, stands there shouting at the dog from behind the barbed wire. But his influence doesn't reach that far.

This morning the radio at work played Bach.[550] A suite I once heard sometime in the past. Slowly the world around us fills up with this magnificent monotony. Far-reaching thoughts, and yet very close to being formulaic. This music has nothing anecdotal like Mozart. It is very near to what all music tends towards. To unfettered music, harmony, no longer carried by anything. But as a result also inaudible. Because our music, which consists of sound, exists by grace of the silence surrounding it. And is therefore limited, anecdotal. The harmony of the spheres is so perfect that you don't hear it. Its element of silence is absent. It has no dwelling, no pace, no shape, it is everything and thus it is nothing. Bach approaches it. But you can still hear him. Beethoven's last works are past the boundary. I said this to Hannie, who is well acquainted with Bach.

She says: "There's a lot of truth in that, but it's not everything. You don't know him well enough."

I also thought: he is a stream, the others have drawn only small, sometimes nicely formed casks of this water. And poetry does the same thing. The magnificent monotony of Homer. The feeling of poetic harmony realizes itself in words, but words are the humble and almost invisible pedestals on which the whole stands.

---

550. Philips had installed a loudspeaker system in their workshop that prisoners referred to as "the radio."

Winter

(December 22, 1943–February 8, 1944)

By the first day of the winter of 1943 over 98,000 Jews had been deported from the Netherlands. But the frequency of the transports had declined: over the fall only four transports had left the Netherlands—all destined for Auschwitz. Three of these, with a total of almost 3,000 people, had departed from Westerbork, and the other, carrying 1,149 Jews, from Vught. The Jewish community had officially ceased to exist on September 28, when the Germans arrested some 5,000 Jews who had been protected by the Jewish Council and the members of the Jewish Council itself. After this date, the only Jews living in the Netherlands were those who were in hiding, those who were interned in Westerbork and Vught, a small group of Portuguese Jews and other Jews whose descent was still being investigated, and Jews in mixed marriages.

[Wednesday] December 22 [1943].[551] Recently Hannie has been indifferent and taciturn when I talk with her. The conversation suddenly halts like a small cart that won't go on. All day long I think about a pretext for a possible new conversation, in the hope that this will be enough. Often it is not. And then Frau Poppert has come between us too. She captivated her for whole days, or so it seemed. For more than one reason I was sad about this. Discovered clearly this in Poppert: simply a will to dominate, which applies in personal "friendship" relations just as much as in other areas. After a week Hannie tells me everything has been merely an experiment. A dangerous and high-stakes game. After a few days P. already seems to have told one of Hannie's girlfriends that she is bisexual. She shows Hannie letters from Richard Süsskind and talks about the relationship. Right away. She says she wants to be Hannie's mother. Invites her to come and

---

551. On December 17, 1943, the Jews in Vught numbered 676, including 17 children younger than sixteen years.

sit next to her. There you are, now you're at home. Saves up cake for her: "You see, I'm thinking of you even when you aren't here." And all this with her eerie vacant face with the brown eyes that try to shroud themselves under the plain blond hair. And her strange gait: a bit bent forward in the lumbar region, something languid and smooth, soft stepped, but there's no one who can see anything [inappropriate] in it. But now, Hannie says, it's hard to get rid of her. A character from Dostoevsky. That obsessed.

If anybody *can* see anything in it, S[anders?] can't. The old Adam is stirring, he's being warned from all sides. But nevertheless he stands behind her chair all day long. Washes her saucepan and gives her rolls with neatly sliced ham. He has qualms, of course. So snarls at the girls on the assembly line. And she is charming and says to a girlfriend: "He's getting on my nerves."[552]

There has been a new development in the situation: one remembers a Mr. N. Aksent.[553] He has a good instinct for having a good time. Here he unerringly found the right direction. And these two made an agreement, P. and Naccent.[554] Day in, day out they'll perform something for the benefit of Mr. S. The situation brings to mind: (1) Falstaff in *The Merry Wives [of Windsor];* (2) some scenes in Molière; (3) prints by Watteau or Biedermeier of the kind that hang in gilded frames in the bedroom at home. Because tall Barend stands leaning diagonally over her, an elegant bend of the hips, head turned sideways, and the leg on the other side thrust forward. Her head inclined, she looks up at him. And S., his face fire-engine red, walks back and forth or, in the best case, sits squarely on his table, legs spread wide. Sometimes beside him the lively G. v. R., talking animatedly and laughing. Cheerful and wise and unobtrusive in appearance in this group: [a play by] Molière, with a wise and cheerful domestic who in such plays is always typically refined. Or Falstaff when he gets into the basket. S. is like him, huge and red. The shepherd boy who always plays the flute in the background is absent. And she isn't dressed like a shepherdess, and he isn't wearing knee breeches and buckled shoes. Sometimes they're having a good time together right at his table, and then he walks back and forth on the other side of the assembly line, red faced, as if he were meditating, the poor infatuated idiot. All the women are

552. With this sentence David had filled the exercise book in which he had kept his diary from November 20. He continued his diary in a new exercise book.

553. N. Aksent or Naccent were the nicknames David gave to Barend Stokvis.

554. David is referring to Hertha Poppert.

enjoying themselves, and P[oppert] is insulted in the rudest of ways. A charming sight.

In the meantime, because of the bombing of B[erlin], the Lorenz prod[uction] has come to Eindhoven.[555] That has focused attention on the fact that the appliances are piling up. They're at their wits' end here now. They're very happy that a lot of hostages have gone home. So they're rid of them. But what to do with us, poor, poor Jews, as the poet says. So all kinds of proposals. It'll probably become: a capacitor factory and a transformer factory, and the people making hand-cranked flashlights will be divided among the Aryan assembly lines. Also some will go to the radio vacuum tubes line, which is on the road to becoming a crowded factory with a poor reputation. Love stories, or what passes for them, I will keep for another occasion.

It is [Tuesday, December] 28 [1943].[556] Nettie's birthday. I think about that a lot, but oh so abstractly. With a light and airy happiness now and then. There are a few small facts to report. Did I already write that the drunk Mr. Kermer, who broke my buttons, has escaped? It seems he had good reason for it. And two weeks later, three fellows who simply walked out and two who failed. Now they're attaching chimes to the barbed wire. People are even claiming that it's going to be electrified. It'll all be very beautiful. But those who walked out were wrong to do so. Because we had a Christmas that made us fear mass execution, they were that nice to us. They repeatedly gave us grits, with a flavor actually fit for humans. They also gave Red Cross parcels to the Jews. Philips distributed charity to the entire camp and to us in particular. And we got two afternoons off but then had to work all day on December 26, Sunday. The gentlemen of Philips showed a very special caring side, and Philips gave us ten cigarettes, ginger cake, molasses, Perl,[557] and a few tidbits. The camp got cigarettes and cake only. Sunday also Philips stew. There was a lighted Christmas tree on the roll-call grounds, and the *Scharführer*, who had earlier threatened me in my role as doorman, saying he was going to knock out my

---

555. C. Lorenz AG, established by Carl Lorenz in 1880, was one of the main manufacturers of radio transmitters and receivers in Germany in the 1930s. The company had production facilities in Berlin. In 1943 it contracted the Philips electronics company to produce parts for its transmitters. They were made in the company's main plant in Eindhoven.

556. On December 24, 1943, Vught held 672 Jews, including 17 children younger than sixteen years.

557. Perl was a fruit-based soft drink.

molars, told someone else that, had it not been Christmas, he would
certainly have hit him in the mouth. Roll call at nine. I was late. What
beat the band: an afternoon visit to the women. S[aathoff?] is back,
that much is clear, but someone else is probably lying on the sofa,
groaning. The visit more or less the way it used to be. The women had
prepared all kinds of things: big cakes: really *thauma idesthai*.[558] Sat at
decorated tables, facing their small stores of food. My heart shrank.
Got the same frozen feeling as during every visit. Don't really care to
enter this dwelling place of my mother and of the others. It was also
a painful affair for the many who have been left here by themselves.
All the same, the mood was greedily festive. Mother said: a bit like a
late-night bar. With it also all that silver (capacitor paper) and red
decoration and pine branches. Really a fairly luxurious arrangement.
I soon left to see H[annie], who was in the recovery barrack [for
people who had just left the hospital], where we talked pleasantly.
Philips sent Christmas trees and lights to the factory. We Jews, who
with this tree had to catch up on all the Christmas trees of previous
years, decorated it gaudily and quarreled about that. That's the way it
is. Observed with ironic enjoyment the Christmas spirit of this flock
of Israel. None of this matters much to me anymore. I've begun to
like "Silent Night" a lot, especially when it's sung by a choir. It was a
[feature] of my childhood years, mysteriously forbidden yet acknowledged to be holy. A hymn that will always remain alien yet sacred to
me, no matter how often I hear it and how beautiful I may find it. My
association: I'm standing in the dark and see a golden glow in the
depth right before me: Christmas Eve.

[Wednesday] December 29, [1943]. Just now a nice scene: in the office. A message boy from the Political Department comes in and says:
"De V[ries], is he here?" "No . . ." "He can go home." First he has
to change. De V[ries] says: "My dentures are being repaired, have
I got time to go to the dentist?" A few people shake his hand. Most
don't. But a lot of people happen to be around at that point, so
among themselves they shake hands and pat each other on the back.
V[an] W[ijk] is at the center of the ovations. De V[ries], staring va-
cantly, bundles up his possessions and leaves. First to the dentist and
then home. B[arend?] has hung a wreath around his neck and calls
through the microphone: "De W[it]?" The microphone stays on for

---

558. Greek for "a marvel to behold"—a recurring phrase in Homer's *Iliad* and *Odyssey*.

a while. People notice it too late. . . . Erich purses his lips and says: "Well, he was greatly loved." There is truer fidelity to be found in this camp than that between man and woman. People forget very quickly here. Some prisoners came along during the visit a few days ago. They were roundly kissed by married women. And that doesn't mean that they don't care about the other one. He's still the one and only great love, they say. And they're greatly moved when they get mail. There was a woman, whose husband was in Amsterdam, who had a close relationship with a prisoner and who provided cover for it by saying that he brought her messages from her husband. No doubt in a graphic manner. Don't they call this the Dalton system?[559] People don't fully understand what's going on. A rather affected lady says to another, who works side by side with her husband, except that he is ill now: "It must seem like a big empty spot in the morning," and the other one answers: "Oh, it's not that bad."

There are three electricians at work there and two men who light the stoves. It took a long time to clear up the misunderstanding. Th. is adorably monogamous, acts as though she knew nothing, and in conversation with R. P. holds up to shame those husbands who have a good time with other women and gratefully accept parcels from their wives and write loving letters home.[560] P. blushes deeply and becomes very ill at ease. In the women's concentration camp the girls and women roll on the floor with the SS at night.

[Thursday] December 30 [1943]. Just now S[anders] was beaten once again by a *Kapo,* this time by [D.] Ali. Slowly but surely he must be callused all over. Once again a girl who is messing around with Ali is the guilty one.

Small facts: after ten weeks they gave us clean clothes. But there was also a bed raid. What remains to me in the way of clothing is two hand towels and *Der jüdische Krieg.*[561] Theo E[nklaar], the head of the clothing department, was present. He has evolved nicely here. Doesn't look at me anymore.

---

559. The Dalton education system is based on giving students assignments that they are invited to tackle whenever they feel ready for them in cooperation with other students. The principles of the system were established by Helen Parkhurst on the basis of her experience as a teacher in Dalton, Massachusetts. The first Dutch school using the Dalton system opened in 1926.

560. David is probably referring to Theresia van Praag. She seems to have survived.

561. David is referring to Lion Feuchtwanger's *Der jüdische Krieg* (published in English as *Josephus*). This was the first volume of Feuchtwanger's Josephus trilogy.

Van W[ijk] told me: among all of us De W[it] likes only Spitz. The others, the Kokers as well, have something scheming about them. He charges me with all kinds of things that I don't have on my conscience. But at bottom he's right. I'm not open, not straightforward. My shyness (I haven't spoken yet about the H[annie] matter) is no excuse, but it's part of it. I was unusually affected. I feel Jewishness as something that must be an enormous burden for an acute, self-aware consciousness. So I had this dream last night: I was out of the camp and had turned into someone, my actual self, whom everyone avoided and threw out of the house. Annie R[omein-Verschoor] and Aunt E[sther] each emptied a garbage can over me from the top of the stairs.[562] A horrible dream. [Jan] Romein resembles De Wit, who yesterday didn't want to speak to me. After this Van Wijk pressed me to go to him again with a general question. I have the same feelings towards both of them. Aunt E[sther] represents Jewish anti-Jewishness. Really a horrible dream. Then there's also the conflict at Rosenberg's, where the A[ryan] women are indignant about the friendly attitude of our women towards K[apos], g[uards] and S[S men]; and about R[osenberg]'s own attitude. That led to strongly anti-Semitic comments, which in turn led R[osenberg] to say to *Kapo* P[iet] that he didn't know whether people approved of his conversations with him. Whereupon P[iet] fetches Erich, who enters half a minute later, wearing gloves, storms up to the lady in question and wants "to give the stupid cow a couple of knuckle sandwiches." At the last moment R[osenberg] is able to prevent it, but the next morning he's soundly raked over the coals by R[iek] S[nel] and is just like a little boy.[563] Germanness is a sensitive point with the gentlemen; not long ago H. got a couple of blows, which undoubtedly would have met with the approval of the clothing industry if a few Aryan women hadn't shouted: "*Mof* [Kraut]," etc. Thus our good friend E[rich]: "I'm going to smash the Aryan women." That we're so much friendlier, that E[rich] was specially addressed by us on his birthday, that we've given him a certificate of appreciation, etc., is not due to the fact that we need them more, K[apos], g[uards], and S[S men]. Much more due to a lack of inner strength, of direction. The women's contempt is beginning to sting me a bit, because I know it's jus-

562. Annie Romein-Verschoor was the wife of the historian Jan Romein and an author in her own right. Esther Santcroos-Presser was a sister of David's mother.
563. David is referring to the non-Jewish prisoner Diederika (Riek) Elsendoorn-Snel. She was imprisoned because of her resistance activities.

tified, even where I'm concerned, even though they see me as one of them.

Superb conversations about this with R[iek] S[nel] and M[argreet] T[asselaar].

Of course it is true that there's a selection of them here, and at Philips a further selection. In the barracks of the women's concentration camp at night you used to have to climb over the women who were lying there with SS and *Kapos*. But the difference can't be entirely explained away in that fashion.

In the meantime it's *1944*. [Thursday, January] 6. Much happiness and prosperity. There hasn't been any trouble in the camp so far. The year is starting well. We got half a day off, so worked all day Sunday. One good turn deserves another. Sunday afternoon, an afternoon I won't soon forget. More later. Saturday evening V[an] W[ijk] addressed us. A speech he had allowed me to read in draft that afternoon. Very impressive. An attempt to help people give meaning to the fortuitousness of being here and having stayed here. Only he knows there aren't many left in Poland. Has suspected it for a long time. Earlier than we did. And doesn't keep in mind that others don't know it. And so he writes about the people in Poland as though we have to write them off. This arouses great commotion. In my view that still has the advantage of making people face the situation squarely, instead of calmly walking across their worn-out feelings of grief and acquiescence. It's not that bad to open up old wounds, some wounds have no right to heal. I've been thinking about this. The goal is neither happiness nor unhappiness. It's the unfolding of human potential. The development of that piece of the universe that you represent, as it were, even when it happens at the expense of what people call the self and their own welfare. Actually, it always happens at their expense. By feeling a lot we expand the world. There have been a lot of attacks on V[an] W[ijk], and he feels rather affected by this. Meanwhile he has been removed from the office. The Jewish departments are a bad horse to bet on.

Next: I'm able to write so much because my table is no longer in such a dangerously exposed place. The capacitor factory is being expanded by twenty machines. The transformer wrapping machines have been installed. Sp[itz?] becomes foreman. S[anders] has gone to the timekeepers but still continues to wear his armband RB IV [Radio Assembly Line IV]. The line has been wound up, with some of

it going to vacuum tubes, some to capacitors, and some to transformers, and some put on hold. But more about that later. First this:

> Ditty of the bitter end. Rondel
>
> A dismal fate we've been accorded
> sheer boredom to the bitter end
> when the last few of us as sordid
> smoke pall from the stack ascend
>
> So too my verse is disappearing
> before that happens though I've penned
> who knows if it will reach your hearing
> this ditty of the bitter end
>
> The smoke ends up by dissipating
> and I have no more strength to spend
> Better to straightway face cremating
> as smoke pall from a stack ascend
> than years of boredom and of waiting
> with even so that bitter end.

I allowed Hannie to read this verse, with which I will pay the wager
with T[ini] L[ansberg]. A silly neighbor looks over her shoulder and
breaks into loud laughter. And after a few minutes Hannie is laughing too, and for a moment there was a lot of jeering. After that she
wants to say something serious, and I tell her I'll speak with her later.
That evening I say it really hit me hard. She confesses that it was
deliberately cruel. The relationship has been tense the last while, I
was irritating her, was ever more strongly drawn to her, had ever less
to say, and kept beginning conversations and then falling silent. Unpleasant to my family and others. After this business of the verse we
talked openly for once. My nervousness bothered her, under these
circumstances she didn't have the strength to take on so much. I tell
her about my Amsterdam girlfriends and how they know all of this.
Tell her about Nettie and how she's above me in a maternal way,
above all my fear and shyness. It's a good conversation. That evening
I write a letter and ask her to make things a bit easier for me. Occasionally give a trivial token of attentiveness, of affection. The next
morning she's a different person, comes up to me, speaks calmly and

kindly. Says that day and the next, at the end of each conversation: "I'll talk to you later." Everything is good and joyful, and my days are totally new again.

The radio assembly line has now been closed down, and she has been accepted for vacuum tube assembly. The glasses she's wearing are really too weak, and after the examination she was half-blind, but all that is not supposed to matter. She doesn't want to and does want to, just a bit. De W[it] orders her to go there. On Sunday afternoon she can still make some effort to get out of it. Now suddenly she definitely wants to go there, and we have a two-hour conversation in which I try gently but urgently to persuade her not to go. A conversation that is dangerous for both of us. Our nerves are stretched to the limit. Each completely focused on the other and expectant, as during physical contact, of which I feel all the sensations at a particular moment. I: "We're flirting dangerously here, with this conversation." She: "You're noticing it too. Oh, just for once. And here you thought you couldn't do it." I: "I can play one more trump. But it's too serious." She: "Go ahead, I consider you capable of anything this afternoon." So I did.

After the break a calm and happy farewell conversation. I've saved up much that's good and tell her that. I tell her a lot of things. She says that in my interactions with other people I behave like a little Rudolf.[564] I suddenly see a lot that has led to this, and get an image of how I appear to her. I give her a few verses. And write a joyful and lucid letter to her that evening. The next day she presents herself at the vacuum tube line. I've made an agreement with the management that I can show up during the break. I do so, but am closemouthed and very nervous. Also because she won't make any effort to get away from there. But above all because of the role I am playing of the disagreeable prisoner who's hanging around. The tensions return and I'm deeply unhappy. She's told me often how others have accused her of playing games. I myself have been warned from all sides. And she has said: "Maybe with everybody else, but not with you." And has given me many proofs and indications of genuine friendship. But I

564. Aart de Leeuw's novel *De kleine Rudolf* (Little Rudolf) is a Dutch bildungsroman published in 1930. At the beginning of the book the reader meets Rudolf as a shy orphan with a small and misshapen body. Rudolf is, however, able to overcome his inferiority complex and after many tribulations find happiness. In a letter to Fré written at this time, David wrote that he was very worried, and that someone had compared him to little Rudolf. "It was said well, too well," David admitted. Letter, David Koker to Fré Samson, January 1944, collection 244 (diaries), file 1657 (Koker), NIOD archive, Amsterdam; De Leeuw, *De kleine Rudolf.*

continue to be suspicious. She's as tight-lipped and passive as N[ettie] can be. But comes out of it less often. And knows only one coercive possibility of reacting, just like me.

Because of the distance that has developed I've been deeply un-happy for a couple of days and have temporarily lost control of all my feelings. I wrote to her that I wanted to give my feelings free play, let them go, and then bottle them up, depending on their nature, mu-tual relationship, and circumstances. It's in the past now, but for a few days it was a passion. One that I knew could appear only in this camp, here, where nothing gives direction, where life meanders on without a goal and finds no footing anywhere. So how do things go? You look for a woman, a girl, and you bring her everything, without holding back. Your good qualities, the thoughts of your best moments, your emotions, your happiness about messages from home: the lot. That's how you find the path for everything, life suddenly gains direction, and one focus holds all the parts of our personality together. But we become monomaniacal, are no longer capable of anything besides this. We think of her under the strangest circumstances, of how she might act, of the possibility of telling her this. After all, it's a good story. . . . And I also thought of this: friendship is always between equals, and usually a woman is simultaneously our superior and infe-rior. Our superior: she has insight and is the repository of happiness. What happens to us depends on her. The inferior: we must seek to win her, so that she will give herself to us and to us alone. Therefore a woman: with the double inequality comes striving: movement from a higher to a lower level, attempts to get from lower to higher. That is why it isn't peaceful, an association like this, but it compels us and strains our will.

Earlier I jotted down some fragments of verse, which I composed in an inchoate rush of feeling during the last few days.

> With doglike faith, doglike docility
> I trail you, where to, mistress, can that be?
>
> At many things that I have said for instance
> you've nodded yes but never got the gist
> but ah, I happen to be biased with a vengeance
> and that gives me the strength to still persist
>
> until I really come to you and ask

And afterwards my heart's full of regret
for tendernesses that remained unspoken
for . . . I repress instead
. . . I'm not always just like this

Often doubts for which there is no reason
. . . ness.

That here I happened to find your dear face

And footfall that I know from far away

And bind the fear and wildness in the space
and the calm measures of the song

And should I go out for an evening walk
. . . to unlock
. . . reproach
ask how much there is still binds

The heart bereft of feeling, the eyes blind
. . . look afar
what is forgotten finds its way again
the selfsame moon the selfsame stars
perhaps the selfsame evening wind.

What harm is there . . . god no more
. . . . .
when . . . rotten to the core
the rest can join it as well

And I who often mar your life
with all my bitterness and lack of trust
you cannot wish . . . I for you
. . . shall be.

. . . look the year is starting
. . . of . . . or of parting

the misty season hanging in the air
and through the sky the geese now fly away

and windows in the afternoon are gray
from cold outside and from the heat within.

(The song) it says so little leaves so much unsaid

There's no peace with my often fickle mood
to you I have avowed the utmost that I could
I would have found words for my tenderness
. . . not always I confess

Verses are pitiful but feelings are
often too powerless to support a word

The choice of words is also not original

The wind blows and your hair is blond and full

I feel my eyes becoming warm and tender
tenderness lightly caught is borne away

Life with all its chances good and bad

For this abode of murderers and thieves
That . . .
and gives two lovers no right to exist

From fear to fear and ever deeper fall

But store it with the rest of what you know
. . . and lock the door.

[Wednesday] January 12 [1944]. Eleven months today. Hurrah, hurrah. One year next month. And still in Holland. With my entire family. I am well satisfied. Mother, whose parcel seems to have been lost,
by the way, got a very nice letter from N[ettie] on the occasion of her
birthday on December 28. The past week I've had a very close feeling
of contact with her. Every afternoon when I go to eat, a girl in a deep-
blue coat comes by. Every afternoon I'm startled in a joyful way. The
same shape and a color that comes close, somewhat lighter perhaps.
I think of her constantly, the way I saw her walking along Rijnstraat:
with a smile of recognition only when she was very near, even when
she had already seen me a lot earlier. If you walk along Berkelstraat
past the sports field, you can just see her pass on Rijnstraat. Often I
position myself there and I almost always run across her.

Now first some facts. I mentioned the beautiful chimes on the
barbed wire. But with them and without them escape is still possible.
Because our friend Black Jack took to his heels while with an external detachment. New Year's Eve. It's happened more than once the
last little while. Not long ago three one evening, at the same time
two in Den Bosch. It's getting empty here. They did bring in a few
profs from Leiden the other day.[565] And there is also the bunker, the
brothel that is temporarily being used as the women's prison. In it is
the woman from the patisserie in Rotterdam, the girlfriend of Frank

565. On January 5, 1944, the Germans took to Vught four hostages from Leiden University: Siegfried Thomas Bok (1892–1964), professor of medicine; Rudolf Pabus Cleveringa
(1894–1980), professor of law and dean of the Faculty of Law; the Surinam-born Paul
Christiaan Flu (1884–1945), professor of tropical hygiene and former president of the university; and Cornelis Weststrate (1899–1961), professor of economics. Ten days later a fifth
academic from Leiden arrived from Buchenwald, Benjamin Telders (1903–45), professor
of international law. The professors were all assigned to the Philips Kommando. All were
anti-Nazi, but Cleveringa and Telders stood out for being among the very few members
of the Dutch establishment who, in November 1940, publicly condemned the dismissal
of Jewish civil servants. Cleveringa and Telders were immediately arrested. Cleveringa was
released in 1941, but Telders was sent to Buchenwald. After more than two and half years
in that camp he was transferred to Vught, and from there the Germans would send him
to Sachsenhausen and Bergen-Belsen, where he succumbed to typhus. See Cleveringa,
Gedenkschriften, 87ff.

Peter, the interpreter. You enter a dark and apparently empty washroom, turn on the light, and then hear from behind the toilet door,
in German, with English and Czech-Jewish, etc. accent: "Please turn
the light off." F[rank] P[eter] is "interpreting" there. But when he
tried to do this on an expanded scale in block 5, together with a few
other companions, they surrounded the block with *Landwacht* and
female guards, so

> There was once a man called Frank Peter
> who was a wonderful interpreter
> but once 'pon a night
> he made fun with his bride
> and now he is sniffing the ether.[566]

In a punishment detachment. But after a week he is back, walking
around in the industrial court, speaking in English to everyone, in
German if he isn't understood, in Polish to T[opel], claims to know
sixteen languages, also some rudiments of Chinese. His mother was
Spanish, his father English. He had an important mission in the Spanish Civil War, was caught in Barcelona, and is a very great poet. He
tells us all of this, and it's all called into question. Right up to his an-
cestry . . . Although people don't really doubt that, . . . He has an unbelievably sharp and insolent face. Wears a very attractive black beret.
And he slaps me on the shoulder, very hard, and says: "Hello, chief."
Three women escaped from the women's bunker not long ago. They
were walking very calmly through the camp. Then they were taken to
the actual prison.[567] Yesterday R[auter?] was here, and he was most
offended by the fact that there was a woman there [in the bunker],
her feet bare and swollen, in the damp. I think he has a point.

   In the evening, when you go past the brothel-bunker, you hear the
sound of singing in that empty space: very shrill and not at all cheerful: "And why should I be sad, the bunker is so big." I can't imagine
anything more dreary than that. The rations there, the official rations in any case, are inadequate. In the large bunker these days is . . .
Theo Vr[ins]. The same fellow who escaped in July. And tried to get
to England for the umpteenth time but was captured 50 kilometers
[30 miles] off the coast. Is in there barefoot, without chair, table, bed,

566. David wrote this limerick in English.
567. This is the main bunker, located in the northern part of the camp.

bedclothes, heat. Six slices of bread per day, and the water is dripping from the walls. That's what people say, I don't know whether it's true.

Yesterday a woman calmly walked past the *Komm[andantur]* and then kept on going, was allowed to pass everywhere, just not past the final checkpoint. A young hostage put on overalls and a beret. But right at the end ran into S[aathoff]. Who recognized him. Too bad.

[Sunday] January 16 [1944]. The matter of that woman is quite different [from the way it appears].[568] This is how it is: she applied from here to become a member of the NSB. As a result they made her block leader, because of pressure from outside, of course. Then she was harassed so much that after three days she officially resigned. . . . At that point she informed the *Kommandantur* that she knew where some Jews were hiding. Then that evening they threw her out of bed, together with her mattress and blankets, so that she hung "like a monkey," or so I was told, from the coils of the upper bed. They assured her that, if she were to report this, she would lose her hair. She spent that night on a bench in the dining hall, without mattress or pillow. In her clothes. And the next day she reported it anyway, so they cut off some of her hair that evening. Thereupon she made an attempt to escape, and now she's in the hospital, having been shot through the lung. We remember her in our prayers. Subsequently the lady who was said to have taken the initiative in the affair was taken to the bunker, which was grounds for the women to send in a list with all their numbers, this on the advice of the guard, because they had all been party to it. A hitch: the Jewish women in the block didn't want to sign it. The other women told them: you were willing to be sheltered by us, but you won't do anything in return. They signed after all. Yesterday evening the women, 93 strong, were put in the bunker. The entire hand-cranked flashlight line has ground to a halt. A couple of women are still sitting there, a bit ashamed, because they had the misfortune of living in another block. I arrived just in time [to see the 93 go in]. They went along cheerfully, somewhat excited of course, but still self-controlled. The guards were on edge. Not least because of that cheerfulness. One to another: "I'm about to hit a couple of them in the face." Girls among themselves can take a few liberties.

568. David is referring to the non-Jewish German-born prisoner Agnes Jedzini (1903–1944). She died on January 23.

There were tears in my eyes. You can say it's senseless, and they were playing games. It's no small thing: sixty strong in a damp cell, without coats, benches, or anything. Some days ago the place was condemned by R[auter] because of the bad conditions. But they're going through with it. I thought: it makes sense to ask what the objective is. [What they're doing] is unwise. They're living here in a calm exaltation, the women. Their life here is directed towards one thing only. They don't have household cares or social responsibilities: they live for each other here, and their presence here represents the same thing for each of them. "They forget they're in a KL here," some smart aleck among us said. The Jews are very sensible. And cowardly.

They do forget that. But this senseless action has just as little in common with everyday life as with the KL. They've created a heaven of their own here, and they lift it high above their heads. These are the best women, of course. There are others as well: the transport of hookers from Rotterdam, for example, who were kept in secure detention for quite a while. Yesterday evening two of them arranged a tryst with Paul [a *Kapo*]. In the industrial courtyard. They had a lot of fun. And S[aathoff] was there too. Now P[aul] is in the bunker. His beautiful hair is gone. And they found a list on him, so it is said, with the names of forty women on it.

[Saturday] January 22 [1944]. I have to tell everything succinctly. A lot has happened. And I didn't feel like writing. I now weigh less than 110 lbs. But I'm healthy. X-rayed, blood tests in the magnificently beautiful hospital. I've stood in front of that X-ray machine before. Seventy-four [women] in a small room for 14 hours. Crammed in. Seventeen elsewhere because there was no room. 60.14.14? The sky with a few stars. Strangle [?]. An eye with a crooked finger through it [?]. And people say it won't be so bad. People are tearing their clothes in mourning. And an old man cautions us to stay calm. As if we could bottle up our feelings.

The story of head [guard Margarethe Maria] G[allinat], who heard airplanes overhead: "Why doesn't the Führer take preventive measures, why does he allow this?" She walks outside and shakes her fist at the heavens. But in a month "we'll be the rulers of the sky." Then they'll build a big KL in E[ngland?] and she'll be H[ead Guard] G[allinat] over there. And Saathoff, who's also standing there: "There they are again, the damned bastards. They never leave us in peace."

But: the new defenses. H. [German SS man] reportedly came back from Frankfurt, completely apathetic. True, I hadn't seen him for a while. And W. [German SS man] came back and said it was time for the war to come to an end. Used to be full of confidence in the victory. Uncle K. says they certainly won't execute him, because he was always very good to the prisoners. In fact, quite a while ago there was a proposal to buy him a dairy store after the war.

The women are back now. There are supposed to have been deaths.[569] Everybody's lips are sealed. But it seems to have been hellish. People were constantly fainting. Prominent members of the women's camp have gone to Den Bosch. The matter seems to have been reported as a mutiny. The c[ommandant]: "We still have entirely different ways [to punish people]." I have the impression they have gone too far, even by their own standards.

I've been through a distressing time. On one occasion I was in [block] 43 to deal with a case of absenteeism. Was shown the door in a very unfriendly manner by J., who thought I was coming to get something. An exchange of words, during which he said that he might well be in the wrong, but that it was in his nature. And I: that his nature was defective. And then I shook his hand all the same. Since then I've been agonizing so much about myself that it isn't funny. I've written H[annie], to whom I haven't spoken since then, a couple of letters exposing all my fears and frailties. It's terribly sad when you see all kinds of people walking through the barracks, free as a bird, see them talk with whomever they want. Cheerful, innocent, carefree. And I myself am drawn to someone, unresistingly, with a thousand fears, a thousand regrets, making every friendly contact impossible because of that inhibition and that fear. And if a third person says something, I fly off, shuddering, the way a swarm of sparrows flies from a field of wheat. Everyone's warning me about Hannie. Generally I always believe what the majority says. But she is good and sensible. And under different circumstances could be a consoling friend. But here everything gets driven to extremes, here people are so bent towards and

569. Seventy-four of the ninety women were locked up in one cell measuring ninety square feet. They all had to stand crowded against one another. In the darkness some of them panicked and began to scream. After fourteen hours the guards opened the door to find that ten women had died from lack of oxygen. News about what came to be known as the bunker tragedy circulated in the underground press. The Higher SS and Police Leader in the Netherlands, Hanns Rauter, became enraged because he had tried to develop Vught as a "model camp." He fired Commandant Adam Grünewald, had him demoted and sent to the eastern front. See also note 503.

away from others, that they feel psychologically forced beyond their limits. A few evenings ago I wrote her a letter in a mood of nervous endearment. She responded defensively. My tone had certainly gone too far. Mother reproached me strongly yesterday and really upset me: "How can you do this when you've got such a nice girlfriend in Amsterdam?" I can't explain it to her. Most of all I'd like to have my own sun and sky. Whatever is outside is abstract, property you can't touch. Nettie, that's the goodness and richness that's in Amsterdam, and I believe my feelings towards her have become very strong. But it's like money you have but can't use. It makes you rich, but the riches are theoretical. Nettie very likely knows and understands this, and this, too, I won't be able to make clear to Mother. But I'm totally out of it.

Prof. Telders, who was arrested near the beginning, has arrived. From Buchenwald, where conditions seem to be better than here. Last week a number of profs showed up. The son of one of them [was] shot to death. That can happen if you're arrested by auxiliary police. Not if the Germans do the arresting. On January 16 the camp had its first anniversary. Lehmann delivered a very long speech, in which he recounted the early history with a lot of humor. He over-rates this camp as something that has intrinsic value, but it was very pleasing all the same. A few kind words about Ettlinger, on whose orders the SS gave up their milk and who in any case had the entire food supply of the children under his control. He also recounted how at the beginning they moved from block 22 to 39. 38 was empty. In 37 were the women, whom they hadn't seen since their arrival. But whoever got too close, even to 38, would be shot, according to Ettlinger. After a day had passed they nevertheless began to peer through the windows in order to look at 37. Ettlinger noticed it, "and then, gentlemen, for the first time we heard one of them really raise his voice," L[ehmann] said. "We thought: now a couple are going to be shot as punishment for sure." Completely dismayed they stayed behind, distraught and dazed, until soon afterwards the barbed-wire gates opened and . . . the children entered. Ettlinger had sent them. "We shall never forget this," L[ehmann] says. And indeed, it is a re-markable event. One of many.

[Tuesday] January 25 [1944]. Vught is a healthy place. For prisoners. Not for commandants. This morning a telegram from Berlin arrives at the *Kommandantur:* the commandant [is] confined to quarters.

R[auter] is coming this afternoon. Earlier this morning people were saying that [Grünewald] had sent his wife and those two annoying boys away. Dark laughter is heard in hell: Chmielewski.[570] In his case it all began with some red rear ends. (A couple of stories I wanted to tell earlier, quickly here.) The commandant's wife always had Ocz make her clothes.[571] People say they never fit properly, because the commandant was present and kept saying: "Speed it up." A story told here: the commandant's wife is walking through the gate one time. Fat Piet storms angrily out of his gatehouse and shouts: "You've got to check in, you stupid bitch. . . ." Later the commandant showed up to complain, and Piet, taken aback, said he was an old man and didn't see well. "I thought she was a Jewess . . . ," he says. A good story, but I don't believe it.

The commandant has two sons who wander through the camp all day long. In *Hitlerjugend* outfits. One is thirteen or thereabouts, the other not yet ten. They salute and want the prisoners to greet them. These say: "Beat it." A while ago they were watching and screaming during roll call. Saathoff, who can be faulted for many things but not for lacking a sense of what is and what is not permissible, is irritated. "Miserable kids," he says to himself. They also come along on visits. And stand there, looking puny, behind their big father, watching the doings of the prisoners, who have no doubt been described to them as villains and criminals and subhumans. Erich and Ali are standing in a corner, the latter is crumpling his cap, looking like shabby scoundrels. They don't know which way to look, they want to laugh [at the scene] behind that broad back, but they're also quite nervous. (Shakespeare at his best.)

The cause of it all: Mrs. Jedzini is dead.[572] People say that 16,000 letters reached R[auter] in The Hague. Already people are said to be on their way over here because they have circulated pamphlets about "the murder in Vught." The International Red Cross has protested in Berlin. The Red Cross concerns itself with everything, sometimes

570. Commandant Karl Walter Chmielewski had been arrested in 1943. It was clear to David that Grünewald was to follow Chmielewski's fate, with an undignified departure in chains.

571. David is referring to the Polish-Jewish tailor Juda Oczeret (1884–1960), who was imprisoned in Vught with his wife, Jenta Oczeret-Feger (1885–1960). Their two sons were killed: one in Auschwitz and the other in Sobibor. In January 1944 Oczeeret was the only Jew in the camp who was not part of the Philips Kommando. The SS had kept him in Vught because of his tailoring skills.

572. Agnes Jedzini had been dead for three days when David wrote this entry.

successfully, but always with impunity. The other day corporal punishment was being meted out: the leader of the protective custody
camp looked at his watch and said: "Oh, shit. The Red Cross is going to protest anyway." In any case the toll is very high. It's still not
known how high. One says 14, another eight.[573] To lose a man in the
camp is bad, but [to lose] a woman is worse. One of the women, who
has been transferred to Den Bosch, escaped but was caught after 16
hours. In the entire affair the staff doctor behaved very humanely in
having mattresses taken to the bunker. People say the commandant
withheld them. Beyond that it seems that one of the women told the
whole story to a Red Cross worker, v. B.,[574] in the presence of the
staff doctor. The Red Cross supplied us with cereal; the commandant
refused it, but the staff doctor brought it in. The 17 who were in the
next cell didn't understand why there was so much noise. But now reproach themselves for not breaking down the door. They had the first
woman [to be put in the bunker] sign a confession of Communistic
mutiny, and made the group sign for mutiny in general. M[argreet]
T[asselaar], who was in the hospital, said she regretted not being in
the bunker. Indeed, you can't blame the women for the business having ended this way. Once again: there are actions in which humans
display themselves truly and do big things, which from a logical social
perspective can only be condemned. Things that can actually happen only in a kind of intoxication. That's not the same as a state of
excitement.

The staff doctor was gathering information this morning about why
so many of our women were sick (15 out of 196 today). M[argreet]
told him a few things about the Philips stew and the bread being held
back. He treats Jews and Aryans the same way, now also takes Jewish
women into the hospital. Three Jews recently got splendid treatment
because they had donated blood for a transfusion. And it was for
an SS *Obersturmführer* [first lieutenant]. This commandant was always
particularly unfriendly to the civilians.[575] A couple of weeks ago they
had to stand neatly in rows of three (after all, they aren't prisoners; we
stand in rows of five) and watch their colleagues undressing and put-

573. The actual number was ten.
574. David is referring to Charlotte van Beuningen-Fentener van Vlissingen (1880–
1976), a wealthy resident of Vught who was one of the women from that village who, under
the auspices of the Dutch Red Cross, supplied inmates in Vught with food parcels, and
family members of the inmates with information. Brouwers, *Broodnodige hulp.*
575. These are civilians who were employed in the camp. They entered and left the
camp at the beginning and end of each workday.

ting on prisoner's uniforms. Letters.[576] Their collars had to be turned down, hands outside their pockets. Well over an hour. But that immediately elicited a report. The *Schutzhaftlagerführer* [leader of the protective custody camp] is also a remarkable presence. Very tall and burly, with a fairly pleasant face. He looks like Max Meiers.[577] In light of the anti-Semitic regime of the most recent commandant, he says some very unusual things: we're standing at roll call; those [Aryans] who don't have sweaters get them from the camp. The Jewish leadership embolden themselves to ask whether we are also eligible. "But of course," he says. At the last Sunday roll call there was yet another inspection. (Numbers and buttons this time, otherwise haircuts and *renbanen*.[578] He appears before the Jewish block and says: "Hopefully you'll do better than these other filthy swine." We've gone through a period of discrimination here. It does feel good to be treated on a basis of equality again, no matter who does it. Today is the day on which the mind reader in block 15 said the invasion would take place. Too bad.

Hannie's birthday was on the 20th; I wrote this poem:

> This evening I have stayed up late
> a present's almost duty bound
> why toil away though to create
> some lines that have a dismal sound?
> And if you find my mood too glum
> no rhyme and rhythm turns it gay.
> For you take life just as it comes
> All I can do is talk away.
>
> You know how I turn things loved well
> quite gloomy. Stupid, needless too?
> Ah, nature cannot be compelled
> or did you think that I chose to
> let everybody get a look
> at this my paltry, sordid fate,
> until my very last friends took
> their leave, let down and quite irate.

576. David is referring to the fact that these civilians had broken the rules by smuggling letters.

577. It is not clear to whom David is referring.

578. A *renbaan* (racing track) was a shaved strip of hair on the head, running from the forehead to the neck.

Since childhood this has always been
my sole and mournful melody.
My better side you won't have seen
only from reading verse by me.
The word's the spirit's bitter foe
it rhymes and reasons till it's poor
a thousand deaths one fears and so
feels lonely, wretched, that's for sure.

Distrustful full of hesitation
at personal bonds of unity
powerless to find conciliation
with any good community,
or in his loved ones' company
from many kinds of fear and fret
to find one human word that he
does not immediately regret.

Friend, who have seen so deep inside me
each secret know that me besets,
the only one I let deride me
who much forgives but naught forgets
is then a song for you to be
an endless train of repetitions
of all that I've avowed of need
and weakness to you, all the sessions
when you encouraged me to speak?

This personal gift is hardly able
to make or break the birthday fun
I doubt you'll put it on the table
when celebrations have begun
as formerly, or place it there
with other gifts displayed with pride.
That's not done in the KZ where
till further notice we reside.

The second and third stanzas are not very strong. Still, it's pretty
good.

[Wednesday] January 26 [1944]. This morning a physiology lecture.[579] I left it in a state of elation. My background is definitely not that of a physiologist, but listening attentively and taking notes, and knowing that the man standing there has mastered his subject fully, are pleasures I had actually quite forgotten. Also: a sparkling spring day today. The sky is an icy blue, but the wind and sun make for radiantly fresh weather. We leave the barrack at 6:30 this morning. I have my breakfast in the industrial courtyard, I put a hunk of dry bread in my pocket and eat it that way. The sky is luxuriantly star covered and people shiver a bit, it's just cold enough. Ten past seven, sometimes a bit later, the women show up. We're already fully settled; they look strange, wrapped up in men's overcoats and head scarves, with lots of stuff hanging around their necks. Entering the light, they look around in a shy and surprised way. In the evening they are first to leave, and recently we've had to wait until they have left. We're not even allowed to stand in the corridor, otherwise we'd see them through the door opening. It is closed now. Not that we don't spend all day with them and work with them, but that doesn't matter.

According to some stories the camp doctor is supposed to have given superfluous patients in Dachau injections of gasoline. Others say, and I'm more inclined to believe this, that he was relieved of his duties there for being soft on prisoners. During his visit to 43 [barrack where the radio tubes were being made], he sat down at one of the mounted magnifying glasses and asked people whether their spectacles were adjusted for this work. Also examined the spectacles and ordered one girl to have her eyes checked frequently.

We are getting curious reports from Buchenwald. Coincidentally Cahen told us last week that they had wanted to take him there for the laboratory in that place. There seems to be an important industrial center in B[uchenwald]. Armament factories. In total 25,000 people, about half of them in external detachments, which are unhealthy because of the nature of the work but are not intended as extermination detachments. Working in mines. People also sleep in the mines and get fresh air only during roll call. The factory detachments have it very easy. The SS consists of ethnic Germans (Sudeten Germans and the like) who couldn't care less and have been doing as little as possible the last couple of years. You can escape work easily there, in

579. This lecture was given by Leiden professor Siegfried Thomas Bok.

contrast with the situation here. The hostages are in civilian dress, just as they were here at the outset. A number of the prisoners as well. There's a library with 8,000 volumes. Everyone has to hand over the books he receives. Everyone is learning English, because there's a big collection of Shakespeare on hand. The good jobs are unattainable for a non-Communist, because the Communist *Kapos* control every-thing (it used to be that way here too. Some say it's still that way, but others deny it). There are still a couple of hundred Jews there, rigidly separated from the rest. But they're not doing badly. In fact, the guys who later went to Mauthausen had an easy time in B[uchenwald], put on a lot of weight, we're told.[580]

B[uchenwald] used to be really dreadful. People were chased over the mountainside in their shirts, in the freezing cold wind. Pneumo-nia was *the* disease there. You had to work in the quarries with a spade that had a very long and narrow blade and a short shaft. With that you had to dig Thuringia loess with large pebbles in it. When the loess has been exposed to the air for an hour, it becomes so hard that you can split it only with a pickax. This work from 5 a.m. until 8 p.m. Anybody who faints gets doused by a *Kapo*. Anybody who can't carry on: finished off. P. A. weighed less than fifty kilos [110 lbs.] when he left there. And he is by nature a big, robust fellow. J. P. was lucky. He had tendinitis in his arm, went to the sick bay. They wanted to amputate his arm, but he was too weak. He stayed there throughout. Sometime in the future I hope to have him dictate the song. *Buchenwald ich kann dich nicht vergessen, weil du mein Schicksal bist* (Buchenwald, I can't forget you, because you are my destiny).[581] I was about to ask E. But St. was approaching and he had to meet him. It belongs here.

Yesterday evening B[ochel] found V. smoking in the washroom. "What should I do to you?" "Please, *Herr Unterscharführer,* just punch me in the mouth a couple of times." "If I report you," B[ochel] pon-ders, "you'll go into the punishment detachment. And then they'll say: 'It's the damn Kraut's fault.'"

580. These were the Jewish men who were arrested in Amsterdam in February 1941. They spent some time in Buchenwald.

581. "Buchenwald, I can't forget you, because you are my destiny," are the two first lines of the refrain of the Buchenwald Song. Created in 1938 by the Jewish inmates Hermann Leopoldi (1888–1959) and Fritz Beda-Löhner (1883–1942), the Buchenwald Song became one of the songs inmates had to sing when marching to work.

[Thursday] January 27 [1944]. The punishment detachment has been abolished: 250 people. The previous commandant also began with positive measures. So wait and see. Yesterday there was a tall *Hauptsturmführer* [captain] here. The commandant? Or perhaps the commandant in Haaren will come here?[582] Because all he can do is say in an affected voice: "This is insolence, unheard of, shameless." So that's very easy. The mood in the camp is one of relief. This evening a roll call under a shining red sky. Nobody knew why, but everybody was laughing. A powerless *Ober-* and *Hauptscharführer* stood facing us, but we talked and grinned and kept our hands in our coat pockets. One great gang of badly raised boys. "The roll call is just about accurate, commandant, sir," Sp[itz] remarked. Yesterday E[rich?] was blind drunk. But he strolled very nicely along the rows with B[ochel]. Only when he gave the order: "Forward, march!" did he stumble, unfortunately. But no one says a word about it. It's getting to be very good here: Sunday work is going to disappear. We're getting Philips stew again, for the first time in a while. But B[ochel] didn't want to sign for bread.

I hear that, to moisten their mouths, the women in the b[unker] licked the sweat off each other's bodies. Also the saltpeter in the condensation that dripped from the walls. I've read: *Der j[üdische] Krieg*.[583] It's psychologically sound enough but not altogether convincing as historical tableau. Also *Macbeth* a while ago. A woman in [block] 43 is messing around with a Polish soldier and has now ditched her husband. No need for him to show up anymore. I wrote about the Aryan women that the single principle governing them was their togetherness here with its political significance. Our presence here has no political significance. All other features of life have collapsed for us, just as they have for them, but we no longer have anything, are becoming rudderless, while they are focused in a single-minded and fixed way. That is not a condemnation (actually the former isn't either).

582. Haaren was a subcamp of Vught located in a former seminary. All the inmates were hostages.

583. Lion Feuchtwanger (1884–1958), the author of *Der jüdische Krieg*, would have agreed with David's judgment. The historic novel was for him a means to describe a contemporary problem. In the case of Josephus it concerned the tension beteen nationalism and internationalism. While he tried to provide accurate details, he resisted pedantry in his historical descriptions and, following Shakespeare, felt free to interpret the past in a bold and even cavalier manner if it brought life to the narrative. See Feuchtwanger, "Vom Sinn des historischen Romans," 641ff.

[Friday] January 28 [1944]. Stokker has become commandant, it seems.[584] Himmler is coming to visit us tomorrow.[585] Everything has to be made to look very beautiful. Last week two parcels for Mother and me were seized because of two irregular parcels received in between [the regular ones]. To my great joy, Van W[ijk]'s wife was visiting K[arel]'s mother and saw my photo there. I often look at her photo here. That's an amusing relationship. Van W[ijk] has left the sick bay and seems to me to be a lot better. Hugo's book is once again going to his friends in Amsterdam.[586] He is particularly happy about that. It is as if he were leaving the camp himself. I feel much better the last few days.[587]

[Saturday] January 29 [1944]. I've been feeling a lot better the last few days. I wrote a letter to H[annie] in response to hers, which I mentioned before. Received a reasonable and sensible answer. I was living in a kind of exaltation from which I needed to be awakened by force. Its result was that I glorified her in a kind of ecstasy, something she couldn't accept. We had to limit our written contact to an occasional letter. I left this up to her, had myself more or less suggested that we might not correspond at all, which is probably how it will end up. I answered her letter but didn't send my answer. I'm attaching it to this entry.[588] The next day I was ill again [and] quite by

584. In fact, August Stokker was serving as acting commandant. Grünewald's successor was to be SS-Sturmbannführer Hans Hüttig.

585. Himmler's visit, which was to take place on February 3, occurred as the result of a struggle between the chief of the Wirtschaftsverwaltungshauptamt, Oswald Pohl, who was in charge of the operation of the concentration camps, and the Higher SS and Police Leader in the Netherlands, Hanns Albin Rauter. Rauter, who had taken the initiative for the creation of Vught in 1942, was responsible for pacifying the Dutch, and in late 1943 he realized that the bad reputation of Vught didn't serve his purpose. Hence he insisted that the camp become a "model camp." Pohl was not interested in the Dutch perception of Vught. He insisted on complete freedom to operate the camp as he saw fit. In early 1944 it became clear that Pohl and Rauter could not find a compromise, and Pohl decided that he would transfer the camp to Rauter and withdraw all his men—that is, the whole SS garrison. Rauter had no men to replace them and resisted taking responsibility for the camp. Both Pohl and Rauter reported to Himmler, and he settled the issue: Pohl was to remain in charge. See Königseder, "Polizeihaftlager," 9:31.

586. This means that another installment of the diary was being smuggled out of the camp.

587. With this sentence David filled the exercise book in which he had kept his diary from December 28. Obviously he was ready to send this, and earlier exercise books, to Amsterdam. Yet the anticipated opportunity to smuggle the diary out of the camp did not materialize until after February 8, 1944. Therefore the dispatch also included the exercise book that contained his diary from January 28 to February 8.

588. This letter is missing from the file.

coincidence spoke with Ruth, her sister, who raised the subject herself and promised to write to me. She said: "You're mistaken about her, and you're not the first." I'm saving her letter, too. Whether I agree with it I don't know. Only at the moment that she spoke I felt how I had drifted away from H[annie]. Floated off. And I'm going to make every effort not to return to her. For the last couple of days I've tried this out, and it's working. There's a spot inside that I don't touch on purpose. I feel its sensitivity, even when nothing touches it. I deliberately avoid it. We see each other occasionally, exchange very friendly greetings. It hurts for a moment, but only just long enough that the sensitive spot betrays its presence. Nothing more. And I can live with that.

Yesterday our dear notary left to go home.[589] I'm very conscious of missing the sound of his voice over the microphone. "Good morning, it's seven o'clock, so . . . let's get to work!" With all the quaint turns of speech he took so much trouble over. Someone remarkably distinguished, this lovable old man. Bochel is reading "Maria Lécina" and finds it most diverting.[590] But he thinks it's pornography and claims it's scandalous to let women read it.

In a nice little speech over the microphone, De W[it] said something about vitality and wisdom. You find these qualities emphatically expressed in the notary's gestures, in an old-fashioned way like everything else about him. De W[it] said too: "He has fallen away from us." And that's how I felt about it as well today.

Now M[argreet] T[asselaar] also has a chance to leave. Yesterday evening: discharge hearing. The last few days I've had the occasional conversation with her. She has something free and lively and something steady at the same time.

The day before yesterday I met Fl[othuis], with whom I talked about Frederika [Samson] and the Reichenfelds [Hans and Dora].[591] In fact, he's a relative of M[argreet] T[asselaar]'s. It's a small world.

Life has become a lot easier. The business with H[annie] is definitively over and done with, I believe. I'm starting to forget her. It hits me when I see her, but mostly I fail to notice her. Yesterday I replied

589. David is referring to the non-Jewish lawyer and notary public Gregorius J. M. Schoenmaeckers, who had become an important person in the Philips Kommando.

590. The reference is to a poem written by Johan Willem Frederik Werumeus Buning (1891–1958).

591. This is the non-Jewish prisoner Marius Flothuis. See the entry on him in the appendix.

to Ruth's letter. She had spoken with Mother and told her that she regretted that we hadn't been in contact for so long. Not long ago I greeted her in the street for the first time, and that had particularly touched her (actually, I don't know for how long I've been suffering the ill effects of forgetting to greet people). Chiefly a question of shyness. In the meantime she had written me a most remarkable short letter. If her health and vigor recover she'll become a remarkable woman. Of course, I know her fiancé. A history student in my year, a friend of Van Peski's, one of the few with whom I used to speak. Written below this was a reply to my letter about H[annie] that did not reveal much. Just one curious thing: her satisfaction that this had ended and that she had contributed to it. "The last while you've been looking much less concerned than I have ever seen you before." And everything comes at the same time: Sp[itz] told me how Mother had expressed her anxiety about the whole matter to him and had talked about Nettie. Actually, he thought it was rather forward of her. It's typically her style, of course. "But," Sp[itz] says, "I'm telling you this now because I can, since enough time has passed," so yesterday it gave me the feeling, all day long, that I haven't heard the last of this.

Dear Nettie, you'll probably soon be reading this. I suddenly happened to see a possibility . . . [of getting this diary out]. The whole history is here, with all its ups and downs. As free and open as I could write it down for my own purposes. Because I didn't think you people would be reading this before the end of the war. That has [been] a great advantage, of course. That's the only way I was able to let myself go completely. And you'll see: in writing down my feelings I've gone just as far as those feelings went. And that was quite far, as you'll also see. I'm glad that you're not reading this earlier rather than after things have clarified themselves. In more than one respect, to this point this diary is a finished whole. This history has come to an end; at Philips I'm now simply a timekeeper, after a period when the group had to be formed and transports were leaving and I had a lot of influence. In my own mind I've really become a prisoner, and so have largely escaped the special problematic position we civilian internees were in for a long time here.

This whole business with Hannie, the girl about whom I've been writing for the last few months (H), can you understand it? That has been an added passion always accompanied by the thought: all of it is the camp that's working within me: that's driving my feelings along to such an extreme (if you ask what content and direction they actually have, you can't tell, they are simply hurried along) and that separates me so much from the world outside, from Nettie, from everything that's out there. All that time you've remained for me what you were when I entered this camp: the beloved, loving abundance that is in Amsterdam but that has become so hard to discern, to which my feelings go out. But I'm losing track of my feelings, I don't know what's happening to them. That's how my letters must sound to you. But I can't write any better than this, and I can't feel any more deeply than this. From the beginning I've walked around reproaching myself about that. You'll recall my letter of April last year. And I talked about it constantly later on. Perhaps you'll find it pusillanimous of me, but I've learned that I am very pusillanimous: where you're concerned I'm ashamed of this passion. Not that it is reprehensible in itself. Every exercise of feelings is valuable, without exception. I've learned that here. Things can get really intense around here, and people are ever more judgmental according to the norm and intensity of the emotion. In regard to that no morality is valid. But this has been much more the consequence of an instinctive *emotional deficit* where you are concerned. Something I knew at once, even at the beginning of last year. This has not been a matter of too much feeling, but too little. And against this stands the fidelity of all of you and your fidelity in its special way: I notice how completely alive I am to you all and how your emotional contact with me is just as strong, or even stronger, than it used to be.

I must ask you to excuse me. Perhaps you judge it to be inappropriate, yet it is the only possibility. Perforate a newspaper, best would be the *Deutsche Zeitung [in den Niederlanden]* [*German Newspaper in the Netherlands*], and wrap it around some item in the parcel (have the others do that as well.[592] I'd really like more overviews from Karel), and say something about it in your regular letter, but not too explicitly.

I'll stop writing now. I don't think it's fair to smuggle a letter when it's only about a diary. But this fits within the framework of everything I've written in this diary earlier.

Do write to me regularly, via newspaper and official mail. Much love from Dick.

The visit by H[immler] didn't come off. The night before we were woken up at around three. A couple of guys were smashing windows

---

592. David is suggesting that Nettie use the simplest of ways to send a coded message by putting pinholes in the letters of a newspaper.

with hammers. All the windows that were broken or cracked were taken out. For some reason that had to be done in the middle of the night, even though a list of all the broken windows in the camp has been available for two weeks. Once again the inmates of block 7 made a terrible racket. In fact, recently the noise has been appalling in the evening. The work of the outside detachments is quite light these days, so that they're unfortunately not sleepy and low-spirited. Their stench, their accent, [and] their jokes make me nauseous and dejected.

I got the coffee this morning. On a big pushcart. A container fell over. It was very nice, that journey through the darkness with the cart, from which you could hear the coffee dripping.

Of course Himmler didn't come. But he's coming tomorrow. And he won't come then either, you'll see.

In the meantime it's a lot more agreeable here now that the commandant is gone. Sunday afternoon roll call had the old hurrah mood. And E[rich?] is particularly human and pleasant and raises hell like a real rascal. On the other hand, they don't want to give us too free a rein. So at roll call the evening of the day before yesterday, two men (Jews), 15 strokes each. Old offenses. Actually 4 were supposed to be beaten: 2 were sick. Evidently a show of force. Just like a sudden inspection of our barrack by a block leader.

The new detachment leader isn't stupid: "In Russia it'll take a while longer before they reach our borders. But the invasion. When and in how many places? That's the most important question. Invading in one place should work."

[Sunday] January 30, 1944. Excerpt from a letter mentioning a letter from Simon Toncman,[593] who left with a transport on October 17, 1942, to the Van der Lee family.

593. Simon Louis Toncman (1915–72) was born in Oss. He trained as an accountant. In 1942 he was deported to Auschwitz. He survived the selection, more than two years of camp life, and the death march that brought him in early 1945 to Buchenwald. That camp was liberated on April 11, 1945. Five days after the liberation of Buchenwald Private Harry Miller of the United States Signal Corps entered block 56. He decided to take a photo showing the many emaciated and naked inmates (inclusive Elie Wiesel) as they were crowded in their bunks. In order to increase the dramatic effect, Miller asked one of them to get up, step forward and lean against a post. This inmate was Simon Toncman. This photo appeared in the New York Times in May 6, 1945. The website of the Buchenwald Memorial carries this photo. Commenting on Toncman the caption observes that "to this day, the photo of the latter's emaciated body in front of the seemingly endless rows of boxes still shapes our image of the crimes committed in the concentration camps." www.buchenwald.de/english/index.php?p=168. Toncman returned to Oss and married Auschwitz survivor Judith Kalker (1923–2001). They had four children.

They're doing well in Beut[h]en, Upper Silesia, near Katowice. That's where they're working. Simon passes on Henri's greetings. They don't know whether they're staying there. You can't write to them directly, but to an acquaintance of theirs. He is curious how Van der Lee and other acquaintances are making out. Quotation(?): Henri is constantly close at hand and sends his best. He's doing well, too. Let's hear from you soon. We don't see many acquaintances anymore. So girl, now you know: are you ever happy, eh?

The letter was dated November 5, 1943, and arrived January 14. If you can manage it, send a parcel, he also wrote.

Id[em]

Simon had a bad cold; otherwise he was doing well under the circumstances. Working near Beuthen. He wrote, Duna would say: "How is that possible?" but I'm very curious how you're all doing, and everyone I know.

[Thursday] February 3 [1944]. In connection with this there's also the following story: the *obershiksa* [head female guard] was at the Aryan women's assembly line and asked who wanted to volunteer for work in Germany. Two wanted time to think about it. The rest refused, of course. And she: "Just wait, if the Russians are here four weeks from now you won't get any food at all."

The mood among the SS is very down. A nice example of favoritism: in the production office of the capacitor factory they're looking for a cost accountant. H[eine?] mentions it to Mother and also says that he doesn't have anyone for the job. Silbermann proposed his friend Pollace, but H[eine?] doesn't want him.[594] Mother says very impulsively: "That would be something for my husband." H[eine?] takes her up eagerly on this; he really looks on us with favor. Some time ago he put me in charge of shipping in order to keep me in barrack 2.

594. David is referring to the German Quaker Manfred Pollatz (1886–1964). Manfred and his wife, Lili Pollatz-Engelsmann (1883–1946), left Germany in 1933 for the Netherlands and, in 1934, established a small boarding school for refugee children in Haarlem. Those who could not pay stayed for free. After the beginning of the deportations the Pollatz couple took in Jewish babies of parents who had been arrested. Their house also became a hiding place for members of the resistance and a distribution point of one of the illegal newspapers. Manfred was arrested in 1943. He spent time in Vught and Dachau but was released in late 1944.

[Friday] February 4 [1944]. In the end it seems that Father will also join us. This being Vught, it's too good to be true. At once fear grips my heart. But S[ilbermann] is angry that his friend P[ollatz] isn't coming and starts intriguing with De W[it], who generally can't stand us. Mother asks H[eine?] to reverse the decision. At first he doesn't want to: it has to be fought out with De W[it]. Peuscher, who takes a particularly kindly view of all of us, has a conversation with Mother and grants her request for Father's return to his old position, after first suggesting to her that if she wanted it, he could stay. Mother and later Father have really given Silbermann a piece of their mind. On my insistence. Because in this matter I'm implacable. He really deserves to be insulted every day of his life.

Meanwhile we always get the short end of the stick. We are completely helpless against all the shady deals and insolence. This morning the whole business here was rearranged (the result of De W[it]'s bullying); without even checking with me, they moved my table while I was still talking about a suitable place for it. Now I'm sitting in an exposed place again. I was upset about that all morning. Not so much because of the fact itself but because of my helplessness in situations in which I should have acted. But I feel myself to be very cowardly and weak here. As far as my self-esteem is concerned, this camp has put an enormous dent in it. Respected from day one and later in a prominent position, but from the outset with that feeling of helplessness, cowardice, shyness towards people. And in the end everyone here sees through the whole show of influence and respect.

In the meantime it has begun to snow, large, gossamer flakes. So much is falling that it is bound to stick even though the snow and the air are moist. All morning long the sky hung down in large, gray bags. Everything here was marvelously small. And later in the day the camp is white. The trees still look a bit black. Some places emerge from under the snow. The blocks seem even lower than otherwise. The roofs are only a little bit brighter than the grubby plain sky behind them. And it is very quiet. But you sense that it's only for a short while. And after a couple of hours everything will be a wet mess. Yesterday I began the day with book T. *The Iliad*.[595] Together with H. de J.,[596] classicist. I still have a marvelous intuition for these verses, still know

595. In Greek-language editions of *The Iliad* chapter 19 is usually referred to as chapter T.
596. H. de J. must be the unnamed head of the shipping department of the Philips workshop mentioned in the entry of December 16, 1943.

many words and sentence constructions.[597] Even feel more at home in them, more in command of the text than H. de J., although he does have the inimitable skill of the professional, in establishing internal relations between different pieces of text. It made my day.

So yesterday the high-ranking visitors came after all. An hour before they came, the girls' mood was already very nervous and giggly. Van Wijk and I at my table. They're in the barrack but don't show up for quite a while. Van Wijk adds up the total through Thursday and by mistake writes it in ink as the total for the week. I make a lot of errors on a daily report that I have to be very careful with, otherwise it's finished too quickly and I won't have anything more to do. Finally they come. H[immler] at their head. A slight, insignificant-looking little man, with a rather good-humored face. High peaked cap, mustache, and small spectacles. I think: If you wanted to trace back all the misery and horror to just one person, it would have to be him. Around him a lot of fellows with weary faces. Very big, heavily dressed men, they swerve along whichever way he turns, like a swarm of flies, changing places among themselves (they don't stand still for a moment) and moving like a single whole. It makes a fatally alarming impression. They look everywhere without finding anything to focus on. One of them takes a couple of steps towards Van Wijk and me, evidently irritated by the fact that, while writing assiduously, we keep talking and paying close attention to the group. One is carrying a very big movie camera and a big leather briefcase. (He's got the whole day's sandwiches in there, says little Herman.) Himmler and De W[it] get into conversation. Rauter, who's also present, turns out to know De W[it]'s case very well.[598] "We Germans," says H[immler], "can't tolerate that a brother people are hiding behind their dikes and flooded defensive lines while we are fighting on the eastern front for *den Endsieg* [the final victory]." [Asks] whether De W[it] is related to the great W.?[599] In any case he gets a handshake. And the whole camp is still talking about that handshake today.

597. David had read *The Iliad* in Greek while in high school.

598. David is referring to Abraham de Wit.

599. Johan de Witt (1625–72) was grand pensionary of the States of Holland (comparable to the position of prime minister today) from 1653 until his murder by a Hague mob in 1672, ostensibly for having betrayed his country. The charge was spurious. While Bram de Wit was not a descendant of Johan de Witt's, he suggested in his conversation with Himmler that there might be a connection. Believing in the importance of genealogy and an admirer of Johan de Witt as an opponent of English power, Himmler decided to personally review the files on Bram de Wit, and a few days after his visit he ordered his release.

M[argreet] T[asselaar] is asked why she's here. To repair things, she says at first. Then: favoritism towards Jews. "The Jews are not our friends," Himmler decrees, "so they're not yours either." The words of such a powerful and wise man silence Margreet. A small, blond, Germanic woman, why is she here: "For distributing *De waarheid [The Truth]*." "Meaning what?" "Communist publications, among them *De waarheid*." Is she still a Communist? "Yes." "Even now?" "Even now." And H[immler] goes on his way. Later, outside the door, he says: "The only one who's honest." As Sp[itz] comments: a remark that characterizes the situation he is in.[600] A lad of 17 is working at the electric razor assembly line. H[immler] asks him his name and why he's here. R[auter] knows the case and says: "Wasn't there shooting on your farm too?" That does indeed turn out to be true.

J[ohnny] van Doorn gets P[euscher] to buttonhole [Himmler] and says: "My discharge is on your desk, *Herr R[eichs]f[ührer]*." P[euscher] says that J[ohnny] van D[oorn] will get a job with Philips as soon as he's free.[601]

The numbers of the boy and of J[ohnny] van D[oorn] have been noted.

In 43 [the barrack housing the Philips laboratory] Frau Dr. Kohn was introduced to him.[602] He asked why the only women there were Jewish. "They can't leave," L[aman] T[rip] said, "and the training period is very long." "So why aren't there more?" "The rest were sent away. But there are some left in Westerbork." "What is that, Westerbork?" It's made clear to him. "So it would only be a transfer from one camp for Jews to another? That can be arranged." Evidently they continued with this topic. "The work is too exacting to do for ten

600. Spitz is suggesting that no one around Himmler dared to speak truth to power. Indeed, the chief of the SS did not have a court jester.

601. David is referring to the non-Jewish Communist Johannes Wilhelmus (Johnny) van Dooren. He was arrested for resistance activities and after his stay in Vught ended up in Dachau. He had lived in England, France, and Germany and as a result had a superb command of the English, French, and German languages. General George S. Patton recognized his talents and used him for some time as an interpreter.

602. David is referring to the German-Jewish refugee Henriette (Henny) J. Cohn (1900–50). Cohn had earned a Ph.D. in physics and began her career at Telefunken. A single mother, she fled to the Netherlands in 1935 and found a job with Philips. In 1942 she became part of the SOBU group, and after her internment in Vught she was in charge of the production of radio tubes. In August 1944 she ended up in Reichenbach, working as a forced laborer for her original employer, Telefunken. She survived the war, but when it was clear she would not obtain Dutch citizenship she emigrated to the United States. Klein and Van de Kamp, *Het Philips-Kommando,* 152.

hours," M[aarschalk] says.[603] "You could," says H[immler], "have the girls work eight hours and have them do something else afterwards. Agriculture, for example." "Can't be done," says M[aarschalk], "because of their hands." H[immler] to St[okker]: "Then it should be possible to find something else." St[okker] agrees.

Around the time of this visit, which turned out to be a big success, and in any case has had no adverse effects for us, we regularly got oatmeal and pea soup. For a moment it became clear what the food here ought to be. Afterwards it became just as thin, disagreeable, and insufficient as it was before.

[Monday] February 7, 1944. Yesterday afternoon and this afternoon, once again the meals were good: I hear that H[immler] said that this is supposed to become the healthiest camp in W. Europe. To begin with, the last three days I've had a terrible itch. It's not lice, because I wash very thoroughly every morning, and moreover [there's] inspection every Sunday. (That is to say, the last few weeks I've passed inspection by stating that I wasn't itching.) Yesterday examined myself closely and verified a complete absence of these friendly animals. Van Wijk has pressed two of them in his diary. I'm still hoping to splice a detailed yet barely decent description of the inspections into this diary. To the clinic yesterday. Obtained the same ointment (sulfur ointment) that so many people are using to rub into themselves. The treatment to be repeated after two or three days. When it has cleared up Van der Hal will tell me what it is.[604] He doesn't have to say any more, because it's undoubtedly scabies. But then that is to be expected, because all those people who are anointing themselves have it. Van Wijk has already had it twice. But it doesn't improve anyone's self-image.

I rather think I can see small irregularities in my skin, but I could be mistaken.

This morning a long conversation with R[iek] S[nel], who has recovered after a fairly long illness. In appearance she is an insignificant, wrinkled little woman. She hides her hands deep in her man's overcoat, thrusts her nonchalant head forward, and shuffles along in her wooden shoes. But she's capable of sharp insights and value judg-

---

603. Philips employee Hans Maarschalk had been the manager of the SOBU group.
604. David is referring to the physician Dr. Isidoor van der Hal.

ments, perhaps a bit too radical. She has the same soundness that all the Aryan women have. It's unimaginable that she already has two grown sons. We prefer to avoid the subject. We did it once and she lost her composure.

This morning we spoke about all the adulterous situations that prevail here and that are simply accepted as commonplace. "M[argreet] thinks differently about it," says Riek, "but I'm old-fashioned and I say to her these things don't happen because people's hearts are too big but because they're too small." And in the course of the conversation she repeats this a couple of times. But I tell her how crazy this camp is: as soon as you're here you only see all your loved ones in a haze. I tell her I already wrote that to people back home after two months, last year. And how all this time that sense of incompetence of feeling has pursued me here as a reproach. And the good things Nettie and Tini have asserted about this: *der Welt abhanden kommen* (to be mislaid by the world).[605] But still: I do experience her words about simplicity and strength of feeling as reproaches. Otherwise I've been very happy recently with that calm feeling that everything is yet to come and that it is waiting for me in Amsterdam. And that Nettie has revealed herself, if you can call it that, through and in this separation. Dear Nettie, I know now that you'll read all of this: you have to picture me at this moment, in the evening in the factory at my table. It's almost time to go: people are just chatting a bit. People are slowly getting ready to go. Everyone is tired. Officially the working day is 12 hours. I think of you with a feeling of calm and affection. You are not angry with me? Everything here is very difficult. I am grateful for every moment of homesickness and loss. Write to me what you think of my diary. I have the sense that I'm passing through incomprehensible adventures, far, far from home. To think I'm less then 200 kilometers [124 miles] away from you!

[Tuesday] February 8 [1944]. Today is the big day. This in haste. Yesterday an unpleasant experience. I have good relations with F[lothuis], an acquaintance of Fr[ederika]'s, after all. And not long ago he sent me to give some bread to a very young married woman, not yet 18 years old. She looks so thin, he says. I think nothing of it. Yesterday he sent me with something again. I still don't suspect anything, he's

---

605. David is referring to a poem by Friedrich Rückert (1788–1866), "Ich bin der Welt abhanden gekommen," set to music of wondrous beauty by Gustav Mahler (1860–1911).

never spoken with her yet . . . There are two cigarettes and a letter. But such a letter. About her beautiful spirit. About his intuition, his wife, his children, his desire for companionship with such a sensitive woman. I return everything without saying a word. He's been in this camp for two months.

I rage at R[iek Snel] for a long time, along the lines of our conversation yesterday morning. And feel myself caught badly in the middle.

Epilogue: The Final Year

David's diary breaks off with the words "[I] feel myself caught badly in the middle." Of course he had been caught between Nettie, who was in hiding, and Hannie, who was in the camp. And he had been in the middle of camp affairs, as a sharp observer of the tragicomedy of human life in extremis. The abrupt ending was the result of the imminent departure of the Philips employee who was going to smuggle the diary out of the camp. David handed him his exercise books, and they found their way to Karel. According to his brother Max, David continued to keep a diary after February 8, but he was unable to smuggle out the next installment. The new commandant, SS-Sturmbannführer Hans Hüttig, imposed a strict regime on the camp. He was known as a troubleshooter, and the bunker tragedy of the night of January 15 had shown Vught to be a badly managed concentration camp. More evidence of this was the discovery on January 25, 1944, that civilian workers had been smuggling prisoners' letters out of the camp. Clearly the Grünewald regime had failed to keep the camp under full control. Hüttig responded with the symbolic gesture that prisoners were to sew up the pockets in their uniforms.

The new commandant was also determined to get rid of the 672 remaining Jews. Hüttig was a hard-core anti-Semite: the Jews should leave and be liquidated. Compared with this, the interests of Philips or the possible economic benefits of the Philips workshop for the SS were of no significance. On March 20 he informed the Philips management that the 285 Jewish men left in Vught would leave for Westerbork immediately.[1] The women would remain in Vught for the time being. Jacques, David, Max, and the other men were given civilian clothes and taken by truck to Vught station, where a train stood ready to take them northeast to Westerbork. They were not allowed to take any personal belongings. These, they were told, would be forwarded to them, but this never happened. David lost all the letters he had received since the beginning of the fall.[2]

When they arrived in Westerbork, they were surprised by the conditions in the camp. In Vught some Jewish functionaries like Arthur Lehmann had exercised authority, but there had been a spirit of egalitarianism among the Jewish inmates. In Westerbork an elite of German-Jewish refugees, interned by the Dutch in 1939, was well entrenched, and an unbridgeable gap existed between them and the other inmates, who could be dispatched to the east at any time. In November 1943, when David, Alfred Spitz, and Hein van Wijk faced the question of whom to save from deportation they found themselves in what was for Vught an extraordinary position. In contrast, trains had been leaving Westerbork for Auschwitz or Sobibor on a weekly basis, filled with deportees selected by the Jewish establishment in the camp. In Vught the inmates had formed a republic of sorts; Westerbork was an absolute and immensely corrupt monarchy headed by the German-Jewish refugee Kurt Schlesinger. The newcomers from Vught found themselves at the bottom of the hierarchy.[3] Furthermore, in Vught they had internalized a sense of discipline, but in Westerbork there was nothing like it. Yet at least David enjoyed meeting old friends he had not seen for a year. In a letter he wrote from Westerbork he mentioned that Leo and Margot Seeligmann, who had sent packages of food to him in Vught when they were still free, were taking care of him.[4]

David would not stay in Westerbork for long. Philips executive Rutger E. Laman Trip worked hard to have the men returned to Vught. His motives were complex: he wanted to keep the Philips workshop productive and profitable, but he also was eager to protect the Jews who worked for Philips. In 1943 he had created the Philips workshop without any intention of saving Jewish lives, but once his creation had become an effective shelter, he had accepted this as a valid and important purpose. Laman Trip quickly contacted senior security police officials in The Hague, and after some haggling they agreed that 90 of the 285 men sent to Westerbork would be allowed to return, and that in addition 22 Jewish women interned in Westerbork would be sent to Vught also.[5] The Germans did not tell Laman Trip that the others were to be deported to the east with the first available train. Laman Trip approached prisoner Hein van Wijk, who remained in Vught, to help him compile a list of the lucky ones. Van Wijk and David were close, and it is not surprising that the list included the names of the three Kokers. On March 22 Laman Trip visited Westerbork and handed camp commandant Albert Konrad Gemmeker the list. He should not think that the 90 men and the 22 women were safe, Gemmeker said: if and when the Allied invasion came, all remaining Jews in the Netherlands would be shipped to the east. Yet a reprieve was better than immediate deportation to Auschwitz. And so, on March 28, David, his father, brother, and 87 other men returned to Vught, accompanied by 22 women who were new to the camp. David's friend Max Cahen recalled that, when they entered the camp, the 90 men were told to stand in the roll-call place. Initially not a single SS officer showed up to "welcome" them. Finally one left the commandant's office and yelled to them: "Weren't you here once before?" David and the others responded in unison: "Yes sir!" "All of you?" "Yes sir! All of us!"[6] This was the sum total of their reinitiation into Vught. They knew the place and did not need threatening speeches or the humiliations that accompanied the reception in a concentration camp. They felt they had returned home.

The Jewish contingent in Vught was down to 499 inmates. David continued to write the poems that were intended to become a cycle named, after Mozart's Serenade no. 13 in G Major, K. 525, *Een kleine nachtmuziek*.[7] He continued to receive letters from Fré Samson and Karel van het Reve. For much of 1943 he had lived in Vught without being too much concerned about his earlier life in Amsterdam. After reconnecting in Westerbork with some of his Amsterdam friends, life outside the camp acquired sharper contours—and also because it seemed ever more likely that the war might end within the next year. Shortly after David's return to Vught, Fré informed him that she had heard from David's onetime friend Philip de Vries, who had been able to obtain his degree shortly before the University of Amsterdam was forced to expel Jewish students. When the deportations began, Philip had told his parents he wanted to escape to Switzerland. They consented and gave him all the ready money they had. He had reached Switzerland and after a brief internment was allowed to take up graduate studies at the University of Bern. In 1944 he earned his second degree and reported the news to Fré. When she informed David about Philip's achievement, he felt envious and depressed. "Childish?" he replied to Fré. "Perhaps, but you who are still active (and ever more so in some respects) can't come close to imagining what this absolute stagnation means. I dream of Amsterdam a lot these days, of being with you all, of working together enthusiastically."[8]

Laman Trip's rescue of the men may have given them the impression that they were safe in the Philips workshop. If so, they were living an illusion: Hüttig remained committed to making Vught Jew free. On May 3, around noon, David and the others were called away from their work and ordered to stand in line for roll call. It was the beginning of Hüttig's second attempt to transfer them to Westerbork. This time Laman Trip intervened immediately.[9] While the men remained in the roll-call square, he phoned Philips headquarters in Eindhoven to report their impending deportation. A senior Philips executive called Ewald Löser in Berlin. Löser was the *Reichstreuhänder* (Reich trustee) of the German branches of the Philips Corporation, and as such he was the liaison between the company and the German government and its institutions. Löser was willing to help, and not only because he valued good relations with Eindhoven. He loathed the Nazi regime. In fact, if the July 20, 1944 assassination attempt against Hitler had succeeded, he would have become minister of finance in the government formed by his friend Carl Goerdeler. He contacted SS-Standartenführer Gerhard Maurer, head of department D2, Arbeits-einsatz (labor deployment) in the SS-Wirtschafts-Verwaltungshauptamt (SS Economic Administrative Main Office) in Oranienburg. Maurer had been a businessman before joining the SS and made his career within the SS as an accountant in the auditing department. This shaped his perspective. He was committed to getting the maximum economic benefit from concentration-camp inmates. When the interests of the economy clashed with those of ideology, Maurer believed the former should trump the latter. He regarded the Jews within the camp system primarily as an economic force to be used to good advantage while they were still alive.[10] Maurer knew the Philips workshop in Vught well, for he had visited it in 1943. He thought the Jews should stay. In the early evening Maurer called Hüttig and ordered him to cancel the transport. Only then, nine hours after the negotiations began, were the men allowed to go back to their barracks. They had been on their feet throughout.

Hüttig had failed in his second attempt to get rid of the Jews. In the weeks that followed he focused on another strategy that centered on the non-Jewish prisoners. The Germans expected an Allied invasion shortly, and if the landings took place on the Belgian or Dutch coasts, Vught would soon be within the theater of operations. The camp was full of members of the resistance, and the SS anticipated an uprising to support the invasion. Hüttig therefore decided to evacuate 1,200 of the most dangerous non-Jewish inmates to Dachau. The group included 250 members of the Philips workshop, including Van Wijk. Because the transfer occurred on the basis of legitimate security concerns, Laman Trip was powerless to prevent the removal of key members of his operation, which was devastated as a result. This gave Hüttig the opportunity to remove the remaining 499 Jews. On the night of June 2 the SS assembled all of them, took them to Vught station, loaded them in cattle cars, locked the doors, and sent the train on its way east.[11]

With a blunt pencil David scrawled a short note to his friends and addressed it to "K. v. h. Reve / Tooropkade 116 / A'dam." When the train passed through the shunting yard of the nearby city of 's Hertogenbosch, he folded it and dropped it out of the window. It was barely legible.

> At the moment we're in the train on the way to somewhere in Germany. We know for certain we'll get through this. We've been familiarizing ourselves with the concept recently. This is the way things are. The entire camp is being vacated. Ph. will keep on protecting us over there. I received L.'s last letter. Lots of love, lots of thanks. Good-bye. D.[12]

Someone found the piece of paper and added a brief comment.

> Found shunting yard Hgb. The whole Vught camp is gone. Men and women were in cattle cars. It was a sad business. They may be Jews [*sic!*], but something like this ought not to happen in this civilization.

The finder put the note in an envelope, but the almost illegible scrawl led him to send it to Rotterdam, not Amsterdam. Only after a postal clerk had opened the envelope—the finder had indicated no return address—did the note find its way to Karel.[13]

While a Dutch postal clerk tried to resolve the mystery of a wrongly addressed letter without a return address, Laman Trip tried to save the people on the train. He knew that by acting swiftly and decisively Hüttig had won this round. The train would not be stopping in Westerbork, so Laman Trip could not intervene at that stage. He also knew that his argument about the importance of maintaining production in Vught had lost its validity: as a result of Hüttig's deportation of twelve hundred inmates to Dachau the Philips workshop had effectively ceased production. But Laman Trip did not give up. He contacted Löser, who called Maurer, who in turn phoned the acting commandant of Auschwitz, SS-Obersturmbannführer Rudolf Höss.[14] Maurer knew Höss well: during Höss's tenure as commandant of Auschwitz (April 1940–November 1943) they had met often to discuss the labor deployment of the inmates. More recently they had been close colleagues in the SS Economic Administrative Main Office in Oranienburg. Höss had been temporarily redeployed to Auschwitz to oversee the murder of four hundred thousand Hungarian Jews, but both men knew that by the end of the summer Höss would return to Oranienburg. Maurer informed Höss that a transport of trained radio technicians was on its way to Auschwitz and that they should not be subject to selection upon arrival but quarantined until he had decided what to do with them. Then Maurer instructed his aides to investigate the need for radio technicians within the concentration camp system.

No one on the train knew about the negotiations that were taking place but, as David's note reveals, they expected that Laman Trip would do his best to help them.[15] At the same time they knew that they were about to cross not only a political but also an existential frontier. They were aware that since the deportations had commenced in July 1942, no Jew who had left the Netherlands had returned. Shortly before the train reached the Dutch-German border David wrote a second and last letter:

> Dear Friends,
> We're very near the frontier. It's disappointing, but we were prepared for it and are full of confidence. I think of you all a lot. I was happy and shocked about L.'s last letter. I have all the letters and photos with me. My dearest possession. When will we see each other again? It will be a long time. But we will get through it. The mood here is good. I am very melancholic. Go to 24 Oosterom Kribbestraat for Spitz. Lots of love, dear friends, thanks for everything. Good-bye. D.[16]

With less difficulty than the first, his letter also found its way to Karel.

David and his companions must have been shocked when their train stopped in a railway shunting yard near Breslau (Wrocław). Parked next to it was an army transport. The soldiers on it yelled: "None of you will be alive tomorrow."[17] They were wrong. Upon arrival in Auschwitz-Birkenau on June 6, the day of the Allied invasion in Normandy, the Jews from Vught did not undergo selection. They were very lucky: more than 228,000 Jews arrived in Auschwitz in May, and more than 169,000 in June, most of them from Hungary. All of these deportees underwent selection, and 90 percent were killed within hours of that ordeal. But the Kokers were not spared the calamity of separation: the SS sent Judith to the women's camp in Birkenau, while they sent the men to the Auschwitz *Stammlager* (main camp). Jacques would never see his wife again; David would never see his mother again. On the day that marked the beginning of the liberation of western Europe from the Nazi nightmare, the Germans destroyed the unity of the Koker family.

When the men were registered, Max Cahen noticed that the clerk checked his data against a list with the heading "Transport of Trained Radio Technicians."[18] Thus he learned that the SS deemed them too valuable to be killed at once. Nevertheless they underwent the usual initiation. All their body hair was removed, and registration numbers were tattooed on their left arms. But after more than a year in Vught, such things had ceased to shock them.

Initially Maurer's protective umbrella continued to work: they were spared heavy labor. However, the SS men mocked them as "the gentlemen from Philips." After a few weeks, they were assigned to labor squads canalizing the Vistula River, or sorted the possessions of those who had been killed in the gas chambers. David had lost neither his arrogance nor his courage. One day he approached an SS officer in charge of labor deployment, reminded him that he and the others were trained radio technicians from Philips, and said that they should be spared for skilled work. Remarkably, this reminder had the desired result: one of the very few occasions in the history of Auschwitz that an inmate successfully petitioned a senior SS man. The Philips Jews were taken out of the labor squads and confined to their quarters.[19]

Of course the SS man very likely relented not because he liked David or was impressed by his argument but because he had learned that "the gentlemen from Philips" were going to be assigned to another camp. Maurer had not forgotten them after his conversation with Höss. Investigating the need for radio technicians, he discovered that the Hagenuk company, located next to the German naval base at Kiel, was moving its production line for radio transmitters from an area that was within reach of the Allied bombers to one that was not, the town of Reichenbach in Lower Silesia.[20] In the nineteenth century Reichenbach had been a center of the Silesian textile industry, but by the 1940s many textile mills had closed. Their buildings offered ample space for companies evacuated from the bomb-ravaged cities in western and northern Germany. Even better: two miles south of Reichenbach, in the municipality of Langenbielau, there were fourteen empty barracks of a former forced-labor camp. It would not take much to transform them into a concentration camp.[21] Maurer had found a destination for the Jews from Vught. They would work in Reichenbach and live in Langenbielau.

At the end of July, a Hagenuk engineer accompanied by one of Maurer's men arrived in Auschwitz. They lined up the "gentlemen from Philips," and after a cursory examination declared them to be useful to Hagenuk. Max remembered that in every case they said: "We can use him." Then the men were sent back to their barracks and held in quarantine for a few more weeks. On August 23, they received new prison uniforms and were shipped to Langenbielau. Most of the women also went to Langenbielau, to be put to work in a Telefunken factory. Judith remained behind because she was considered too old. Somehow she survived her imprisonment in Birkenau to be liberated by the Red Army on January 27, 1945.

The living and working conditions were harsh. The distance between the factory and the camp created an extra burden: wearing wooden clogs, the prisoners had to walk two and a half miles to the Hagenuk factory, work a twelve-hour shift, and walk back. But for the rest of 1944 the inmates received enough food to keep from starving. In January 1945, however, the infrastructure supporting the camps collapsed as the Red Army launched its final attack on the German heartland. Both public morale and public order broke down. Nazi fanatics arbitrarily identified and executed German civilians and soldiers accused of defeatism, but these acts of violence did not stop the collapse. Fleeing German civilians clogged the roads. Cities, towns, and villages emptied. Food supplies ran out. The prisoners now had to try to survive on a starvation diet. Meanwhile the Hagenuk factory in Reichenbach continued production, and the labor regime did not soften. In addition, snow and bitter cold turned the daily trek to and from the factory into a cruel ordeal. Starvation and exhaustion brought disease and death in their wake. Jacques declined quickly, and on February 4 he died, aged fifty-eight. He was buried in a mass grave.[22]

By this time both David and Max were in bad shape. A few weeks after Jacques's death, Max became ill, and after some time in the Langenbielau sick bay he, his friend Albert Joachim (Fedush) Herz, and Max Cahen were taken, on March 20, to what the SS promised to be an *Erholungslager* (recovery camp). It turned out to be completely different. They ended up in a so-called *Krepierungslager* (camp for croaking) located in a former carpet factory in Dörnhau, where the Germans left both Jewish and non-Jewish prisoners to die.

Throughout the Holocaust, Jewish prisoners had always remained at the bottom in the concentration-camp system, and their chances of survival had been much smaller than those of non-Jewish prisoners. Only very few had been exempted from this general rule, determined by the SS leadership in Berlin. Once they became valuable members of the Philips group, the Kokers had belonged to those few. If Nazi racist logic had determined in 1942 that all Jews were to die, German business logic had decided in 1944 that Jews with skills important to the war effort should remain alive, at least for the duration. This had saved the Kokers from the gas chamber in June 1944. But in early 1945, amid the apocalyptic collapse of Germany, the last vestiges of ideological consistency or economic rationality disappeared. Amid chaos and random violence, the only thing that mattered was luck.[23]

For most inmates, Dörnhau meant death. But the two Maxes and Fedush had luck: Hertz's cousin, Fritz Wissbrun, worked as the chief clerk in the nearby camp of Wüstegiersdorf, where the conditions were at least tolerable. Wissbrun had been interned in Vught, sent to Westerbork in March 1944, but unlike the Koker men and Cahen he had not returned to Vught, but instead he had been deported to Auschwitz to end up as a prisoner functionary in Wüstegiersdorf. As such, he had received a copy of the list of inmates who had been transferred on March 20 from Langenbielau to Dörnhau, and noticed the names of his cousin Fedush and some of his Vught comrades. He knew well that Dörnhau meant a death sentence, and he decided to get them out of there—something that would have been inconceivable just a month earlier but that had become possible in the fluid conditions that prevailed in the last months of the war. Wissbrun convinced the *Kommandant* of Wüstegiersdorf that he needed qualified assistants in his secretariat, and that he believed some good people could be found in Dörnhau. Accompanied by a guard he walked to Dörnhau, where he collected Fedush, Max Cahen, Max Koker, and a few other former Vught inmates, and took them to Wüstegiersdorf. There they remained until their liberation by the Red Army on May 8, 1945.[24]

As for David, in the last days of January 1945 a *Kapo* had caught him as he tried to rustle up extra food for Jacques. David no longer had the physical reserves to recover from the beating he received. Furthermore, and perhaps more important, Jacques's death must have shaken him profoundly. David had to deal with the death of his father while the world was falling apart around him. Like all the inmates in Langenbielau, he had been close to the edge for months. Jacques's death may have pushed him over it.

Within a week after Jacques's death, David's health had deteriorated to the point that Hagenuk had no more use for him. Once he became a "useless mouth" the SS wanted to get rid of him. Six months earlier, the sick would have been sent to Auschwitz, to be gassed. But since January 27 Auschwitz was under control of the Red Army. Some lower official in the Gross-Rosen camp system decided to commandeer a freight train, fill it with sick inmates, and send it in the freezing cold without any supplies on an almost four-hundred-mile-long journey to Dachau. It is likely that this official did not give the matter much thought. If he did, he might have uttered the neologism proper to the occasion: *Krepierungszug* (death train).

Max Cahen witnessed the departure of David and his comrades when he returned to Langenbielau from his shift in Reichenbach. Some of them were walking, he recalled, and some sat on a wagon: "I still see them passing by: Asscher, Heilmann, and Spitz in front, supporting each other. Spitz with hollow eyes but also with a gaze of resignation. On the wagon I saw Sanders and David Koker. I sensed that their *levaya* passed by."[25]

In Reichenbach, David and his comrades were put on a train already filled with sick inmates from other camps in the Gross-Rosen concentration-camp system. The train crawled southward to Dachau. When the transport finally arrived at its destination, exposure to the winter cold had killed 80 percent of the men. On February 28, 1945, the writer Eduard Hoornik, a Dutch inmate in Dachau and an acquaintance of David's, learned of the arrival of a transport from Lower Silesia. There were few survivors, he wrote twenty years later. "The corpses were laid on the platform in rows of five—by force of habit—which caused some trouble because several were frozen together and could not be separated simply by yanking them apart. Someone soon got hold of some small easy-to-use axes that did the job and also provided a break to the crematorium workers, who sometimes complained about the monotony of their work." A few of those who were still alive were admitted to the camp. The rest were brought to the courtyard of the crematorium. That night Hoornik took a walk through the camp, darkened because of an air-raid alarm. Approaching the crematorium, he came across "a jumble of bodies, lying not next to but over and under one another, all mixed up together, with most limbs paralyzed, but others quivering and others again shaking." One of those still alive elevated his head. Hoornik noticed "the still burning eyes." And he added, as an afterthought: "They will pursue me afterward."[26] By daybreak all were dead.

Under normal circumstances the corpses would have been cremated in the ovens built for that purpose. But by the end of February the crematorium had run out of coke. On February 28 the camp authorities sent inmates to the Leitenberg, a hill near the nearby village of Etzenhausen, where they were ordered to dig a mass grave.[27] Then they brought the corpses to the Leitenberg and buried them.

David was not admitted to the camp. He died on the train, on the platform, or in the yard of the crematorium. His corpse ended up with 7,608 other corpses in the mass graves on the Leitenberg. Between 1955 and 1959 the mass graves were exhumed and the remains of a few hundred victims were identified and sent back for burial in their countries of origin. David's body was not among them. The remains of the bodies that could not be identified were reburied on the Leitenberg, which was then landscaped like an English garden. Half a century later, the Leitenberg cemetery, located along Route 2339, has become a beautiful and peaceful site.

David left behind him a dozen articles in school magazines and Zionist publications, a couple of published translations of psalms, a book of translations of contemporary Hebrew poems, a book of articles written by Jacob Israël de Haan that he had edited, the poem "Sabbath," a bundle of letters, the diary of his year in Vught, and a memory in the minds of those who had known him. He also left some unfinished lines of verse written shortly before his arrest and collected by Karel van het Reve, who, after David's deportation to Vught, broke into the Biesboschstraat apartment to salvage some of his friend's most precious possessions. These lines are the rudimen-

tary material for a poem that, like his life, remains caught in an infi-
nitely suspended beginning.

> Departed now the final train
> in total darkness and in rain
>
> the world has suffering to spare
> I hear the weariness, despair
> when neighbors talk to one another
>
> no Jew's left in existence
>
> The falling rain would not subside
> I sat at my open doors staring
> at all that was cheerless outside
> and thought: Seen it all, I'm past caring.
>
> No need for more self-promising
> there's never been all that much here
> it's over and that's just as well
> I also look now without fear
>
> on what will be the bitter end
> and concern myself no more with dangers
>
> though I have no desire to die.
>
> to have been born at such a cursèd time
>
> Maybe it's festive there outdoors
> I'm fearful though and worn
> Where can I go?
> Never before have I felt so
> Forlorn.
>
> Forgive me
> Forgive this cheerless song full of regret
> Forgive me thousands of unpleasantnesses
> Forgive me everything but don't forget.[28]

Notes

1. It is unclear exactly how many men left. After the war Rutger Laman Trip claimed that the number was 317. The lower number is based on a comparative analysis of the weekly reports of the number of Jews in Vught sent to the headquarters of the security police in The Hague, and on research done in the NIOD archive by Hans de Vries. Letter, Hans de Vries to Robert Jan van Pelt, September 22, 2010.

2. Letter, David Koker to Fré Samson, March 1944, Koker family archive, Santpoort-Zuid, Netherlands.

3. The main sources for my account are M. Koker, "Nawoord"; Klein and Van de Kamp, *Het Philips-Kommando*, 159–68; Cahen, *Ik heb dat alles opgeschreven*, 101–3; and oral histories with Max Koker conducted in August 2008.

4. Letter, David Koker to Fré Samson, March 1944, Koker family archive, Santpoort-Zuid, Netherlands.

5. The evidence concerning the number and identity of those who were sent from Westerbork to Vught on March 28, 1943, is confusing. It appears that eighty-three civilian male internees and six protective custody prisoners were sent back to Vught, accompanied by twenty-two women who had not been in interned in Vught before.

6. Cahen, *Ik heb dat alles opgeschreven*, 103.

7. Letters, David Koker to Fré Samson, April 2 and April 28, 1944, collection of Max Koker. None of the poems written in this period survived.

8. Letter, David Koker to Fré Samson, April 2, 1944, collection of Max Koker. Letters David sent to Fré in 1943 were destroyed, but those written in 1944 survived.

9. Klein and Van de Kamp, *Het Philips-Kommando*, 155ff.

10. On Maurer, see Tuchel, *Die Inspektion der Konzentrationslager*, 118ff.

11. Fifty years later Max Cahen took the initiative in having a memorial placed in Vught railway station. The text of the monument reads "In 1943 and 1944 14,000 mostly Jewish men and women, including 1,800 children, were taken from this spot to the extermination camps."

12. With "Ph" David refers to Philips. Letter, David Koker to Karel van het Reve, June 3, 1943. Koker family archive, Santpoort-Zuid, Netherlands.

13. Historically, part of the confusion resulted from the fact that there was no Tooropkade in Amsterdam until the Germans began to "Aryanize" Dutch society by deporting its Jewish citizens and expunging the evidence of their existence. Until 1942 (and after the liberation in 1945) this quay was called the Josef Israëlskade, after the well-known nineteenth-century Dutch-Jewish realist painter. Furthermore David had written that the addressee lived in "A'dam," but his *A* resembled an *R*, so the finder interpreted it as "R'dam."

14. Klein and Van de Kamp, *Het Philips-Kommando*, 167.

15. My account of the stay of the Koker men in Auschwitz and Langenbielau and Max's stay in Dörnhau and Wüstegiersdorf is based on various oral histories with Max Koker conducted in August 2008; M. Koker, "Nawoord"; and Cahen, *Ik heb dat alles opgeschreven*.

16. Letter, David Koker to Karel van het Reve, June 3, 1943, collection of the Jewish Historical Museum, Amsterdam.

17. Quoted in Cahen, *Ik heb dat alles opgeschreven*, 109.

18. Ibid., 110.

19. M. Koker, "Nawoord," 244.

20. Hagenuk is an acronym for Hanseatische Apparatebau Gesellschaft, vormals Neufeld und Kuhnke.

21. Langenbielau camp, located between the towns of Langenbielau (Bielawa) and Reichenbach (Dzierżoniów), had been built in 1942 as a camp for Jewish forced laborers employed by the Schmelt organization. Its location was an area that had been part of a former SA [Sturmabteilung] sports school, and hence the camp was often referred to as the Langenbielau Sportschule, or the Reichenbach Sportschule. It consisted of fourteen two-story barracks surrounded by a ten-foot-high electrified barbed-wire fence and eight guard towers. When the Schmelt organization was dissolved in 1944, the SS took over the facilities and made them into a subcamp of Gross-Rosen concentration camp. The SS divided the camp into two parts. The men's camp held two thousand inmates, and the women's camp eight hundred. See Konieczny, "Langenbielau I (Bielawa)"; Konieczny, "Langenbielau [aka Reichenbach, Reichenbach Sportschule]"; Gutterman, *Narrow Bridge to Life*.

22. In 1997 Max Koker and his wife, Nina, visited the grave site. They found a Polish memorial to the camp, but it did not contain any names. Max and Nina took the initiative to create a memorial for the Netherlanders who were buried there. They contacted the Dutch Oorlogsgravenstichting (War Graves Foundation), and in cooperation with this organization they created a memorial that takes the form of an oversized granite headstone. The text states, in Dutch and Polish: "In memory of those who are buried here . . ." The monument records the names, birth, and death dates of thirteen people. The seventh entry reads "Jesaja Koker / 21-12-1886 Amsterdam 4-2-1945." The memorial was unveiled in 2003.

23. See Blatman, *The Death Marches: The Final Phase of Nazi Genocide*, 416–18.

24. On Dörnhau and Wüstegiersdorf, see Sula "Dörnhau (Kolce)" and "Wüstegiersdorf / Tannhausen"; Sula, "Riese / Dörnhau" and "Riese / Wüstegiersdorf"; Gutterman, *Narrow Bridge to Life*, 128ff.; the account of the rescue of Max Koker from Dörnhau is based on Cahen, *Ik heb dat alles opgeschreven*, 129–32, and on Max Koker, oral history conducted by Robert Jan van Pelt, August 4, 2008, Santpoort-Zuid, Netherlands.

25. Cahen, *Ik heb dat alles opgeschreven*, 125; *levaya* is the Hebrew term for "funeral." Those in the group were, apart from David Koker, Johnny Asscher (1916–45), Eugene L. Heilmann (1914–45), Alfred Spitz (1917–45), and Levie Sanders (1920–45).

26. Hoornik, "Voor altijd Dachau," 5. Translation by Michiel Horn.

27. Zámečnik, *Das war Dachau*, 370.

28. Karel van het Reve printed these lines in his introduction to David's diary. Van het Reve, "Inleiding," 17.

David wrote his diary amid an unfolding genocide. All his family members, many of his friends and acquaintances from before his internment, and all the Jewish inmates in Vught were targeted for murder, while the non-Jewish prisoners of the camp faced considerable risk. Some readers of David's diary may want to know the fate of his fellow inmates mentioned in the text and some of David's family, friends, and acquaintances. This edition of the diary gives that information in two ways. If David mentioned the person only once, a footnote provides the information. If David mentioned the person more than once, the information appears in this section of the book.

Research on the identity of the inmates David met in Vught was greatly facilitated by the unique electronic resource of the Digital Monument to the Jewish Community in the Netherlands. Established in 2000 by Ies Lipschits, this database provides the names and, as far as available, basic biographical information for the more than one hundred thousand men, women, and children who were persecuted as Jews during the Nazi occupation of the Netherlands and who did not survive the Holocaust. This digital library has been administered since 2006 by the Jewish Historical Museum in Amsterdam and is available at http://www.joodsmonument.nl/. The Central Database of Shoah Victims' Names, created and maintained by Yad Vashem, the Holocaust Martyrs' and Heroes' Remembrance Authority in Jerusalem, also provided useful information. This database is available at http://www1.yadvashem.org/.

David, his father, Jacques, and the majority of people mentioned in the diary were murdered. In the words of the Jewish memorial prayer, as transliterated and translated by Rabbi Nosson Scherman,

> *B'Gan Ayden t'hay m'nuchatam;*
> *la-chayn Ba-al Harachamim*
> *yas-tiraym b'sayter k'nafav l'olamim,*

v'yitz-ror bitz-ror hacha-yim et nishmotay-hem,
Ado-nay Hu na-chalatam,
v'yanuchu b'shalom al mishk'votay-hem.
V'nomar: Amayn.

May their resting place be in the Garden of Eden;
therefore may the Master of Mercy
shelter them in the shelter of His wings for Eternity;
and may He bind their souls in the Bond of Life.
Hashem [God] is their heritage,
and may they repose in peace on their resting place.
Now let us respond: Amen.

Aardewerk, Samuel

Born in Amsterdam, Samuel Aardewerk (1910–43) was married to Bertha van der Broek and worked as a teacher in the town of Alphen aan den Rijn. Samuel and Bertha were sent to Vught on February 23, 1943. They were taken to Westerbork on July 2, included in a transport to Poland on July13, and killed in Sobibor on July 16, 1943.

Aptroot family

Isidoor Simon Aptroot (1910–71) was born in London of Dutch-born parents. At the beginning of World War I nationals of neutral states were no longer welcome in Britain, and the Aptroot family returned to the Netherlands. In 1934 Isidoor married Lucie Lewy, a German-Jewish refugee. Isidoor and Lucie had three children, Alida, Joseph Benno, and Ruth. The Aptroot family was taken to Vught in the same transport as the Koker family. They stayed for just a month. In an attempt to remove young families from Vught, the Germans sent the Aptroots and 157 other inmates to Westerbork on March 11. They were not sent on to Sobibor or Auschwitz, but remained at Westerbork, protected by Isidoor's British ties and the fact that one of the camp officials came from Lucie's hometown of Aplerbeck and was concerned about her well-being. He advised her to destroy her German papers so that she would be better protected by Isidoor's claim to British nationality. On January 11, 1944, the Aptroots were transported with 1,032 other Jews to Bergen-Belsen, where they were held in a special section of the camp designated for Jews who might be exchanged for Germans interned abroad. Such an exchange never took place, and in April 1945 the entire Aptroot family was put on a transport to Theresienstadt. After a journey of a week a unit of the U.S. Army intercepted the train near Magdeburg. In June 1945 the family returned to the Netherlands. Lucie's brother Eric Lewy had moved to South Africa in 1934, which led the Aptroots to move there in 1947. By the time Isidoor died, Alida and Joseph had settled in Israel, and in 1974 Lucie joined Kibbutz Kfar-Hanassi in the Upper Galilee, where she died two years later. Ruth moved to Germany. E-mail messages from Ruth Aptroot-Polonksi to Robert Jan van Pelt, August 16, 22, and 24, 2009.

Asscher, Henri Abraham

Henri Abraham Asscher (1921–45) was the younger brother of David's friend Louise (Loes) Asscher. He had been a classmate of David's in the Vossius Gymnasium, but Henri and David had not been close. Henri married Esther Rosa Pinkhof. He was brought to Vught on April 22, 1943, transferred to Westerbork on July 2, and taken to Bergen-Belsen. In early 1945 he was put on a train to Theresienstadt. Like many of the deportees, he did not survive the journey.

Asscher, Louise

Louise (Loes) Asscher (1920–99) and Tini Israël became best friends in primary school. Tini introduced Loes to David, and the two became friends also. Loes became a member of Zichron Ja'akov and there she met Jacob (Jaap) van Amerongen (1913–95) The two married in 1940. They survived the war in hiding. In March 1948 they moved with their son Arie to Palestine where they adopted the name Arnon. Jaap became a senior civil servant in the Israeli Ministry of Finance. Lewin, *Vorig jaar in Jeruzalem.*

Assou, Philip

Philip Assou (1896–1945) was a manager of a diamond factory in Amsterdam. Philip, his wife, Vrouwtje Assou-Polak, and their two daughters, Anna and Marja, arrived in Vught on January 16, 1943. They remained in the camp until June 1944, when they were deported to Auschwitz. Philip died in Dörnhau; his wife and daughters survived the war. See "Verklaring van Mevr. Vrouwtje Assou-Polak," n.d., collection 250g (Vught), file 528, NIOD archive, Amsterdam.

Barber, Jakob Samson

Jakob Samson Barber (1896–1944) was born in Wieliczka, Poland. He lived in Amsterdam and worked as a manager in a fur business. Together with his wife, Chane Barber-Lieblich, and his daughter, Edith, Jakob was taken to Vught on January 16, 1943. On November 15, 1943, they were sent to Auschwitz. The Barbers were murdered shortly after their arrival.

Beck, Erich Max

Erich Max Beck was born in Mittweida, Saxony. It appears that he was a convicted thief. He arrived in Vught on January 11, 1943, and became chief *Kapo* of the Philips Kommando. He abused his power, and the women of the Philips Kommando were afraid of him. The Dutch arrested him after the war for having maltreated the Vught inmates. In September 1945 he escaped from custody and was never found.

Beek, Philip

Philip Beek, born in Amsterdam in 1915, became a teacher in Haarlem. He planned to escape to England by sailboat early in 1942, but he was betrayed and arrested on January 7, 1942. First imprisoned in Amersfoort concentration camp, Philip was sent on to Buchenwald, where he died on June 17, 1942.

Bialek, Abram Moisze

Abram Moisze Bialek (1895–1945) was born in Pajęczno, near Warsaw. After World War I he moved to the Netherlands, where he worked as a butcher and cook. He was taken to Vught on February 20, 1943, and put to work in the SS kitchen. There he remained exempt from deportation for a long time. Ultimately he was deported to the east and ended up in the Dachau satellite camp in Munich-Allach, where he died shortly after the end of the war.

Biedermann, Sigmund

Sigmund Biedermann was born in 1911 in Vienna. He fled to the Netherlands after the *Anschluss* and married Vogeline Haringman. Deported to Vught in January 1943, the Biedermanns became part of the Philips Kommando and remained in Vught until June 1944, when they were put on a train to Auschwitz. Vogeline ended up in Bergen-Belsen. She died shortly after the liberation of that camp. Sigmund survived the war and married Eveline Susan.

Blüth, Conrad

Conrad [Kurt] Blüth was born in Germany and moved to the Netherlands in 1919 and became a Dutch citizen in 1935. He was married to Erika Blüth-Henschel, and they had two daughters. In 1942 Blüth became the head of the department of the Jewish Council that sent supplies to internees in Westerbork and Vught; Mrs. Blüth was in charge of the Jewish Council's department of Youth Aliyah. Blüth made regular visits to the camps and tried to improve conditions to the best of his abilities. In October 1943 Blüth and his family were interned in Westerbork, and from there they were sent to Theresienstadt, where they survived the war. The Blüths then moved to Israel.

Cahen, Max

Max Cahen (1905–95) trained as an electrical engineer. Upon the death of his father in 1938, Max became CEO of the family's paper factory in 's Hertogenbosch. In 1940 he married Jet Elion. The couple settled in Vught. There Max became involved with the Jewish Council. When the deportations began, Max obtained an exemption. The Cahen house was located close to the station and became an informal office for Kurt Blüth and other members of the Jewish Council when they visited the Vught camp. As a result Max became involved in attempts to improve the situation for the Jewish inmates. In March 1943 Blüth and Philips engineers Rutger Egbert, Laman Trip, and Carl Braakman asked Max to become a purchaser for the Philips workshop to be created in the camp, and as a result he became a regular visitor to the camp. In June the Cahens were ordered to report to Westerbork, but Max was able to get himself admitted to Vught, while Jet, pregnant but diagnosed by an understanding physician with a severe concussion, was admitted to a local hospital. From there she went into hiding, where she delivered a daughter. Max joined the Philips group and quickly resumed his job as purchaser, which allowed him to periodically leave the camp. In the camp he joined a *praatgroep* (conversation group) that included David and Max Koker. On June 3, 1944, Max was deported with the Kokers to Auschwitz. On August 23, they left Auschwitz for the Langenbielau camp near Reichenbach. Unlike Jacques and David Koker, Max Cahen survived the ordeal. On his return to Vught, he was greeted by Jet and their daughter, Truusje. Max Cahen wrote an important memoir of his time in Vught, *Ik heb dat alles opgeschreven.*

Caransa, Barend

Barend Caransa (1922–43) was born in Amsterdam. He was married to Hettij Kuit. Interned in Vught on January 16, 1943, they were transported to Westerbork on July 16. Four days later Barend and Hettij were loaded on a train that took them and 2,207 other Jews to Sobibor. They were murdered upon arrival on July 23.

Cohen, David

David Cohen (1882–1967) studied classics and earned a doctorate in 1912. That year he married Cornelia (Corrie) Slijper. They had one son and two daughters. From 1926 to 1940 and from 1945 to 1953 Cohen held the chair of ancient history at the University of Amsterdam. He was active in the relief of Jewish refugees from eastern Europe and Belgium (1914–18) and also became one of the leaders of the Dutch Zionist movement. Between 1933 and 1940 Cohen took leadership of the efforts of the Dutch-Jewish community to help Jewish refugees from Germany and later Austria. At this time he gained an international reputation for his humanitarianism. After the German invasion Cohen saw the need for Dutch Jews to unite to confront the danger they faced, and he established, in late 1940, the Joodsche Coördinatie Commissie (Jewish Coordination Committee). In 1941 Cohen became, with the industrialist Abraham Asscher, cochairman of the Joodsche Raad (Jewish Council), the German-imposed body that represented first the Jews of Amsterdam and later all Dutch Jews. Considering his role in the Jewish Council as a continuation of his charitable activities in the 1930s, Cohen believed that he had an obligation to negotiate with the Germans with the aim "to prevent worse." After the beginning of the deportations in July 1942, Asscher and Cohen initially believed the German assurances that the deported would be put to work in Poland. Nevertheless, they tried to obtain exemptions from deportation for as many people as possible. They decided who received those exemptions and, when the Germans tightened the screws, which exemptions became null and void. In the fall of 1942 Cohen requested permission from the Germans to visit the Dutch Jews in Auschwitz. The Germans refused his request. By the beginning of 1943 Cohen and Asscher realized that Auschwitz meant death, and now their aim became to preserve "a core" (that is businessmen and intellectuals like themselves), deemed necessary to rebuild the Jewish community after the war. In September 1943 the Germans closed down the Jewish Council and interned Asscher and the Cohens in Theresienstadt. All three survived the war. The Dutch authorities arrested Cohen in 1947 on suspicion of collaboration, but after a month he was released, and the case against him was dropped. A Council of Honor established by the Jewish community censured Asscher and Cohen for their decisions in 1942 and 1943. In 1953 Cohen retired as a professor, but he remained active as a scholar until his death in 1967. Schrijvers, *Rome, Athene, Jeruzalem.*

David, Netty (Nettie)

Nettie David (1920–2000) was David Koker's girlfriend. She was born in the German town of Cleve. She fled with her parents to the Netherlands in 1938 and lived in Amsterdam on Roerstraat, near the Koker family. David met Nettie in the Zionist youth organization Zichron Ja'acov. According to Max Koker, David was attracted to her intelligence, strong will, and kindness; and Nettie was smitten with David's brilliance. But their relationship was difficult. Max believes that the very strong friendship between David and Karel van het Reve left little room for Nettie. In the fall of 1942 Nettie's parents were taken into custody while she was out of the house, and she immediately went into hiding. She later obtained false papers. On these papers her given name was Lydia. In his letters from Vught, David often referred to her as Lydia. Nettie was very angry that David had not gone into hiding. Max believes that her anger was due in part to David's decision to accompany his family to the camp instead of joining her in hiding. Yet she tried to help him to the best of her ability, and through the mediation of mutual friends she sent many food parcels that also included secret letters. Nettie survived the war and in 1949 married the German-Jewish refugee and camp survivor Leo Hess. Max Koker and Frederika Samson, oral history conducted by Robert Jan van Pelt, August 9, 2008, Santpoort-Zuid, Netherlands; telephone interview and e-mail exchanges with Nettie's daughter Evelyn Berger-Hess, June 4 and 21, 2009.

Dekker, Simon

Simon Dekker (1892–1945), who made his living as an actor, was married to Mina Felicitas da Silva Rosa. Their daughter, Renée, was born in November 1942. The family was taken to Vught on February 10, 1943, sent on to Westerbork in May, and finally to Bergen-Belsen. Renée and Simon died in that camp before its liberation by the Allies, and Mina shortly after Germany's surrender.

De Kleyn, Johannes (Jan)

Johannes (Jan) de Kleyn was born in 1900 in Amsterdam. A Communist, he was arrested in 1942 and sent to Amersfoort. Transferred to Vught in March 1943, he was deported to Dachau in May 1944. It appears that he survived the war.

De Vries, Barend

Barend de Vries (1883–1943), a well-known member of the board of the Amsterdam Diamond Exchange, and his wife, Jansje de Vries-Duim, arrived in Vught with the same transport that took the Koker family there. They remained in Vught for only a week. In his February 20 entry, David notes that Barend (Bernhard) has left. That day Barend and Jansje were part of a transport of 179 mostly elderly and sick inmates who were taken to Westerbork. There they stayed until February 23, when they were put on a train to the east. The train carried 1,101 Jews. The train arrived in Auschwitz on the night of February 25. Eighty-seven of the deportees were admitted to the camp. The other 1,104 were murdered within hours. Barend and Jansje were among them.

De Vries, Philip

Philip de Vries (1921–2001) was the only son of Aaron de Vries, who had a hardware business in Amsterdam, and Sarah Teeboom. Philip attended the Vossius Gymnasium, where he became part of the circle that included David, Karel van het Reve, Erik Jan Romein, Fré Samson, and Tini Israël. While David was known as the most gifted of the friends, Philip was considered to be the most learned. From the outset Philip and David were very competitive. As time progressed, they grew to dislike each other. Philip studied history at the University of Amsterdam and passed his *kandidaats* exam in the spring of 1942—an achievement that was to fill David with envy when in September Jews were forbidden to take all exams. In the summer of 1942 Aaron gave Philip all the money he had been able to save from confiscation so his son might escape to Switzerland. After an adventurous journey Philip reached Switzerland, was interned there, escaped, and crossed the border back into France hoping to go to Spain. He was arrested in Dijon, escaped, and returned to Switzerland, where he was interned for a second time. Eventually he was allowed to attend the University of Bern, where he graduated with a second degree in 1944. When the Allied armies liberated the south of the Netherlands in the fall of 1944, Philip obtained a commission in the Dutch military government in the liberated areas. In 1945 he returned to his studies, and in 1947 he received his doctorate. He joined the Department of History at the University of Amsterdam in the 1950s and retired in 1981.

De Wilde-Asscher, Sarlieni

Sarlieni de Wilde-Ascher (1906–43) was married to Salomon de Wilde (1904–45). Both were diamond workers. They had three daughters: Branca Henriette (1929–43), Henriette (1932–43) and Jacoba (1937–43). Interned in Vught on February 20, 1943, Sarlieni and her daughters were sent to Westerbork on June 6, 1943 and deported to Sobibor a few days later. They were killed on June 11. Salomon died shortly after the liberation in Bergen-Belsen.

De Wit, Abraham

Abraham de Wit was born in 1904. He trained as an engineer and was employed by the province of Groningen. In February 1943 he openly called for resistance against forced labor of Dutch men in Germany. He was arrested and sent to Vught. Because of his technical training he acquired a leading position in the Philips workshop. When Himmler visited Vught on February 3, 1944, he met De Wit and, deeming him to be of excellent racial background, ordered his release. De Wit went into hiding. He survived the war.

Dresel, Willy

Willy Dresel, born in the Sauerland (a mountainous region close to the Ruhr area), was married to a non-Jewish woman. He fled to the Netherlands in the 1930s. On January 16, 1943, he was taken to Vught, where he became the *Appellverantwortlicher des Judenlagers* (literally: [The man] responsible for the roll call in the Jewish camp). Because of his marriage he was released from Vught on July 16, 1943, and survived the war.

Drukker family

Born in Amsterdam, Willem (Wolf) Drukker (1897–1944) married Marie Schaap. She gave birth to a son, Sylvain (Syl) Drukker (1924–45). A talented musician, he played in the Tuschinski movie theater accompanying silent movies. In 1933 he became the conductor of the Cinetone Orchestra. It produced the music for twenty-one movies and also issued records. During the occupation the Germans ran the Cinetone as a satellite of the Universum Film AG (UFA) in Berlin, the main film studio in Germany. By that time Drukker had been fired. On February 12, 1943, the Drukker family was sent to Vught. Drukker obtained, for his family and himself, places on the Barneveld list, exempting from deportation Jews considered to have made a contribution to Dutch society. Initially it appeared that this list would protect them. When on July 2, 1943, the Drukkers were sent with 1,367 other Jews from Vught to Westerbork, they were among the very few who were not sent on to Sobibor four days later. Willem Drukker died in Sachsenhausen in December 1944. Marie and Syl ended up in Bergen-Belsen. Marie survived and returned to the Netherlands. Syl died in Bergen-Belsen shortly after the liberation.

Duizend family

Diamond worker Herman Duizend (1890–1943), his wife, Jeannette Duizend-Witmondt (1889–1943), and their son, Joseph (Joey) (1920–43), a rabbinical student, lived in Amsterdam. They were taken to Vught on February 17, 1943. The Duizend family was transported to Westerbork on June 6. Two days later they and 3,014 other Jews boarded a train that took them to Sobibor on June 11. All deportees were killed on their day of arrival.

Einhorn, Burech

Polish-Jewish Burech (Bolo) Einhorn (1896–1945) was born in Oświęcim. His family had moved before the war to Antwerp, and from there they moved to the Netherlands. They established a bank in Amsterdam and became Dutch citizens in 1924. Bolo became known in the 1930s as one of the world's best bridge players. When the Germans began to confiscate the assets of Dutch Jews, Bolo and his two brothers, Juda (Julius) and Chaim (Heinrich), tried to shelter much of their wealth by giving it in safekeeping to non-Jewish business partners. When the Germans discovered this, they were imprisoned as protective custody prisoners in Vught. Bribing the SS, Bolo and his brothers were able to lead a life of comfort in the camp. They had their own food supply and maintained a small court of people who were willing to be of service. Hence David referred to him as the king of the concentration camp. Bolo remained in Vught until May 1944, when he was deported to Westerbork and finally to Mauthausen, where he died shortly after the liberation of the camp.

Engelander family

Jakob (Jacques) Engelander, born in 1910 in Antwerp, moved to Amsterdam and earned a living in the diamond trade. He was married to Betty Gerarda van der Kar; their son, Robert, was born in 1941. They were taken to Vught on February 12, 1943, and sent on to Westerbork on July 2. The subsequent fate of the family cannot be established.

Färber family

Chaim Färber was born on May 23, 1883, in the Galician town of Dukla. In 1911 he moved to Germany, where he married Chaja Turner. She bore him nine children. In 1933 the Färbers left for the Netherlands, where Chaim established himself as a furrier in The Hague. Two of their sons left for the Americas in the late 1930s. One son died a natural death in 1941. Because the Färbers were stateless they were the among the first to be sent to Westerbork when the deportations started in the summer of 1942. The two remaining sons were deported to Auschwitz on August 31 and put to work as slave laborers; one died in the Fürstengrube camp in 1943, and the other in the Gräditz camp in 1944. Chaja and her four daughters were deported to Auschwitz on October 19, 1942, and they were all killed upon arrival. Chaim remained in Westerbork because of his skill as a furrier. When the Germans decided to create a fur workshop in Vught they transferred Chaim to this camp. There he remained until he was sent to Auschwitz on March 23, 1944. Chaim Färber did not survive.

Flothuis, Marius

Marius Flothuis (1914–2001) attended the same high school as David. After a few years of university studies Flothuis decided to make his passion for music into a profession: he became the assistant of the conductor of the Concertgebouw Orchestra. In 1941 he refused to join the Nazi Culture Chamber and was dismissed from his job. Flothuis and his Jewish wife, who was protected through her marriage to him, provided a hiding place for Jews facing deportation. In 1943 the Germans arrested Flothuis. In Vught he organized a chamber ensemble and composed a number of relevant pieces. Flothuis had a great influence on the world of classical music in the postwar Netherlands.

Fränkel, Fritz

The German-Jewish refugee Fritz Israel Fränkel (1901–45) was born in Berlin. He was a chemical engineer by training. In the Netherlands he married Esther Aronson. They were brought to Vught on February 24, 1943. Both worked for Philips. On June 3, 1944, they were sent to Auschwitz, and from there Fritz went to Langenbielau. He died in the Dörnhau "camp for croaking."

Frank-Palm, Sariena

Sariena Frank-Palm (1916–44) trained as a teacher. She married the German-Jewish merchant David Frank. The Franks went into hiding but were betrayed and sent to Vught on February 20, 1943. On July 2 of that year they were sent to Westerbork. They stayed a few months in Westerbork and in August were deported to Auschwitz. David was killed on arrival. Sariena survived until April 1944, when she too was murdered.

Frederikstadt, Israel Alexander (Roland)

Israel Alexander (Roland) Frederikstadt (1921–45) was born in Amsterdam. David knew him from the Zionist movement. Frederikstadt was married to Vera Bos. He was interned in Vught on February 20, 1943. Deported to Auschwitz later that year, Roland ended up in early 1945 in the Flossenbürg concentration camp, where he died on April 13, 1945.

Friedländer family

Born in Berlin, Adolf Friedländer (1909–44) fled to the Netherlands in 1938. In 1940 he met Maria Koen, and in August 1941 she bore him a son, Max. Adolf and Maria married in 1942. On January 20, 1943, Adolf, Maria, and Max were taken to Vught, where Adolf joined the Orde Dienst (OD). Adolf was able to protect Maria and Max from deportation in June 1943, when almost all children under the age of sixteen were sent to Westerbork. But a month later he was unable to shield his family, and Maria and Max left for Westerbork on July 16, 1943. They were murdered in Auschwitz on September 3, 1943. Adolf Friedländer remained in Vught until November 15, 1943, when he was taken to Auschwitz. He was murdered there in January 1944.

Gersons-van der Hove, Josephine Anna

Josephine Anna Gersons-van der Hove (1910–43) was married to the fur and leather wholesaler Roedolph Jacob Gersons. They had two children, Peter and Ine Henriëtte. The Gersons family was taken to Vught on February 20, 1943. In the camp Josephine acquired responsibility for the school. On July 2 she and her family were sent to Westerbork. Four days later they boarded a train to Sobibor, where they were gassed on July 9, 1943.

Glazer-Cohen, Martha

Born in 1908 in Amsterdam, Martha Cohen was a diamond worker who also worked as a singer. She married diamond worker Joseph

Salomon Glazer. They were interned in Vught on February 26, 1943. Joseph was quickly sent on to Westerbork and Sobibor and killed on April 23, but the Germans kept Martha in Vught. She became a member of the Philips group. She was sent to Westerbork on May 21, 1944, and deported a month later to Auschwitz. She survived the war.

Grewel, Israel (Ies)

Israel (Ies) Grewel (1885–1943) and his wife, Anna Grewel-Bolle, were good friends of Jacques and Judith Koker, and since they lived close by, they were regular and welcome visitors. David and Max referred to them as Uncle Ies and Aunt Anna. They were deported to Sobibor on June 1, 1943, and killed on arrival three days later.

Groen, Max

Born as Meier Groen (1918–2004), Max trained as a newsreel cameraman. As a part-time entertainer he became, in the late 1930s, a well-known performer of songs by Maurice Chevalier and Charles Trenet in the Tip Top Theater on the corner of Joodenbreestraat and Uilenburgerstraat in Amsterdam. Arrested in September 1942 when he broke the curfew to visit his mother, Max Groen was sent to Vught as a *Schutzhäftling*. In the camp, he gave a few solo performances and played the guitar in the camp orchestra. On November 15, 1943, he was sent to Auschwitz. He was able to convince the SS that he was a skilled printer and was sent to Sachsenhausen to join a select group of Jewish printers who were promised survival if they helped the Germans to counterfeit British currency (the story of Operation Bernhard is told in the Austrian movie *The Counterfeiters*). After some time Max was transferred to Mauthausen and was liberated in Ebensee. See Kors, *De tocht opnieuw*.

Hess family

Siegfried Hess (1896–1944) married Alice (Liesel) Reis (1898–1944) in 1920. They lived in Stuttgart. They had two children, Ruth (b. 1922) and Hannelore (b. 1924). In the 1930s the Hess family fled to the Netherlands and settled in Enschede. Siegfried became the manager of a clothing factory. They were interned in Vught in April 1943. David became romantically involved with Hannie. Siegfried and his wife were sent to Auschwitz on November 15, 1943. They were murdered shortly after their arrival. Ruth and Hannie were sent to Auschwitz on June 2, 1944. Like the Koker men they were sent to Langenbielau, but they weren't put to work in the Hagenuk factory in Reichenbach but in the adjacent Telefunken factory. On February 18 Ruth and Hannie joined a three-day death march that brought them to Parschnitz, and from there they traveled in open railway carriages to the west to be dumped, on March 3, in Porta Westfalica, a small subcamp of Neuengamme near Minden. They were put to work in a newly established radio workshop, created with equipment brought directly from Vught, and operated by the so-called Hammerwerke company, the code name of the Philips plant located in a partly completed underground aircraft factory. On April 1, they were evacuated, and after a weeklong stay in the notorious Beendorf camp near Helmstedt they were sent on to Hamburg, where they were interned in one of the many Gross-Rosen subcamps. From there they were sent, on April 30, to the Danish town of Padborg, where they were picked up, on May 3, by the Swedish Red Cross. They arrived a day later in Malmö, where they were nursed back to health. In the summer of 1945 Ruth and Hannie returned to the Netherlands. Both sisters married, emigrated, and established families overseas—Ruth in Surinam and Hannie in New Zealand.

Hollander, Hartog (Han)

Hartog (Han) Hollander (1886–1943) was a famous radio sportscaster who became the voice of Dutch soccer. He had the ability to make his listeners feel as though they were at the game, and his voice became the most famous in the country. He was fired from his job at the beginning of the German occupation. In 1943, Han and his wife, Leentje Hollander-Smeer, were interned in Westerbork, and on July 6 they were shipped with 2,416 other Jews to Sobibor, where they were killed on July 9.

Knoche, Gerhard Dagobert

Born in Berlin, Gerhard Dagobert Knoche (1893–1945) was a teacher who had a Ph.D. and the title of *Privatdozent,* which gave him the right to teach at a university. In 1935 Knoche married a Dutch woman and moved to Amsterdam. He was taken to Vught on February 10, 1943, and deported to Theresienstadt on April 20, 1943. On September 28, 1944, he was sent to Auschwitz, where he was gassed.

Koker family.

Jesaja [Jacques] Koker (1886–1945) and Judith Presser (1892–1979) married in 1920 in Amsterdam. Jesaja was a highschool graduate, had trained as a calligrapher and jewelry designer, and worked as a manager in an atelier producing jewelry. Judith was a bookkeeper, but gave up her career after her marriage. They had two sons: David (1921–45) and Max (born 1927). In 1930 the Koker family moved to the newly built Rivers Quarter where Jacques became a key person in establishing the Jewish community which, in 1937, was to inaugurate a new synagogue in the Lekstraat. From 1933 to 1939 David attended the Vossius Gymnasium where he received a thorough education that included a high level of literacy in English, German, French, Latin, and classical Greek. At the Vossius he became friends with Karel van het Reve (1921–1999). David and Karel stimulated in each other a literary ambition.

From 1937 onwards David became involved with various Jewish youth organizations, and he adopted what was known as a radical Zionist position. He published articles in various Zionist publications. He learned Hebrew, and translated both Biblical and modern Hebrew poetry into Dutch. In 1939 David enrolled at the University of Amsterdam to study sociography. In 1940 he quit sociography, and began to study history. During the first two years of the German occupation of the Netherlands David became the literary executor of the estate of the Dutch-Jewish poet Jacob Israël de Haan (1881–1924). In 1941 he published a small book with a selection of de Haan's essays and, with Jozeph Melkman, a volume of translations of modern Hebrew poetry written in Palestine. At that time David met the German-Jewish refugee Nettie David (1920–2000). In 1942 David was forced to leave the university. By that time Max had been also kicked out of school.

When in the summer of 1942 the deportations to Auschwitz began, the Koker family was initially protected because Jacques had obtained an exemption. Nettie went into hiding. On the night of February 11, 1943, the Koker family was arrested and interned in the Herzogenbusch concentration camp near Vught. In that camp David kept on loose pages and in exercise books a diary with the purpose of recording his experiences for Nettie. In July 1943 and February 1944 he was able to smuggle this diary to Karel van het Reve in Amsterdam. In the summer of 1943 the Koker family was put to work in a detachment that was to provide forced labor for the Philips Electronics Corporation in workshops created in the camp. This assignment protected them from deportation to the death camps in the east until June 2, 1944, when they and all the other Jews from the Philips detachment were deported to Auschwitz.

Upon their arrival in Auschwitz on June 6, 1944, the Kokers were spared selection and death because the skills they had acquired in the Philips detachment were deemed to be useful for the German war industry. Judith was imprisoned in the women's camp. She became ill with typhus, but narrowly escaped the routine "cure" for Jewish inmates who fell ill: death in the gas chambers. Because she was too ill to walk she remained in the camp when the SS began to evacuate the inmates towards the West. As a result she witnessed the liberation of the camp by the Red Army on January 27, 1945. The Russians nursed her back to health, and she returned to the Netherlands in September 1945. She had great difficulty rebuilding a life. In the 1960s and 70s the trauma of her years in Vught and Auschwitz and unrelenting sense of loss caused by the death of David increasingly crippled her ability to enjoy life. She died in 1979.

On June 6, 1944, Jacques, David, and Max were admitted to the men's camp of Auschwitz. In August they were brought to the Langenbielau camp, which was a satellite of the Gross-Rosen concentration camp, and put to work in the Hagenuk factory in Reichenbach. The conditions were bad to begin with, and dramatically worsened. Jacques died on February 4, 1945. David became ill, and on about February 20 he was put on a train transporting sick prisoners to Dachau. He did not survive the journey.

Max remained imprisoned until his liberation by Red Army soldiers in May 1945. After a month in a hospital used by the Red Army he was repatriated to the Netherlands. Unlike his mother, Max adjusted to the new situation. He finished high school, earned a degree in economics, and made a career working for the National Bank of the Netherlands (1953–59), the National Investment Bank (1959–64), and the Hoogovens steel works (1964–91), where he became chief financial officer and chairman of the aluminum division. In 1970 Max married Nina Tordjman (born 1941), and they had two children: David (born 1971) and Ralph (born 1974). Max took responsibility for David's legacy, and in 1977 he and Karel van het Reve organized the publication of David's diary. Thirty years later Max and Nina were instrumental in advocating for this English-language edition.

Koker, Roza

Roza (Rootje) Koker was born in 1927 as the daughter of Jacob Koker (1890–1943), Jacques Koker's younger brother, and Sara Koker-Gobetz (1896–1943). Because she was an only child, she became quite close to David and Max. In 1934 she and her parents moved to Hilversum because Rootje was asthmatic, and the air in Hilversum was supposed to be better for her. In 1942 they returned to Amsterdam on the order of the Germans. Because the family had only a single room, Rootje moved in with her cousins. By that time Rootje was an ardent Zionist. When the deportations started, she obtained a job in the Jewish Council, where she worked for Kurt Blüth. On May 18, 1943, the Germans arrested Rootje and her parents and took them to the Hollandse Schouwburg. There Rootje was able to contact Zionist friends, who contacted Jacob and Sara to ask their permission to smuggle her out of the theater and hide her. Realizing that they were unable to protect their daughter, Jacob and Sara agreed, and as a result Rootje escaped and spend the rest of the war in hiding. On May 22 Jacob and Sara were sent to Westerbork to be deported to Sobibor on May 25. They were murdered on arrival three days later. In 1946 Rootje traveled to Palestine on an illegal *aliyah* (literally "ascent," *aliyah* denotes the immigration of Jews to the Land of Israel). There she adopted the name Michal. As a pioneer she helped found the city of Eilat (1950). In Israel she married Chaim Elata, who became a well-known academic. They had two daughters and two sons, naming their oldest son David, in memory of David Koker. He is a professor of mechanical engineering at the Technion, Haifa.

Krieker family

The diamond polisher Abraham Krieker (1909–43), his wife, Sara Krieker-Mathijse (1907–43), and their two-year-old daughter, Nanny, were taken to Vught on February 12, 1943. They were sent to Westerbork on June 7 in a transport that was intended to remove the remaining families with young children from Vught. Six weeks later, on July 20, they were forced on a train destined for Sobibor. The transport held 2,209 deportees. It arrived in Sobibor on July 23. The Kriekers and the other passengers were murdered upon arrival.

Lansberg family

The Lansberg family came from The Hague. Ten members of the family were imprisoned in Vught: Rebecca Lansberg-Fresco (1891–1943) and her nine children. According to the Vught records, Rebecca's husband was non-Jewish, but he had died in July 1942, and as a result the family lacked the protection that came with his "Aryan" status. David became good friends with Albertine (Tini) Lansberg (b. 1917). Tini and four of her siblings survived the war. Rebecca and three of her children were deported to Westerbork in July 1942 and, in November 1943, sent on to Auschwitz, where they were murdered. Martin Victor Lansberg (1925–43) died on September 2, 1943, in Vught while asleep in a barrack that was fumigated with Zyklon-B. His death was an accident. He was the only fatality resulting from gassing in the history of the Vught camp.

Lehmann family

Arthur R. Lehmann was a German-Jewish refugee. Born in 1892 in Berlin, he fled to the Netherlands with his wife, Gertrude Lehmann-Sternberg (1897–1945), his children, Franz (1921–42) and Marianne (1922–42), and Gertrude's mother, Babette Sternberg-Mayer (1870–1943), and settled in Amsterdam. As young, stateless Jews, Franz and Marianne were called up for the first transport that left Amsterdam on July 15, 1942. They were gassed in Auschwitz in August. Arthur, Gertrude, and Babette were arrested on January 15, 1943, and arrived in Vught the next day. Four days later Babette was included in a transport to Westerbork, and from there she was deported to Auschwitz, where she was killed on February 5. Trained as a lawyer, Arthur was appointed *Leiter der Inneren Verwaltung und Lagerschreiber I* (chief of the Internal Administration and chief camp clerk) of the Jewish section of Vught. Arthur and Gertrude were sent to Westerbork on March 20, 1944 and then on to Auschwitz. Gertrude succumbed to the hardships of imprisonment in April 1945. Arthur survived. After his return to the Netherlands, he wrote an important and as yet unpublished account of Vught. Arthur Lehmann, "Das Lager Vught

(16.1.43– 20.3.1944),” collection 250d (camps and prisons), file 633, NIOD archive, Amsterdam.

Levie family

Rolf Walter Levie (1911–44) was born in Frankfurt am Main. In the 1930s he left Germany for the Netherlands, where he married Carolina Rozette Catharina van Biene. They lived in the provincial capital of Arnhem, where Rolf made a living as a manager of a cinema and in advertising. Carolina gave birth to a son, Rolf Jules Charles, in October 1940. The Germans separated the family in February 1943: the elder Rolf had been stateless since 1941, while Carolina and the younger Rolf claimed Portuguese-Jewish descent. In the summer of 1942 efforts had been made to convince the Germans that Portuguese Jews were really of largely Aryan blood, and hence four hundred were held back from deportation. The elder Rolf was interned in Vught on February 10, 1943. But the family was reunited in April when Carolina and the younger Rolf were sent to Vught as a result of the decision to intern the hitherto protected Portuguese Jews. On July 16 the family was sent to Westerbork. Because of Carolina’s Portuguese-Jewish origin they were not sent on to Sobibor but kept in Westerbork, where senior SS officers were to examine the Portuguese Jews. This inspection took place on February 20, 1944. The SS officers decided that the Portuguese Jews in the camp were “a subhuman race” and ordered that they were to share the fate of other Jews. Most of them were sent to Theresienstadt five days later. From there they were deported to Auschwitz. The Levie family was kept back for a week and finally deported with 729 others on March 3, 1944, to Auschwitz. They arrived on March 5. Mother and son were murdered on arrival, together with 475 other Jews. The elder Rolf belonged to the 255 Jews considered “useful” to the Germans. Two weeks later he also died.

Mackay, Jan

Jan Mackay was arrested for having helped Jews. Taken to Vught on April 2, 1943, he was released on July 16.

Meijer, Jaap

David met Jaap Meijer (1912–93) in Zichron Ja’akov. Jaap had received his high school education at the Dutch Rabbinical Seminary.

At the University of Amsterdam he studied Dutch language and literature and Hebrew, and in 1941 he earned a doctorate for his study of the Dutch-Jewish writer Isaac da Costa (1798–1860). In the late 1930s he was an occasional dinner guest at the Kokers. He and his wife, Liesje Meijer-Voet (1918–93), survived deportation to Bergen-Belsen. After the war Jaap became a history teacher and a very prolific and polemical author of books and articles on Dutch-Jewish history and literature. See E. Gans, *Jaap en Ischa Meijer.*

Meijers, Benjamin Theodoor

Benjamin Theodoor Meijers or Meyers (1915–42), born in 1915, studied medicine and became a physician in 1940. That year he also earned a Ph.D. in physics and in 1941 a Ph.D. in medicine. On March 21, 1942, he was apprehended while attempting an escape to England. He was tried, condemned to death, and executed on August 15, 1942. His wife, Sofia van Gelder, was deported to Auschwitz and killed on October 12, 1942.

Meisler family

Maijer Meisler (1890–1944) and his younger brother, Albert (1899–1944), were born in the Russian Empire. Maijer married Jetti Kerkrut and Albert, Chaje Meisler. The Meislers fled to Germany because of the postwar pogroms in Ukraine. The two brothers settled in Leipzig, where Jetti gave birth to Paul and Chaje to Ruth and Isaac. In 1933 the stateless Meislers fled to the Netherlands. All were interned in Vught in January 1943. Maijer, Jetti, and Paul had papers for Palestine, and for a time they were held for possible exchange. On November 15, they were taken to Auschwitz, where they were killed in the gas chambers. By that time Chaje and her children had already been murdered. Albert was the last of the family to die. He had survived the selection but was killed in March 1944.

Melkman, Jozeph

Jozeph Melkman (1914–2009) was born in Amsterdam. In 1929 he joined Zichron Ya'acov and became a leader of the radical wing of this organization and, in the 1930s, of the Joodsche Jeugdfederatie (Jewish Youth Federation). As such he was one of David's mentors. Melkman studied classical languages at the University of Amsterdam.

A committed Zionist, he applied for a Palestine Certificate. Jozeph taught David Koker Hebrew, and in 1941 they published an anthology of modern Hebrew poetry with translations. When the deportations started Jozeph and his wife, Frederika de Pauuw, hid their son, Awraham, with non-Jewish friends. In 1943 they were arrested and, after a sojourn in Westerbork, were interned in Bergen-Belsen on the strength of Jozeph's application for a Palestine Certificate. They survived the war. From 1945 to 1957 Jozeph played a central role in the rehabilitation of the Jewish community in the Netherlands. He and his family, joined by two of the children of Jozeph's murdered sister, Lenie, moved to Israel in 1957, where Melkman became general director of Yad Vashem. In 1960 he joined the Ministry of Education and Culture and served as director of the Department of Culture. He testified at the Eichmann trial. In 1965 he Hebraized his family name to Michman. Three years later he established the Center for Research on Dutch Jewry, and for the next thirty-five years he was the leading expert on the history of Dutch Jewry. See Michman, *Ma'aglei Hayim ve-Zehut.*

Monnikendam, Philip

Philip Monnikendam (1916–43) was born in Amsterdam. He arrived in Vught on April 2, 1943. By that time Philip's sister Elzina had already been murdered in Auschwitz. On April 9, 1943, Philip's father, Barend, his mother, Marianna, and his sisters Henrietta and Dina were murdered in Sobibor. Philip was the last of his family to lose his life. He was murdered on May 28, 1943, in Sobibor.

Mossel, David Alexander

David Alexander Antonius Mossel (1918–2004) studied medicine at the University of Leiden, and in 1942 worked at the University of Amsterdam, which was located behind the Oudemanshuispoort (The gate to the home of old men), which explains David's reference to "Mossel from Oudemanshuispoort" in his entry of March 13, 1943. He was taken to Vught on March 20, 1943. While in Vught and in subsequent camps, he worked as a male nurse and became very interested in water- and food-transmitted diseases. He survived the war, earned a doctorate in microbiology (1949), and became a leading expert on the growth of microorganisms in food.

Nemet, Leizer

Leizer Nemet (1892–1943) was born in Jezupol (Ukraine). With his wife, Malka Drachtenberg, he moved to Germany after World War I. After 1933 they and their daughters, Rosa and Klara, took refuge in The Hague. The Nemet parents were taken to Vught on February 20, 1943; Rosa and Klara followed in April. On July 2, 1943, Leizer and Malka were taken to Westerbork. Later that month they were deported to Sobibor and killed upon arrival. Rosa and Klara were put to work in the Philips Kommando. Both survived the war.

Neumann, Josef

Josef Neumann, his wife, Gertrud Neumann-Löwenthal, and their fourteen-year-old son, Peter Neumann, were German-Jewish refugees. They arrived in Vught on February 12, 1943. Peter was sent to Westerbork on September 11, 1943, and from there he was deported to Auschwitz, where he was killed. Josef and Gertrud stayed behind because they were working for Philips. It seems that they survived the war.

Nikkelsberg, Gerrit

Gerrit Nikkelsberg was born in 1901 in Amsterdam. He became a dancer and well known as the partner of the dancer Johannes Marinus Cornelis Bouman, who introduced tap dancing to the Netherlands and became, after the war, a prominent choreographer. Bouman and Nikkelsberg performed as Bow and Nicholson. Nikkelsberg retired from dancing in the late 1930s and turned to fashion design. In 1942, aware that neither retired dancers nor fashion designers had much future in a time of deportations, Nikkelsberg redefined himself as a tailor. Because Vught was to manufacture fur-lined winter coats for the *Wehrmacht,* Nikkelsberg ended up in that camp on January 27, 1943. David and Gerrit became friends, and the latter wrote poems for David. Sent on to Auschwitz on November 15, 1943, Nikkelsberg was killed in January 1944.

Nordheim, Lion

Lion Nordheim (1910–45) was David's mentor in the Jewish youth movement. He and his wife, Marianne Branka (Jeanne) Nordheim-van Amerongen (1912–2000), went into hiding in the summer of 1942. On March 19, the Germans raided their hiding place and they were arrested. On April 15, 1945, Lion was executed in reprisal for an attack by the resistance on the rail line between Amsterdam and Haarlem. Hoogewoud-Verschoor, *Lion*.

Pais, Abraham (Bram)

David met Abraham Pais (1918–2000) in the Jewish youth movement. Bram studied physics and completed his dissertation in 1941 just before the Germans decreed that Jews could not obtain a doctorate. Bram went into hiding in 1943. In early 1945 he ended up in the same house where Geertruida (Truus) van Amerongen, her sister Jeanne van Amerongen, and Jeanne's husband, Lion Nordheim, had found refuge. They were betrayed in March. The Germans executed Lion but spared the lives of the others. After the war Bram moved to Denmark to work with Niels Bohr, who had been impressed by his dissertation. Bram moved to the Institute for Advanced Studies in Princeton in 1947, and for the next forty years he built a distinguished career as a theoretical physicist and historian of physics. See Pais, *Tale of Two Continents*.

Poppert-Speier, Hertha

The milliner Hertha Speier (1913–91) and her husband, the hatmaker Erich Poppert (1912–43), left Germany for the Netherlands in 1933. They established a successful hatmaking business in the provincial town of Zaandam. In March 1941 the firm was Aryanized (expropriated). In early 1942 the Poppert family was forced by the Germans to relocate to Amsterdam. When the security police raided the Poppert house in July 1942, Erich was able to hide; their daughter, Sonja, was in a Catholic school, but Hertha was arrested. She spent six months in the jail on Amstelveenseweg. While she was in jail the Germans caught Erich and sent him to Westerbork. On May 11, 1943, Erich was deported to Sobibor and killed on arrival. On March 3, 1943, Hertha arrived in Vught. She became secretary to Dr. Arthur Lehmann and gained a reputation for her fearless manner of dealing with the SS, which earned her three months of hard labor. From November 1943 to June 1944 she worked in the Philips Kommando, and then shared the fate of her fellow prisoners: first Auschwitz, then forced labor in the Telefunken factory in Reichenbach. As in Vught she became a prison functionary. Like Ruth and Hannie Hess, she began, on February 18, a three-day death march that brought her to Parschnitz, and from there to Porta Westfalica, Beendorf, Hamburg, and finally Denmark, where she was picked up, on May 4, by the Swedish Red Cross. Fellow prisoners have testified that they owe their lives to Hertha's courageous and effective intercession on their behalf in the last months of captivity. In the summer of 1945 she returned to the Netherlands, where she was reunited with her daughter. She married twice more and died a wealthy woman in Cannes. Ligtvoet, *Ik heb een heel tijdje niets van me laten horen;* letters, Ellen Goudsmit to Robert Jan van Pelt, March and April 2010.

Ricardo, Eljakim

Eljakim Ricardo (1911–45) was born in Amsterdam, where he established a practice in family medicine in 1939. He was interned in Vught on March 5, 1943, and sent to Westerbork on July 16, 1943. From there he was deported to Auschwitz. He survived until January 1945. Coppenhagen, *Anafiem Gedoe'iem.*

Roman, Martin

Martin Leopold Roman (1910–68) was born in Berlin. He played for the famous Marek Weber Dance Orchestra and the Rudolf Nelson Revue Orchestra in Berlin in the late 1920s but fled to the Netherlands after 1933. On February 17, 1943, he was interned in Vught, where he became the leader of the camp orchestra. He was sent to Westerbork on October 18, 1943, and then to Theresienstadt. He survived the war and moved to the United States, where he lived until his death.

Rosenberg, Max

Max Rosenberg was born in 1913 in Amsterdam. He married Ida Frankenstein. Max was a furrier. On February 20, 1943, Max and Ida were interned in Vught. They were assigned to the Philips Kommando. In June 1944 they were shipped to Auschwitz. Both survived the war.

Samson family

David met Frederika (Fré) Samson (born 1921) at the Vossius Gymnasium, and they became close friends. Fré and her parents, the architect Frederik (Frits) Edward Samson (1891–1988) and Wilhelmine Samson-Rens (1895–1949), remained loyal friends throughout David's internment in Vught. They sent packages to the Koker family on a regular basis. They also hid Nettie David for a time. Frits's father was Jewish, but because his family had come from Surinam, Frits and Fré did not bother to register as a half and a quarter Jew as their ethnicity could not be checked.

Sanders, Combrecht Bernard (Gerard)

Gerard Sanders (1902–45) had been a senior manager at a large textile mill in Enschede and, beginning in 1941, secretary of the local Jewish Council. He lost his job in 1942 when a German trustee took charge. The latter began his tenure with the production of half a million cloth Jewish stars. Sanders was interned in Vught in April 1943 and became a highly valued member of the Philips Kommando. He was deported to Auschwitz in June 1944 and died in Langenbielau in February 1945. See J. de Haan, *Een eigen patroon.*

Schrijver, Joachim

Dr. Joachim Schrijver (1871–1951) was born in Amsterdam and trained as a gastroenterologist. In 1903 he married the non-Jewish painter Ida IJzerman. They had one daughter and two sons. Schrijver became an expert in the interpretation of handwriting (ironic since the name Schrijver means "writer" in Dutch). His *Leerboek der graphologie (Manual on Graphology)*, first published in 1934 and issued in various expanded editions for the next thirty years, became the standard work on the topic in the Dutch language. Because his children were half-Jewish, Schrijver's position was unclear when the deportations started. Generally Jewish spouses in so-called mixed marriages were exempt from deportation if such marriages had produced children. But Schrijver's position was shaky because he had divorced his non-Jewish spouse in 1924. The cause for his arrest on February 17, 1943 was an infraction: Joachim's unmarried sister, Marianne, had moved in with him without permission from the authorities. When this was discovered, Joachim was sent as a *Schutzhäftling* to Vught. Marianne went into hiding. She was soon betrayed, sent as a "punishment case" to Westerbork, and on April 6 to Sobibor, where she and 2,019 other Dutch Jews were murdered upon arrival on April 9, 1943. For reasons that remain unclear, Joachim did not enter the *Schutzhaftlager* but the *Judenauffangslager*. He was released a month later because of his mixed marriage. The umbrella of protection offered by Ida (deceased by then) and their three children remained intact. After some months he was arrested a second time and sent to Theresienstadt, where he survived the war. See Stuhldreher, *De legale rest,* 193ff, 223ff.

Seeligmann, Leo

Isaac Leo Seeligmann (1907–82) studied classical languages, taught at the Jewish seminary, and was active in the Mizrahi movement. In 1939 he married the German-Jewish refugee Margot Darmstädter. She bore him two daughters, Judith (born 1939) and Mirjam (born 1942). In the first years of the war he was deputy chairman of the Central Cultural Committee of the Jewish Council, and David got to know him well. Leo and his family were deported to Theresienstadt, where they survived the war. In Theresienstadt Leo served as librarian, and this allowed him to work on a study of Isaiah which became the basis of the doctoral dissertation he defended at the University of Leiden in 1947. In 1950 Leo became a professor of biblical studies at the Hebrew University in Jerusalem.

Silbermann, Arnold

The Polish-born engineer Arnold Silbermann (1901–45) belonged to the Philips Kommando. He was deported to Auschwitz in June 1944, and along with the Koker men he ended up in Langenbielau. He died there shortly before the end of the war.

Smit, Christiaan (Chris)

The non-Jewish Communist prisoner Chris Smit spent time in Amersfoort before his transfer to Vught in January 1943. He became a member of the Philips Kommando and survived the war.

Spitz, Alfred Abraham

Alfred Abraham Spitz (1917–45) trained as an engineer. In September 1941 he became a teacher of mechanics and drawing at the Jewish High School in Hilversum. In July 1942 the school closed following the departure of all its students. He was interned in Vught in February 1943 and was instrumental in establishing the Philips workshop. Deported to Westerbork on March 20, 1944, he was sent to Auschwitz, and from there to Langenbielau. He became ill in early 1945 and was included in the sick transport that also brought David to Dachau. It appears that he was one of the few to survive the journey, but he did not live to see liberation: Alfred died in Dachau in April 1945.

Spitz, Frederik

David met Frederik Spitz (1914–63) in the Zionist movement. Frederik worked as a purchaser for the Bonneterie fashion house. He survived the war in hiding. In 1946 he married Edith Deborah Polak (born 1921). She bore him two daughters: Lena (born 1947) and Sarah (born 1949). In the 1950s the Spitz family moved to Israel.

Splitter family

The Splitter family, originally from Galicia, owned Splitter Frères, a well-known and prosperous fur business in The Hague. In 1940 the core of the clan consisted of Baruch (Bernhard) Splitter (1886–1945), his wife, Ida Splitter-Splitter (1884–1944), and their two sons, Max (1913–45) and Henri (1918–45). In 1941 the Splitter business was put under German *Verwaltung* (administration), but Bernhard, Max, and Henri remained involved. In December 1941 the Splitter firm became an important supplier of fur-lined clothing to the German military. Bernhard, Max, and Henri were arrested in September 1942 and imprisoned in the Scheveningen prison. In October of that year they were sent to Westerbork, together with Ida and Max's wife, Amelie. In January 1943 the Germans decided to create fur workshops in Vught, which were to be managed by the Escotex firm from Amsterdam. Skilled furriers were in demand, and thus Bernhard, Max, Henri, and all the other members of the extended Splitter family were sent there on February 20, 1943. The Splitters worked in the Escotex workshops for almost a year. On March 20, 1944, the male Splitters were sent to Westerbork and then to Auschwitz. Max and Bernhard most likely died on the death march in late January 1945, and Henri died in early February in a subcamp of Sachsenhausen. Ida and Amelie remained in Vught to work for Philips. With the other "Philips Jews," among them the Kokers, they were deported to Auschwitz in June 1944. The sixty-year-old Ida died after a few months in the camp. Amelie was sent to Reichenbach and survived the war. Weinreb, *Collaboratie en verzet*, 1:353ff, 384ff; Axelrod, *In the Camps*, 42ff.

Süsskind, Richard

Richard Süsskind (1910–44) was born in Berlin and fled to the Netherlands with his wife, Elisabeth Süsskind-Ballin (1908–44), after Hitler's rise to power. On January 16, 1943, the Süsskinds arrived in Vught with the first Jewish transport. Richard became *Lagerälteste* (senior inmate) of the *Judenauffangslager* (reception camp for Jews), which after some weeks was renamed the *Judendurchgangslager* (transit camp for Jews) section of the Vught camp. Süsskind acted as liaison between the Jewish inmates and the commandant, and he was in charge of the Ordedienst. The Germans removed Süsskind from his position in October 1943, and, together with 1,150 other inmates, Richard and Elisabeth were sent on November 15, 1943, to Auschwitz. Elisabeth died there in March 1944 and Richard in July.

Susan, Eveline

Eveline Susan was born in 1922 and trained as a nurse. She worked in a Jewish old-age home that was, on January 14, 1943, emptied of all its inhabitants by the notorious Sam Olij (see note 59). One of those taken was Eveline's mother, and although Eveline had a valid exemption, she decided to remain with her mother. Both were sent to Vught on January 16, 1943. Upon her arrival she stood out for her resolute behavior, and the Germans appointed her senior inmate of the women's section of the camp. In the summer of 1943 she became a member of the Philips Kommando. She was deported to Auschwitz on June 2, 1944, and, like the Kokers, was sent to Reichenbach in August. There she continued to work as a nurse. She survived the war and married Sigmund Biedermann. See "Verklaring van mej: Eveline Susan," December 2, 1947, collection 250g (Vught), file 751, NIOD archive, Amsterdam.

Topel family

Simon Szaja Topel (1896–1975) was born in Cracow. He moved to the Netherlands, settled in 's Hertogenbosch, and, in 1923 married

Kaatje Boers (1902–59). They were interned in Vught in April 1943. Protected by Palestine Certificates, they became members of the Philips group. On June 2, 1944, the Topels were deported to Auschwitz. Both survived and were reunited after the war.

Van Amerongen family

David met Geertruida (Truus) van Amerongen (1921–87) and her brother Jacob (Jaap) (1913–95) in Zichron Ja'akov. The Van Amerongens belonged to the inner circle known as the Catacombs. According to Max Koker, Truus fancied David, but David did not reciprocate her feelings. Truus survived the war in hiding in the town of Alkmaar, north of Amsterdam. Jaap survived in hiding with his wife, Louise (Loes) van Amerongen-Asscher (1920–99). After the war Jaap, Loes, and Truus moved to Israel. While still in the Netherlands, Truus met Ben-Zion Be'eri, a member of the Jewish Brigade. She entered Palestine illegally in March 1948, adopted Tirtsah as her first name, and in 1949 married Be'eri. The couple had three daughters. Max Koker, oral history conducted by Robert Jan van Pelt, August 8, 2008, Santpoort-Zuid, Netherlands; letters, Ben Zion Be'er to Robert Jan van Pelt, October 31 and November 2, 2009.

Van Doorn, Johannes

Johannes van Doorn was born in 1905. Imprisoned as a *Schutzhäftling* in Vught in January 1944, he was assigned to the Philips Kommando. His attempt to humour Himmler backfired (see p. 332), and he was assigned to work in the *Aussenkommando* in Breda, in which inmates worked on the expansion of the Gilze-Rijen Luftwaffe base. Van Doorn survived the war.

Van het Reve, Karel

Karel van het Reve (1921–99) was born in Amsterdam. Both his parents were Communists, and as a teenager he was active in the Communist youth movement. Later Karel would turn away from Communism, but a fascination with Russia and Russian literature, nurtured in his youth, was to shape his life and career. From 1933 to 1939 he attended the Vossius Gymnasium. He was a classmate of Jozina (Tini) Israël (b. 1921), who became his girlfriend, and David Koker, who became his bosom friend. Karel and David stimulated each other's literary ambitions, which expressed themselves in articles written for the two school journals in circulation at the Vossius: Vulpes (Fox) and De Ventilator (The Fan). After passing their final exams in 1939, Karel, Tini, and David were admitted to the sociography program of the University of Amsterdam. All of them dropped out after a few months, Karel and Tini in order to attend lectures given by the Russian émigré scholar Bruno Becker. As a result, they switched to Slavic Studies in 1940. From 1941 to 1944 Karel trained as a graphic designer and a typesetter. He remained closely involved with David before the latter's arrest in February 1943, and supported him and his family for the seventeen months they were interned in Vught by means of letters and packages. Karel and especially Tini also helped Nettie David and other Jews in hiding. The recipient of David's diary in July 1943 and February 1944, Karel gave it to Max Koker upon his return to Amsterdam in the summer of 1945, the same year that Karel married Tini. They had two children, Jozina Jannetta (born 1947) and David (born 1950). In 1945 Karel and Tini resumed their studies with Becker, who had obtained the Chair of Slavonic Studies in 1945. In 1951 Karel obtained the Dutch equivalent of a master's degree, and in 1954 he earned his doctorate with a thesis on Soviet literary criticism. By that time he had drifted away from Communism. In the 1950s, as the result of his columns and essays for a great variety of Dutch newspapers and literary magazines, Karel began to acquire a reputation as a public intellectual. His literary style was unique: concise, lucid, simple, and witty—characteristics in short supply in the Dutch literary world of that time. He also became known for his translations of Russian authors in the so-called "Russian Library" published by Geert van Oorschot.

In 1957 Karel was appointed to the Chair of Slavic Literature at the University of Leiden. A few years later he became closely involved with Russian dissidents like Andrej Amalrik and Andrej Sacharov, and in 1969 established the Alexander Herzenstichting (Alexander Herzen Foundation) to publish their works. His activism on behalf of the dissidents and his work as an essayist stymied the production of original scholarship and prevented him from making good on his promise made to Max Koker to produce a critical edition of David Koker's diary. Finally, after much prodding by Max, he sent the transcript of the diary made by Toet Hiemstra-Timmenga in the late 1940s, together with a short memoir of his friendship with David, to Van Oorschot, who published the book as *Dagboek geschreven in Vught* (1977). Although his career as a scholar did not live up to expectations, he was popular as a teacher and there was general acknowledgement of his great contribution to Dutch letters. In 1982 Karel received the highest literary award given in the Netherlands, the P.C. Hooft Prize, for his essays. He retired from his professorship in 1983, but continued his literary activities until 1996, when Parkinson's disease crippled his ability to write. He died three years later.

Van Maarseveen, Johanna

The non-Jewish physician Johanna van Maarseveen (1872–1946) married the homosexual Jewish writer Jacob de Haan in 1907. She did not join him in 1918 when he moved to Palestine. David got to know her well in 1940, when she appointed him to be the literary executor of her late husband's estate.

Van Praag, Siegfried E.

Siegfried E. van Praag (1899–2002) was a prominent journalist, novelist, and essayist who introduced the work of Franz Kafka into the Netherlands. Having escaped to England in 1940, he worked as a war correspondent for the Dutch radio service in London.

Van Wijk, Jan Hendrik (Hein)

Jan Hendrik van Wijk (1907–81) studied law and worked as a journalist from 1933 and as a lawyer from 1938. A radical socialist and well-known pacifist, he helped political opponents of the Hitler regime find refuge in the Netherlands. After the German invasion he became active in the resistance. When the deportations began in 1942 Van Wijk helped Jews find hiding places. In 1942 the Germans arrested him, and in 1943 they sent him to Vught as a prisoner. In the fall of 1943 he became chairman of the prisoners' committee of the Philips Kommando. In May 1944 the Germans deported van Wijk to Dachau and later to the satellite camp at Kottern. He survived the war, and upon his return to the Netherlands reestablished his legal practice. He became known as an advocate for conscientious objectors to military service, whom he always defended free of charge. Van Wijk also helped Max Koker make a new beginning after his return from Langenbielau. In 1966 he became a member of the *Eerste kamer* (first chamber) of the *Staten Generaal* (Estates General or the Dutch parliament) and leader of the Pacifist Socialist Party in that body, serving until 1974.

Verduin family

Born in Belgium, Abraham (Albert) Verduin (1902–45) arrived in Amsterdam with his parents and siblings as a refugee in 1914. He became an apprentice hatmaker. In 1924 Albert, his wife, Anna, and his brother Leo established a small hatmaking shop that quickly became a large enterprise. In 1941 Albert lost his business as a result of the Aryanization (expropriation). In January 1943 the Verduins were taken to Vught, where Albert became a barrack leader and the key figure in the initially successful effort to establish a school. Albert and Anna's son, Ernst, became a close friend of Max Koker's. On November 15, 1943, Albert was deported to Auschwitz. In 1944 he was transferred to the Auschwitz subcamp of Blechhammer, where he was put to work on the construction of a synthetic gasoline factory. It appears he was still alive when the Germans began evacuating Blechhammer on January 21, 1945. The four thousand inmates were ordered to walk to Gross-Rosen concentration camp; some eight hundred died on the way. It is likely that Albert Verduin was one of them, for he was never heard of again. Anna and Ernst survived the war.

Vrins, Theodor

Theodor (Theo) Vrins (1917–2000) served with the Dutch air force in May 1940. His plane was shot down during the Grebbeberg Battle, and he became a prisoner of war. After the armistice (May 15, 1940) he was released. In 1942 and '43 Vrins made three attempts to reach England by crossing the North Sea. After the third time he was sentenced to death by a German military court. Luftwaffe general Friedrich Christiansen pardoned him as a fellow air-force officer. Vrins spent the rest of the war in German prisons. After the war he again served in the Dutch air force.

Zwaap family

Salomon Zwaap (1906–44) was born in Amsterdam. He passed his medical exams in 1931 and became a family doctor in Hilversum. He married Rotterdam-born Esther Jeanette Zwaap-Philipse, a well-known cabaret singer who often performed on Dutch radio. They had two sons. The family was taken to Vught on February 17, 1943. There Dr. Zwaap worked in the sick bay. In July 1943 the Zwaap family was sent to Westerbork, but they were saved from transportation to Poland when Esther joined the popular cabaret group that performed with the German commandant's permission. In August 1944, however, the group was disbanded, the commandant considering it inappropriate that Jews should be entertained while German cities were being bombed, and on September 4, 1944, all members and their families were deported to Theresienstadt. The Zwaap family stayed there for a month before being sent to Auschwitz and to their deaths.

Alakus, Baris, Katharina Kniefacz, and Robert Vorberg, eds. *Sex-Zwang-sarbeit in nationalsozialistischen Konzentrationslagers*. Vienna: Mandel-baum Verlag, 2006.

Arendt, Hannah, "The Image of Hell." *Commentary* 2, no. 3 (September 1946): 291–95.

———. *The Origins of Totalitarianism*. New York: Harcourt, Brace, 1951.

Axelrod, Toby. *In the Camps: Teens Who Survived the Nazi Concentration Camps*. New York: Rosen, 1999.

Bakels, Floris. *Verbeelding als wapen*. Haarlem: Tjeenk Willink, 1947.

Bauer, Fritz, et al. *Justiz und NS-Verbrechen: Sammlung deutscher Strafurteile wegen nationalsozialistischer Tötungsverbrechen, 1945–1966*. 50 vols. Mu-nich: K. G. Saur Verlag; Amsterdam: Amsterdam University Press, 1968–2010.

Bauman, Zygmunt. "A Century of Camps?" In *Life in Fragments: Essays in Postmodern Morality*, 192–205. Oxford: Blackwell, 1995.

Berghuis, Corrie K. *Joodse vluchtelingen in Nederland, 1938–1940: Documenten betreffende toelating, uitleiding en kampopname*. Kampen: J. H. Kok, 1990.

Berkelbach van der Sprenkel, Jan Willem ed. *De pelgrimstocht der mensch-heid: geïllustreerde wereldgeschiedenis van de oudste tijden tot heden*. Utrecht: De Haan, 1937.

Blanken, Ivo J. *The History of Philips Electronics N.V.* Vol. 4, *Under German Rule*. Translated by C. Pettiward. Zaltbommel: European Library, 1999.

Blatman, Daniel. *The Death Marches: The Final Phase of Nazi Genocide*. Translated by Chaya Galai. Cambridge, Mass.: Harvard University Press, 2011.

Blom, Johan Cornelis Hendrik, Renate Gertrud Fuks-Mansfield, Ivo Schöffer, eds. *The History of the Jews in the Netherlands*. Translated by Arnold J. Pomerans and Erica Pomerans. Oxford: Littman Library of Jewish Civilization, 2002.

Boas, Jacob. *Boulevard des Misères: The Story of Transit Camp Westerbork*. Hamden, Conn.: Archon Books, 1985.

Bolle, Mirjam. *Ik zal je beschrijven hoe en dag er hier uitziet: Dagboekbrieven uit Amsterdam, Westerbork en Bergen-Belsen*. Amsterdam: Pandora, 2003.

Brasz, Chaja, and Yosef Kaplan. *Dutch Jews as Perceived by Themselves and Others: Proceedings of the Eighth International Symposium on the History of the Jews in the Netherlands.* Leiden: Brill, 2001.

Brouwers, Jan, *Broodnodige hulp: Organisatie van de materiële hulpverlening aan het kamp Vught, 1943-1944.* Vught: Nationaal Monument Vught, 1996.

Cahen, Max. *Ik heb dat alles opgeschreven: Vught-Auschwitz-Vught.* 's Hertogenbosch: Wolfaert, 2010.

Cleveringa, Rudolf Pabus. *Gedenkschriften Prof. Mr. R.P. Cleveringa.* Leiden: Brill / Universitaire Pers Leiden, 1983.

Convenant-Commissie in de Nederlandse Mizrachie. "Rapport." *De Joodsche wachter* 36, no. 11 (March 15, 1940): 77–78.

Coppenhagen, Jacob Hyman. *Anafiem Gedoe'iem: Overleden Joodse artsen in Nederland, 1940–1945.* Rotterdam: Erasmus, 2000.

De Haan, Jacob. *Pijpelijntjes.* Amsterdam: Van Cleef, 1904.

De Haan, Jacob Israël. *Brieven uit Jeruzalem.* Edited by David Koker. Amsterdam: Joachimsthal, 1941.

———. *Het Joodsche lied.* Amsterdam: Versluys, 1915.

———. *Libertijnsche liederen.* Amsterdam: Van Kampen, 1914.

———. *Verzamelde gedichten.* 2 vols. Edited by Kees Letterkerker. Amsterdam: Van Oorschot, 1952.

De Haan, Johanna. *Een eigen patroon: Geschiedenis van een Joodse familie en haar bedrijven, ca. 1800–1964.* Amsterdam: Aksant, 2002.

De Jong, Louis. *Een sterfgeval te Auswitz.* Amsterdam: Querido, 1967.

———. *Het Koninkrijk der Nederlanden in de Tweede Wereldoorlog.* 14 vols. The Hague: Martinus Nijhoff, 1969–1991.

De Koster, Charles. *De legende en de heldhaftige, vrolijke en roemrijke daden van Uilenspiegel.* Amsterdam: Becht, 1927.

De Leeuw, Aart. *De kleine Rudolf.* Rotterdam: Nijgh & Van Ditmar, 1930.

De Moei, Janneke. *Joodse kinderen in het kamp Vught.* Vught: Stichting Vriendenkring Nationaal Monument Vught, 1999.

De Vries, Hans. "Herzogenbusch Main Camp (aka Vught)." In *Encyclopedia of Camps and Ghettos, 1933–1945,* edited by Geoffrey P. Megargee, 1b:814–18. Bloomington: Indiana University Press, 2009.

———. "Herzogenbusch (Vught)—Stammlager." In *Der Ort des Terrors: Geschichte der nationalsozialistischen Konzentrationslager,* edited by Wolfgang Benz, Barbara Distel, and Angelika Königseder, 7:133–50. 9 vols. Munich: C. H. Beck, 2005–9.

———. "Sie starben wie Fliegen im Herbst." In Alice B. van Keulen-Woudstra, ed. *Mauthausen 1938–1998,* 7–18. Translated by Herman Vinckers. Westervoort: Van Gruting, 2000.

De Vries, Simon Ph. "Openingsrede." *Mizrachie: Maandblad van de Nederlandsche afdeeling der wereldorganisatie "Mizrachie"* 23, no. 1 (February 1940): 1–3.

De Wolff, L. "Spanningen tusschen 'jongeren' en 'ouderen.'" *Baderech: Maandblad—Officieel orgaan van de Nederlandsche Zionistische Studentenorganisatie en leidersorgaan van de Joodsche Jeugdfederatie in Nederland* 13, no. 5 (Siwan 5698): 1–2.

De Zwarte-Walvisch, Klaartje. *Alles ging aan flarden: Het oorlogsdagboek van Klaartje de Zwarte-Walvisch.* Edited by Ariane Zwiers. Amsterdam: Balans, 2009.

Dickens, Charles. *The Pickwick Papers.* Edited by James Kinsley. Oxford: Clarendon Press, 1986.

Dwork, Debórah, and Robert Jan van Pelt. *Auschwitz: 1270 to the Present.* New York: Norton, 1996.

Elzas, Abraham. "De synagoge aan de Lekstraat te Amsterdam." *Bouwkundig weekblad architectura* 59 (1938): 429–34.

Erikson, Erik H. *Identity: Youth and Crisis.* New York: Norton, 1968.

Feuchtwanger, Lion. *Der jüdische Krieg.* Berlin: Propyläen, 1932.

———. "Von Sinn des historischen Romans." *Das neue Tage-Buch* 3 (1935): 640–43.

Frank, Anne. *De dagboeken van Anne Frank.* Edited by David Barnouw and Gerrold van der Stroom. The Hague: Staatsuitgeverij; Amsterdam: Bert Bakker, 1986.

Friedman, Leon, ed. *The Law of War: A Documentary History.* 2 vols. New York: Random House, 1972.

Gans, Evelien. *De kleine verschillen die het leven uitmaken: Een historische studie naar Joodse sociaal-democraten en socialistisch-zionisten in Nederland.* Amsterdam: Vassallucci, 2002.

———. *Jaap en Ischa Meijer: Een Joodse geschiedenis, 1912–1956.* Amsterdam: Bert Bakker, 2008.

Gans, Mozes Heiman. *Het Nederlandse jodendom: De sfeer waarin wij leefden.* Baarn: Ten Have, 1985.

———. *Memorboek: Platenatlas van het leven der joden in Nederland van de middeleeuwen tot 1940.* Baarn: Bosch & Keuning, 1971.

Gastelaars, Marja. *Een geregeld leven: Sociologie en sociale politiek in Nederland, 1925–1968.* Amsterdam: SUA, 1985.

Giebels, Ludy. *De Zionistische beweging in Nederland, 1899–1941.* Assen: Van Gorcum, 1975.

———. *Jacob Israël de Haan: Correspondent in Palestina, 1919–1924.* Amsterdam: De Engelbewaarder, 1981.

Gitter, Sieg. "De Mizrachistische Jeugd: Zichron Jaäkov, Amsterdam." *Mizrachie: Maandblad van de Nederlandsche afdeeling der wereldorganisatie "Mizrachie"* 21, no. 6 (March 1938): 61–62.

———. "Zichron Jaäkov en de Joodse Jeugdfederatie." *Pitchon peh: Officieel orgaan van de Mizrachistische Jeugdvereniging Zichron Jaäcov te Amsterdam,* no. 7 (November/December 1939): 6–8.

Gitter, Sieg, and Jaap Meier. "De sjoeldiensten van Zichron Jaäkov." *Mizrachie: Maandblad van de Nederlandsche afdeeling der wereldorganisatie "Mizrachie"* 21, no. 8 (May 1938): 71–72.

Goethe, Johann Wolfgang von. *Götz von Berlichingen.* Leipzig: Seemann, 1871.

Greshoff, Jan. *In alle ernst: Overpeinzingen op een reis.* Amsterdam: Querido, 1938.

Gross, Karl Adolf. *Zweitausend Tage Dachau: Erlebnisse eines Christenmenschen unter Herrenmenschen und Herdenmenschen: Berichte und Tagebücher des Häftlings Nr. 16921.* Munich: Neubau-Verlag, 1946.

Grüter, Regina. *Een fantast schrijft geschiedenis: De affaires rond Friedrich Weinreb.* Amsterdam: Balans, 1997.

Gutterman, Bella. *A Narrow Bridge to Life: Jewish Forced Labor and Survival in the Gross-Rosen Camp System, 1940–1945.* New York: Berghahn, 2008.

Hanssen, Léon. *Menno ter Braak, 1902–1940—Leven en werk van een polemist.* Amsterdam: Meulenhoff, 2003.

Hartog, Karel. and Gien Maykels. "Bij het 40-jarige regeeringsjubileum van H.M. Koningin Wilhelmina." *Tikwath Israel* 19, no. 10 (August 1938): 1.

Heine, Heinrich. *The Harz Journey and Selected Prose.* Translated by Ritchie Robertson. London: Penguin, 1993.

Herzberg, Abel. *Between Two Streams: A Diary from Bergen-Belsen.* Translated by Jack Santcross. London: Tauris; New York: European Jewish Publication Society, 1997.

———. *Verzameld werk.* 3 vols. Amsterdam: Querido, 1996.

Hilbrink, Coen. *"In het belang van het Nederlandse volk . . .": Over de medewerking van de ambtelijke wereld aan de Duitse bezettingspolitiek, 1940–1945.* The Hague: Sdu, 1995.

Hillesum, Etty. *The Letters and Diaries of Etty Hillesum, 1941–1943.* Edited by Klaas D. Smelik, translated by Arnold J. Pomerans. Grand Rapids, Mich.: Eerdmans, 2002.

Hirschfeld, Gerhard. *Bezetting en collaboratie: Nederland tijdens de oorlogsjaren 1940–1945.* Translated by Piet Jaarsma. Haarlem: H.J.W. Becht, 1991.

———. "Niederlande." In *Dimension des Völkermords: Die Zahl der jüdischen Opfer des Nationalsozialismus,* edited by Wolfgang Benz, 137–65. Munich: Oldenbourg, 1991.

Hoofdbestuur der Nederlandsche Mizrachie. "Onze verantwoordelijkheid voor de toekomst der Mizrachistische gedachte." *Mizrachie: Maandblad van de Nederlandsche afdeeling der wereldorganisatie "Mizrachie"* 22, no. 5 (May 1939): 33–35.

Hoogewoud-Verschoor, Ruth M. M. "The First Years of the Zionist Youth Movement in the Netherlands." In *Dutch Jewish History: Proceedings of the Fifth Symposium on the History of the Jews in the Netherlands, Jerusalem, November 25–28, 1991,* edited by Jozeph Michman, 309–19. Assen: Van Gorcum, 1993.

———. "Idealisten en fanatici: Radicale jonge Zionisten in Nederland en hun strijd om de Joodse identiteit in de jaren 1933–1940." In *Balanceren op de smalle weg,* edited by Lies Brussee-van der Zee et al., 36–48. Zoetermeer: Boekencentrum, 2002.

———. *Lion: Een schets van het leven van Lion Nordheim 1910–1945 en een keuze uit zijn artikelen.* Jerusalem: Awraham Yinnon, 1995.

———. "Rabbijn Simon Philip de Vries (1870–1944) en de Mizrachi in Nederland." In *Markante Nederlandse Zionisten,* edited by Francine Püttmann et al., 38–49. Amsterdam: De Bataafsche Leeuw, 1996.

Hoornik, Eduard. *Kritisch proza.* Amsterdam: Meulenhoff, 1978.

———. "Voor altijd Dachau." *Vrij Nederland,* May 1, 1965, 5.

Huizinga, Johan. *Verzamelde werken.* 9 vols. Haarlem: Tjeenk Willink & Zoon, 1948–53.

International Military Tribunal. *Trial of the Major War Criminals.* 46 vols. Nuremberg: Secretariat of the International Military Tribunal, 1947.

In 't Veld, Nanno Klaas Charles Arie, ed. *De SS en Nederland: Documenten uit SS archieven, 1935–1945.* 2 vols. The Hague: Martinus Nijhoff, 1976.

———. ed. "Jahresbericht 1942 des Befehlshabers der Sicherheitspolizei und des SD für die besetzten Niederländische Gebiete." In *Nederlandse historische bronnen I,* edited by Anton Carl Frederik Koch et al., 277–416. The Hague: Martinus Nijhoff, 1979.

Huizing, Bert, and Koen Aartsma. *De zwarte politie, 1940–1945.* Weesp: De Haan, 1986.

Jacobsen, Jens Peter. *Niels Lyhne.* Translated by Tiina Nunnally. Harmondsworth, U.K.: Penguin, 2006.

Kahn, Charles H. *The Art and Thought of Heraclitus: An Edition of the Fragments with Translation and Commentary.* Cambridge: Cambridge University Press, 1979.

Kelder, Jan Jaap. *De Schalkhaarders: Nederlandse politiemannen naar nationaal-socialistische snit.* Utrecht: Veen, 1990.

Kertész, Imre. *Fatelessness.* Translated by Tim Wilkinson. New York: Random House, 2004.

Klarsfeld, Serge. *Vichy-Auschwitz: Die "Endlösung der Judenfrage" in Frankreich.* Darmstadt: Wissenschaftliche Buchgesellschaft, 2007.

Klatzkin, Jakob. *Krisis und Entscheidung im Judentum.* Berlin: Jüdischer Verlag, 1921.

Klee, Ernst. *Das Personenlexikon zum Dritten Reich: Wer war was vor und nach 1945?* Frankfurt: Fischer, 2003.

Kleerekoper, Salomon. "Het Tsionisme en het staatsburgerschap." *Cheroetoenoe: Zionistisch maandblad* 14, no. 5 (1938–39): 60–63.

Klein, Peter Wolfgang, and Justus van de Kamp. *Het Philips-Kommando in kamp Vught.* Amsterdam: Contact, 2003.

Kogon, Eugen. *The Theory and Practice of Hell.* New York: Berkley Books, 1984.

Konieczny, Alfred. "Langenbielau [aka Reichenbach, Reichenbach Sportschule]." In *Encyclopedia of Camps and Ghettos, 1933–1945,* edited by Geoffrey P. Megargee, 1a:759–60. Bloomington: Indiana University Press, 2009.

———. "Langenbielau I (Bielawa)." In *Der Ort des Terrors: Geschichte der nationalsozialistischen Konzentrationslager,* edited by Wolfgang Benz, Barbara Distel, and Angelika Königseder, 6:377–79. 9 vols. Munich: C.H. Beck, 2005–9.

Königseder, Angelika. "Polizeihaftlager." In *Der Ort des Terrors: Geschichte der nationalsozialistischen Konzentrationslager,* edited by Wolfgang Benz, Barbara Distel, and Angelika Königseder, 9:19–52. 9 vols. Munich; C.H. Beck, 2005–9.

Koker, David. *Dagboek geschreven in Vught.* Amsterdam: Van Oorschot, 1977.

———. "Dagboek geschreven in Vught." *Hollands maandblad* 18, no. 349 (December 1976): 3–10.

———. "De honingactie van Zondag 10 September a.s." *Pitchon peh: Officieel orgaan van de Mizrachistische Jeugdvereniging Zichron Jaäcov te Amsterdam,* no. 5 (September 1939): 13–14.

———. "Fragmenten uit Jesaja." *De Joodsche wachter* 42, no. 21 (September 26, 1951): 20.

———. "Franse stemmen over de emancipatie." *Tikwath Israel* 21, no. 2 (November 1939): 19–21.

———. "De 20ste algemene vergadering van de federatie." *Tikwath Israel* 21, no. 1 (October 1939): 10–11.

———. "Help Toch!" In *Tisjrie 5702,* edited by Arie de Jong, 30–31. Amsterdam: Hoofdbestuur der Nederlandsche Mizrachie, 1941.

———. "Het Joodse gezin en zijn Joodse traditie." In Bestuur van de Nederlandse Zionistenbond, *Rondschrijven* (10 March 1941/11 Adar 5701), 1–6.

———. "In alle ernst." *De ventilator,* no. 5 (1938): 16–20.

———. "In alle ernst." In *De jongste generatie over J. Greshoff,* edited by Adrianus van der Veen, Eduard Hoornik, and Henri Albert Gomperts. 25–28. The Hague: Leopold's Uitgevers Maatschappij, 1938.

———. "Kritiek in dienst van de gemeenschap en in dienst van het individu." *De ventilator,* no. 3 (1938): 17–18.

———. "Mizmoriem." *De Joodsche wachter* 42, no. 20 (September 7, 1951): 10–11.

————. "Na de ontbinding der collectiviteit." *De ventilator,* no. 5 (1938): 9–12.

————. "Sjabbath." In *Menorah 5702: Joods jaarboek,* edited by Hugo Heymans and Jo Melkman, 113. Amsterdam: Allegro, 1941.

————. "Strijd voor het Galoeth." *Tikwath Israel* 21, no. 4 (January 1940): 69.

————. "Wat betekent Palestina op het ogenblik voor ons?" *Tikwath Israel* 21, no. 4 (January 1940): 70–71.

Koker, David, and Jozeph Melkman. *Modern-Hebreewse poëzie.* Amsterdam: Joachimsthal, 1941.

[Koker, David, and Jacob Vleeschhouwer]. "Het Galoeth in verval." *Pitchon peh: Officieel orgaan van de Mizrachistische Jeugdvereniging Zichron Jaäcov te Amsterdam,* no. 6 (October 1939): 13–15.

[————.]. "Onze taak." *Pitchon peh: Officieel orgaan van de Mizrachistische Jeugdvereniging Zichron Jaäcov te Amsterdam,* no. 5 (September 1939): 1–2.

Koker, Max. "Nawoord." In David Koker, *Dagboek geschreven in Vught,* 241–46. 3rd expanded ed. Amsterdam: Van Oorschot, 1993.

Kors, Ton. *De tocht opnieuw.* Amsterdam: Van Gennep, 1990.

Kupfer-Koberwitz, Edgar. *Die Mächtigen und die Hilflosen: Als Häftling in Dachau.* 2 vols. Stuttgart: Friedrich-Vorwerk-Verlag, 1957.

Kwiet, Konrad. *Reichskommissariat Niederlande: Versuch und Scheitern nationalsozialistischer Neuordnung.* Stuttgart: Deutsche Verlags-Anstalt, 1968.

Lammers, Han. Review of *Ondergang,* in *De groene Amsterdammer,* April 24, 1965.

Laqueur, Renata. *Schreiben im KZ: Tagebücher, 1940–1945.* Bremen: Donat, 1992.

Lessing, Gotthold Ephraim. *Nathan the Wise: A Dramatic Poem in Five Acts.* Translated by Bayard Quincy Morgan. New York: Frederick Ungar, 1955.

Levi, Primo. *The Drowned and the Saved.* Translated by Raymond Rosenthal. New York: Summit Books, 1988.

Lévy-Hass, Hanna. *Inside Belsen.* Translated by Ronald Taylor. Brighton, U.K.: Harvester Press, 1982.

Lewin, Lisette. *Vorig jaar in Jeruzalem: Israël en de Palestinapioniers.* Amsterdam: Nijgh & Van Ditmar, 1996.

Leydesdorff, Julius. *Bijdrage tot de speciale psychologie van het Joodsche volk.* Groningen: M. de Waal, 1919.

————. "De Nederlandse Joden." In *De Nederlandse volkskarakters,* edited by Pieter Jacob Meertens and Anne de Vries, 483–500. Kampen: Kok, 1938.

Ligtvoet, Pim. *Ik heb een heel tijdje niets van me laten horen: Joden in de Zaanstreek, 1940–1945.* Wormerveer: Uitgeverij Noord Holland, 2007.

Lindwer, Willy. *Het fatale dilemma: De Joodsche Raad voor Amsterdam, 1941–1943.* The Hague: Sdu, 1995.

Lipstadt, Deborah. *Beyond Belief: The American Press and the Coming of the Holocaust, 1933–1945.* New York: Free Press, 1986.

Mak, Geert. *Amsterdam: A Brief Life of the City.* Translated by Philipp Blom. London: Harvill Press, 1999.

Mann, Klaus. "Amsterdam." *Die Sammlung,* no. 6 (1934): 326–28.

Mann, Thomas. *The Magic Mountain.* Translated by H. T. Lowe Porter. 2 vols. London: Martin Secker, 1927.

———. *Royal Highness: A Novel of German Court Life.* Translated by A. Cecil Curtis. New York: Knopf, 1916.

Mechanicus, Philip. *Year of Fear: A Jewish Prisoner Waits for Auschwitz.* Translated by Irene R. Gibbons. New York: Hawthorne Books, 1968.

Meershoek, Augustinus Johannes Jacobus. *Dienaren van het gezag: De Amsterdamse politie tijdens de bezetting.* Amsterdam: Van Gennep, 1999.

———. "The Amsterdam Police and the Persecution of the Jews." In *The Holocaust and History: The Known, the Unknown, the Disputed, and the Reexamined,* edited by Michael Berenbaum and Abraham J. Peck, 284–300. Bloomington: Indiana University Press, 1998.

Meijer, Jaap. *De zoon van een gazzen: Het leven van Jacob Israël de Haan, 1883–1924.* Amsterdam: Atheneum–Polak & van Gennep, 1967.

———. *Onze taal als een bare schat: Jacob Israël de Haan en het Hebreeuws.* Amsterdam: De Engelbewaarder, 1981.

Meijer, Jaap, and Lion Nordheim. "De trots van Israel: Ongewenschte vreemdelingen." *Tikwath Israel* 19, no. 8 (May 1938): 117–19.

Melkman, Jozeph. "Mizrachistisch jeugdwerk." *Mizrachie: Maandblad van de Nederlandsche afdeeling der wereldorganisatie "Mizrachie"* 22, no. 3 (February 1939): xi–xii.

Mendes-Flohr, Paul R., and Jehuda Reinharz. *The Jew in the Modern World: A Documentary History.* (New York: Oxford University Press, 1980.

Michman, Jozeph. *Ma'agley Hayim ve-Zehut [Cycles of Life and Identity].* Edited by Dan Michman. Tel Aviv: Gvanim, 2004.

———. "Nederlands zionisme in de branding: Herinneringen aan zionisten uit de jaren dertig." In *Markante Nederlandse Zionisten,* edited by Francine Püttmann et al., 28–37. Amsterdam: De Bataafsche Leeuw, 1996.

Moore, Bob. *Refugees from Nazi Germany in the Netherlands, 1933–1940.* Dordrecht: Martinus Nijhoff, 1986.

———. *Victims and Survivors: The Nazi Persecution of the Jews in the Netherlands, 1940–1945.* London: Arnold, 1997.

Morgenstern, Soma. *Flucht in Frankreich: Ein Romanbericht.* Edited by In-
golf Schulte. Lüneburg: zu Klampen, 1998.

Morsch, Günter, ed. *Murder and Mass Murder in Sachsenhausen Concentration Camp, 1936–1945.* Berlin: Metropol, 2005.

Multatuli [Eduard Douwes Dekker]. *Max Havelaar; or, The Coffee Auctions
of the Dutch Trading Company.* Translated by Roy Edwards. Leiden:
Sijthoff, 1967.

———. *Woutertje Pieterse.* Edited by G. Stuiveling. Amsterdam: Van Oorschot, 1952.

No. 469 [Albertus Santegoeds]. *De hel op de Vughtse heide.* Utrecht: Kemink,
1945.

Nordheim, Lion. "De heerschappij van het geweld." *Cheroetoenoe: Zionistisch maandblad* 15, no. 2 (1939/40): 2–5.

———. "De verdorde beenderen." *Cheroetoenoe: Zionistisch maandblad* 14,
no. 2 (1938/39): 34–35.

———. "Het zionisme in Nederland." *Cheroetoenoe: Zionistisch maandblad*
15, no. 2 (1939/40): 23–25.

———. "Humanisme en zionisme." *Cheroetoenoe: Zionistisch maandblad*
14, no. 2 (1938/39): 8–12.

———. "More Derech: De plaats van de Joodsche cultuur in de Zioni-
stische jeugdbeweging." *Baderech: Maandblad—Officieel orgaan van de
Nederlandsche Zionistische studenten-organisatie en leidersorgaan van de
Joodsche Jeugdfederatie in Nederland* 11, no. 6 (Ijar 5696): 3–4.

———. "Om de Joodse traditie." *Cheroetoenoe: Zionistisch maandblad* 14,
no. 5 (1938/39): 97–100.

Novac, Ana. *The Beautiful Days of My Youth: My Six Months in Auschwitz and
Plaszow.* Translated by George L. Newman. New York: Holt, 1997.

[Oorlogsgravenstichting]. *In Memoriam—L'zecher.* The Hague: Sdu, 1995.

Oppenheim, Abraham Naftali. *The Chosen People: The Story of the "222 Transport" from Bergen-Belsen to Palestine.* London: Vallentine Mitchell, 1996.

Pais, Abraham. *A Tale of Two Continents: A Physicist's Life in a Turbulent
World.* Princeton: Princeton University Press, 1997.

Ponsonby, Arthur. *Falsehood in War-Time: Containing an Assortment of Lies
Circulated Throughout the Nations During the Great War.* London: Allen
& Unwin, 1928.

Presser, Jacob [Jacques]. *The Destruction of the Dutch Jews.* Translated by
Arnold Pomerans. New York: Dutton, 1968. The British edition appeared as *Ashes in the Wind: The Destruction of Dutch Jewry,* trans. Arnold Pomerans. London: Souvenir Press, 1968.

———. *Ondergang: De vervolging en verdelging van het Nederlandse jodendom,
1940–1945.* 2 vols. The Hague: Staatsuitgeverij / Martinus Nijhoff,
1965.

Read, James Morgan. *Atrocity Propaganda, 1914–1919*. New Haven: Yale University Press, 1941.

Rijksinspectie van de Bevolkingsregisters. *Statistiek der bevolking van Joodschen bloede in Nederland*. The Hague: Algemeene Landsdrukkerij, 1942.

Rijksinstituut voor Oorlogsdocumentatie. *Het woord als wapen: Keur uit de Nederlandse ondergrondse pers, 1940–1945*. The Hague: Martinus Nijhoff, 1952.

Rilke, Rainer Maria. *Gesammelte Werke*. 6 vols. Leipzig: Insel-Verlag, 1930.

———. *Letters to a Young Poet*. Translated by Stephen Mitchell. New York: Random House, 1984.

———. *Levensinzicht: Menselijk waardevolle overdenkingen uit de brieven van Rilke*. Edited by G. Mencken, translated by J. W. Kuiper. Graveland: De Driehoek, n.d.

Rost, Nico. *Goethe in Dachau: Literatuur en werkelijkheid*. Amsterdam: L. J. Veen, 1948.

Sadan, Dov. "Alter Terakh: The Byways of Linguistic Fusion." In *The Field of Yiddish: Studies in Language, Folklore and Literature*, edited by Uriel Weinberg, 134–42. New York: Linguistic Circle of New York, 1954.

Saint-Clair, Simone. *Ravensbrück: L'enfer des femmes*. Paris: Fayard, 1967.

Schmitz-Berning, Cornelia. *Vokabular des Nationalsozialismus*. Berlin: de Gruyter, 1998.

Schopenhauer, Arthur. *Parerga and Paralipomena*. Translated by Eric F. J. Payne. 2 vols. Oxford: Oxford University Press, 2001.

Schrijvers, Piet. *Rome, Athene, Jeruzalem: Leven en werk van Prof. Dr. David Cohen*. Groningen: Historische Uitgeverij, 2000.

Seeligmann, Sigmund. "Die Juden in Holland: Eine Charakteristik." In *Festskrift i anledning af professor David Simonsens 70-aarige fødseldag*, edited by J. Fischer et al., 253–57. Copenhagen: Hertz, 1923.

Siebesma, Pieter Anne. "Zichron Yaakov and the Struggle for the Sephardic Pronunciation." *Studies on the History of Dutch Jewry* 3 (1981): 223–46.

Siertsema, Bettine. *Uit de diepten: Nederlandse egodocumenten over de nazi concentratiekampen*. Vught: Skandalon, 2007.

Sitniakowsky, Ivan. "Uniek dagboek van Koker uit kamp van Vught." *De telegraaf*, April 1977.

Spies, Gerty. "Diary, September 1944." In *My Years in Theresienstadt*, translated by Jutta R. Tragnitz, 127–44. Amherst, N.Y.: Prometheus, 1997.

Steiner, George. *In Bluebeard's Castle: Some Notes Towards the Re-definition of Culture*. London: Faber & Faber, 1971.

Steinmetz, Sebald Rudolf. "Wat is sociographie?" *Mensch en maatschappij* 1 (1925): 280–82.

Storrs, Ronald. *The Memoirs of Sir Ronald Storrs*. New York: Putnam, 1937.

Stuhldreher, Coenraad Johannes Franciscus. *De legale rest: Gemengd gehu-wede Joden onder de Duitse bezetting.* Amsterdam: Boom, 2007.

———. "Deutsche Konzentrationslager in den Niederlanden: Amers-foort, Westerbork, Herzogenbusch." *Dachauer Hefte* 5, no. 5 (Novem-ber 1989): 141–73.

Sula, Dorota. "Dörnhau (Kolce)" and "Wüstegiersdorf / Tannhausen." In *Der Ort des Terrors: Geschichte der nationalsozialistischen Konzentration-slager,* vol. 6, *Natzweiler, Gross-Rosen, Stutthof,* edited by Angelika Kö-nigseder, 275–78 and 461–67. Munich: C.H. Beck, 2007.

———. "Riese / Dörnhau" and "Riese / Wüstegiersdorf." In *Encyclopedia of Camps and Ghettos, 1933–1945,* edited by Geoffrey P. Megargee, 1a:784, 798–99. Bloomington: Indiana University Press, 2009.

Tacitus, Cornelius. *The Annals of Imperial Rome.* Translated by Michael Grant. Harmondsworth, U.K.: Penguin, 1966.

Tas, Louis [Loden Vogel]. *Dagboek uit een kamp.* Amsterdam: Van Oor-schot, 1965.

Ter Braak, Menno. *Verzameld werk.* 7 vols. Amsterdam: Van Oorschot, 1951.

Terentianus Maurus. *Terentiani Mauri De litteris, de syllabis, de metris.* Ed-ited by Chiara Cignolo. 2 vols. Hildesheim, Ger.: Olms, 2002.

Ter Veen, Henri Nicolaas. *De Haarlemmermeer als kolonisatiegebied: Proeve eener sociaal-geographische monographie.* Groningen: Noordhof, 1925.

———. "Van anthropogeografie tot sociografie." *Mensch en maatschappij* 3 (1927): 298–312.

Tuchel, Johannes. *Die Inspektion der Konzentrationslager.* Berlin: Hentrich, 1994.

Tucholsky, Kurt. *Castle Gripsholm: A Summer Story.* Translated by Michael Hofman. London: Chatto & Windus, 1985.

Van Bruggen, Carry. *Verhalend proza.* Amsterdam: Delta / Van Oorschot, 2007.

Van de Mortel, Jan. *Kamp Vught: Januari 1943–september 1944.* Vught: Stichting Archieven, 1940–45, 1990.

Van de Kamp, Justus, and Jacob van Wijk. *Koosjer Nederlands: Joodse woor-den in de Nederlandse taal.* Amsterdam: Contact, 2006.

Van der Heijden, Chris. *Joodse NSB'ers: De vergeten geschiedenis van Villa Bouchina in Doetinchem.* Utrecht: Begijnekade18, 2006.

Van der Zee, Nanda. *Om erger te voorkomen: De voorgeschiedenis en uitvoering van de vernietiging van het Nederlandse jodendom tijdens de Tweede Werel doorlog.* Amsterdam: Meulenhoff, 1997.

Van Goirle, Concordius. *Gedachten in Steen: De kathedrale basiliek van St. Jan te 's-Hertogenbosch.* Utrecht: Van Rossum, 1941.

Van het Reve, Karel. "Inleiding." In David Koker, *Dagboek geschreven in Vught,* 5–23. Amsterdam: Van Oorschot, 1977.

Van Opzeeland, ed. *Ben Bril: Davidster als ereteken*. Rotterdam: De Buiten-spelers, 2006.

Van Peype, Dirk Cornelis Jacob. *Wat is sociologie?* Hilversum: W. de Haan, 1965.

Van Voolen, Edward, and Paul Meijer. *Synagogen van Nederland*. Zutphen: Walburg Pers, 2005.

Verrips, Ger. *Denkbeelden uit een dubbelleven: Biografie van Karel van het Reve*. Amsterdam: Arbeiderspers, 2004.

Vom Holt, Heinrich Eduard. *Weltfahrt ins Herz: Tagebuch eines Arztes*. Cologne: Balduin-Pick-Verlag, 1947.

"Voorwoord der redactie." *Tikwath Israel* 21, no. 1 (October 1939): 1.

Warmbrunn, Werner. *The Dutch Under German Occupation, 1940–1945*. Stanford: Stanford University Press, 1963.

Weinreb, Friedrich. *Collaboratie en verzet, 1940–1945: Een poging tot ontmy-thologisering*. 3 vols. Amsterdam: Meulenhoff, 1989.

Wibaut-Guilonard, Tineke. *Zo ben je daar: Kampervaringen*. Amsterdam: Ploegsma, 1983.

Wijnberg, Sylvain. *De Joden in Amsterdam: Een studie over verandering in hun attituden*. Assen: Van Gorcum, 1967.

Wilde, Oscar. *Complete Works*. Introduction by Vyvyan Holland. London: Collins, 1966.

Yudkin, Leon I. *Isaac Lamdan: A Study in Twentieth-Century Hebrew Poetry*. Ithaca: Cornell University Press, 1971.

Zámečnik, Stanislav. *Das war Dachau*. Translated by Peter Heumos and Gitta Grossmann. Frankfurt am Main: Fischer, 2007.

Zweig, Arnold. *De Vriendt Goes Home*. Translated by Eric Sutton. New York: Viking, 1933.

David Koker was transported to the Vught Concentration Camp in 1943. During his time in Vught, David recorded on an almost daily basis his observations, thoughts, and feelings. Unlike Anne Frank, who had a purposefully made diary book available in her hiding place, David did not have such a luxury in the camp. In the first month of his imprisonment he wrote his entries on whatever scraps of paper he was able to find. Later he used the exercise books supplied for the children who, after a short sojourn in Vught, were sent on to Poland to be murdered. Until early February 1944, David was able to smuggle some 73,000 words from the camp to his best friend Karel van het Reve, a non-Jew. The part of the diary that David kept between February 8, 1944 and June 1944, when he was deported to Poland, did not survive the war.

Robert Jan van Pelt was born and educated in the Netherlands. He is university professor at the University of Waterloo where he teaches in the School of Architecture. He has published widely on the history of Auschwitz, the Holocaust, and Holocaust denial.

Michiel Horn was born in the Netherlands and grew up in Canada. He is professor emeritus of history and university historian at York University, Toronto. He has translated fiction and nonfiction.

John Irons has translated Danish, Swedish, Norwegian, German, and Dutch poetry into English. He lives in Odense, Denmark.